THE GUI...

CONTINENTAL
EUROPE
GOLF
COURSE
GUIDE

THE GUINNESS

CONTINENTAL EUROPE GOLF COURSE GUIDE

MALCOLM HAMER

GUINNESS PUBLISHING

This book is dedicated to Jill

Published in Great Britain by Guinness Publishing Ltd,
33 London Road, Enfield, Middlesex

Maps by Peter Harper
Illustrations by Sarah Silvé

Cover design by Ad Vantage Studios
Text design and layout by Stonecastle Graphics Ltd,
Marden, Kent

Typeset in Century Schoolbook by Ace Filmsetting Ltd,
Frome, Somerset

Printed and bound in Great Britain by The Bath Press,
Bath, Avon

ISBN 0-85112-509-3

THE AUTHOR

Malcolm Hamer has been an agent for professional sportsmen for over twenty years. He has represented many leading golfers and his experiences led him to begin another career as a writer.

His first two novels have recently been published and the third in the series will appear soon. *Sudden Death* and *A Deadly Lie* are thrillers set in the world of professional golf. His account of the famous series between the golfers of Europe and the United States, *The Ryder Cup – The Players*, was published in 1992.

Together with his wife, Jill Foster, he has written a successful series of guide books. *The Family Welcome Guides* are now in their tenth year of publication.

Malcolm is an enthusiastic golfer with a moderate handicap.

ACKNOWLEDGEMENTS

I owe a great debt to P & O European Ferries, whose help was both timely and generous.

My thanks to all those who helped me with the research for this guide, especially to Des Austin, who also helped with the editing; also to Tim Brooke-Taylor, Bjorn Clason, Nick Edmund, Ivor Gillhespy, David Haynes, Chris Honnor, George Jones, Philip Olsen, Alan Palmer and Roger Thomas.

The various national golf associations, federations and unions were unstinting in their provision of essential information; my thanks to the associations of Austria, Belgium, Denmark, France, Germany, Greece, Italy, Luxembourg, Netherlands, Norway, Portugal, Spain, Sweden and Switzerland.

Finally, my thanks to all those club officials who filled in questionnaires and provided information; and above all to those who welcomed me and my inspectors to their courses.

CONTENTS

INTRODUCTION

A GREAT surge of enthusiasm for golf has occurred during the last few years at all levels in Europe. Just as the sponsors have poured their money into the professional game, so have people taken up the game in huge numbers. The waiting lists at private clubs have never been longer, likewise the waiting times on the first tees at public courses.

Most people who aspire to play golf regularly are no doubt attracted by a sport that usually takes place in pleasant surroundings away from the noise and pressures of their everyday lives. "There is a pleasure in the pathless woods, there is a rapture on the lonely shore" might find an echo in many golfers' minds. Golf is also a game that can last for the whole of your life and, because of the handicap system, you can compete against anybody, from Nick Faldo downwards.

The successes of European golfers, in winning major golf tournaments and in defeating the mighty American teams in the Ryder Cup, has also generated enormous enthusiasm. In Europe, the building of golf courses has increased dramatically in the last few years. Enlightened national golf federations and entrepreneurs have tried to meet some of the demands. In the past five years the stock of courses in Europe has increased by about 50% and by the end of 1993 there should be 2000 courses in play.

Most of the European countries have participated in this course-building boom, especially the Netherlands, Germany and Sweden. Spain, the traditional haven of the sun-starved British golfer, has also added many new courses, especially on the Costa del Sol. Really remarkable growth has been seen in France; at the end of 1987 there were less than 200 courses available for play, but there are now over 400, with many more in the pipeline.

Nor has this growth of facilities meant 'more is less'. Even if many clubs have been built to meet a very pressing demand and have simple designs and facilities, many captivating courses, both in visual and golfing terms, have been built.

There are many golfing jewels, both old and new, upon which the golfing tourist can gaze and which he can enjoy in Europe; and there are many more varied destinations than the Algarve and the Costa del Sol, where the golf can be expensive and the welcome uncertain. Belgium and the Netherlands, easy of access by car and ferry, have some wonderful courses; Denmark is an interesting and different country in which to play golf; the Alpine courses offer magnificent scenery; in Austria you can combine the charms of Salzburg or Vienna with the fun of some excellent golf courses; in France, a favoured country for holiday makers, the choice of golf courses is unrivalled on the continent.

One of the pleasures of visiting a club in Europe is the warm welcome that is offered, often from a chic and smartly-dressed lady secretary. It is a refreshing change from the traditional British club secretary, usually a crusty military gentleman lately retired perhaps from the Royal Artillery. It should also be said that the eating and drinking facilities at European clubs are generally first-class. Sustenance is available throughout the day and the food is often of very high quality. There is no formality either; jackets and ties are rarely needed.

Visitors should remember two things:

1. Book a starting time well in advance, especially in August when continental clubs have competitions almost every day.

2. Take your handicap certificate, which is usually required. It will also enable you to join in some of the competitions.

In this first edition of the Guide we have listed every golf course which, according to our research, is open for play at the end of 1992. Short courses (i.e. under 4000 metres in length) have not been listed.

THE ENTRIES

We have tried to present the information in its simplest form, without the use of irritating symbols. Below is a sample Course guide:

① **Club de Chamonix (1982)**   **9**

    Phone: 50 530628

    74400 Les Praz de Chamonix

②   Just north of Chamonix, off the N506

③   *Holes*   18 Par 72 6087m.

④   *Visitors*   Welcome. Course closed November to April

⑤   *Fees*   FFr200–250

⑥   *Facilities*   Bar and restaurant; driving range

⑦   *Pro*   J C Bonnaz

⑧   The celebrated winter sports resort of Chamonix has a golf course which is something of an oddity – not surprisingly, since it was designed by Robert Trent Jones. Under the towering heights of Mont Blanc, it is rather flat and might have been flown in from Florida. It shows Jones's inevitable penchant for small plateau greens of bizarre shape, protected by huge bunkers and streams. Never mind, the views are magnificent.

① The clubs are listed in alphabetical order, with the year in which they were founded in brackets. A reference number for the map at the start of the chapter follows, and the address and telephone number are shown underneath. The primary name of the club is predominant. For example, Royal Zoute is listed under Z, and Chateau de la Bawette under B. The courses in France and Germany, because of their large numbers, have been split into regions.

② Directions are given; you should combine these with a good map.

③ The number of holes, the par, and the length of the course in metres.

④ Any restrictions on visitors are given, and any closing times. Many continental courses close on one day a week and some have to close during the winter, owing to the weather.

⑤ Fees. These are given in the domestic currency. Many clubs were unable to predict their charges for 1993 and you should check when you book your tee times.

⑥ Facilities. Availability of food and drink and other facilities such as swimming pools, tennis courts, etc. You can usually get something to eat and drink at any time of the day at European clubs.

⑦ Professional. His or her name is given when known.

⑧ We have given short descriptions of many of the courses in the Guide, in an effort to convey their character and appeal.

At the back of the book I have included some forms for the reader to use. Please send me your comments about any of the courses in the Guide or on any aspect of the Guide. I would welcome your views, especially about the nature of European golf courses; the more the debate with our readers, the more interesting the next edition of the Guide will be.

As an encouragement to you to seize your pens, I will give away a bottle of champagne for the six most interesting, amusing or controversial letters.

Malcolm Hamer

AUSTRIA

A LTHOUGH Austria is as synonymous with skiing as is its neighbour, Switzerland, there is a significant stock of golf courses – over 70 in number. The majority of them are laid out over 18 holes and many are well-established clubs. Over 20 of them were built before 1980 and the 'senior' clubs include the Golfclub Wien (1901), Kantner (1927), Semmering (1926), Salzkammergut (1933) and the Innsbruck and Kitzbuhel clubs (1950s).

The general growth of interest in golf during the last two decades has been aided by the great success of Bernhard Langer, someone with whom Austrians can identify. Despite the shortened golf season (usually April to October), this has encouraged the building of more courses, especially during the last five or six years when more than 20 new ones have opened for play.

There are few more attractive countries than Austria: on the one hand the magnificent Alpine countryside with its thick forests and glittering lakes, on the other the cultural and culinary delights of the great cities of Vienna and Salzburg. From those two bases alone a golfer would have a fine selection of golf courses, usually located in magnificent countryside.

It is worth noting that no golfing expedition to Austria would be complete without a visit to Seefeld, a spectacular course in an idyllic setting.

Unit of currency: Austrian Schilling (AS)
Rate of exchange (approx. at 1.1.93): 17AS–£1
International dialling code: 010 43

GLC Achensee (1934)   **1**

Phone: 05243 5377

6213 Pertisau/Achensee

North east of Innsbruck off the B181 at Pertisau

Holes	9 Par 31 1938m.
Visitors	Welcome. Course closed December to March
Fees	300–400AS
Facilities	Bar and restaurant; driving range; swimming pool; tennis courts

Golf Club Amstetten-Ferschnitz (1981)   **2**

Phone: 07473 8293

Gut Edla 18, 3325 Ferschnitz

South east of Amstetten off the A1 (Vienna to Linz). Follow signs for Ferschnitz and then to the club.

Holes	9 Par 35 2950m.
Visitors	Welcome
Fees	300–400AS
Facilities	Bar and restaurant; driving range
Pro	Alexander Reiss

Golfclub Austria Worthersee (1988)   3

Phone: 43 4272 83450

Golfstrasse 2, 9062 Moosburg

Between Villach and Velden; take the Velden-West exit off the main Klagenfurt road

Holes   18 Par 72 6216m.

Visitors   Welcome. Course closed December to March

Fees   500AS

Facilities Bar and restaurant

Pro   Mike Sullivan

Golf Club Bad Gleichenberg (1984)   4

Phone: 03159 3717

Am Hoffeld 3, 8344 Bad Gleichenberg

South east of Graz, off the B66 at Bad Gleichenberg

Holes   9 Par 36 2850m.

Visitors   Welcome. Course closed December to March

Fees   250–300AS

Facilities Bar and restaurant; driving range

Pro   John Mee

AUSTRIA

Golf Club Bad Kleinkirchheim-Reichenau
(1977)   **5**

Phone: 04275 594

9546 Bad Kleinkirchheim

North of Villach, and just east of Bad
Kleinkirchheim, on the B88

Holes	18 Par 72 6127m.
Visitors	Welcome. Course closed November to April
Fees	450AS
Facilities	Bar and restaurant; driving range
Pro	Gordon Manson

Golf & Country Club Brandlhof (1983)   **6**

Phone: 06582 2176

Am Steinermen Meer, 5670 Saalfelden

Just north of Saalfelden off the B311

Holes	18 Par 72 6218m.
Visitors	Must book. Course closed November to April
Fees	500–600AS
Facilities	Bar and restaurant; practice ground; swimming pool; squash and tennis courts; riding stables
Pro	H J Lumpi

A luxury hotel with all manner of amenities lies
at the heart of this sporting estate. Serious

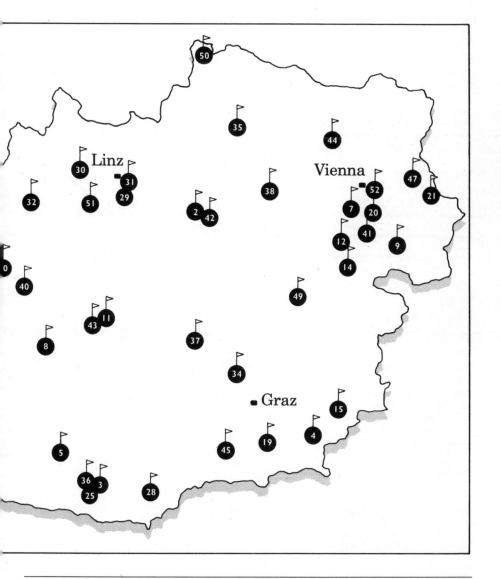

golfers should at all costs avoid horse riding (indoor and outdoor), the swimming pool, and the squash and tennis courts. Concentrate instead on avoiding the water hazards presented by the Saalach River, which wends its way through the golf course.

Golf Club Brunn am Gebirge (1988) 7

Phone: 02236 31572

Rennweg, 2345 Brunn am Gebirge

Off the A2 south of Vienna; in Modling turn on to the Vienna/Perchtoldsdorf road

Holes	18 Par 72 6088m.
Visitors	Welcome
Fees	400/600AS
Facilities	Bar and restaurant; practice ground; swimming pool
Pro	Rafael Jerman

Dachstein–Tauern Golfclub (1990) 8

Phone: 03686 2630

Coburgstrasse 626, 8970 Schladming/Oberhaus

Off the B146 east of Schladming; head for Oberhaus

Holes	18 Par 71 5727m.
Visitors	Welcome. Course closed November to April
Fees	500–600AS
Facilities	Bar and restaurant; practice ground
Pro	Roger Andrews

Designed by Bernhard Langer, the course is set amidst thickly wooded terrain, with views of distant mountains. There are water hazards to test the golfer and the rolling contours of the course also pose their problems.

Golfclub Donnerskirchen (1988) 9

Phone: 02683 8110

7082 Donnerskirchen

North east of Eisenstadt, off the B50 at Donnerskirchen

Holes	18 Par 72 6261m.
Visitors	Welcome
Fees	480–570AS
Facilities	Bar and restaurant; practice ground
Pro	Nick Conrad

There is more than a suggestion of a traditional links course to this demanding venue, which is situated well south of Vienna near the Neusiedler See. The presence of over eight acres of ponds, and the prevailing winds, add to the challenge which the golfer faces (and to the fun).

Golfclub Drachenwand (1989) 10

Phone: 43 6232 4437

Keuschen 166, 5310 Mondsee

Just east of Salzburg off the A1; take the Mondsee exit. One kilometre after the exit, turn right to Tahlgau and the golfcourse is just over 1km away

Holes	18 Par 68 5316m.
Visitors	Must book. Course closed mid-November to March
Fees	300–400AS
Facilities	Bar and restaurant; practice ground
Pro	Shaun Cunningham

GLC Ennstal-Weissenbach (1978) 11

Phone: 03612 24774

Postfach 76, 8940 Liezen

South west of Liezen; off the B146 at Aigen

Holes	9 Par 35 2802m.
Visitors	Welcome
Fees	300AS
Facilities	Bar and restaurant; driving range

Golf Club Enzesfeld (1970) 12

Phone: 02256 812721

2551 Enzesfeld

South of Vienna. From the A2 take the B18 to Berndorf, and then turn to Enzesfeld.

Holes	18 Par 72 6048m.
Visitors	Welcome on weekdays; by introduction at weekends. Course closed November to March
Fees	450–600AS
Facilities	Bar and restaurant; practice ground
Pro	Richard Morris

Golf Club Europa Sport Region (1983) 13

Phone: 06542 6161

Golfstrasse 25, Zell am See

Between Zell am See and Kaprun off the B168

Holes	18 Par 72 6218m;
	9 Par 36 2825m.
Visitors	Welcome. Course closed November to March
Fees	420–530AS
Facilities	Bar and restaurant; driving range; tennis courts
Pro	David Shaw

The course, designed by Donald Harradine, has an idyllic position at the foot of the Kitzsteinhorn glacier; you can take a cable car to the summit. From the first tee the fairway seems to run away into the mountains, and the course is very demanding, especially since the lush fairways make the holes play longer than the scorecard suggests and there are many natural hazards. Whatever the state of your golf you cannot but enjoy the gorgeous scenery: the vast tranquil lake and the fine trees which line the fairways. There are many other facilities here, including tennis, all-year-round skiing, swimming and walking.

Golf Club Fohrenwald (1968) 14
Phone: 02622 29171
Postfach 105, 2700 Wr Neustadt
South of Vienna near Wr Neustadt. Take the S4 to Mattersburg, and then head for Pitten
Holes   18 Par 72 6043m.
Visitors   Welcome
Fees   400–500AS
Facilities   Restaurant (April to November) closed Monday; practice ground
Pro   Adrian Andrews

Golfclub Furstenfeld (1984) 15
Phone: 03382 8533
8282 Gillersdorf 50
From the A2 east of Graz take the B65 to Furstenfeld and follow signs for Loipersdorf, Dietersdorf and Gillersdorf
Holes   18 Par 72 6192m.
Visitors   Welcome
Fees   400–500AS
Facilities   Bar and restaurant; driving range
Pro   Alastair Neilson

Golf Club Gastein (1960) 16
Phone: 06434 2775
Postfach 59, 5640 Badgastein
On the B167 just north of Bad Hofgastein
Holes   9 Par 32 2932m.
Visitors   Must book. Course closed December to March
Fees   350–450AS
Facilities   Bar and restaurant; practice ground
Pro   Andy Mayer

Golf Club Goldegg (1987) 17
Phone: 06415 8585
Postfach 6, 5622 Goldegg
South of Salzburg. Take the B311 towards Zell am See, and then turn off to Goldegg
Holes   9 Par 33 2228m.
Visitors   Welcome. Course closed December to April.
Fees   300–400AS
Facilities   Bar and restaurant; driving range
Pro   Rodney Richards

Golf & Country Club Gut Altentann (1986) 18
Phone: 06214 6026
5302 Henndorf am Wallersee
North east of Slazburg; take the Wallersee exit off the A1 to Henndorf (B1). There are signs to the club
Holes   18 Par 72 6173m.
Visitors   Weekdays only and must book. Course closed November to April
Fees   800AS
Facilities   Bar and restaurant; practice ground
Pro   Jonathan Mannie

Designed by Jack Nicklaus, Gut Altentann is a very severe test of any golfer's skills, and its quality led to its hosting the 1992 Austrian Open. The course is built on a generous scale with several dogleg holes, and water compounds the player's problems on many holes. In the Austrian Open, the Ryder Cup player Mark James took a *thirteen* at the 16th hole. The final hole is a monster, with a vast expanse of sand in front of the green and a lake behind. You have been warned!

Golfclub Gut Murstatten (1989) 19
Phone: 03182 3555
8403 Lebring 58
30km south of Graz off the A9; take the Lebring exit and then head for Schloss Murstatten
Holes   18 Par 74 6417m; 9 hole public course Par 36 3060m.
Visitors   Welcome. Closed during winter
Fees   450–550AS
Facilities   Bar and restaurant; practice ground; 9 hole pitch and putt
Pro   Wayne Tyrie

This relatively new course was conceived by the architect as a links course, albeit designed around a large lake and with many trees in evidence. The fairways have a true links character with their humps and hollows and the traditional pot bunkers are also in place. Murstatten is a stiff test, especially when the wind blows.

Colony Club Gutenhof (1988) 20
Phone: 02235 88055
2325 Himberg-Gutenhof
South of Vienna off B15 at Himberg
Holes   (West Course) 18 Par 73 6397m; (East Course) 18 Par 73 6335m
Visitors   Welcome
Fees   500–650AS
Facilities   Bar and restaurant; driving range
Pro   Tony Cox

Golf Club Hainburg/Donau (1977)   21

Phone: 02165 2628

A/d Heide 762, 2410 Hainburg

East of Vienna off the B9; the club is to the
north east of Hainburg.

Holes	18 Par 70 5950m.
Visitors	Welcome
Fees	300–500AS
Facilities	Bar and restaurant; 6 practice holes
Pro	Kevin Fontaine

Golfclub Innsbruck-Igls (1956)   22

Phone: 05223 8177

Oberdorf 11, 6074 Rinn

Just east of Innsbruck. Take the Hall-Tirol exit
off the A12, follow the road to Rinn.

Holes	18 Par 71 5935m; holes 9 Par 33 2329m.
Visitors	Welcome. Course closed November to March
Fees	400–500AS
Facilities	Bar and restaurant; driving range
Pro	Ian Shaw

Only a few kilometres from the resort of
Innsbruck, the course is encircled by the
magnificent Alpine mountains, snow-capped and
thickly forested. The course also has its share of
trees, since the undulating fairways are cut
through lines of fires. It is a splendid holiday
course, with excellent facilities.

Golfclub Innsbruck-Lans (1956)   23

Phone: 05222 77165

6072 Lans, Sperberegg

Take the Innsbruck-O exit off the A12 and follow
the signs to Lans

Holes	9 Par 33 2350m.
Visitors	Welcome. Course closed November to March
Fees	200–300AS
Facilities	Bar and restaurant; driving range

Kaiserwinkl Golfclub Kossen (1988)   24

Phone: 05375 2122

7345 Kossen, Muhlau 1

Off the B172 near Kossen

Holes	18 Par 73 5927m.
Visitors	Welcome
Fees	450–550AS
Facilities	Bar and restaurant; practice ground
Pro	Chuck de Castro

The holes thread their way through thick forest
and are characterised by elevated tees and
greens well protected by bunkers. There are
many dog-legged holes, made all the more
difficult to negotiate by the presence of water
hazards. It is an excellent test for any golfer.

Karntner Golf Club (1927)   25

Phone: 04273 2515

Dellach 16, 9082 Maria Worth

East of Villach off the B83. After Velden, head
for Dellach-Maria Worth

Holes	18 Par 70 5745m.
Visitors	Welcome
Fees	500AS
Facilities	Bar and restaurant; driving range; swimming pool
Pro	David Marsh

Quiet and secluded, the Karntner course is close
by the lake of Worthersee in the middle of
delightful Alpine countryside. Surprisingly the
course is rather flat but the holes offer plenty of
variation and several of them run near the lake.
As well as golf you can enjoy the water sports
which are available on the lake. A legacy of
World War II is that the 'British Troops in
Austria Cup' is contested here every August.

Golfclub Kitzbuhel (1955)   26

Phone: 05356 3007

6370 Kitzbuhel

Off the B161 at Kitzbuhel

Holes	9 Par 36 3022m.
Visitors	Welcome. Course closed November to March
Fees	450–550AS
Facilities	Bar and restaurant
Pro	Gordon Thomson

This is one of Austria's oldest courses, and was
built along the side of a hill. The golfers are
blessed with superb views of the town and of the
magnificent Kitzbuhel Alps. Despite its being a
9-hole course, the club has played host to many
championships. The approaches to the elevated
greens are challenging and the putting surfaces
are fast and true.

Golfclub Kitzbuhel-Schwarzsee (1988)   27

Phone: 05356 71645

Schwarzsee/Reith, Am Golfplatz

North of Kitzbuhel towards Going

Holes	18 Par 72 6247m.
Visitors	Welcome. Course closed November to April
Fees	550–650AS
Facilities	Bar and restaurant; driving range
Pro	John Larrad

Golf Club Klopeinersee-Turnersee (1989)   **28**

Phone: 04239 3800

Grabelsdorf 94, 9122 St Kanzian

East of Klagenfurt. Turn off the B70 towards St Kanzian and then head for Grabelsdorf. The club is a few kilometres south east of St Kanzian

Holes	18 Par 72 6109m.
Visitors	Welcome. Course closed November to March
Fees	500AS
Facilities	Restaurant; practice ground

Golfclub Linz (1960)   **29**

Phone: 07223 2873

Tillysburg 28, 4490 St Florian

South east of Linz. Take the St Florian exit off the A1. In Asten head for Schloss Tillysburg

Holes	18 Par 72 6091m.
Visitors	Welcome. Course closed December to March
Fees	450–580AS
Facilities	Bar and restaurant; driving range
Pro	Jonathan Crisp

The city of Linz sits astride the Danube and the surrounding countryside is one of hills and thick forest. Donald Harradine's course is cut through the woods, an attractive and quite long parkland course with well-placed bunkers.

Open Golf Linz Feldkirchen (1991)   **30**

Phone: 07233 7676

Postfach 17, 4101 Linz

20km from Linz, 30km from Wels towards Badesea Feldkirchen

Holes	9 Par 37 2867m
Visitors	Welcome
Fees	230–480AS
Facilities	Bar and restaurant; practice ground
Pro	Roger Andrews

Linzer Golfclub Muhlviertel (1990)   **31**

Phone: 07237 3893

Am Luttenberg 1, 4222 St Georgen

Just east of Linz, at St Georgen

Holes	9 Par 35 2924m.
Visitors	Welcome
Fees	400–500AS
Facilities	Bar and restaurant; driving range
Pro	Peter Kreier

Golfclub Maria Theresia (1991)   **32**

Phone: 07732 3944

Letten 5, Haag-Goboltskirchen, 4680 Haag am Haustruck

West of Linz, off the A8 at Haag

Holes	18 Par 72 6282m.
Visitors	Welcome. Course closed mid-November to March
Fees	450–550AS
Facilities	Bar and restaurant; practice ground; swimming pool; tennis courts
Pro	Ellen Wright

Golf Club am Mondsee (1986)   **33**

Phone: 06232 3835

5310 St Lorenz-Brachensee

East of Salzburg. Take the Mondsee exit off the A1; head for Scharfling on the B154

Holes	18 Par 72 6036m.
Visitors	Welcome. Course closed November to March
Fees	400–600AS
Facilities	Bar and restaurant; driving range
Pro	S Schrolnberger

Golfclub Murhof (1963)   **34**

Phone: 03127 2101

8130 Frohnleiten-Murhof

North of Graz off the S35. In Peggau turn left for Murhof

Holes	18 Par 72 6167m.
Visitors	Welcome. Course closed December to March
Fees	450–700AS
Facilities	Bar and restaurant; driving range; swimming pool; tennis courts
Pro	Richard Paul Austin

Situated in the foothills of the Alps in Styria, the course sits in secluded and tranquil territory, encircled by bosky hills. Murhof is a long and demanding course with some very testing par 4s. It is always in first-class condition and is notable for its fine trees and arrays of flowering bushes. The hotel has excellent facilities including tennis courts and a swimming pool.

Golf Club Ottenstein (1991)   **35**

Phone: 02826 7476

3532 Niedergrunbach 1

North west of Krems off the B37

Holes	18 Par 74 6048m.
Visitors	Welcome
Fees	300–400AS
Facilities	Bar and restaurant; driving range
Pro	Astrid Kleine

Golf Club Portschach (1960)   36

Phone: 04272 83486

Stallhofen 2, 9602 Moosburg

Off the main road between Villach and Klagenfurt. Take the Portschach West exit and then turn to Moosburg

Holes	18 Par 72 6216m.
Visitors	Welcome. Course closed November to March
Fees	500AS
Facilities	Bar and restaurant; practice ground
Pro	Mike Sullivan

Golf & Country Club Reiting (1991)   37

Phone: 0663 833308

Golfplatzweg 1, 8793 Schardorf/Gai

North east of Graz. Head for Trofaiach and the club is west of it at Schardorf/Gai

Holes	9 Par 36 3131m.
Visitors	Welcome. Closed December to March
Fees	450AS
Facilities	Bar and restaurant; practice ground; squash and tennis courts
Pro	Noel James Adams

Golf Club St Polten Schloss Goldegg (1988) 38

Phone: 02741 7360

3100 St Polten, Goldegg

Take the St Polten exit off the A1 west of Vienna, then the B1 towards Melk

Holes	18 Par 73 6258m.
Visitors	Welcome
Fees	400–500AS
Facilities	Bar and restaurant; driving range
Pro	John Dockray

Golf & Country Club Salzburg-Klessheim (1955)   39

Phone: 0662 850851

5071 Salzburg-Wals

On the west side of the city. Take the Salzburg-Klessheim exit off the A1; head for Schloss Klessheim

Holes	9 Par 35 2350m.
Visitors	Welcome
Fees	300–400AS
Facilities	Bar and restaurant; driving range; swimming pool; tennis
Pro	Paul Mackenzie

This appealing golf course meanders through avenues of ancient and stately trees close to the historic Schloss Klessheim, a baroque state building. The trees make the course a real test of the golfer's accuracy. The club is on the outskirts of the city and has tennis courts and a swimming pool.

Salzkammergut Golfclub (1933)   40

Phone: 06132 6340

Postfach 145, 4820 Bad Ischl

West of Bad Ischl, off the B158. The club is signposted

Holes	18 Par 71 5900m.
Visitors	Welcome. Course closed November to end of March
Fees	550AS
Facilities	Restaurant; practice ground
Pro	Ian Hay

Close to the renowned resort and spa of Bad Ischl, Salzkammergut is an interesting and challenging course in lovely surroundings of meadows, woods and hills. Ancient trees, tricky slopes, ponds and a stream make it a tough test for any golfer.

Golf Club Schloss Ebreichsdorf (1988)   41

Phone: 02254 3888

Schlossallee 1, 2483 Ebreichsdorf

Off the A2 south of Vienna; take the B210 to Ebreichsdorf.

Holes	18 Par 72 6246m.
Visitors	Welcome. Course closed December to March
Fees	500–650AS
Facilities	Bar and restaurant; driving range
Pro	Keith Preston

Golf & Country Club Schloss Ernegg (1988) 42

Phone: 07488 214

3261 Steinakirchen am Forst

Off the A1 between Vienna and Linz. Take the Ybbs exit and turn right off the B25 to Steinakirchen and the club.

Holes	18 Par 72 5699m.
Visitors	Welcome. Course closed November to April
Fees	300–400AS
Facilities	Bar and restaurant; driving range; 9 hole short course
Pro	Jim Graham

Golfclub Schloss Pichlarn (1972)   43

Phone: 03682 2841

8952 Irdning/Aigen in Ennstal

Off the B146 south west of Liezen. From Trautenfels head for to Irdning and then Aigen

Holes	18 Par 72 6158m.
Visitors	Welcome
Fees	500–650AS
Facilities	Bar and restaurant; practice ground; swimming pool; tennis courts
Pro	Alan Mitchell

Golf Club Schloss Schonborn (1987) **44**

Phone: 02267 2879

2013 Schonborn

North of Stockerau off the B303. Go towards Viendorff and then follow the signs to the club

Holes	18 Par 73 6370m; 9 Par 35 2895m.
Visitors	Welcome. Course closed December to March
Fees	500–700AS
Facilities	Bar and restaurant; driving range
Pro	Ossi Gartenmaier

Golf Club Schloss Frauenthal (1988) **45**

Phone: 03462 5717

Ulrichsberg 3, 8530 Deutschlandsberg

South of Graz. Off the B76 just east of Deutschlandsberg

Holes	9 Par 36 2810m.
Visitors	Welcome. Course closed December to March
Fees	300–400AS
Facilities	Bar and restaurant; driving range
Pro	Mark Thompson

Jagd und Golf Club Schloss Fuschl (1964) **46**

Phone: 06229 2390

5322 Hof bei Salzburg

East of Salzburg off the B158 at Fuschlsee

Holes	9 Par 31 1825m.
Visitors	Welcome. Course closed November to March
Fees	250–300AS
Facilities	Bar and restaurant; driving range
Pro	Franco Torrano

Golfclub Schonfeld (1990) **47**

Phone: 02213 2063

2291 Schonfeld

On the east side of Schonfeld

Holes	18 Par 72 6175m.
Visitors	Welcome. Closed December to February
Fees	400–500AS
Facilities	Bar and restaurant; practice ground
Pro	Manfred Muller

Golfclub Seefeld/Wildmoos (1969) **48**

Phone: 05212 3003

6100 Seefeld

West of Innsbruck. Take the B177 to Seefeld and then head for Mosern/Wildmoos

Holes	18 Par 71 6155m.
Visitors	Must book. Course closed November to mid-May
Fees	500AS
Facilities	Bar and restaurant; practice ground
Pro	Mike Mawdsley

Situated 4300 feet above sea level in a setting dominated by the Hohe Munde mountain, here is alpine golf personified. Seefeld is where drives soar through crisp thin air and where the fairways are framed by a dazzling array of colours as they rollercoast their way against a stunning mountain backdrop. Golf at Seefeld is nothing if not exhilarating! A famous skiing resort, Seefeld is located midway between Innsbruck and Garmisch. The club has a noted teaching centre including two driving ranges; not surprisingly Seefeld has established itself as one of Austria's premier golf clubs.

Golf Club Semmering (1926) **49**

Phone: 02664 8154

Hochstrasse 108, 2680 Semmering

Off the S6 at Semmering

Holes	9 Par 31 1930m.
Visitors	Welcome. Course closed November to April
Fees	300–400AS
Facilities	Bar and restaurant; driving range
Pro	Thomas Kabietadiko

Although the Golf Club of Vienna is the oldest club, Semmering is the oldest existing golf course. It has an idyllic position; from the fairways the golfers can see the distant hills across broad vistas of rolling, thickly wooded countryside. It is a short course but has some tough bunkers and hazards; many tournaments are organised through the season.

Golf Club Waldviertel (1988) **50**

Phone: 02865 8490

3874 Haugschlag/Littschau

North west of Vienna; off the B5 at Littschau

Holes	18 Par 72 6319m.
Visitors	Welcome
Fees	450–600AS
Facilities	Bar and restaurant; practice ground; 18 hole pitch & putt
Pro	Billy Mahaffy

Golf Club Wels (1981)   **51**

Phone: 07243 6038

Weyerbach 37, 4512 Weisskirchen

South east of Wels at Weisskirchen

Holes	18 Par 72 6098m.
Visitors	Welcome. Course closed December to March
Fees	400–500AS
Facilities	Bar and restaurant; driving range

Golfclub Wien (1901)   **52**

Phone: 0222 2189564

Freudenau 65a, 1020 Wien

The club is near the Hippodrome on the east side of Vienna

Holes	18 Par 70 5861m.
Visitors	Welcome
Fees	700AS
Facilities	Bar and restaurant; driving range
Pro	Tom Rogerson

The oldest Austrian golf course is located in the famous Vienna park, the Prater, with its giant wheel. The terrain is fairly flat, though relieved by some elevated greens, with well-situated bunkers. The many old and majestic trees are a delight to the eye but a peril to the golfer.

Golf Club Wienerwald (1981)   **53**

Phone: 0222 823111

Forstof 211, Klausenleopoldsdorf/Laaben

South west of Vienna off the A1; take the B19 to Laaben

Holes	9 Par 34 2326m.
Visitors	Welcome. Course closed November to April
Fees	300–500AS
Facilities	Bar and restaurant

BELGIUM

L IKE many other European countries, Belgium has seen a great increase in the number of courses available during the last five or six years. During that time 35 new clubs have been opened and the country can now claim over 50 golf courses. Several of these new courses are notable additions, in particular Golf du Chateau de la Bawette, Golf du Bercuit and Cleydael.

There is a fine golfing tradition in Belgium, aided by the abiding enthusiasm of their Royal Family; King Badouin was good enough to play for the Belgian amateur team, for example. Most of the older courses embody the finest traditions of golf course architecture, designed as they were by some of the great names such as Tom Simpson and Harry Colt. Royal Antwerp, the Royal Golf Club des Fagnes ('a fine and beautiful examination of golf'), Royal Waterloo, Royal Zoute and Royal Latem can be favourably compared with any course in Europe. The jewel in the crown is the Royal Club de Belgique, an immaculately presented and testing course amid beautiful surroundings.

Belgium is a splendid country in which to play golf and it is surprising that more British golfers do not make their way there. It is easy to reach by ferry (and relatively inexpensive); the road system is excellent; it is very easy to reserve tee times; the clubhouse facilities are excellent; and most of the people understand English.

Unit of currency: Belgian Franc (BF)
Rate of exchange (approx. at 1.1.93): BF50–£1
International dialling code: (010 32)

Golf Club d'Andenne (1988)   **1**

Phone: 085-84 34 04

Ferme du Moulin 52, 5220 Andenne

East of Namur off the N90; or take Junction 9 off the E42 to Andenne. Then go towards Bonneville

Holes	9 Par 34 2446m.
Visitors	Welcome at any time
Fees	BF500–700
Facilities	Bar and restaurant; practice ground
Pro	Fréderic Dupont

Royal Amicale Anderlecht Golf Club (1987)   **2**

Phone: 025 21 16 87

Drève Olympique 1, 1070 Bruxelles

On the outskirts of Brussels. Take exit 15 or 16 off the ring road

Holes	9 Par 36 2660m.
Visitors	Welcome
Fees	BF750–1000
Facilities	Bar and restuarant closed Mondays; covered practice ground
Pro	Pierre Michielsen

BELGIUM & LUXEMBOURG

Antwerp

Bruges

Brussels

Brussels

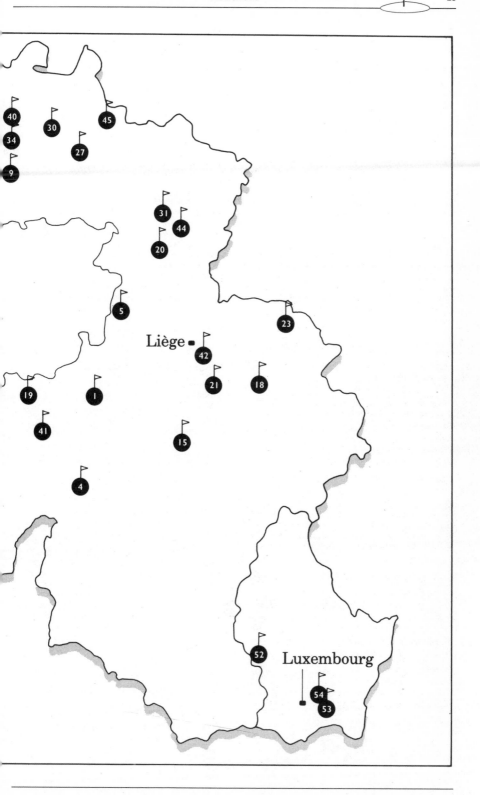

Royal Antwerp Golf Club (1888)   3

Phone: 03-666 84 56

G Capiaulei 2, 2950 Kapellen

North of Antwerp, off the N4

Holes	18 Par 72 6155m.
Visitors	Must book
Fees	BF1500–3000
Facilities	Bar and restaurant; practice ground
Pro	John Halliwell

This is the oldest golf club in Belgium and the second oldest in continental Europe, founded as it was in 1888 and originally laid out by Willie Park. The course was redesigned by Tom Simpson in 1930. Accuracy is demanded from the tees, since the landing areas are extremely narrow and the trees which line every hole will exact a severe penalty if a shot is hit off-line. Many of the holes, especially during the middle part of the course, are dog-legs and this puts a further premium on accuracy and sensible tactics. It is a very testing golf course (which was rated by Pat Ward-Thomas as 'a masterpiece of its kind') in beautiful surroundings, where the holes wend their way through groves of majestic trees.

Golf Club du Château Royal d'Ardenne (1900)   4

Phone: 082-66 62 28

Tour Leopold, 5560 Houyet

South east of Dinant, off the main Brussels to Neufchateau road; turn opposite Restaurant La Marquisette for the club

Holes	18 Par 71 5333m.
Visitors	Welcome
Fees	BF1000–1500
Facilities	Bar and restaurant closed Tuesdays; practice ground
Pro	Pierre Delmas

The course was built at the turn of the century and is unusual in that there are only 12 greens. This necessitates the use of different tees on six of the holes in order to provide 18 holes.

Avernas Golf Club (1990)   5

Phone: 019-51 30 66

Route de Grand Hallet 21, 4280 Hannut (Avernas le Bauduin)

Take Exit 27 off the E40 Brussels to Liège road, which runs past the course

Holes	9 Par 34 2674m.
Visitors	Welcome
Fees	BF500–700
Facilities	Bar and restaurant; practice ground
Pro	Maurice Duhamel

Golf du Château de la Bawette (1988)   6

Phone: 010-22 33 32

Chaussée du château de la Bawette 5, 1300 Wavre

Just of Exit 5 of the E411 (Brussels to Namur) motorway.

Holes	18 Par 72 6049m.
	9 Par 33 1876m.
Visitors	Welcome
Fees	BF1000–2000
Facilities	Bar and restaurant; practice ground
Pro	Ken Murray

The course opened in 1988 and is built in the grounds of the Beaulieu estate, at the heart of which is the delightful family château. Built in the glorious wooded Brabantine countryside, in the foothills of the Ardennes, the fairways swoop and roll through deep forest. Some of the drives through the trees demand great accuracy and the eccentrically-shaped bunkers, which are splashed on the fairways, offer further protection. Water hazards also come into play on several of the holes. It is a most appealing and demanding course in beautiful surroundings. There is a beginners' course and an extensive practice area.

Royal Golf Club de Belgique (1906)   7

Phone: 02-767 58 01

Château de Ravenstein, 3080 Tervuren

Off the N3 at Tervuren, east of Brussels

Holes	18 Par 73 6082m.
Visitors	Must book
Fees	BF1550–2550
Facilities	Bar and restaurant; practice ground; short course
Pro	Flory Van Donck

The course was built in the early years of the century at the behest of King Leopold II and was designed by Tom Simpson. A superb 18th-century château makes a most imposing clubhouse.

The course can only be described as idyllic. From the moment you survey the first hole, which is shaped through an avenue of beautiful trees, you cannot but be captivated. The trees themselves are a constant wonder in their variety; rhododendrons, cedars, willows, beeches, Japanese cherry trees and dozens of others make the course into a fascinating botanical garden. The course, manicured to perfection, is a great test for any golfer and is full of interesting challenges.

Golf du Bercuit (1967)   8

Phone: 010-84 15 01

Les Gottes 3, 1390 Grez-Doiceau

Off the E40 (Brussels to Namur) motorway at Exit 8. The club is close to Dion-le-Val

Holes	18 Par 72 5931m.
Visitors	Welcome at any time

Fees   BF1500–2500

Facilities Bar and restaurant; practice ground; swimming pool

Pro   P Toussaint

Tall and stately trees line many of the fairways of this charming golf course. Amateur golfers will be relieved to hear that, although a shot hit off line will usually mean the loss of a shot, the ball will usually be found quite easily. The course, built in the sixties, was designed by Robert Trent Jones and bears many of his trademarks, such as steeply contoured fairways, long kidney-shaped bunkers and the use of water on several holes. The 9th and 18th holes share a huge double green. The course is immaculately maintained and is set in delightful, undulating countryside. The spacious modern clubhouse has an open air swimming pool.

Bossenstein Golf & Polo Club (1987)   9

Phone: 03-485 64 46

Bossenstein Kasteel, 2520 Broechem

East of Antwerp, off the E34/E313; take Exit 19 towards Lier

Holes   18 Par 72 6232m

Visitors   Welcome

Fees   BF100–1500

Facilities Bar and restaurant closed Monday; practice ground; 9 hole short course

Pro   Alain Christiaens

Brabantse Golf (1982)   10

Phone: 02-751 82 05

Steenwagenstraat 11, 1820 Melsbroek

North of Brussels off the E19. Take the Vilvoorde/Brucargo exit, turn left at next crossroads; the club is on the left

Holes   18 Par 69 4648m.

Visitors   Welcome

Fees   BF800–1500

Facilities Bar and restaurant closed Monday; practice ground

Pro   Eugenio Rovnar

Brasschaat Open Golf Center (1991)   11

Phone: 03653 10 20

Miksebaan 248, 2930 Brasschaat

North of Antwerp, off the Breda road

Holes   9 Par 36 2915m.

Visitors   Welcome

Fees   BF400–600

Facilities Bar and restaurant; practice ground

Pro   Colin Mackay

There are over sixty tees, under cover, on the practice range, which is open until midnight. As well as the 9 hole course, there is a pitch and putt course.

Cleydael Golf Club (1988)   12

Phone: 03-887 00 79

Kasteel Cleydael, Cleydaellaan 36, 2630 Aartselaar

Off the N177 south of Antwerp

Holes   18 Par 72 6059m.

Visitors   Must book. The course is reserved for members at weekends from 8am to 2pm

Fees   BF1500–2000

Facilities Bar and restaurant, closed Monday in winter; practice ground

Pro   Richard Lovelady

The clubhouse, a moated medieval castle, is well worth a visit and has marvellous facilities. It sits at the heart of an excellent golf course, which was designed by Paul Rolin and opened in 1990. The fairways wander through avenues of trees and are generous in width, but canals and lakes affect the play on many of the holes.

Damme Golf & Country Club (1987)   13

Phone: 050-35 35 72

Doornstraat 16, 8340 Sijsele-Damme

East of Bruges, just off the N9 at Sijsele

Holes   18 Par 72 6016m.

Visitors   Welcome at any time (handicap 28)

Fees   BF1300–1700

Facilities Bar and restaurant, closed Monday; practice ground; indoor practice area; 9 hole short course

Pro   Graham Pearce

The course was opened in 1987 and its notable feature is the profusion of water, which affects the play on almost every hole. This, combined with the massed ranks of beautiful mature trees (and many newly planted ones), makes it an exacting course to play.

As well as an extensive outdoor practice area there is a remarkable indoor practice facility. Housed in a huge hanger, there is room for at least a dozen people to hit golf balls, plus a 9 hole putting green and a practice bunker.

Golf & Country Club De Palingbeek (1992)   14

Phone: 057-20 04 36

Eeckhofstraat 14, 8902 Hollebeke-Ieper

Take Exit 3 off the A19 west of Kortrijk, turn right to Ypres and sharp left into Hollebeke Street. The club is on the right

Holes   18 Par 72 6120m

Visitors   Welcome

Fees   BF1200–1700

Facilities Bar and restaurant; driving range

Pro   David Petrie

Golf de Durbuy (1990)　　15

Phone: 086-21 44 54

Route d'Oppagne, 6940 Barvaux-Durbuy

South east of Namur. At Marche en Famenne on the E411, take the N86 to Barvaux then sharp right onto N286. The club is on the right

Holes	18–Par 72　5964m.
Visitors	Welcome
Fees	BF1200–1500
Facilities	Bar and restaurant; practice ground; tennis courts; short course
Pro	Cedric Bertrand

Edegemse Golf Club (1990)　　16

Phone: 03-440 64 30

Drie Eyckenstraat 546, 2650 Edegem-Antwerpen

South of Antwerp off the E19. After the tunnel take the UIA exit

Holes	9　Par 35　2547m.
Visitors	Welcome, but must book
Fees	BF600
Facilities	None

Golf de l'Empereur (1991)　　17

Phone: 067-77 15 71

Rue Emile François, 1474 Ways (Genappe)

South of Brussels off the N5. Take the exit towards Ways, and then turn left at the crossroads

Holes	18　Par 72　6527m.
Visitors	Welcome
Fees	BF800–1200
Facilities	Bar and restaurant; practice ground
Pro	Marcel Vercruyce

Royal Golf Club des Fagnes (1930)　　18

Phone: 087-79 16 13

Chemin du Golf 1, 4900 Spa

Off the N629 north of Spa

Holes	18　Par 72　5948m.
Visitors	Welcome, but must book
Fees	BF1200–1600
Facilities	Bar and restaurant; practice ground
Pro	W Robertson

The course, close to the resort of Spa, opened for play in 1930 when Henry Cotton and Archie Compston played a match against Massy and Boyer. Cotton described the course as a 'continental Sunningdale', as well he might since it was designed by Harry Colt and bears many of his hallmarks. The fairways meander in captivating style through avenues of delightful trees, and Pat Ward-Thomas rightly called the course 'a fine and beautiful examination of golf'.

Golf de Falnuée (1991)　　19

Phone: 081-63 30 90

55 rue E Pirson, 5032 Mazy

West of Namur off the N33

Holes	18　Par 70　5500m.
Visitors	Welcome, but must book at weekends
Fees	BF800–1300
Facilities	Bar and restaurant closed Monday; practice ground
Pro	Hervé Ladmirant

Flanders-Nippon Golf & Business Club (1988)　　20

Phone: 011-22 37 93

Vissenbroek Straat 15, 3500 Hasselt

On the east side of Hasselt, off Universiteitslaan (the road to Genk)

Holes	18　Par 72　5992m. Public course: 9 holes　Par 32　1779m
Visitors	Welcome
Fees	BF1000–1500
Facilities	Restaurant closed Monday in winter; practice ground
Pro	John Gulesserian

International Gomzé Golf Club (1986)　　21

Phone: 041-60 92 07

Sur Counachamps, 4140 Gomzé-Andoumont

On the E25 Liège to Ardennes autoroute, take Exit 44 to Gomzé-Andoumont

Holes	18　Par 72　6034m.
Visitors	Welcome
Fees	BF1000–1250
Facilities	Bar and restaurant closed Monday; practice ground
Pro	Leslie J Cain

Royal Golf Club du Hainaut (1933)　　22

Phone: 065-22 94 74

4 Rue de la Verrerie, 7050 Erbisoeul

Take Exit 23bis off the E42 Paris–Brussels autoroute, then the N6 towards Mons and follow signs for Ath. The club is signposted

Holes	18　Par 72　6108m 9　Par 36　3233m.
Visitors	Welcome, but must book
Fees	BF1000–1500
Facilities	Bar and restaurant; practice ground
Pro	John Wilkinson

Golf & Business Club Henri-Chapelle (1933) **23**

Phone: 087-88 19 91

Rue du Vivier 3, 4841 Henri-Chapelle

The club is off the N3 Battice to Aachen road

Holes	18 Par 72 6061m.
Visitors	Welcome
Fees	BF1200–1500
Facilities	Bar and restaurant; practice ground; 9 hole short course
Pro	Henk Timmer

Golf Club Hulencourt (1991) **24**

Phone: 067-78 01 24

Bruyère d'Hulencourt 15, 1472 Vx Genappe

North east of Nivelles, off the N27

Holes	18 Par 72 6215m.
Visitors	Welcome. Course closed Tuesday
Fees	BF1200–1800 (1992)
Facilities	Bar and restaurant; 9-hole pitch and putt; practice ground
Pro	Fabrice Masson

Golf & Business Club Kampenhout (1990) **25**

Phone: 016-65 12 16

Wildersedreef 56, 1910 Kampenhout

North east of Brussels, off the N21 and N26

Holes	18 Par 72 6142m.
Visitors	Must book
Fees	BF1000–1500
Facilities	Bar and restaurant closed Monday; practice ground
Pro	Vance Waters

Keerbergen Golf Club (1979) **26**

Phone: 015-23 49 61

Vlieghavenlaan 50, 3140 Keerbergen

East of Mechelen off the N21. At the Keerbergen junction, head for the lake. The club is behind the lake

Holes	18 Par 70 5530m.
Visitors	Welcome
Fees	BF1000–1400
Facilities	Bar and restaurant closed Monday in winter; driving range
Pro	W Van Begin

Kempense Golf Club (1990) **27**

Phone: 014-81 62 34

Kiezelweg 78, 2400 Mol-Rauw

East of Antwerp off the N71 and to the east of Geel

Holes	18 Par 72 5816m.
Visitors	Welcome, but must book
Fees	BF1000–1400
Facilities	Bar and restaurant; practice ground
Pro	Xavier Pagnanini

Golf La Bruyère (1990) **28**

Phone: 071-87 72 67

Rue de Jumere 1, 1495 Sart-Dames-Avelines

Off the N93, Nivelles to Namur road

Holes	18 Par 71 5805m.
Visitors	Welcome
Fees	BF600–1000
Facilities	Bar and restaurant; practice ground
Pro	Patrick Vandermoot

Royal Latem Golf Club (1909) **29**

Phone: 91-82 54 11

Latemstraat 120, 9830 Saint-Martens-Latem

Off the E40 autoroute just west of Ghent

Holes	18 Par 72 5767m.
Visitors	Must book
Fees	BF1300–1750
Facilities	Bar and restaurant closed Monday; practice ground
Pro	Jan Verplancke

This delightful golf course was designed by Tom Simpson in the early years of this century. With its rolling fairways, the landing areas well protected by bunkers, and immaculate greens, it is a splendid and very testing course to play. Its appeal is greatly enhanced by the towering old trees; there is a profusion of beeches, oaks and birches. A fine clubhouse stands at the centre of the course and from its windows and terraces you have fine views of this most attractive course.

Lilse Golf Club (1988) **30**

Phone: 014-55 19 30

Haarlebeek 3, 2275 Lille

Take Exit 22 off the E34 from Eindhoven to Antwerp. Turn left to Gierle, bear right and left at crossroads to find the club

Holes	9 Par 33 2331m.
Visitors	Welcome
Fees	BF500–700
Facilities	Bar and restaurant closed Sunday
Pro	Fabien Van Damme

Limburg Golf & Country Club (1966)   31

Phone: 011-38 35 43
Golfstraat 1, 3530 Houthalen
North of Hasselt; off the N715

Holes	18 Par 72 6101m.
Visitors	Welcome
Fees	BF950–1250 (1992)
Facilities	Bar and restaurant closed Monday; practice ground
Pro	Joop Renders

Golf Club de Louvain-la-Neuve (1991)   32

Phone: 032-10-45 05 15
Rue A Hardy 68, 1348 Ottignies L-L-N
Take Exit 7 off the E411 (Brussels to Namur)
onto RN 4. The club is on the right

Holes	18 Par 72 6047m.
Visitors	Welcome
Fees	BF1200–2400
Facilities	Bar and restaurant closed Tuesday; practice ground
Pro	Mrs P Xhardez

Golf du Mont Garni (1990)   33

Phone: 065-62 27 19
Rue du Mont Garni 3, 7331 Saint-Ghislain
From the E19 take Exit 25 and take the road to
Herchies. The club is on the left

Holes	18 Par 74 6353m.
Visitors	Welcome
Fees	BF900–1300
Facilities	Bar and restaurant; driving range
Pro	Jerome Lafon

Olen Golf Club (1965)   34

Phone: 014-22 25 90
Britslaan, 2250 Olen
Off the N152 between Antwerp and Hasselt

Holes	9 Par 34 2492m.
Visitors	Welcome, but at weekends can only play with a member
Fees	BF400
Facilities	Bar and restaurant

Koninklijke Golf Club Ostende (1903)   35

Phone: 059-23 32 83
Koninklihke Baan 2, B8420 De Haan
North of Ostend on the coast road to De Haan

Holes	18 Par 70 5285m.
Visitors	Welcome
Fees	BF1250–1850
Facilities	Bar and restaurant; practice ground
Pro	G Niven

This club is also known as the Royal Ostend Golf Club and is the only links course in Belgium. It was created at the turn of the century on the initiative of King Leopold II and the players have sweeping views of the beaches and the sea. The course is quite short but the winds off the sea frequently impose severe problems on the average golfer.

Golf & Country Club Oudenaarde (1976)   36

Phone: 055-31 54 81
Kortrijkstraat 52, 9790 Wortegem-Petegem
West of Oudenaarde off the N453

Holes	18 Par 72 6172m; Holes 9 Par 34 2536m.
Visitors	Welcome
Fees	BF1000–1500
Facilities	Bar and restaurant closed Wednesday; practice ground
Pro	Chris Morton

Overijse Golf Club (1988)   37

Phone: 02-687 50 30
Gemslaan 55, 3090 Overijse
South east of Brussels. Off the N4 or E40
(Brussels to Namur) motorway, exit 2

Holes	9 Par 36 2876m.
Visitors	Welcome
Fees	BF1200
Facilities	Bar; practice ground
Pro	Pierre Crepin

Pierpont Golf Club (1990)   38

Phone: 071-85 14 19
Chemin de Pierpont, 6210 Frasnes-Lez-Gosselles
North of Charleroi, just off the N5 close to its
junction with the N93

Holes	18 Par 72 6297m.
Visitors	Welcome
Fees	BF1000–1600
Facilities	Bar and restaurant; driving range; short course; tennis courts

Golf de Rigenée (1983)   39

Phone: 071-87 77 65
62 Rue du Chatelet, 1495 Villers-la Ville
Near Exit 19 of the E19 (Brussels to Mons).
Rigenée is off the N93 towards Namur

Holes	18 Par 72 5936m.
Visitors	Welcome
Fees	BF950–1900, BF1500 before 10am
Facilities	Bar and restaurant closed Tuesdays; practice ground, 3 tennis courts
Pro	Hervé Ladmirant

Rinkven Golf & Country Club (1982)   40

Phone: 033-84 07 84

Sint Jobsteenweg 120, 2970 Schilde
North of Antwerp, off the E19 towards
Gravenwesel. Turn right at T junction and the
club is on the left beyond a farm

Holes	27 Par 72 About 6100m.
Visitors	Must book
Fees	BF1300–2600
Facilities	Bar and restaurant; practice ground
Pro	Mike Waldron

Also known as the Antwerp International Golf
Club, there are three loops of nine holes at
Rinkven. The various combinations make up
courses of just over 6000 metres, which meander
through avenues of trees. Water affects the play
on several holes.

Golf de Rougemont (1989)   41

Phone: 0811-41 14 18

Chemin du Beau Vallon 45, 5170 Profondeville
South of Namur off the N92

Holes	18 Par 72 5621m.
Visitors	Welcome
Fees	BF600–800 (1992)
Facilities	Bar and restaurant closed Monday; practice ground
Pro	Ringo Braems

Royal Golf Club du Sart-Tilman (1939)   42

Phone: 041-36 20 21

541 Route du Condroz, 4031 Angleur-Liège
South of Liège off the Route du Condroz (N63)

Holes	18 Par 72 6000m.
Visitors	Welcome, but must book
Fees	BF1050–1550
Facilities	Bar and restaurant; practice ground
Pro	Mme Agathe Fransolett

Golf Club de Sept Fontaines (1988)   43

Phone: 02-353 02 46

1021 Chaussée d'Alsemberg, 1420 Braine l'Alleud
Take Exit 2 off the N5 (Brussels–Waterloo), or
Exits 15 or 17 off the E19

Le Château:

Holes	18 Par 72 6057m.

La Forêt:

Holes	18 Par 66 4438m.
Visitors	Welcome
Fees	BF1000–1800
Facilities	Bar and restaurant closed Mondays; practice ground; swimming pool; tennis courts; 9 hole short course
Pro	Wayne Cunliffe

Spiegelven Golfclub (1988)   44

Phone: 32 11 35 96 16

Wiemesmeerstraat 109, 3600 Genk
Take exit 32 off the E314 Aken–Brussels
autoroute, and follow signs for Zutendaal. The
Club is on the left

Holes	18 Par 72 6198m
Visitors	Welcome, but must book
Fees	BF1000–1500
Facilities	Bar and restaurant; practice ground
Pro	Andre van Pinxten

Steenhoven Country Club (1986)   45

Phone: 014-37 72 50

Eerselseweg 40, 2400 Mol-Postel
West of Eindhoven; take exit 26 and head for
Postel. The course is a little east of Postel

Holes	18 Par 72 6010m.
Visitors	Welcome, but must book
Fees	BF1500–2500
Facilities	Bar and restaurant closed Tuesday; practice ground
Pro	Terry Welch

Ternesse Golf & Country Club (1976)   46

Phone: 03-353 02 92

Uilenbaan 15, 2160 Wommelgem
From Antwerp, take the first Exit off the E313 to
Wommelgem

Holes	18 Par 72 5813m.
Visitors	Must book
Fees	BF1250–2500
Facilities	Bar and restaurant closed Monday in winter; practice ground; short course
Pro	Sylvain Bouillon

Golf du Château de la Tournette (1992)   47

Phone: 067-21 95 25

Chemin de Baudemont 21, 1400 Nivelles
South of Brussels; close to exit 18 of the E19

Holes	36 Par 71/72 5950/6050m.
Visitors	Welcome
Fees	BF1000–1500
Facilities	Bar and restaurant closed Monday; practice ground
Pro	Freddy Swaelens

Waregem Happy Golf Club (1988)   48

Phone: 056-60 88 08

Bergstraat 41, 8790 Waregem

East of Kortrijk. Take exit 5 off the E17; turn left at American Cemetery and follow signs for the Mercedes Center

Holes   18 Par 72 6038m.

Visitors   Welcome

Fees   BF900–1500

Facilities   Bar and restaurant; practice ground

Pro   François Gabias

The sports centre has comprehensive facilities, including tennis and squash courts, an athletics track and a fitness centre.

Royal Waterloo Golf Club (1959)   49

Phone: 02-633 18 50

50 Vieux Chemin de Wavre, 1380 Ohain

South of Brussels off the N253 – signposted

La Marache:

Holes   18 Par 73 6276m.

Le Lion:

Holes   18 Par 73 6269m.

Le Bois Heros:

Holes   9 Par 33 2143m.

Visitors   Welcome except summer weekends

Fees   BF1800–3000

Facilities   Bar and restaurant closed Mondays; practice ground; pitch and putt

Pro   George Will

The two present courses were built in 1959 by Fred Hawtree not far from the famous battlefield of Waterloo, but the club was founded in 1923 and has had several distinguished professionals including Henry Cotton, Aubrey Boomer and Donald Swaelens.

    The fine clubhouse overlooks the courses, which differ in character. La Marache is an undulating course which, during the second half, weaves its way between beech and chestnut trees, while Le Lion is flatter and more open and has views of the old battleground. The short course, Bois Heros, requires great accuracy.

Winge Golf & Country Club (1988)   50

Phone: 016-63 40 53

Wingerstraat 6, 3390 Sint-Joris Winge

East of Leuven, off the N2

Holes   18 Par 72 6159m.

Visitors   Welcome, but must book

Fees   BF1300–1800

Facilities   Bar and restaurant closed Mondays; practice ground

Pro   Flory Van Donck

Royal Zoute Golf Club (1946)   51

Phone: 050-60 12 27

Caddiespad 14, 8300 Knokke-Heist

On the outskirts of Knokke

Holes   18 Par 72 (and a par 64 course) 6172m.

Visitors   Welcome, but must book

Fees   BF1700–2500

Facilities   Bar and restaurant closed Monday; practice ground

Pro   Guy Maxwell

Golf was first played at Knokke at the turn of the century when the club was an offshoot of Bruges Golf & Sports Club. It assumed its own identity in 1909 and the current courses were designed after World War II by Lt. Col. Allen. The quality of the main course, laid out over undulating ground with a profusion of trees – pines, birches and poplars – is such that the Belgian Open was held there in 1992. It is a delightful course; the humps and hillocks of the fairways and the excellent greens, which are well protected by bunkers, make it a good test for any golfer, especially when the wind blows.

LUXEMBOURG

Unit of currency: Luxembourg franc
Rate of exchange (approx. at 1.1.93): LF50–£1
International dialling code: (010 352)

Golf Gaichel (1991)   **52**
Phone: 352-39 71 08
Rue de Eischen, L8469 La Gaichel
Off the N34, in the north of Luxembourg

Holes	9 Par 34 2207m.
Visitors	Welcome. Course closed Monday
Fees	LF700–900
Facilities	Bar and restaurant; practice ground
Pro	Philippe Georges

Kikuoka Country Club (1991)   **53**
Phone: 352-35 61 35
Scheierhaff, L 5412 Canach
Off the E29, east of the airport

Holes	18 Par 72 6340m.
Visitors	Must be introduced by a member
Fees	LF2060–2560
Facilities	Bar and restaurant; driving range
Pro	John Pickford

Golf Club Grand Ducal de Luxembourg (1935)
54
Phone: Luxembourg 34090
Route de Treves 1, 2633 Senningerberg
East of the city and close to the airport

Holes	18 Par 71 5765m.
Visitors	Welcome
Fees	LF1600–2650
Facilities	Bar and restaurant closed Monday; practice ground
Pro	Etienne Saquet

The club was founded in 1935 and was, until 1991, the only golf club in Luxembourg. The steeply pitched roof with its row of dormer windows gives a charming aspect to the rather grand clubhouse, which was once a hunting lodge. It has a large terrace from where you can gaze along several of the holes.

The course has altered little since 1935 and is not particularly long but the narrow fairways, lined with beautiful mature trees, demand accuracy as do the tight, well-bunkered greens. There are some long par threes, and these are balanced by a couple of shorter par 4s.

DENMARK

D ENMARK is not an obvious destination for golfers who feel the urge for a change of scene. But there are over 60 courses in being and about two thirds are of 18 holes. It is worth noting that nearly half of the courses have attained a good degree of maturity, since they were built before 1970.

The oldest course in the country is the Copenhagen Golf Club, established in 1898 and well worth a visit. Other notable courses include Holstebro, Himmerland, Rungsted, SCT Knuds and Silkeborg, and there are many other excellent courses in attractive surroundings.

Denmark is a country with much delightful countryside, notable for its massive pine forests, lakes and the famous fjords. Golf can be played virtually the whole year round, since the climate is similar to that of Britain. Above all the prices are eminently sensible; it is rare to pay much more than £20 for a day's golf and often the green fees are much lower than this. Accommodation is also reasonably priced, especially at the Danish inns, and the majority of the Danish people speak English.

Unit of currency: Danish Krone
Rate of exchange (approx. at 1.1.93): DKr10–£1
International dialling code: (010 45)

Aalborg Golfclub (1908)   **1**

Phone: 98 34 1476

Jaegersprisvej 35, Restrup Enge, 9000 Aalborg
West of Aalborg off the Northholm road; turn south after Restrup Enge

Holes	18 Par 70 5711m.
Visitors	Welcome; must book at weekends
Fees	DKr150–200
Facilities	Bar and restaurant;
Pro	Morten Thuen

This parkland course offers reasonably spacious fairways but a bad shot will usually find one of the many bunkers or streams or end up behind one of the fine old trees. There are two excellent finishing holes; at the short 17th hole you must play over a lake to a green charmingly encircled by silver birches and azaleas, while the dog-leg 18th is bounded by a stream which flows into a lake in front of the green. It's a card-wrecker.

Aarhus Golfklub (Moesgaard-banen) (1931)   **2**

Phone: 86 27 6322

Ny Moesgaardvej 50, 8270 Hojbjerg
South of Aarhus off the B541

Holes	18 Par 71 5796m.
Visitors	Welcome
Fees	DKr180–220
Facilities	Bar and restaurant; practice ground
Pro	Per Greve

A well-established and interesting course which presents a real challenge to the golfer by dint of its elevated tees, tree-lined fairways, water hazards and tricky two-tiered greens.

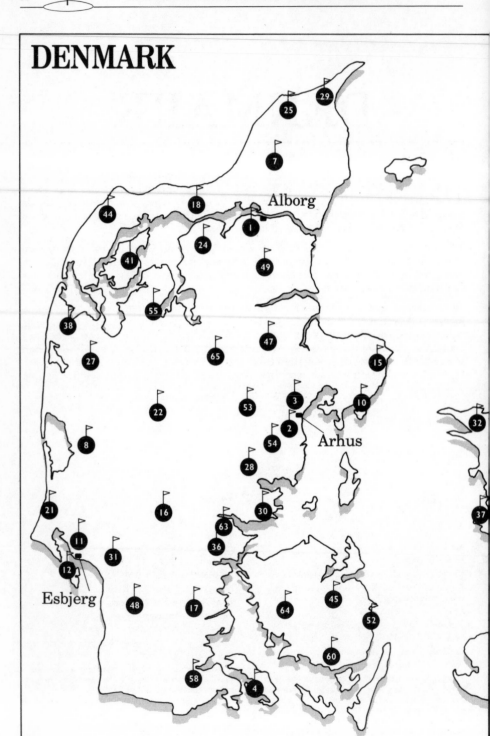

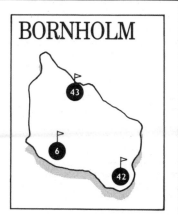

BORNHOLM

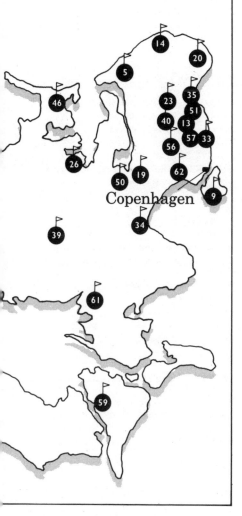

Copenhagen

Aarhus Golfklub (Mollerup-banen) (1931) 3
Phone: 86 27 6322
Mollerupvej, 8240 Risskov
North of Aarhus, off the E3 towards Randers
Holes   9 Par 36 3037m.
Visitors   Welcome
Fees   DKr100–150
Facilities Bar and restaurant; driving range
Pro   Michael Jacobsen

Alssund Golfklub (1980) 4
Phone: 74 41 6238
Vestermark, Skydebanevej, 6400 Sonderborg
North of Sonderborg, close to Kaer
Holes   9 Par 32 2172m.
Visitors   Welcome
Fees   DKr50–95
Facilities Driving range

Asserbo Golfklub (1946) 5
Phone: 42 12 1490
Bodjergaardsvej, 3300 Frederiksvaerk
North of Frederiksvaerk at Asserbo
Holes   9 Par 34 2594m.
Visitors   Welcome
Fees   DKr150–200
Facilities Bar and restaurant; driving range
Pro   John Nielsen

Bornholms Golfklub (1973) 6
Phone: 53 95 6854
Plantagevej 3b, Robbedale, 3700 Ronne
Off the A38 east of Ronne
Holes   18 Par 68 4789m.
Visitors   Welcome
Fees   DKr160
Facilities Bar and restaurant; practice ground
Pro   Erling Pedersen

Bronderslev Golfklub (1971) 7
Phone: 98 82 3281
Golfvejen 83, 9700 Bronderslev
On the north west side of Bronderslev
Holes   18 Par 71 5783m.
Visitors   Welcome, except Saturday (10am to
             2pm) and Sunday
Fees   DKr150
Facilities Bar and restaurant; practice ground
Pro   Lars Jacobsen

Dejbjerg Golfklub (1964)   8

Phone: 97 35 0959
Letagervej 1, Dejbjerg, 6900 Skjern
North of Skjern. Turn for Dejbjerg before you reach Hanning

Holes	18 Par 69 5275m.
Visitors	Welcome
Fees	DKr130–160
Facilities	Driving range; par 3 course
Pro	Jens Veje

Dragor Golfklub (1989)   9

Phone: 32 53 8975
Kalvebodvej, 2791 Dragor
West of Dragor at Kongelund (on the island of Amager)

Holes	18 Par 71 5854m.
Visitors	Welcome
Fees	DKr160–190
Facilities	Bar; driving range; par 3 course
Pro	Jens Kristensen

Ebeltoft Golfklub (1966)   10

Phone: 86 36 1064
Strandgardshoj 8a, 8400 Ebeltoft
On the north side of Ebeltoft

Holes	18 Par 68 4925m.
Visitors	Welcome
Fees	DKr120–150
Facilities	Practice ground
Pro	Gerry Gardiner

Despite its relative lack of length Ebeltoft is a tough course on which to score well, by dint of its excellent bunkers, tight dog-leg holes, variety of hazards and tricky greens. It is a distinct challenge and is situated in a delightful area.

Esbjerg Golfklub (1921)   11

Phone: 75 26 9219
Sonderhedevej, Marbaek, 6710 Esbjerg
North west of Esbjerg, off the B463 at Kravsno

Holes	18 Par 70 5728m.
Visitors	Welcome
Fees	DKr160
Facilities	Bar and restaurant; driving range
Pro	Arne Tinning

Esbjerg is judged to be one of the best of the Danish courses and has been the venue for several important professional tournaments. Encircled by the Marbaek Pine Plantation and laid out on heathland with a profusion of heather and fern, it is reminiscent of many of the best Scottish inland courses.

Fano Vesterhavsbads Golfklub (1901)   12

Phone: 75 16 2236
6720 Nordby
West of Esbjerg on Fano Island; take the ferry

Holes	18 Par 65 4450m.
Visitors	Welcome
Fees	DKr125
Facilities	Practice ground
Pro	Henry Aafeldt

Fureso Golfklub (1974)   13

Phone: 42 81 7444
Hestkobvaenge 4, 3460 Birkerod
25km north of Kobenhavn. Take the Farum exit off the A16 onto the B207 to Birkerod

Holes	18 Par 71 5692m.
Visitors	Welcome
Fees	DKr180–250
Facilities	Bar and restaurant; practice ground
Pro	Colin Smith

Gilleleje Golfklub (1970)   14

Phone: 49 71 9516
Ferlegard, Ferlevej 52, 3250 Gilleleje
South east of Gilleleje off the B227

Holes	18 Par 72 6040m.
Visitors	Welcome
Fees	DKr200–250
Facilities	Bar and restaurant; driving range
Pro	Peter Dangerfield

Grena Golfklub (1981)   15

Phone: 86 32 7929
11 Vestermarken 1, 8500 Grena
Off the A16 just west of Grena-Randers, at Enslev

Holes	9 Par 35 2884m.
Visitors	Welcome
Fees	DKr100
Facilities	Bar and restaurant; practice ground
Pro	Graham Townhill

Gyttegard Golfklub (1978)   16

Phone: 75 33 5649
Billundvej 43, 7250 Hejnsvig
South east of Grindsted. Take the B425 for Hejnsvig

Holes	9 Par 35 2855m. 9 more holes to be opened in 1993
Visitors	Welcome
Fees	DKr100
Facilities	Bar and restaurant; practice ground
Pro	Svend Jensen

Haderslev Golfklub (1971)   **17**

Phone: 74 52 8301

Egevej 22, 6100 Haderslev

Just west of Haderslev; head for Sommersted and there are signs for the club

Holes	18 Par 69 5137m.
Visitors	Welcome
Fees	DKr130–160
Facilities	Bar and restaurant; practice ground
Pro	Stephen Smith

Near the pleasant cathedral town, Haderslev golf club has a fairly open course over slightly undulating ground. Good bunkering and the water hazards which affect eight holes make it an interesting test, as do the small well-protected greens.

Han Herreds Golfklub (1987)   **18**

Phone: 98 21 1444

Vestergade 48, 9690 Fjerritslev

Just west of Fjerritslev

Holes	9 Par 32 2014m.
Visitors	Welcome
Fees	DKr90
Facilities	Driving range

Hedeland Golfklub (1984)   **19**

Phone: 42 13 6188

Staerkendevej 232a, 2640 Hedehusene

South east of Roskilde at Reerslev

Holes	18 Par 72 5735m.
Visitors	Welcome
Fees	DKr150–180
Facilities	Practice ground; par 3 course
Pro	Allan Kristensen

Helsingor Golfklub (1927)   **20**

Phone: 49 21 2970

G1 Hellebaekvej, 3000 Helsingor

North west of Helsingor. Take the coast road (B237) towards Alsgarde

Holes	18 Par 71 5705m.
Visitors	Welcome
Fees	DKr160–240
Facilities	Bar and restaurant; practice ground
Pro	Russell Taylor

This is not a long course, but with its narrow fairways menaced by trees, it calls for accuracy and a good touch on the greens. It is well worth a visit, not least for its fine views of the sea. This is also one of the most interesting parts of Denmark with some superb castles, including the royal Fredensborg and Kronborg, the setting for Shakespeare's *Hamlet*.

Henne Golfklub (1989)   **21**

Phone: 75 25 5610

Hennebysvej 30, 6854 Henne

North west of Varde, near the coast at Kirkeby

Holes	18 Par 69 6193m.
Visitors	Welcome
Fees	DKr150
Facilities	Driving range; 9 hole short course
Pro	Neil Elston

Herning Golfklub (1964)   **22**

Phone: 97 21 0033

Golfvej 2, 7400 Herning

Off the A15 just east of Herning

Holes	18 Par 70 5669m.
Visitors	Welcome
Fees	DKr150–200
Facilities	Bar and restaurant; practice ground
Pro	Morten Stendorf

Hillerod Golfklub (1966)   **23**

Phone: 42 46 5046

Nysogardsvej, Ny Hjammershold, 3400 Hillerod

On the south west side of Hillerod at Ny Hjammershold

Holes	18 Par 70 5452m.
Visitors	Welcome
Fees	DKr160–230
Facilities	Bar and restaurant; driving range; par 3 course
Pro	Mike Tulloch

Himmerlands Golfklub (1981)   **24**

Phone: 98 66 1600

Centervej 1, Gatten, 9670 Logstor

South west of Logstor, off the B29. The club is west of Gatten

Holes	18 Par 69 5220m. (Old Course)
	18 Par 73 6050m. (New Course)
Visitors	Welcome
Fees	DKr170–200
Facilities	Bar and restaurant; driving range; par 3 course
Pro	Robert Kristensen

The golf courses of West Jutland are rapidly becoming a popular destination for holiday golfers; there are several reasons for this, chief among which must be the fact that all courses in the region offer value for money combined with genuine seclusion, peace and quiet. The Himmerland Golf and Country Club is a prime example, though it has only been in existence since 1981 (when it was opened by Tony Jacklin) and its second 18-hole course was completed as recently as 1990. Open competitions are regularly staged throughout the summer on Himmerland's not-too-demanding courses, both of which are surrounded by the mature woods and lakes of an attractive nature reserve.

Hjorring Golfklub (1990)   25

Phone: 98 91 1828

Vinstrupvej 30, 9800 Hjorring

Off the A55 north of Hjorring; head for Vidstrup and then follow the signs to the club

Holes	18 Par 71 5886m.
Visitors	Welcome
Fees	DKr150
Facilities	Bar and restaurant; practice ground
Pro	Alvah Routledge

Holbaek Golfklub (1964)   26

Phone: 53 43 4579

Dragerupvej 50, Kirsebaerholmen. 4300 Holbaek

North west of Kalundborg, on the fjord

Holes	9 Par 35 2870m.
Visitors	Welcome
Fees	DKr120–150
Facilities	Bar and restaurant; driving range
Pro	Tim Card

Holstebro Golfklub (1970)   27

Phone: 97 48 5155

Rasted, 7570 Vemb

South west of Holstebro off the A16. After Idom turn right to Rasted

Holes	18 Par 72 6002m.
Visitors	Welcome
Fees	DKr170–200
Facilities	Restaurant; driving range; 9 hole course
Pro	Roy Howett

Widely acclaimed as the leading course in Denmark, Holstebro reminds many visiting British golfers of some of their own heathland courses. There is a hint of Blairgowrie and possibly of Slaley Hall about Holstebro with its picturesque, well manicured fairways which weave a path amid secluded avenues of firs and scattered heather. Although many fairways are generous, the wayward hitter is heavily punished and most of the greens are protected by cunningly positioned bunkers. There are 27 holes at Holstebro; the championship course is complemented by a shorter, easier 9-hole layout. Holstebro is a welcoming club and its courses are guaranteed to charm.

Horsens Golfklub (1972)   28

Phone: 75 61 5151

Silkeborgvej 44, 8700 Horsens

Just north west of Horsens off the A52

Holes	18 Par 72 6020m.
Visitors	Welcome
Fees	DKr140
Facilities	Bar and restaurant; practice ground
Pro	Graham Oakley

Hvide Klit Golfklub (1972)   29

Phone: 98 48 9021

Hvideklitvej 28, Bunken, 9982 Aalbaek

Just north of Aalbaek on the A40

Holes	18 Par 72 5875m.
Visitors	Welcome
Fees	DKr180
Facilities	Bar and restaurant; driving range; par 3 course
Pro	Ole Smidt

Juelsminde Golf & Tennisklub (1973)   30

Phone: 75 69 3492

Boolbroholtvej 11a, 7130 Juelsminde

On the west side of Juelsminde

Holes	9 Par 36 3025m.
Visitors	Welcome, but must book
Fees	DKr100
Facilities	Self-service café; driving range; par 3 course; tennis courts
Pro	Hans Larsen

Kaj Lykke Golfklub (1988)   31

Phone: 75 10 2246

Porsholtvej 13, 6740 Bramming

Just to the north of Bramming

Holes	18 Par 72 6043m.
Visitors	Welcome
Fees	DKr120–140
Facilities	Bar and restaurant; practice ground; 6 hole short course
Pro	Jamie Elkins

Kalundborg Golfklub (1974)   32

Phone: 53 51 5350

Rosnaesvej 225, 4400 Kalundborg

North west of Kalundborg, on the coast at Nostrup

Holes	9 Par 34 2532m.
Visitors	Welcome
Fees	DKr100–120
Facilities	Driving range
Pro	James Darroch

Kobenhavns Golfclub (1898)   33
Phone: 31 63 0483
Dyrehaven 2, 2800 Lyngby
Take the coast road from Kobenhavn to
Rungsted; the club is to the left after Tarbek
Holes   18 Par 71 5898m.
Visitors   Welcome except Tuesday
Fees   DKr150–200
Facilities   Bar and restaurant closed Monday;
               practice ground
Pro   Ole Pedersen
This is Denmark's oldest golf course and was
originally laid out over 8 holes in a stretch of
parkland. A year later the club moved to the
Klampenborg deer park, a delightful setting with
its magnificent old trees and excellent turf. The
grazing deer add to the charm of the course,
which has been the venue for many senior
Danish tournaments.

Koge Golfklub (1969)   34
Phone: 53 65 1000
G1 Hastrupvej 12, 4600 Koge
South of Koge at Hastrup
Holes   18 Par 72 5924m.
Visitors   Welcome
Fees   DKr140–200
Facilities   Restaurant; driving range
Pro   Peter Taylor

Kokkedal Golfklub (1971)   35
Phone: 42 86 9959
Kokkedal Alle 9, 2980 Kokkedal
Just north of Rungsted
Holes   18 Par 72 5958m.
Visitors   Welcome
Fees   DKr170–220
Facilities   Bar and restaurant; driving range
Pro   Nigel Willett

Kolding Golfklub (1933)   36
Phone: 75 52 3793
Emerholtsvej, 6000 Kolding
Just north of Kolding off the E3. Take the
Bramdrupdam exit and in Kolding follow signs
for the club
Holes   18 Par 69 5465m.
Visitors   Welcome
Fees   DKr140–200
Facilities   Bar and restaurant; practice ground
Pro   Frank Atkinson

Korsor Golfklub (1964)   37
Phone: 53 57 1836
Tarnborgparken Ornumvej 8, 4220 Korsor
Just north of Korsor, by the lake (Korsor Nor)
Holes   18 Par 71 5998m.
Visitors   Welcome
Fees   DKr150–180
Facilities   Bar and restaurant; practice ground
Pro   Mark Irving

Lemvig Golf Club (1986)   38
Phone: 97 81 0920
Sogardevejen 6, 7620 Lemvig
North west of Leming, off the B513
Holes   9 Par 35 2822m.
Visitors   Welcome
Fees   DKr140–160
Facilities   Bar and restaurant; driving range
Pro   Ian Appleyard

Midtsjaellands Golfklub (1980)   39
Phone: 53 63 3767
Ringstedvej, 4180 Soro
On the east side of Soro
Holes   9 Par 30 1880m. New course ready
               in 1993.
Visitors   Welcome
Fees   DKr90–110
Facilities   Practice ground

Molleaens Golfklub (1970)   40
Phone: 42 18 8631
Stenbaekgard, Rosenlundvej 3, Bastrup, 3540
Lynge
Off the B207 south of Lynge, at Bastrup
Holes   18 Par 70 5730m.
Visitors   Welcome
Fees   DKr160–230
Facilities   Bar and restaurant; driving range
Pro   Richard Jackson

Morso Golfklub (1984)   41
Phone: 97 72 2044
Rolstrupvej, 7900 Nykobing Mors
On Mors Island, to the west of Nykobing
Holes   9 Par 34 2485m.
Visitors   Welcome
Fees   DKr90
Facilities   Driving range

Nexo Golfklub (1982)   42

Phone: 53 98 8987
Strandmarksvejen 14, Dueodde, 3730 Nexo
In the south east of Bornholm, towards
Snogebaek and Dueodde

Holes	18 Par 70 5715m.
Visitors	Welcome
Fees	DKr120
Facilities	Bar; driving range; par 3 course
Pro	B B Jensen

Nordbornholms Golf Klub (1983)   43

Phone: 56 48 4050
Spellingvej 3, 3760 Gudhjem
West of Gudhjem on the Ro road. The club is
near the airport

Holes	18 Par 71 5512m.
Visitors	Welcome. Course closed November to March
Fees	DKr130
Facilities	Bar and restaurant
Pro	L Karlsenn

Nordvestjysk Golfklub (1972)   44

Phone: 97 92 2164
Nystrupvej 19, 7700 Thisted
North west of Thisted between Vang and
Klitmoller

Holes	9 Par 35 2803m.
Visitors	Welcome
Fees	DKr100–120
Facilities	Driving range; par 3 course
Pro	Karsten Maas

Odense Golfklub (1979)   45

Phone: 65 95 9000
Hestehaven 210, 5220 Odense 50
South east of Odense, off the E66. Take the
Odense-C exit

Holes	18 Par 72 5990m.
Visitors	Welcome
Fees	DKr180
Facilities	Bar and restaurant; practice ground; 9 hole short course (2057m)
Pro	Peter Dixon

Odsherred Golfklub (1965)   46

Phone: 59 30 2076
Strarupvej 2, 4573 Hojby Sjaelland
South west of Nykobing, at Hojby

Holes	18 Par 71 5710m.
Visitors	Welcome
Fees	DKr140–160
Facilities	Driving range; par 3 course
Pro	Michael Moller

Randers Golfklub (1958)   47

Phone: 86 42 8869
Himmelbovej, Fladbro, 8900 Randers
On the west side of Randers ringroad, off the
B525

Holes	18 Par 71 5453m.
Visitors	Welcome
Fees	DKr150–180
Facilities	Bar and restaurant; driving range
Pro	Karsten Maas

Ribe Golfklub (1979)   48

Phone: 75 44 1230
Ronnehave, Snepsgardevejh 14, 6760 Ribe
On the A24 east of Ribe, and close to Favrlund

Holes	9 Par 35 2558m.
Visitors	Welcome
Fees	DKr100–120
Facilities	Driving range; par 3 course
Pro	Peter Thompson

Rold Skov Golfklub (1991)   49

Phone: 98 39 2677
Golfvej 1, 9520 Skorping
On the east side of the town

Holes	18 Par 72 5890m.
Visitors	Welcome
Fees	DKr150
Facilities	Bar and restaurant; practice ground
Pro	Morten Thuen

The course is located in one of the most
attractive areas of Denmark and is only ten
miles from the city of Aalborg. Rold Skov has
the classic golf design of four par 3 holes, four
par 5s and ten par 4s, and the rolling fairways
are guarded at strategic points by streams and
other water hazards.

Roskilde Golfklub (1978)   50

Phone: 42 37 0180
Kongemarken 34, 4000 Roskilde
West of Roskilde at Boserup Skov

Holes	12 Par 46 3448m.
Visitors	Welcome
Fees	DKr100–150
Facilities	Driving range
Pro	Steen Kaas

Rungsted Golf Klub (1937)   51

Phone: 42 86 3444

Vestre Stationsvej 16, 2960 Rungsted Kyst

Off the B207 at Rungsted

Holes   18 Par 72 5900m.

Visitors   Welcome, but pm only at weekends

Fees   DKr300

Facilities Bar and restaurant; practice ground

Pro   Marcus Brown

The club is situated to the north of Copenhagen and close to the sound which separates Denmark from Sweden. Designed by Major C A Mackenzie it has staged many important tournaments, including the first Scandinavian International Amateur Championship in 1956, in which both Michael Bonallack and Henry Longhurst participated.

Rungsted is a fine parkland course, whose narrow fairways meander through avenues of beech trees. Streams add to the dangers on virtually every hole and the 17th has real claws; with an out of bounds area on the left, deep rough and woods on the right and a plateau green with ravines awaiting a misdirected shot.

SCT Knuds Golfklub (1954)   52

Phone: 65 31 1212

Slipshavnsvej 16, 5800 Nyborg

In Nyborg on the peninsula

Holes   18 Par 71 5863m.

Visitors   Welcome

Fees   DKr150–200

Facilities Bar and restaurant; practice ground

Pro   Herluf Hansen

The course was built in a wonderful setting on a wooded peninsula on the island of Fyn, close to the town of Nyborg and was designed by Frank Pennink. It is a nicely varied lay-out, with many of the holes running through dense woodland and others alongside the Nyborg fjord. The 16th is a notable hole, a very difficult dog-legged par 5, and part of a stern finish to the course.

Silkeborg Golfklub (1966)   53

Phone: 86 85 3399

Sensommervej 15c, Porskaer, 8600 Silkeborg

Just east of Silkeborg, before you reach Resenbro

Holes   18 Par 71 6204m.

Visitors   Welcome

Fees   DKr180–220

Facilities Bar and restaurant; practice ground

Pro   Mike Kelly

In woodland near the River Gudenaa and surrounded by the Jutland hills, this challenging course, with its heathland character, is reminiscent of some of the celebrated Scottish courses. The fairways are narrow ribbons through the forest and the rough is punishing stuff; the SSS of 72 against a par of 71 indicates its severity.

Skanderborg Golfklub (1990)   54

Phone: 86 53 8688

Hylkemollevej 2, 8660 Skanderborg

South of Skanderborg off the E3

Holes   9 Par 34 2668m.

Visitors   Welcome

Fees   DKr100

Facilities Restaurant; driving range; par 3 course

Pro   Jes Petersen

Skive Golfklub (1973)   55

Phone: 97 51 1554

Resen, 7800 Skive

North of Skive off the A26. The club is signposted

Holes   9 Par 35 2841m.

Visitors   Welcome

Fees   DKr100

Facilities Driving range

Pro   Karsten Maas

Skovlunde Golfklub (1980)   56

Phone: 44 66 5585

2740 Skovlunde

On the western outskirts of Copenhagen at Skovlunde

Holes   9 Par 35 2509m.

Visitors   Welcome

Fees   DKr100–170

Facilities Bar and restaurant; practice ground

Sollerod Golfklub (1972)   57

Phone: 42 80 1784

Overodvej 239, 2840 Holte

North of Copenhagen, off the E4 at Holte

Holes   18 Par 72 5872m.

Visitors   Welcome. Only after noon at weekends.

Fees   DKr170–230

Facilities Bar and restaurant closed Mondays and in January; practice ground; par 3 course

Pro   Jorgen Korfitsen

Sonderjyllands Golfklub (1968)   **58**

Phone: 74 68 7525

Uge Hedegard, 6360 Tinglev

Off the A42 north east of Tinglev

Holes	18 Par 70 5843m.
Visitors	Welcome
Fees	DKr140–160
Facilities	Restaurant; driving range
Pro	Tim Mitchell

There are two distinctly different facets to this course, laid out on undulating territory amid the Artoft Plantation. The front nine holes stretch across open heathland, whereas the second nine wander through more wooded terrain. It offers splendid and relaxing holiday golf for players of all standards.

Storstrommen Golfklub (1969)   **59**

Phone: 53 83 8080

Kollegarden, Virketvej 44, 4863 Eskilstrup

North east of Nykobing at Virket

Holes	18 Par 72 5945m.
Visitors	Must book
Fees	DKr150–200
Facilities	Restaurant; practice ground; par 3 course
Pro	Angus Mackay

Svendborg Golfklub (1970)   **60**

Phone: 62 22 4077

Tordensgaardevej 5, Sorup, 5700 Svendborg

Off the A44 north west of Svendborg

Holes	18 Par 71 5692m.
Visitors	Welcome
Fees	DKr150
Facilities	Bar and restaurant; driving range
Pro	Lars Jensen

Sydsjaellands Golfklub (1977)   **61**

Phone: 53 76 1555

Praesto Landevej 39, Mogenstrup, 4700 Naestvod

South east of Naestved at Mogenstrup

Holes	18 Par 71 5965m.
Visitors	Welcome
Fees	DKr140–160
Facilities	Restaurant; driving range
Pro	Simon Dicksee

Vallensbaek Golfklub (1985)   **62**

Phone: 42 62 1899

Tofteveje 30-34, 2626 Vallensbaek

Off the E4 west of Kobenhavn at Vallensbaek

Holes	18 Par 71 5895m.
Visitors	Welcome
Fees	DKr160–220
Facilities	Bar and restaurant; driving range; par 3 course
Pro	Richard Perthen

Vejle Golfklub (1972)   **63**

Phone: 75 85 8185

Faellessletgard, Ibaekvej, 7100 Vejle

South east of Vejle off the B421

Holes	18 Par 73 6277m. A further 9 holes should now be open.
Visitors	Welcome, but must book
Fees	DKr200
Facilities	Bar and restaurant closed Monday; driving range; par 3 course
Pro	Derek Chad

Located in an appealing part of Denmark, the course winds its way through the Munkebjerg Forest, but some of the fairways are reasonably generous; the excellent bunkering and water hazards add to the fun.

Vestfyns Golfklub (1974)   **64**

Phone: 64 72 2124

Ronnemosegaard, Krengerupvej 27, 5620 Glamsbjerg

East of Assens. Take the B329 exit off the E66; turn for Krengerup just before Glamsbjerg

Holes	9 Par 35 2886m.
Visitors	Welcome. Course closed October to April
Fees	DKr150
Pro	Svend Tinning

Viborg Golfklub (1975)   **65**

Phone: 86 67 3010

Mollevej 26, Overlund, 8800 Viborg

East of Viborg towards Randers

Holes	18 Par 72 5902m.
Visitors	Welcome
Fees	DKr150–180
Facilities	Bar and restaurant; practice ground; par 3 course
Pro	Andrew Martin

This is another open heathland lay-out, where problems are posed primarily by the pine trees, and the lakes which affect play on some of the middle holes.

FRANCE

T HE popularity of golf in France has grown in a remarkable way during the last decade, but especially during the last five years. At the end of 1987 there were around 175 golf courses and now, at the beginning of 1993, there are over 400 courses in play with many more scheduled to open this year.

The French Golf Federation have had an influential role in this extraordinary expansion. Not only do they wish to ensure that the availability of courses keeps pace with the growing demand but also that the enthusiastic public have access to them at reasonable prices. The National Golf Centre near Paris is an example of their initiative: a splendid complex with a magnificent golf course, the Albatross, which anyone with a handicap can play for around £20. It is by no means unusual in France to pay the equivalent of £20 or less for a day's golf; an instructive contrast to Spain or Portugal where a round of golf is often grossly over-priced at £50 or more. The food, the wine and the service are usually a lot better in France, too.

In addition the French Tourist Boards have provided their own impetus to the French Federation's endeavours. Both bodies rightly promote France as a first-class destination for golfing tourism and they provide excellent information about the available facilities. Discounts are also offered to tourists, who should take advantage of the 'green pass' and other incentives. Many hotels and self-catering complexes offer discounts at nearby courses, for example.

By dint of the many cross-Channel ferry routes, France is an easy and inexpensive place to reach. Those golfing jewels of northern France, Hardelot and Le Touquet, are only three hours or so from London, for example. From there you can play the great courses around and to the north of Paris: Chantilly, St Cloud, St Nom-la-Breteche and the National. From the Brittany ports there are many fine courses within reach: La Baule, Le Bretesche, Savenay and St Laurent.

If you decide to go further afield you are spoiled for choice: the classy resort of Biarritz has a superb selection of golf courses including Hossegor, Seignosse and the Biarritz club itself; the Côte d'Azur has an ever-increasing choice of excellent courses from the senior ones of Cannes Mougins, Mandelieu and Monte Carlo to newer designs like Barbarosse, La Grande Bastide and Roquebrune; the Alps in summer is an enticing prospect with its wonderful climate and such courses as Evian, Chamonix and Bossey to enjoy.

For the touring golfer there is enormous variety and interest in France; in a country which is notable for the excellent quality of its food and accommodation, quality which is accompanied by eminently reasonable prices.

Because of their large number the courses in France have been listed by region, and we have in general used the same categories as the Fédération Française de Golf.

Unit of currency: French Franc
Rate of exchange (approx. at 1.1.93): FFr8–£1
International dialling code: (010 33)

NORTH-WEST FRANCE

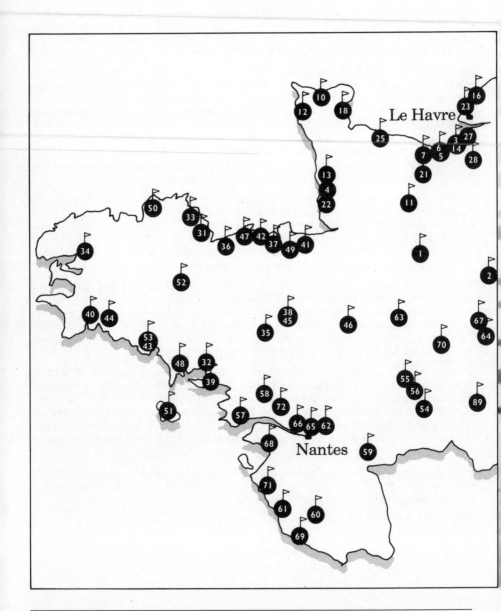

Normandie

Golf Club de Bagnoles (1927) I
Phone: 33 378142
Rte de Domfront, 61140 Bagnoles de l'Orne
Just west of Bagnoles de l'Orne
Holes	9 Par 33 2299m.
Visitors	Welcome
Fees	FFr150
Facilities	Bar and restaurant; driving range
Pro	P Jacob

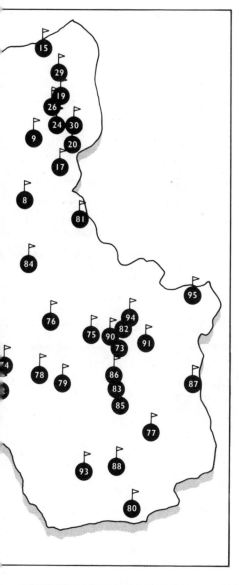

Golf de Bellême St Martin (1989) 2
Phone: 33 730007
Les Sablons, 61130 Bellême
North of Bellême in the forest
Holes	18 Par 72 5970m.
Visitors	Welcome. Closed Tuesday
Fees	FFr150–220
Facilities	Bar and restaurant; driving range; tennis
Pro	Peter Mackland

Golf de Beuzevat (1980) 3
Phone: 31 248049
Gonneville-sur-Mer, 14510 Houlgate
East of Houlgate off the D24
Holes	18 Par 73 5769m.
Visitors	Welcome. Course closed Tuesday
Fees	FFr200–240
Facilities	Bar and restaurant; driving range
Pro	Andrew Forrester

Golf Municipal de Bréhal (1964) 4
Phone: 33 515888
50290 St Martin de Bréhal
15 km north of Granville off the D971
Holes	9 Par 31 2057m.
Visitors	Welcome. Course closed Tuesday
Fees	FFr110
Facilities	Bar and restaurant; driving range

Golf Public de Cabourg (1988) 5
Phone: 31 917053
Ave de l'Hippodrome, 14390 Cabourg
In Cabourg follow signs to the hippodrome
Holes	9 Par 36 2860m.
Visitors	Welcome
Fees	FFr100–170
Facilities	Bar and restaurant; driving range
Pro	Didier Carion

Golf de Cabourg Le Home (1907) 6
Phone: 31 912556
Rte de Sallenelles, 14390 Le Home Varaville
Just west of Cabourg on the D514
Holes	18 Par 68 5269m.
Visitors	Welcome
Fees	FFr160–260
Facilities	Bar; driving range
Pro	Luc Allain

Golf de Caen (1990)   7

Phone: 31 947209

Le Vallon, 14112 Biéville-Beuville

North of Caen, on the coast at Lion-sur-Mer

Holes	18 Par 72 6155m.
Visitors	Welcome. Course closed Tuesday
Fees	FFr140–240
Facilities	Bar and restaurant; driving range

This course is located less than 10 minutes from the ferry terminal at Ouistreham and is an ideal starting/finishing point for a golf holiday in France. This is a new course, opened in 1990 and designed by Hawtree, and its existing 18 holes will be increased to 27 by 1994. An undulating attractive course, planted with numerous beech and wild cherry trees, water comes into play on the 1st and 10th holes and the highlights of the course are the pretty 12th, 13th and 14th holes. Already reasonably mature, this course can only improve.

Golf de Center Parcs (1989)   8

Phone: 32 235002

Les Barils, 27130 Verneuil sur Avre

South west of Verneuil; follow the signs to the Center Parcs

Holes	9 Par 37 3250m.
Visitors	Welcome
Fees	FFr135–175
Facilities	Bar and restaurant; driving range; swimming; tennis; squash

Golf du Champ de Bataille (1988)   9

Phone: 32 350372

Château du Champ de Bataille, 27110 Le Neubourg

North west of Le Neuborg, on the D39 at Champ de Bataille

Holes	18 Par 72 5983m.
Visitors	Welcome
Fees	FFr230–330
Facilities	Bar and restaurant; driving range
Pro	Pierre Vedrinelle

The club is situated in one of the loveliest parts of France and its focal point is a magnificent chateau which dates from the time of Louis XIV. It is the clubhouse and it is no surprise to learn that the magazine, 'France Golf', voted Champs de Bataille the most beautiful course in France. It plunges and rolls through superb woodland, with valleys and lakes and streams adding to the challenges the golfers face. It is not to be missed.

Golf de Cherbourg (1973)   10

Phone: 33 444548

Dom. des Roches, 50470 La Glacerie

South of Cherbourg, off the D122 at La Glacerie

Holes	9 Par 35 2791m.
Visitors	Welcome
Fees	FFr100–120
Facilities	Bar closed Tuesday; driving range
Pro	Arnaud Cagniel

Golf du Clécy Cantelou (1988)   11

Phone: 31 697272

Manoir de Cantelou, Cantelou, 14570 Clécy

South of Clécy off the D562

Holes	18 Par 72 5975m.
Visitors	Welcome
Fees	FFr130–200
Facilities	Bar and restaurant; driving range
Pro	Alain Quibeuf

Situated in the Suisse Normand, this new course offers breathtaking views of the Normandy countryside. A notable feature is the very small greens which make this a difficult course. The clubhouse is a converted château where accommodation is offered at very reasonable rates.

This is a mountainous course and those not in the peak of fitness ought perhaps to avail themselves of the motorised cars available for hire.

Golf de la Côte des Isles (1990)   12

Phone: 33 934485

Chemin des Mielles, 50270 St Jean de la Rivière

South of Barneville Carteret; head for Barneville beach

Holes	9 Par 33 2295m.
Visitors	Welcome. Course closed Tuesday
Fees	FFr100
Facilities	Bar; driving range

Golf de Coutainville (1925)   13

Phone: 33 470331

50230 Agon-Coutainville

By the beach at Coutainville

Holes	9 Par 34 2605m.
Visitors	Welcome
Fees	FFr120–150
Facilities	Bar and restaurant; driving range
Pro	Ivan Folliot

Golf de Deauville (1927) 14

Phone: 31 882053

St Arnoult, 14800 Deauville

3 km south of Deauville off the D278

Holes	18 Par 71 5934m.
	9 Par 36 3031m.
Visitors	Welcome, but must book. Course closed Tuesday in winter
Fees	FFr230–330
Facilities	Bar and restaurant; driving range; swimming pool; tennis
Pro	C Hausseguy

There is a fine golfing pedigree to these courses, since Tom Simpson designed the Red and the White and Henry Cotton the Blue. Traditional in design, they are notable for their tree-lined fairways and fast greens, which are well protected by bunkers. Between the mouth of the Seine and the Touques valley, the views are a delight.

Golf de Dieppe (1897) 15

Phone: 35 842505

Rte de Pourville, 76200 Dieppe

Just west of Dieppe at Pourville

Holes	18 Par 72 5763m.
Visitors	Welcome. Course closed Tuesday in winter
Fees	FFr190–250
Facilities	Bar and restaurant; driving range
Pro	Sebastien Ortiz

Golf Marin d'Etretat (1908) 16

Phone: 35 270489

Rte du Havre, 76790 Etretat

On the west side of Etretat, on the D940

Holes	18 Par 72 6026m.
Visitors	Welcome. Course closed Tuesday
Fees	FFr200–300
Facilities	Bar and restaurant; driving range
Pro	Jean Morea

The course sits on top of the limestone cliffs overlooking the Channel and the views are wonderful. Like any links course, the winds are an inherent part of its challenge. Without the wind the 10th, a par 5 up a hill, is tough enough; and the 6th imposes a positively traumatic tee shot on the player, who must carry his ball over 150 metres across a deep chasm to the fairway beyond.

Golf d'Evreux (1990) 17

Phone: 32 396622

Hippodrome Navarre, 27001 Evreux

In Evreux. Follow the signs to the hippodrome

Holes	9 Par 32 2100m.
Visitors	Welcome. Course closed Tuesday
Fees	FFr80
Facilities	Driving range
Pro	Emmanuel Bizet

Golf de Fontenay-en-Cotentin (1972) 18

Phone: 33 214427

Fontenay-sur-Mer, 50310 Montebourg

On the coast just south of Quinéville

Holes	9 Par 36 2980m.
Visitors	Welcome. Course closed Tuesday except July/August
Fees	FFr100–130
Facilities	Bar and restaurant; driving range

Golf de la Forêt Verte (1991) 19

Phone: 35 336294

Bosc-Guérard, St Adrien, 76710 Montville

North of Rouen in the Forêt Verte

Holes	18 Par 72 5967m.
Visitors	Welcome
Fees	FFr120–180
Facilities	Bar and restaurant; driving range
Pro	J F Guillerm

Green Golf Gaillon (1988) 20

Phone: 32 538940

Rte d'Aubevoye, 27600 Gaillon

Take exit 17 off the A13 Paris–Rouen road to Gaillon

Holes	9 Par 32 2254m.
Visitors	Welcome
Fees	FFr100–150
Facilities	Bar and restaurant; driving range

Golf de Garcelles (1989) 21

Phone: 31 390858

Rue de Lorguichon, 14540 Garcelles Secqueville

South of Caen; take the D41 to Garcelles

Holes	9 Par 35 2892m.
Visitors	Welcome
Fees	FFr70–160
Facilities	Bar and restaurant; driving range; short course; tennis; archery
Pro	Didier Carion

Golf de Granville (1955)   22

Phone: 33 502306

Bréville, 50290 Bréhal

North of Granville at Breville

Holes	18 Par 70 5950m.
	9 Par 33 2210m.
Visitors	Welcome
Fees	FFr200–300
Facilities	Bar and restaurant closed Tuesday; driving range; swimming; tennis; horseriding
Pro	Alain Quibeuf

Golfers who warm to a traditional links course should try Granville, set amongst the dunes facing Grouin Point. There is only one water hazard (on the 14th hole) and the well-bunkered greens make it an excellent test of golf.

Golf du Havre (1931)   23

Phone: 35 463650

Hameau St Supplix, 76930 Octeville sur Mer

North of Le Havre off the D940 at St Supplix

Holes	18 Par 70 5770m.
Visitors	Welcome
Fees	FFr150–300
Facilities	Bar and restaurant closed Tuesday; driving range
Pro	Roy Truman

Golf de Léry-Poses (1989)   24

Phone: 32 594742

Base de Plein Air et de Loisirs, 27740 Poses

North of Louviers at Léry-Poses

Holes	18 Par 72 6220m.
Visitors	Welcome
Fees	FFr150–200
Facilities	Bar and restaurant; driving range; short course
Pro	Helen Lecuellet

Golf de Bayeux Omaha Beach (1986)   25

Phone: 31 217294

14520 Port-en-Bessin

North west of Bayeux. Off the D514 west of Port-en-Bessin

Holes	18 Par 72 6229m.
Holes	9 Par 35 2875m.
Visitors	Welcome. Course closed Tuesday in winter
Fees	FFr180–260
Facilities	Bar and restaurant; driving range
Pro	Marc Eve

Opened in 1985 Omaha Beach comprises three separate and distinct 9 hole golf courses. The Sea course is easily the most enjoyable with several holes perched high above the Channel. The 'signature' hole is the 6th, 427 metres long, and straight out to sea. The drive has to be threaded between two large bunkers, right and left, and the green itself is surrounded by seven bunkers. It requires two very long and accurate shots to find the green. Hackers taking the more scenic route will enjoy stupendous views of the beaches where the US forces landed in 1944.

The other two nine holes are a little disappointing after La Mer. L'Etang is American in style and water comes into play on several holes; Le Bocage is a more traditional, open parkland course. Both are perhaps too new to be fully enjoyed.

The whole course is long and hilly, with long walks between the holes and is therefore not recommended for those seeking a gentle stroll.

Golf Club de Rouen (1911)   26

Phone: 35 763865

Chemin de Communaux, 76130 Mont St-Aignan

North of Rouen off the D43 at Mont St-Aignan

Holes	18 Par 70 5556m.
Visitors	Welcome
Fees	FFr160–250
Facilities	Bar and restaurant closed Tuesday; driving range
Pro	Jean Pierre Quibeuf

Golf de St Gatien (1989)   27

Phone: 31 651999

Mont St Jean, 14130 St Gatien-des-Bois

South east of Deauville, close to St Gatien

Holes	18 Par 72 6174m.
	9 Par 36 3120m.
Visitors	Welcome
Fees	FFR180–270
Facilities	Bar and restaurant; driving range
Pro	J P Turin

Thick forest, deep bunkers, water hazards, switchback fairways and plateau greens make this course a fine and entertaining test of golf. The views of the Seine estuary are an added attraction.

Golf de St Julien (1988) 28

Phone: 31 643030
St Julien-sur-Calonne, 14130 Pont-l'Évêque
South east of Pont-l'Évêque at St Julien-sur-Calonne

Holes	18 Par 73 6286m.
Visitors	Welcome. Course closed Tuesday in winter
Fees	FFr250–280
Facilities	Bar and restaurant; driving range; short course; tennis
Pro	Raymond Etchenic

This is quite a hilly course with greens which are well-protected by numerous bunkers. Several ponds add to the fun and notable holes include the short 6th with its tricky green and the par 5 10th.

Golf de St Saëns (1987) 29

Phone: 35 342524
Domaine du Vaudichon, 76680 St Saëns
North west of St Saëns off the D154

Holes	18 Par 71 5951m.
Visitors	Welcome. Course closed Tuesday in winter
Fees	FFr125–250
Facilities	Bar and restaurant; driving range
Pro	J P Quibeuf

Golf du Vaudreuil (1961) 30

Phone: 32 590260
27100 Le Vaudreuil
North east of Louviers; cross the River Eure and head for the Parc Résidentiel

Holes	18 Par 73 6388m.
Visitors	Welcome. Course closed Tuesday in winter
Fees	FFr150–250
Facilities	Bar and restaurant; driving range
Pro	J Lecuellet

Bretagne (Brittany)

Golf des Ajoncs d'Or (1976) 31

Phone: 96 719074
Kergrain-en-Lantic, 22410 St Quay Portrieux
South west of St Quay Portrieux, near Lantic

Holes	18 Par 72 6230m.
Visitors	Welcome
Fees	FFr170–190
Facilities	Bar; driving range
Pro	P R Maisonneuve

Golf de Baden (1989) 32

Phone: 97 571896
Kernic, 56870 Baden
South west of Vannes off the D101 at Baden

Holes	18 Par 72 6112m.
Visitors	Welcome
Fees	FFr140–220
Facilities	Bar and restaurant closed Tuesday; driving range
Pro	Joel Piron

Golf du Boisgelin (1987) 33

Phone: 96 223124
Pléhédel, 22290 Lanvollon
North of Lanvollon, off the D6/D7

Holes	18 Par 72
Visitors	Welcome
Fees	FFr60–120
Facilities	Bar and restaurant; driving range

Golf de Brest-Iroise (1976) 34

Phone: 98 851617
Parc de Lann-Rohou, 29220 Landerneau
Off the D770 near Landerneau

Holes	18 Par 72 5885m.
Holes	9 Par 37 3329m.
Visitors	Welcome
Fees	FFr100–200
Facilities	Bar and restaurant; driving range; tennis

This very demanding course is characterised by dog-leg holes, plenty of trees and gorse, well-bunkered greens with slippery surfaces, all at the mercy of the wind. The 4th hole at around 600 yards is a tiger, as is the short 17th at well over 200 yards.

Golf de Cicé Blossac (1990) 35

Phone: 99 527979
Domaine de Cicé Blossac, 35170 Bruz
South west of Rennes off the D177 to Redon. There is a sign (near Bruz) to Cicé Blossac

Holes	18 Par 72 6343m.
Visitors	Welcome
Fees	FFr150–250
Facilities	Bar and restaurant; practice ground
Pro	Sydney Kershaw

Golf de la Crinière (1990)   **36**

Phone: 96 327260

La Ville Gourio, Morieux, 22400 Lamballe

9 km northwest of Lamballe

Holes   9 Par 36 2970m.

Visitors   Welcome

Fees   FFr100–160

Facilities Bar and restaurant; driving range

Golf de Dinard (1887)   **37**

Phone: 99 883207

35800 St Briac-sur-Mer

West of Dinard on the coast, off the D786 near
St Briac

Holes   18 Par 68 5137m.

Visitors   Welcome

Fees   FFr220–250

Facilities Bar; driving range

Pro   Antoine Rosinski

Golf de la Freslonnière (1989)   **38**

Phone: 99 608409

Le Bois-Briand, 35650 Le Rheu

West of Rennes off the N24

Holes   18 Par 71 5671m.

Visitors   Welcome

Fees   FFr180–220

Facilities Bar and restaurant closed Tuesday;
             driving range

Pro   David Wakeford

The course was made in the grounds of a
magnificent château originally built in the 13th
century and the 18th green is in its shadow. The
holes wind through avenues of stately trees and
the many dog-leg holes (the 16th and 18th turn
very sharply indeed) demand sensible tactics and
accuracy; water also comes into play on twelve
of the holes. The comfortable clubhouse was
built in the château's farm buildings around a
courtyard.

Golf de Kerver (1989)   **39**

Phone: 97 453009

Domaine de Kerver, 56730 St Gildas de Rhuys

West of Sarzeau, off the D780

Holes   18 Par 73 6147m.

Visitors   Welcome

Fees   FFr150–240

Facilities Bar; driving range

Pro   Jean Luc Leroux

With the Gulf of Morbihan just to the north of
the course, Kerver is one of the very few links
courses in Brittany. It was opened in 1989 and
already adds up to a fascinating test of golf.
     Water meanders through the course and
influences most of the holes, especially when you
reach the lake, across which you must play on

several occasions. The twelfth hole poses some
particularly tricky questions, and the short holes
are very challenging. The course has been
designed with imagination and wit; the greens
are superb and, like the bunkers, are
eccentrically shaped. It is a marvellous golf
course in a lovely holiday area.

Golf de l'Odet (1986)   **40**

Phone: 98 548788

Clohars-Fouesnant, 29950 Bénodet

Just north of Bénodet off the D34 at Clohars

Holes   18 Par 72 6235m.

Visitors   Welcome

Fees   FFr140–220

Facilities Bar and restaurant; driving range;
             short course; tennis

Pro   Ken Strachan

This is a very tough course which will either
intrigue or irritate the golfer, depending on his
view of golf or, more probably, on how he
scored. Although designed by a Frenchman, it is
of the school of Trent Jones with bizarrely
shaped bunkers, sloping greens with protective
mounds and many water hazards.

Golf des Ormes (1989)   **41**

Phone: 99 484027

Château des Ormes, 35120 Dol-de-Bretagne

South of Dol-de-Bretagne, off the D795

Holes   18 Par 72 6070m.

Visitors   Welcome

Fees   FFr160–225

Facilities Bar and restaurant; driving range;
             short course; swimming pool; tennis

Pro   Olivier Cheron

An elegant stone château of 18th century
vintage lies at the heart of the estate on which
the course was built and the old manor farm
buildings now house the clubhouse. The course
is full of charm, set amid fine old trees and
natural lakes, and if your game is not at its best
you can enjoy the peace and beauty of the
surroundings.

Golf de Pen Guen (1960)   **42**

Phone: 96 419120

22380 St Cast Le Guildo

South of St Cast, at Pen Guen

Holes   18 Par 67 4589m.

Visitors   Welcome

Fees   FFr140–200

Facilities Bar closed outside holiday season;
             practice ground

Golf de Ploëmeur Océan (1990) **43**

Phone: 97 328182

St Jude-Kerham, 56270 Ploëmeur

West of Lorient, off the D163 at Kerhan

Holes	18 Par 72 5957m.
Visitors	Welcome
Fees	FFr150–300
Facilities	Bar and restaurant; driving range
Pro	Mario Zimmermann

Alongside the sea this has the characteristics of a links course, with its springy fairways, stretches of sand and scrub, and large, fast running greens. When the wind blows it is a tough proposition.

Golf de Quimper et de Cornouaille (1959) **44**

Phone: 98 569709

Manoir de Mesmeur, 29133 La Forêt Fouesnant

North east of Bénodet off the D44 in La Forêt Fouesnant

Holes	9 Par 35 2820m.
Visitors	Welcome
Fees	FFr100–200
Facilities	Bar and restaurant; driving range

Golf de Rennes (1989) **45**

Phone: 99 642418

35000 St Jacques de la Lande

Off the D34 south of Rennes

Holes	18 Par 72 6135m.
Visitors	Welcome
Fees	FFr180
Facilities	Bar and restaurant; practice ground; short course; pitch & putt course

This new and busy course is lent a rather high-tech appearance by its modern clubhouse, a spacious place with a curved wall of windows overlooking the course. The fairways are wide and generally flat but the course is made interesting by the many trees and the presence of water on most of the holes. The greens are excellent and well bunkered.

Golf des Rochers Sévigné (1990) **46**

Phone: 99 965252

Château des Rochers, 35500 Vitré

South of Vitré, off the D88

Holes	18 Par 71 5986m.
Visitors	Welcome
Fees	FFr160–220
Facilities	Bar; driving range
Pro	Guillaume Frangeul

The course was built in the grounds of an extraordinarily appealing castle, built of sandstone and with steep roofs and priapic towers crowded together over the main building. It was once the home of the 17th century writer,

Madame de Sévigné. The course winds its way through alleys of chestnut trees and ancient beeches, and incorporates many water hazards and some tricky greens. It is a delight to play golf in such surroundings.

Golf des Sables-d'Or-les-Pins (1925) **47**

Phone: 96 414257

22240 Fréhel

South of Sables-d'Or near Plurien

Holes	18 Par 71 5585m.
Visitors	Welcome
Fees	FFr150–200
Facilities	Bar; driving range; tennis
Pro	Christophe Houbé

A Scotsman built the original 9 hole course in 1925 and the design is still reminiscent of a links, and has now been expanded to 18 holes. It is a good holiday course, with wide fairways and good sandy soil, pretty woodland and some water hazards.

Golf de St Laurent-Ploëmel (1975) **48**

Phone: 97 568518

St Laurent-Ploëmel, 56400 Auray

West of Auray off the D105 at St Laurent

Holes	18 Par 72 6112m.
	9 Par 35 2665m.
Visitors	Welcome
Fees	FFr140–220
Facilities	Bar and restaurant closed Tuesday in winter; driving range; tennis
Pro	Dominique Jouare

Between the Gulf of Morbihan and Quiberon bay, the club is close to the attractive resort of Carnac (with its famous megalithic stones). The parkland course is challenging by dint of its lovely old pines scattered over the terrain, its narrow fairways, several lakes and streams. There is a splendid modern clubhouse and the club is a busy and well-organised place.

Golf de St Malo le Tronchet (1986) **49**

Phone: 99 589669

Le Tronchet, 35540 Miniac-Morvan

East of Dinan, of the D73 and D9 at Le Tronchet

Holes	18 Par 72 6049m.
	9 Par 36 2684m.
Visitors	Welcome
Fees	FFr220
Facilities	Bar, driving range
Pro	Cyril Bourakhowitch

This attractive parkland course has plenty of water and acres of bunkers; the sand which runs along the 18th hole is reputedly the largest bunker in Europe. The water affects about ten of the holes and entails some spectacular and nerve-racking carries.

Golf de St Samson (1963)   50

Phone: 96 238734

Rte de Kérénoc, 22560 Pleumeur-Bodou

North of Lannion, off the D11 near Tregastel

Holes	18 Par 71 5700m.
Visitors	Welcome
Fees	FFr120–200
Facilities	Bar and restaurant closed Tuesday in winter; driving range; swimming pool; tennis
Pro	Eric Alvarez

Located on the 'pink granite coast', golfers have magnificent views from this rugged heathland course, which is dotted with heather and gorse and great chunks of granite, as well as water hazards (on the par 3 14th hole, for example). The greens are kept to the very highest standards and the clubhouse was converted from a traditional Breton farmhouse.

Golf de Sauzon (1985)   51

Phone: 97 316465

Quai de Sauzon, 56360 Belle-Ile

On Belle Ile island at Sauzon

Holes	18 Par 71 5800m.
Visitors	Welcome
Fees	FFr180
Facilities	Bar and restaurant; driving range
Pro	Gregory Minassian

Golf de Tir Na N'Go (1990)   52

Phone: 96 365344

Trémargat, 22110 Rostrenen

North of Rostrenen, off the D87 at Tremergat

Holes	9 Par 33 2450m.
Visitors	Welcome
Fees	FFr100
Facilities	Bar and restaurant; driving range

Golf du Val Quéven (1989)   53

Phone: 97 051796

Keruiruisseau, 56530 Quéven

North west of Lorient, off the D6 near Queven

Holes	18 Par 72 6127m.
Visitors	Welcome
Fees	FFr140–220
Facilities	Bar and restaurant; driving range
Pro	Luc Miriel

There is a pleasant rural feel to this course as it take you on your way through woodland, up and down hills (some not so gentle), past water and through valleys. It is so peaceful, despite its proximity to the large town of Lorient.

Pays de Loire

Golf d'Angers (1964)   54

Phone: 41 919656

Moulin de Pistrait, 49320 St Jean des Mauvrets

South east of Angers on the D751 at St Jean

Holes	18 Par 70 5460m.
Visitors	Welcome. Course closed Tuesday
Fees	FFr160–210
Facilities	Bar and restaurant; driving range
Pro	Jerome Bourel

Anjou Golf & Country Club (1988)   55

Phone: 41 420101

Rte de Cheffes, 49330 Champigné

North of Angers and close to Champigné

Holes	18 Par 72 6195m.
Visitors	Welcome. Course closed Tuesday in winter
Fees	FFr180–240
Facilities	Bar and restaurant; driving range; pitch & putt course
Pro	Dominique Dalies

Golf d'Avrillé de la Perrière (1988)   56

Phone: 41 692250

49240 Avrillé

North west of Angers, off the N162 (just after the airport)

Holes	18 Par 71 6120m.
Visitors	Welcome
Fees	FFr200–230
Facilities	Bar and restaurant closed Tuesday; driving range; short course
Pro	C Gassiat

From the steps of the old château, which is now the clubhouse, the whole panorama of the golf course faces you. Trees and lakes are the great challenge here, especially the latter since they threaten at least nine of the holes.

Golf de la Baule (1976)   57

Phone: 40 604618

Domaine de St Denac, 44117 St André-des-Eaux

Just north of La Baule, off the D47

Holes	18 Par 72 6157m.
Visitors	Welcome. Course closed Tuesday in winter
Fees	FFr170–320
Facilities	Bar and restaurant; driving range; swimming pool;
Pro	Eric Mauger

Close to the delightful resort of La Baule with its vast sandy beach and excellent facilities, this well-established course, which was designed by Peter Alliss and David Thomas, has staged the

French Open Championship and offers a good test for any golfer. Many of the holes thread their way through avenues of stately trees and the later holes are played around a large lake. They present a stern finish; the 17th is a tough par 3 across water to a tight and well-bunkered green and the 18th is a very stiff par 4.

Golf de la Bretesche (1965) 58

Phone: 40 883003

441650 Missillac

Between Ponchâteau and La Roche-Bernard, off the N165

Holes	18 Par 72 6080m.
Visitors	Welcome
Fees	FFr140–280
Facilities	Bar and restaurant; driving range; swimming pool; tennis
Pro	Thierry Mathon

The club has an idyllic situation amid hundreds of acres of forest and parkland. The beautiful château, built on the lake, gives the whole place a fairy tale aura. Any lack of accuracy, especially off the tees, will take its toll since the rolling fairways are fringed by mature and variegated trees which also form natural amphitheatres around the greens. The later holes are designed around the lake and you will have views of the château.

The hotel is very comfortable and has an excellent restaurant. The course gets very busy in the summer and also attracts great numbers of British visitors. La Baule with its huge, sandy beach and many facilities is close.

Golf de Cholet (1988) 59

Phone: 41 710501

Le Bois Lavau, Allée du Chêne Landry, 49300 Cholet

Just north of Cholet off the D752. The club is signposted

Holes	18 Par 72 6083m.
Visitors	Welcome. Course closed Tuesday
Fees	FFr200–220
Facilities	Bar; driving range; tennis
Pro	Olivier Canhapé

One of the Golf Espace courses, this is a delightful lay-out designed by Olivier Brizon. The many dog-legs through the serried ranks of oak and chestnut trees make the golfer think about his shots, and there is some water around too.

Golf de la Domangère (1988) 60

Phone: 51 076015

Route de Nesmy, 85310 Nesmy

South of La Roche, off the D746 at Nesmy

Holes	18 Par 72 6500m.
Visitors	Welcome
Fees	FFr140–230
Facilities	Bar and restaurant; driving range; tennis;
Pro	Michel Uchurbide

The club has already hosted the French Professional Championship, a mark of the quality of the course. The Yon river crosses the course and water hazards threaten nine of the holes. The golfer must be prepared to make some long carries, especially at the 7th hole, a fiendish double dog-leg of 580 metres with water menacing the second shot.

Golf des Fontenelles (1990) 61

Phone: 51 541394

85220 l'Aiguilllon-sur-Vie, Coëx

South east of St Gilles Croix de Vie at L'Aiguillon

Holes	18 Par 72 6185m.
Visitors	Welcome
Fees	FFr100–220
Facilities	Bar and restaurant; driving range
Pro	Laurent Bernis

Just across the water from the island of Yeu, the course offers a familiar and very attractive mixture of woods and water. The holes are nicely varied with several dog-legs and many of them are threatened by water.

Golf de l'Ile d'Or (1988) 62

Phone: 40 985800

Le Cellier, 44850 Ligné

North east of Nantes; take the D84 to Vandel and the ferry

Holes	18 Par 72 6292m.
Visitors	Welcome. Course closed Tuesday
Fees	FFr180–250
Facilities	Bar and restaurant; driving range; short course
Pro	Jean Louis Lucas

Golfclub de Laval (1972) 63

Phone: 43 531603

Le Jariel, 53810 Changé-les-Laval

North of Laval off the D561 at Changé-les-Laval

Holes	18 Par 72 6095m.
Visitors	Welcome
Fees	FFr120–150
Facilities	Bar; driving range; short course
Pro	E Hopu

Golf Club du Mans (1962)   64

Phone: 43 420036

Rte de Tours, Mulsanne, 72230 Arnage

South of Le Mans, off the N138 at Mulsanne

Holes	18 Par 70 5825m.
Visitors	Welcome. Course closed Tuesday in July/August
Fees	FFr150–220
Facilities	Bar and restaurant; driving range; tennis
Pro	Daniel Dugue

Golf de Nantes Erdre (1990)   65

Phone: 40 592121

Rond Point Jean Moulin, Chemin du Bout des Landes, 44000 Nantes

North of Nantes, off the D69 at Sucé-sur-Erdre

Holes	18 Par 71 6025m.
Visitors	Welcome. Course closed Tuesday
Fees	FFr170–220
Facilities	Bar and restaurant; driving range

Golf de Nantes Vigneux (1969)   66

Phone: 40 632582

44360 Vigneux-de-Bretagne

North west of Nantes; from the N165 turn on to the D81 to Vigneux

Holes	18 Par 72 5850m.
Visitors	Welcome
Fees	FFr150–240
Facilities	Bar and restaurant closed Tuesday; driving range
Pro	Pascal Bonhomme

Designed by Frank Pennink, the Nantes Club is only a few miles from the city centre. The course is of the familiar undulating parkland type, with some steeply sloping fairways which sometimes entail testing shots uphill to tight greens. The trees are delightful and a stream and a lake add to the fun. Do not omit a good look at the stately Château de Buron, alongside the 10th hole.

Golf de la Petite Blanchardière (1990)   67

Phone: 437-62507

Sargé-lès-le-Mans

North of Le Mans at Sargé-lès-le-Mans

Holes	18 Par 72 6013m.
Visitors	Welcome (public course)
Fees	FFr60–120
Facilities	Bar and restaurant; driving range

Golf de Pornic (1912)   68

Phone: 40 820669

49 bis Bd de l'Océan, Ste Marie/Mer, 44210 Pronic

West of Pornic, on the coast road at Ste Marie sur Mer

Holes	9 Par 35 2560m.
Visitors	Welcome. Course closed Tuesday in winter
Fees	FFr115–180
Facilities	Bar and restaurant; driving range; tennis
Pro	Cyril Duplessis

Golf de Port-Bourgenay (1990)   69

Phone: 51 222987

SMAT, 35440 Talmont St Hilaire

South east of Les Sables d'Olonne on the coast road (D32b) at Bourgenay

Holes	18 Par 72 5920m.
Visitors	Welcome
Fees	FFr60–120
Facilities	Bar and restaurant closed Tuesday in winter; driving range; swimming pool; tennis
Pro	Richard Triaire

Golf de Sablé (1991)   70

Phone: 43 952878

Domaine de l'Outinière, Rte de Pincé, 72300 Sablé-sur-Sarthe

South of Sablé off the D306

Holes	3 x 9 holes Par 36 (all) 3010/3069/3197m.
Visitors	Welcome
Fees	FFr230–320
Facilities	Bar and restaurant; driving range
Pro	Serge Huguenot

Golf de St Jean de Monts (1988)   71

Phone: 51 588273

Ave des Pays de Monts, 85160 St Jean-de-Monts

Just east of St Jean-de-Monts off the D38

Holes	18 Par 72 5962m.
Visitors	Welcome
Fees	FFr150–250
Facilities	Bar and restaurant; driving range; swimming pool; tennis
Pro	J J Lecornue

This splendid course has two separate faces. The first few holes run in typical parkland style along undulating fairways lined by tall trees, and the course then changes character into a links alongside the sea. The winds off the Atlantic can make it a tough test.

Golf de Savenay (1991)   **72**

Phone: 40 568805

44260 Savenay

Just east of Savenay, off the Chateaubriant road

Holes	18 Par 73 6335m.
Visitors	Welcome
Fees	FFr140–220
Facilities	Bar and restaurant closed Tuesday (except July/August); driving range; swimming pool; tennis
Pro	Hubert Pro

Centre

Golf des Aisses (1991)   **73**

Phone: 38 648087

45240 Le Ferté St Aubin

Just south of La Ferté St Aubin

Holes	3 x 9 Par 36 (all) 3234/3270/3308m.
Visitors	Welcome
Fees	FFr200–300
Facilities	Bar and restaurant; practice ground; swimming pool; tennis

Golf d'Ardrée (1988)   **74**

Phone: 47 567738

37360 St Antoine-du-Rocher

North of Tours, off the D2 at St Antoine

Holes	18 Par 71 5804m.
Visitors	Welcome
Fees	FFr210–260
Facilities	Bar and restaurant; driving range
Pro	Christophe Blot

One of Golf Espace's courses, this was built in the grounds of an elegant 18th century château. It is a lovely parkland course where good use is made of the fine old woodland and of water which menaces several of the holes.

Golf International Les Bordes (1987)   **75**

Phone: 54 877213

41220 St Laurent Nouan

South of Beaugency, off the D925 at Bel Air

Holes	18 Par 72 6412m.
Visitors	Welcome
Fees	FFr400–700
Facilities	Bar and restaurant; driving range; swimming pool; tennis

This must be the most exclusive club in the world, since it only has two members: the owner, Baron Bich, and Mr Sakurai. But it is open to the public and is rated as one of the best courses in Europe. It was designed by Robert Von Hagge and is a daunting lay-out on which water comes into play on 15 of the holes; when you add the thick woodland, mammoth bunkers, the

undulations of the terrain and the small, fast-running greens, you have a magnificent test of a golfer's skills. It is definitely not for beginners.

Golf de la Bosse (1987)   **76**

Phone: 54 230260

La Guignardière, 41290 Oucques

East of Vendôme, off the D924 at Oucques

Holes	9 Par 36 2996m.
Visitors	Welcome. Course closed Tuesday except July/August
Fees	FFr105–150
Facilities	Bar and restaurant; driving range
Pro	Michel Couet

Golf de Bourges (1988)   **77**

Phone: 48 212001

Rue de Lazenay, Val d'Auron, 18000 Bourges

Just south of Bourges at Lazenay

Holes	9 Par 36 3036m.
Visitors	Welcome. Course closed Tuesday
Fees	FFr100–150
Facilities	Bar and restaurant; driving range
Pro	Philippe Brehier

Golf de la Carte (1989)   **78**

Phone: 54 204900

Rte Nationale 152, 41150 Onzain

South west of Blois, off the N152 in Chouzy-sur-Cisse

Holes	9 Par 36 3010m.
Visitors	Welcome
Fees	FFr100–150
Facilities	Bar and restaurant; driving range; swimming pool; tennis
Pro	Alain Gaultier

Golf du Château de Cheverny (1987)   **79**

Phone: 54 792470

La Rousselière, Cheverny, 41700 Contres

South of Cheverny off the D102

Holes	18 Par 71 6272m.
Visitors	Welcome. Course closed Tuesday in winter
Fees	FFr180–250
Facilities	Bar and restaurant; driving range
Pro	P Rault

Close to the city of Blois, the Cheverny course was built on delightful terrain of forest and lakes, once the hunting grounds for the charming château, which can be glimpsed through the trees occasionally. There are some excellent holes; for example, the short 7th which is defended by six bunkers and the 18th, with woods on the one side and water on the other.

Golf des Dryades (1988)   80

Phone: 54 302800

36160 Pouligny-Notre-Dame

South of La Châtre, off the D940 at Guéret

Holes	18 Par 72 6120m.
Visitors	Welcome
Fees	FFr200–250
Facilities	Bar and restaurant; driving range; short course; swimming pool; tennis
Pro	Luc Moise

A large modern hotel was built to accommodate visitors to the golf course and there are many other leisure facilities including indoor and outdoor swimming pools and many tennis courts. The course, running through charming woodland and with several lakes, is a delight. The greens are superb and it is a fair test for all standards of golfer.

Golf du Château de Maintenon (1989)   81

Phone: 37 271809

Rte de Gallardon, 28130 Maintenon

On the south side of Maintenon

Holes	18 Par 72 6393m.
Visitors	Welcome, but must book. Course closed Tuesday
Fees	FFr240–450
Facilities	Bar and restaurant; driving range; short course
Pro	Laurent De Miol

Golf de Marcilly (1987)   82

Phone: 38 761173

Domaine de la Plaine, 45240 Marcilly-en-Villette

South of Orléans, off the D108 at Marcilly

Holes	18 Par 72 6324m.
Visitors	Welcome. Course closed Tuesday
Fees	FFr110–170
Facilities	Bar and restaurant; driving range
Pro	Georges Raison

Golf de Nançay (des Meaulnes) (1992)   83

Phone: 48 518380

18330 Nançay

Southeast of Salbris; close to Nançay off the D944

Holes	9 Par 35 2925m.
Visitors	Welcome
Fees	FFr100–150
Facilities	Bar and restaurant; driving range
Pro	Chris Philipps

Golf du Perche (1987)   84

Phone: 37 291733

Vallée des Aulnes, 28400 Souancé-au-Perche

South east of Nogent-le-Rotrou on the D955; the course is signposted

Holes	18 Par 72 6073m.
Visitors	Welcome. Course closed Tuesday in winter
Fees	FFr150–250
Facilities	Bar and restaurant; driving range
Pro	Bill Owens

Golf Club de la Picardière (1988)   85

Phone: 48 752143

18100 Vierzon

North east of Vierzon, off the D926 (in the forest of Vierzon)

Holes	18 Par 72 6077m.
Visitors	Welcome
Fees	FFr140–200
Facilities	Bar and restaurant; driving range
Pro	Frederic Larretche

Golf de Salbris (1987)   86

Phone: 54 972185

Château de Rivaulde, 41300 Salbris

Just to the north east of Salbris, off the D724

Holes	9 Par 35 2600m.
Visitors	Welcome. Course closed Tuesday
Fees	FFr100–200
Facilities	Bar and restaurant; driving range

Golf de Sancerrois (1988)   87

Phone: 38 541122

St Thibault, 18300 Sancerre

Northwest of Sancerre, off the D955

Holes	18 Par 71 5820m.
Fees	FFr150–200
Facilities	Bar and restaurant closed Tuesday; driving range; swimming pool; tennis
Pro	Philippe Gioux

This attractive parkland course is located on the banks of the Loire river and it has its fair share of water hazards and some testing bunkers. The Sancerre hills form an eye-catching background as do the ancient trees on the course.

Golf des Sarrays (1989) **88**
Phone: 54 495449
Les Sarrays, Ste Fauste, 36100 Issoudun
South west of Issoudun. Take the N151 and turn off to Neuvy-Pailloux

Holes	9 Par 36 2593m.
Visitors	Welcome. Course closed Tuesday
Fees	FFr100–130
Facilities	Bar and restaurant; driving range

Golf du Château des Sept Tours (1991) **89**
Phone: 47 246975
37330 Coucelles de Touraine
South of Château la Vallière off the D3

Holes	18 Par 72 6310m.
Visitors	Welcome. Course closed Tuesday
Fees	FFr100–200
Facilities	Bar and restaurant; driving range

The marvellous château makes a compelling centrepiece for this excellent course, which runs through a forest of ancient oaks. Water hazards on nine of the holes and rolling greens make it a very good test.

Golf de Sologne (1955) **90**
Phone: 38 765733
Rte de Jouy-le-Potier, 45240 La Ferté St Aubin
North west of La Ferté St Aubin, off the D18 at Jouy-le-Potier

Holes	18 Par 72 6400m.
Visitors	Welcome
Fees	FFr140–240
Facilities	Bar and restaurant; driving range; tennis
Pro	Brian Lawson

The golf club is part of the Country Club des Olleries, where you can fish, play tennis or shoot game. The course is a delight; it runs through beautiful parkland with masses of trees and the river and the five lakes impose their own problems.

Golf de Sully-sur-Loire (1966) **91**
Phone: 38 365208
L'Ousseau, 45600 Viglain
South west of Sully-sur-Loire, off the D120

Holes	3 x 9 Par 36 (all) 2927/2965/3097m.
Visitors	Welcome. Course closed Tuesday
Fees	FFr160–220
Facilities	Bar and restaurant; driving range
Pro	Christopher Gaunt

Golf de Touraine (1972) **92**
Phone: 47 532028
Château de la Touche, 37510 Ballan Mire
South west of Tours, off the D751 at Ballan

Holes	18 Par 71 5671m.
Visitors	Welcome
Fees	FFr180–270
Facilities	Bar and restaurant closed Tuesday; driving range; tennis
Pro	Marc Vol

Golf du Val de l'Indre (1989) **93**
Phone: 54 265944
Parc du Château de Villedieu, 36320 Villedieu-sur-Indre
North west of Châteauroux at Villedieu

Holes	18 Par 72 6225m.
Visitors	Welcome (public course). Course closed Tuesday except July/August
Fees	FFr140–190
Facilities	Bar and restaurant; driving range
Pro	Serge Lesne

Golf Club du Val de Loire (1953/1988) **94**
Phone: 38 592515
Château de la Touche, 45450 Donnery
East or Orléans, off the D709 at La Touche

Holes	18 Par 71 5771m.
Visitors	Welcome. Course closed Tuesday in winter
Fees	FFr180–250
Facilities	Bar and restaurant closed Tuesday; driving range
Pro	J M Duboc

Situated in the grounds of the beguiling 16th century Château de la Touche, in the lovely valley of the Loire, the original nine holes were designed through the woods by Robert Trent Jones. The second nine were added in 1988 and are even more American in character with many water hazards and large bunkers. It is well worth a visit and, since the manager is English and the professional speaks English, there are no language problems.

Golf Club de Vaugouard (1987) **95**
Phone: 38 957185
Chemin des Bois, Fontenay-sur-Loing, 45210 Ferrières
North of Montargis on the N7 at Fontenay

Holes	18 Par 72 5914m.
Visitors	Welcome
Fees	FFr200–330
Facilities	Bar and restaurant; swimming pool; tennis
Pro	Vincent Loustaud

NORTH-EAST FRANCE

France Nord

Aa-Saint-Omer Golf Club (1989)   1
Phone: 21 385990
Chemin des Bois, Acquin-Westbécourt, 62380 Lumbres
West of St Omer. Take the N42 to Lumbres, and turn on to the D225 to Acquin

Holes	18 Par 72 6313m.
Holes	9 Par 31 2003m.
Visitors	Welcome
Fees	FFr190–270
Facilities	Bar and restaurant; driving range
Pro	Sylvain Raout

The course is located high above the town and there are excellent views from the well-designed clubhouse. Sloping fairways and plenty of trees entail caution, especially on the dog-leg holes, if you are to have a chance of making your pars. If the wind blows, the course becomes a tough opponent, and strong and accurate iron play is needed, to avoid the many water hazards.

Golf d'Abbeville (1990)   2
Phone: 22 249858
Route du Val, 80132 Grand Laviers
North west of Abbeville off the D40

Holes	18 Par 72 6120m.
Visitors	Welcome
Fees	FFr130–180
Facilities	Bar; driving range
Pro	Eulge Hotab

Golf de l'Ailette (1985)   3
Phone: 23 248399
Cerny-en-Laonnois, 02860 Laon
South of Laon, off the D967. At Cerny, follow signs to Vallée de l'Ailette

Holes	18 Par 72 6127m.
Visitors	Welcome. Course closed Tuesday a.m.
Fees	FFr170–220
Facilities	Bar and restaurant closed Tuesday; driving range
Pro	Eric Censier

Golf d'Amiens (1951)   4
Phone: 22 930426
Route d'Albert, 80115 Querrieu
North east of Amiens; off the D929 at Querrieu

Holes	18 Par 72 6124m.
Visitors	Welcome. Course closed on Tuesday
Fees	FFr150–250
Facilities	Bar and restaurant; driving range
Pro	Bruno Dachicourt

Golf d'Arras (1990)   5
Phone: 21 502424
Rue Briquet-Taillandier, 62223 Anzin-St-Aubin
North west of Arras. Off the D60 at Anzin St Aubin

Holes	18 Par 72 6161m.
Visitors	Welcome Monday to Saturday. Course closed on Tuesday
Fees	FFr180–240
Facilities	Bar and restaurant; driving range
Pro	Roger Pollet

Golf du Bois de Ruminghem (1990)   6
Phone: 21 853033
1613 rue St Antoine, 62370 Ruminghem
North west of St Omer; turn off the N43 at Nordausqes

Holes	18 Par 72 6040m.
Visitors	Welcome
Fees	FFr130–150
Facilities	Bar; driving range

Golf de Bondues (1956)   7
Phone: 20 232062
Château de la Vigne, 59910 Bondues
North of Lille, off the N17 at Bondues

Holes	18 Par 73 6245m.
Holes	18 Par 72 6012m.
Visitors	Welcome. Course closed Tuesday
Fees	FFr200–300
Facilities	Bar and restaurant; driving range
Pro	P Itturioz

The courses are built around a charming 18th century château and comprise a fine course of 18 holes designed by Hawtree and a further course by Trent Jones, which opened recently. The Hennessy Cup match was played on Hawtree's course in 1976.

Golf de Brigode (1969) 8

Phone: 20 911786

36 Ave du Golf, 59650 Villeneuve-d'Ascq

East of Lille at Villeneuve

Holes	18 Par 72 6106m.
Visitors	Welcome. Course closed Tuesday
Fees	FFr200–300
Facilities	Bar and restaurant; driving range

The quality of the course is such that the French PGA Championship has been staged here. It is always in top class condition and is notable for its cunningly placed bunkers; the lake guarding the 4th green also adds to the difficulties.

Golf des Bruyères (1990) 9

Phone: 21 589542

Chemin de l'Enfer, 62118 Pelves

East of Arras, off the A26 at Pelves

Holes	18 Par 72 5864m.
Visitors	Welcome
Fees	Ffr100–200
Facilities	Bar; practice ground;
Pro	Raymond Wattinne

Golf de Champagne (1991) 10

Phone: 23 716208

Villers-Agron, 02130 Fère-en-Tardenois

South east of Fère-en-Tardenois

Holes	18 Par 72 6030m.
Visitors	Welcome
Fees	FFr120–190
Facilities	Bar and restaurant; driving range

Golf de Chantilly (1906) 11

Phone: 44 570443

60500 Vineuil St Firmin

Just north of Chantilly off the D924

Holes	18 Par 72 6432m (Les Longeres)
	18 Par 71 6408 (Le Vineuil)
Visitors	Welcome, but by introduction only at weekends. Courses closed on Thursday
Fees	FFr350
Facilities	Bar and restaurant; driving range; tennis
Pro	André Chardonnet

The club is one of the most renowned in France and has staged the French Open on many occasions: Henry Cotton, Roberto de Vicenzo and Nick Faldo have won here. Tom Simpson re-designed the championship course, Le Vineuil, in the Twenties and laid down the second course. All is peace and tranquillity here amid a great forest: 'not the slightest glimpse of an alien world', as Pat Ward-Thomas put it. The holes constantly change in character, some more open than others but with the omni-present bunkers always a threat. The finish is stern, especially the 18th across a valley; it is one of the great closing holes in golf.

Golf de Chaumont-en-Vexin (1963) 12

Phone: 44 490081

60240 Chaumont-en-Vexin, Chateau de Bertichere

Just west of Chaumont off the D923

Holes	18 Par 72 6195m.
Visitors	Welcome
Fees	FFr200–300
Facilities	Bar and restaurant; driving range

Golf de Compiègne (1896) 13

Phone: 44 401573

Ave Royale, 60200 Compiègne

In the south east of Compiègne

Holes	18 Par 71 5834m.
Visitors	Welcome. Course closed Thursday.
Fees	FFr200–350
Facilities	Bar and restaurant; practice ground; tennis
Pro	Michel Amat

Like the golf courses at Ludlow and Kelso, Compiègne is encircled by the local race track: at least it helps you to find the place. It is a flat and open course, without the ubiquitous trees which are found on the neighbouring courses. It is fun and different.

Golf de Dunkerque Fort Vallières (1986) 14

Phone: 28 610743

Coudekerque Village, 59380 Bergues

South of Dunkerque, off the D916 at Coudekerque

Holes	18 Par 71 5750m.
Visitors	Welcome. Public course; closed Tuesday in winter
Fees	FFr160–200
Facilities	Bar and restaurant; driving range
Pro	R Itturioz

Club des Flandres (1956) 15

Phone: 20 722074

137, Bd Clémenceau, 59800 Marcq-en-Baroeul

North of Lille, off the N350. Head for Le Croisé-Laroche and then the hippodrome

Holes	9 Par 33 2275m.
Visitors	Welcome. Course closed Monday
Fees	FFr180
Facilities	Bar
Pro	Philippe Delobelle

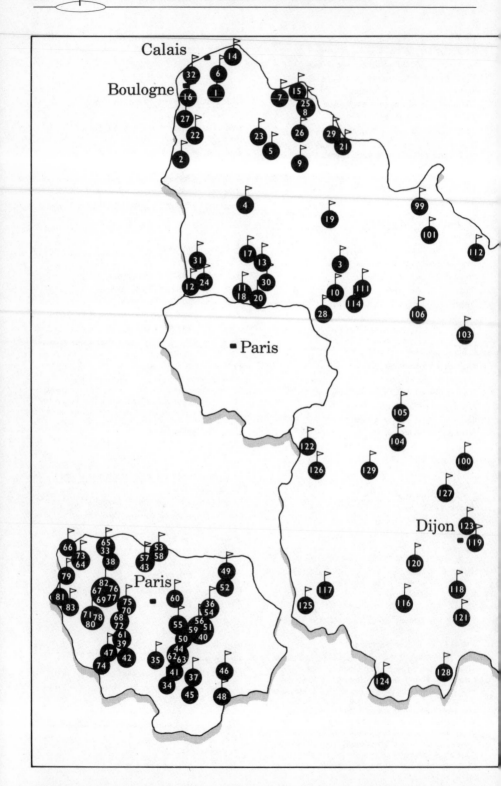

FRANCE
NORTH-EAST

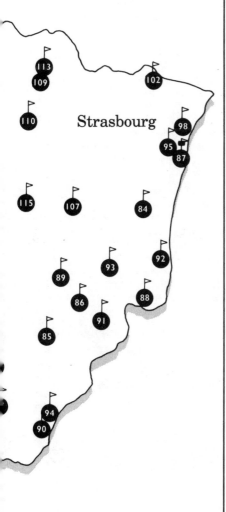

Strasbourg

Golf de Hardelot (1931)   16
Phone: 21 837310
Ave du Golf, 62152 Neufchatel-Hardelot
Off the D940 at Hardelot-Plage

Holes	18 Par 73 6014m (Les Dunes)
	18 Par 72 5871m (Les Pins)
Visitors	Welcome
Fees	FFr200–300
Facilities	Bar and restaurant; driving range; swimming; tennis; horseriding
Pro	Peter Dawson

This is almost the closest golf course to England and, designed as it was by Tom Simpson, bears many resemblances to the Berkshire. It is a beautiful and challenging golf course, threaded through avenues of stately trees, which will punish any erratic shots. There are some blind tee shots, some dog-legs and a superb 9th hole which demands a very accurate drive. The second half opens out a little but has a very stern finish with an intimidating short 17th hole and an even more menacing 18th hole, with the tee seemingly buried in the woods. It's a great course and a second one, Les Dunes, has now been opened. This has not met with universal approval because of the profusion of blind shots which are demanded.

Golf d'Humières (1990)   17
Phone: 44 423951
Chateau d'Humières, 60113 Monchy-Humières
North west of Compiègne off the D935

Holes	18 Par 73 6641m.
Visitors	Welcome
Fees	FFr240
Facilities	Bar and restaurant; driving range; tennis
Pro	Philippe Boyre

International Club du Lys (1929)   18
Phone: 44 212600
Rond-Point du Gr Cerf, Lys-Chantilly, 60260 Lamorlaye
South west of Chantilly. Off the D924 or N16

Holes	18 Par 70 6022m (Les Chênes)
	18 Par 66 4770m (Les Bouleaux).
Visitors	Welcome, but by introduction only at weekends at Les Chênes. Courses closed on Tuesday
Fees	FFr270–470
Facilities	Bar and restaurant; swimming pool; tennis;
Pro	F Saubaber

Golf du Mesnil St Laurent (1987)   19

Phone: 23 681948

Rue de Cambrie, 02720 Mesnil St Laurent
South east of St Quentin, off the D12 at Mesnil

Holes	9 Par 36 3084m.
Visitors	Welcome. Course closed Tuesday
Fees	FFr100–180
Facilities	Driving range
Pro	Dominique Riccau

Golf de Morfontaine (1926)   20

Phone: 44 546827

Morfontaine, 60128 Plailly
South of Senlis, off the A1 or the N17 at
Morfontaine

Holes	18 Par 72 6063m.
	9 Par 35 2585m.
Visitors	By introduction only
Fees	FFr200–300
Facilities	Bar and restaurant;

This is one of the best golf courses in Europe,
but access for visitors is limited, since you can
only play as the guest of a member. This is Tom
Simpson's masterpiece, a beautiful and tranquil
place to soothe any golfer's mind. The fairways
are narrow and there is quite a lot of heather to
trap an inaccurate shot; and there are the pine
trees to avoid as well.

Golf Club de Mormal (1991)   21

Phone: 27 631520

Bois St Pierre, 59144 Preux au Sart
South east of Valenciennes off the N49; after
Wargnies and Preux au Sart, follow signs to golf

Holes	18 Par 72 6022m.
Visitors	Welcome
Fees	FFr170–220
Facilities	Bar and restaurant; driving range
Pro	Olivier Noudeu

Golf de Nampont St Martin (1978)   22

Phone: 22 250020

801230 Nampont St Martin
South of Montreuil off the N1 at Nampont St
Martin

Holes	18 Par 71 5850m.
	18 Par 70 5033m.
Visitors	Welcome. Course closed Tuesday in winter
Fees	FFr130–180
Facilities	Bar and restaurant; driving range
Pro	Hubert Courtessi

Golf d'Olhain (1988)   23

Phone: 21 279179

Parc Dép. de Nature et de Loisirs, 62150
Houdain
South of Bethune off the D301; head for the Parc
d'Olhain

Holes	9 Par 35 2716m.
Visitors	Welcome
Fees	FFr100–150
Pro	S Muka

Golf Club de Rebetz (1988)   24

Phone: 44 491554

Route de Noailles, 60240 Chaumont-en-Vexin
Just west of Chaumont

Holes	18 Par 73 6409m.
Visitors	Welcome
Fees	FFr200–400
Facilities	Bar and restaurant; driving range
Pro	Michel Meyrat

Golf du Sart (1910)   25

Phone: 20 720251

5 rue J-Jaurès, 59650 Villeneuve-d'Ascq
North east of Lille and near Wasquehal

Holes	18 Par 71 5750m.
Visitors	Welcome. Course closed Monday
Fees	FFr200–300
Facilities	Bar and restaurant
Pro	R Wattinne

Golf de Thumeries (1933)   26

Phone: 20 865898

Bois Lenglart, 59239 Thumeries
South of Lille; take the Seclin exit off the A1
and head for Thumeries

Holes	9 Par 35 2310m.
Visitors	Welcome
Fees	FFr150–220
Facilities	Bar and restaurant closed Tuesday
Pro	Bruno Tiradon

Golf Club du Touquet (1904)   **27**

Phone: 021 056847

Ave du Golf, 62520 Le Touquet

On the outskirts of Le Touquet

Holes	18 Par 72 6082m. (La Mer)
	18 Par 71 5912m. (La Forêt)
Visitors	Welcome
Fees	FFr180–320
Facilities	Bar and restaurant; driving range; short course
Pro	Christian Dachicourt

Le Touquet has been a holiday haunt of the British for nearly a century and in the Twenties it was a favourite destination of the smart set, including the Prince of Wales.

The Forest course was opened in 1904 by Arthur Balfour, the British Prime Minister, and is a parkland course which rolls and loops through avenues of pine trees. The Sea course is an entirely different proposition, a very demanding links course which, after a relatively docile start, runs through the dunes. Between the wars, the great writer P G Wodehouse lived in a house which backs on to the course and is situated close to Le Manoir Hotel.

Golf du Val Secret (1988)   **28**

Phone: 23 830725

Ferme de Farsoy, 02400 Château-Thierry

Just north of Château-Thierry off the D1

Holes	9 Par 35 2887m.
Visitors	Welcome. Course closed Tuesday
Fees	FFr80–160
Facilities	Bar and restaurant; driving range
Pro	Gilles Arnaud

Golf de Valenciennes (1904)   **29**

Phone: 27 463010

Chemin Vert, 59770 Marly-les-Valenciennes

On the eastern side of Valenciennes, off the D44 near Marly

Holes	9 Par 33 2380m.
Visitors	Welcome
Fees	FFr150–200
Facilities	Bar closed Monday; driving range
Pro	Pierre Itturioz

Golf du Valois (1988)   **30**

Phone: 44 547061

Château du Raray, 60810 Barbery

North east of Senlis off the D932a at Raray

Holes	9 Par 35 2941m.
Visitors	Welcome
Fees	FFr200–300
Facilities	Bar and restaurant

Golf du Vivier (1990)   **31**

Phone: 44 842411

60650 Ons-en-Bray

West of Beauvais. Off N31 at Ons-en-Bray

Holes	9 Par 32 2200m.
Visitors	Welcome. Course closed on Tuesday.
Fees	Ffr70–100
Facilities	Bar and restaurant; driving range
Pro	H Joly

Golf de Wimereux (1907)   **32**

Phone: 21 324320

Route d'Ambleteuse, 62930 Wimereux

North of Wimereux off the N940

Holes	18 Par 72 6150m.
Visitors	Welcome
Fees	FFr170–250
Facilities	Bar and restaurant closed Tuesday; driving range
Pro	Hugues Marconi

The original 9 hole course was built on the Aubergue race course and a British industrialist took the club over betweeen the wars and built a championship course. It is an extremely demanding links course, which overlooks the Channel; on a clear day you can see the cliffs of Dover. When the wind blows it is a great test, especially the 509 metre 7th hole. The French Ladies Open and the French Professional Championships have been played here.

Ile de France

Golf d'Ableiges (1989)   **33**

Phone: 34 660605

Ableiges, 95450 Vigny

East of Vigny, off the D28 near Ableiges

Holes	18 Par 72 6261m.
Holes	9 Par 33 2137m.
Visitors	Welcome, but must book
Fees	FFr200–350
Facilities	Bar and restaurant; driving range
Pro	Philippe Guy

Golf de Bélesbat (1991)   **34**

Phone: 63 231910

91820 Boutigny sur Essonne

Off the D153 west of Boutigny

Holes	18 Par 72 6039m.
Visitors	Welcome
Fees	FFr300–600
Facilities	Bar and restaurant; driving range
Pro	Daniel Mercier

Golf de Bondoufle (1990)　　35

Phone: 60 864171
D31, 91070 Bondoufle
South west of Evry, at Bondoufle

Holes	18 Par 71 6161m.
Visitors	Welcome
Fees	FFr200–350
Facilities	Bar and restaurant; driving range
Pro	Yves Bechu

Golf de Bussy-St-Georges (1988)　　36

Phone: 64 660000
Promenade des Golfeurs, 77600 Bussy-St-Georges
Just south of Lagny at Bussy

Holes	18 Par 72 5924m.
Visitors	Welcome. Course closed Thursday am.
Fees	FFr160–320
Facilities	Bar and restaurant; driving range
Pro	Anne Le Coniat

Golf du Cély (1988)　　37

Phone: 64 380307
Le Château, Rte de St Germain, 77930 Cely-en-Bière
In Cély, north west of Fontainebleau

Holes	18 Par 72 6026m.
Visitors	Welcome. Course closed Tuesday
Fees	FFr400–600
Facilities	Bar and restaurant; practice ground

Golf de Cergy-Pontoise (1991)　　38

Phone: 34 210348
2 Allée de l'Obstacle d'Eau, 95000 Vauréal
South west of Pontoise, off the D922 near Cergy

Holes	18 Par 72 6035m.
Visitors	Welcome. Course closed Tuesday
Fees	FFr150–250
Facilities	Bar and restaurant; driving range; swimming pool
Pro	Patrice Merel

Golf Public de Chevry (1976)　　39

Phone: 60 124033
91190 Gif-sur-Yvette
North west of Limours, off the D988 at Chevry

Holes	18 Par 69 6125m.
Visitors	Welcome (public course)
Fees	FFr75–200
Facilities	Bar and restaurant; driving range; swimming pool; tennis
Pro	Philippe Maréchal

Golf Clément Ader (1991)　　40

Phone: 64 073410
Av Isaac Pereire, 77220 Gretz-Armainvilliers
Near Gretz, east of Paris, off the N4

Holes	18 Par 72 6323m.
Visitors	Welcome. Course closed Tuesday
Fees	FFr300–500
Facilities	Bar and restaurant; driving range
Pro	Tom Murphy

Golf du Coudray (1960)　　41

Phone: 64 938176
91830 Le Coudray Montceaux
South of Corbeil at Coudray

Holes	18 Par 71 5622m.
Visitors	Welcome. Course closed Tuesday
Fees	FFr250–500
Facilities	Bar and restaurant; driving range; short course
Pro	Claude Langlois

Golf de Courson-Monteloup (1991)　　42

Phone: 64 588080
91680 Bruyère-Le-Châtel
West of Bruyère-le-Châtel at Courson

Holes	4 loops of 9 Par 36 (all) 3056/3115/3149/3415m.
Visitors	Welcome during the week
Fees	FFr250–450
Facilities	Bar and restaurant; practice ground
Pro	Michael Wolseley

Golf de Domont-Montmorency (1966)　　43

Phone: 39 910750
Route de Montmorencyy, 95330 Domont
Just south of Domont, off the N309

Holes	2 x 18 Par 71 5008/5871m.
Visitors	Welcome. Course closed Tuesday
Fees	FFr260–480
Facilities	Bar and restaurant; driving range
Pro	Roger Changart

Golf d'Etiolles (1990) 44
Phone: 60 754949
Carrefour du Trou Rouge, 91450 Etiolles
East of Evry at Etiolles

Holes	18 Par 73 6240m.
	9 Par 36 2665m.
Visitors	Welcome, but must book
Fees	FFr240–360
Facilities	Bar and restaurant; driving range; tennis
Pro	Eric Hemberger

Golf de Fontainebleu (1909) 45
Phone: 64 222295
Route d'Orléans, 77300 Fontainebleau
On the south west side of Fontainebleau, off the N152

Holes	18 Par 72 6074m.
Visitors	Welcome. Course closed Tuesday
Fees	FFr350–640
Facilities	Bar and restaurant; driving range; tennis
Pro	J P Hirigoyen

This is quite a senor club in age and the original design was modified by the ubiquitous Fred Hawtree in the Sixties. It is a beautiful lay-out which runs through avenues of stately oaks and pines, and the springy turf, reminiscent of the downlands of Sussex, is a joy on which to stride.

Golf de Fontenailles (1991) 46
Phone: 64 605100
Domaine des Bois Boudran, 77370 Nangis
West of Nangis, off the D408 at Fontenailles

Holes	18 Par 72 6263m.
	9 Par 35 2925m.
Visitors	Welcome
Fees	FFr250–450
Facilities	Bar and restaurant; driving range; tennis
Pro	Sam Lau Chang

Golf de Forges-les-Bains (1989) 47
Phone: 64 914818
Rte du Général Leclerc, 91470 Forges-les-Bains
South of Paris, off the A10 and D97 at Forges

Holes	18 Par 72 6167m.
Visitors	Welcome
Fees	FFr200–300
Facilities	Bar and restaurant; driving range
Pro	Sydney Kershaw

Golf de la Forteresse (1987) 48
Phone: 60 969510
77156 Thoury-Ferrottes
South of Montereau, off the D219 at Thourry

Holes	18 Par 72 6025m.
Visitors	Welcome
Fees	FFr200–380
Facilities	Bar and restaurant; driving range
Pro	Joel Schilling

Another formidably attractive golf course, laid out partly through avenues of ancient trees, will charm the golfer's eye. Some of the holes lie in more open terrain, but there are many water hazards. The old stone clubhouse was converted from a 12th century farm building.

Golf du Lac de Germigny (1989) 49
Phone: 64 350287
Chemin des Vignes, 77910 Germigny l'Évêque
North east of Meaux at Gemigny

Holes	9 Par 34 2500m.
Visitors	Welcome
Fees	FFr100–250
Facilities	Bar and restaurant; driving range
Pro	Joel Sepchat

Golf de Marolles-en-Brie (1990) 50
Phone: 45 951818
Mail de la Justice, 94440 Marolles-en-Brie
North west of Villecresnes, off the N19

Holes	9 Par 33 2300m.
Visitors	Welcome
Fees	FFr130–160
Facilities	Bar and restaurant; driving range
Pro	Pascal Audoin

Golf de la Marsaudière (1987) 51
Phone: 64 254439
RN 371, 77173 Chevry Cossigny
North of Chevry off the N371

Holes	9 Par 36 2760m.
Visitors	Welcome
Fees	FFr100–200
Facilities	Bar and restaurant

Golf de Meaux-Boutigny (1985)   52

Phone: 60 256398
Le Bordet, Boutigny, 77470 Trilport
South east of Meaux, near Nanteuil

Holes	18 Par 72 6010m.
Visitors	Welcome. Course closed Tuesday
Fees	FFr180–300
Facilities	Bar and restaurant; driving range; short course; tennis
Pro	Nicolas Cecille

Les Golfs de Montgriffon (1990)   53

Phone: 34 681010
Chemin des Rouliers, BP 7, 95270 Luzarches
West of Luzarches, off the D922

Holes	18 Par 72 5765m.
Visitors	Welcome
Fees	FFr200–350
Facilities	Bar and restaurant; driving range; swimming pool; tennis
Pro	Dominique Fournet

Golf de Montpichet (Crécy-La-Chapelle) (1988)   54

Phone: 64 047075
Ferme de Montpichet, 77580 Crécy-La-Chapelle
Near Crécy-La-Chapelle, off the N34

Holes	18 Par 73 6211m.
Visitors	Welcome
Fees	FFr100–200
Facilities	Bar and restaurant; driving range

Golf d'Ormesson (1918/1968)   55

Phone: 45 762071
Belvédère du Parc, 94490 Ormesson
Off the D185 in Ormesson

Holes	18 Par 71 6130m.
Visitors	Welcome. Course closed Tuesday
Fees	FFr230–400
Facilities	Bar and restaurant; driving range
Pro	Franck Leclerq

Golf d'Ozoir-la-Ferrière (1928)   56

Phone: 60 026079
Château des Agneaux, 77330 Ozoir-la-Ferrière
East of Paris, off the N4 at Ozoir-la-Ferrière

Holes	18 Par 72 6085m.
	9 Par 35 2628m.
Visitors	Welcome. Course closed Tuesday
Fees	FFr250–400
Facilities	Bar and restaurant; driving range
Pro	Gerard Henichard

Paris International Golfclub (1991)   57

Phone: 34 699000
95570 Bouffemont
North of Paris, off the D44 near Chauvry

Holes	18 Par 72 6319m.
Visitors	Welcome on weekdays, but must book; with a member at weekends. Course closed Wednesday
Fees	FFr400–600
Facilities	Bar and restaurant; driving range; swimming pool; tennis
Pro	Marc-Antoine Farry

The course was designed by Jack Nicklaus and is a suitably tough proposition as it meanders through thick woodland. There is a familiar American penchant for water hazards and startlingly large bunkers. It is an interesting course with a splendid clubhouse.

Golf du Plessis (1988)   58

Phone: 34 710502
Rue du Petit Paris, 95270 Luzarches
South east of Luzarches, off the D922

Holes	18 Par 72 6120m.
Visitors	Welcome
Fees	FFr200–300
Facilities	Bar and restaurant; driving range; tennis

Golf du Réveillon (1990)   59

Phone: 60 021733
Ferme des Hyverneaux, 77150 Lésigny
In Lésigny, south east of Paris off the N4

Holes	18 Par 72 6136m.
Holes	9 Par 35 2861m.
Visitors	Welcome (public course)
Fees	FFr150–220
Facilities	Bar and restaurant; driving range; short course
Pro	Bruno Antoine

Golf de Rosny-sous-Bois (1988)   60

Phone: 48 940181
Parc de Nanteuil, 93110 Rosny-sous-Bois
East of Paris off the A3 at Rosny

Holes	9 Par 32 2040m.
Visitors	Welcome
Fees	FFr180–210
Facilities	Bar and restaurant; driving range
Pro	J P Seres

Golf Public de St Aubin (1976)   **61**
Phone: 69 412519
Route du Golf, 91190 St Aubin
South east of Paris, off the N306 at St Aubin
Holes	18 Par 70 5817m.
Visitors	Welcome
Fees	FFr100–200
Facilities	Bar and restaurant; driving range

Golf de St Germain-lès-Corbeil (1991)   **62**
Phone: 60 758154
6 Ave du Golf, 91250 St Germain/Corbeil
North west of Melun, off the N447 at St Germain
Holes	18 Par 70 5758m.
Visitors	Welcome
Fees	FFr220–380
Facilities	Bar and restaurant; driving range
Pro	M Laredo

Golf Public de St Pierre-du-Perray (1974)   **63**
Phone: 60 751747
Ville Nouvelle de Melun-Sénart, 9100 Corbeil
Just east of Corbeil at St Pierre
Holes	18 Par 72 6217m.
Visitors	Welcome (public course)
Fees	FFr50–100
Facilities	Bar and restaurant; driving range

Golf de Seraincourt (1967)   **64**
Phone: 34 754728
Gaillonnet, 95450 Vigny
North west of Meulan, off the D913
Holes	18 Par 70 5811m.
Visitors	Welcome
Fees	FFr210–420
Facilities	Bar and restaurant; driving range; swimming pool; tennis
Pro	Jean Paul Gachet

The original nine holes were laid down by Fred Hawtree in 1964 but the course was abandoned for several years until new owners added a further nine holes and re-opened it in 1982. It is an accommodating course and has the useful added facilities of tennis courts and a swimming pool.

Golf Club des Templiers (1989)   **65**
Phone: 44 087372
60173 Ivry-le-Temple
North of Marines at Ivry
Holes	18 Par 72 6310m.
Visitors	Welcome
Fees	FFr100–200
Facilities	Bar and restaurant; driving range

Golf de Villarceaux (1970)   **66**
Phone: 34 677383
Chaussy, 95710 Bray-et-Lu
South of Magny-en-Vexin, off the N183 at Chaussy
Holes	18 Par 72 6128m.
Visitors	Welcome. Course closed Thursday in winter
Fees	FFr175–375
Facilities	Bar and restaurant; driving range; tennis
Pro	R Suguren

Yet another gorgeous château forms the clubhouse for this excellent course, an archetypal parkland course which runs through woodland. The fairways and greens are maintained in superb condition.

Paris

Béthemont Chisan Country Club (1989)   **67**
Phone: 39 755113
Rue du Parc de Béthemont 12, 78300 Poissy
South west of Poissy at Béthemont
Holes	18 Par 72 6035m.
Visitors	Welcome. Course closed Wednesday
Fees	FFr350–650
Facilities	Bar and restaurant; driving range
Pro	Conor Young

Golf de la Boulie (1952)   **68**
Phone: 39 505941
La Boulie, 78000 Versailles
Just to the south east of Versailles
Holes	18 Par 71 5963m (La Vallée).
	18 Par 72 6277m (La Forêt).
Visitors	By invitation only.
Fees	FFr400–500
Facilities	Bar and restaurant; driving range; short course; tennis
Pro	C Bonardi

It is difficult to play this course since you must be invited by a member. But it is worth the effort to cull an invitation since the French Open has been played here many times over La Vallée, even if the course is not rated as an exceptional one.

Golf de Fourqueux (1963) 69

Phone: 34 514147

36, rue de St Nom, 78112 Fourqueux

South west of St Germain en Laye, off the D98 at Fourqueux

Holes	3 x 9 Par 36/36/37 2744/2861/3179m.
Visitors	Welcome on weekdays only. Course closed Tuesday
Fees	FFr350–400
Facilities	Bar and restaurant; driving range; swimming pool; tennis;
Pro	Hugues Gioux

Golf du Haras Lupin (1988) 70

Phone: 47 011504

131 av de la Celle-St-Cloud, 92420 Vaucresson

West of the city at Vaucresson (near St Cloud)

Holes	9 Par 32 2077m.
Visitors	Welcome
Fees	FFr240–320
Facilities	Bar and restaurant; driving range
Pro	Didier Audin

The compact golf course runs around the boundaries of a sports complex, where rugby, football and hockey are played.

Golf Isabella (1969) 71

Phone: 30 541062

Sainte-Appoline, RN12, 78370 Plaisir

West of Versailles, off the N12 at Ste Appoline

Holes	18 Par 71 5629m.
Visitors	Welcome during the week. Course closed Tuesday
Fees	FFr250
Facilities	Bar and restaurant; driving range
Pro	Paddy Fabry

Golf National (1990) 72

Phone: 30 433600

2 Ave du Golf, 78280 Guyancourt

South of Versailles, off the D91 near Guyancourt

Holes	18 Par 72 6515m (Albatros)
	18 Par 72 5936m (Aigle)
Visitors	Welcome, but must book
Fees	FFr200–500
Facilities	Bar and restaurant; driving range; short course; swimming pool; tennis
Pro	J P Pinel

Golf National was built on the initiative of the French Golf Federation to provide first-class golf facilities for the public in an area where private clubs charge visitors inflated fees. It will also be a home for the French Open and other tournaments and a place to train golfers.

The Albatros course ('Florida in Paris' as Nick Faldo termed it) was inspired by the American concept of the stadium course and, designed by Robert Von Hagge, is a magnificent success with its dunes and knolls made from millions of tons of rubble, its water hazards and superb greens. The Aigle suits less accomplished players and there is also a short course and numerous practice areas, including a driving range with 220 bays.

Golf du Prieure (1965) 73

Phone: 34 767012

Sailly, 78440 Gargenville

North west of Meulan, off the D193 at Sailly

Holes	18 Par 72 6157m.
	18 Par 72 6274m.
Visitors	Welcome
Fees	FFr225–375
Facilities	Bar and restaurant; driving range; swimming pool; tennis
Pro	Gilles Bourdy

Rochefort Chisan Country Club (1966) 74

Phone: 30 413181

78730 Rochefort-en-Yvelines

North of Dourdan, off the D10 near Rochefort

Holes	18 Par 71 5735m.
Visitors	Welcome, but must book. Course closed Thursday
Fees	FFr300–500
Facilities	Bar and restaurant; driving range; tennis
Pro	Michel Berthouloux

The club has a magnificent location on high ground on the edge of the Rambouillet forest, and a ruined medieval manor lies in the grounds. Yet another Fred Hawtree design, the course wends its secluded way through the forest. Deep bunkers and elevated greens pose their problems, but the peace and quiet does the golfer's soul good.

Golf de St Cloud (1913/1928) 75

Phone: 47 010185

Parc de Buzenval, 60 rue du 19 Janvier, 92380 Garches

On the west side of the city at St Cloud

Holes	18 Par 67 4857m.
	18 Par 71 5980m.
Visitors	Welcome, but must book. By invitation only on the longer course
Fees	FFr330–600
Facilities	Bar and restaurant; driving range; tennis
Pro	J P Tairraz

St Cloud is one of the most notable clubs in France, partly because of the many international tournaments which have been staged there, including the French Open. It was won there by Aubrey Boomer in 1926 and he was the professional at St Cloud, as was another Ryder Cup player, Peter Butler, in the Sixties. The two courses are situated in the forest of Buzenval and are rolling parkland courses, their fairways threaded through chestnut and beech trees. The championship course, designed by Harry Colt, is a severe test for any golfer.

Golf de St Germain (1920)   76

Phone: 34 517590

Rte de Poissy, 78100 St Germain en Laye
West of St Germain, off the N190

Holes	18 Par 72 6024m.
Visitors	By introduction only
Fees	FFr400
Facilities	Bar and restaurant; driving range; short course
Pro	D Hausseguy

The French Open has been played here on many occasions and you can tread in the steps of such winners as George Duncan, Bobby Locke, Sandy Lyle and Seve Ballesteros, who scored a 62 and a 64 in 1985. St Germain is a lovely parkland course which everyone can enjoy owing to the wide fairways and large greens.

Golf de St Nom-la-Bretêche (1959)   77

Phone: 34 625400

Hameau de la Tuilerie-Bignon, 78860 St Nom-la-Bretêche
Just south of St Nom-la-Bretêche, off the N307

Holes	18 x 2 Par 72 6165/6128m.
Visitors	Welcome on weekdays. Course closed Tuesday
Fees	FFr350–550
Facilities	Bar and restaurant; driving range; swimming pool
Pro	R Golias

Fred Hawtree designed the courses, and the club stages the Lancome Trophy each year. A fine 18th century manor house overlooks the courses, which run through undulating countryside, the one (the Red course) on slightly higher ground than the other (the Blue). A notable feature of the Red course is the lake that separates the 9th and the 18th greens.

Golf de St Quentin (1980)   78

Phone: 30 508640

Base de Loisirs, RN12, 78190 Trappes
South west of Versailles, off the N10 at Trappes

Holes	18 Par 72 6048m.
	18 Par 70 5753m.
Visitors	Welcome (public course)
Fees	FFr150–250
Facilities	Bar and restaurant; driving range; tennis
Pro	Herve Goddard

Golf sur Seine (1990)   79

Phone: 30 924545

La Plagne, 78930 Guerville
On the N13 south of Mantes at La Plagne

Holes	9 Par 35 2885m.
Visitors	Welcome
Fees	FFr75–150
Facilities	Bar and restaurant; driving range
Pro	Vincent Hervé

Golf du Tremblay sur Mauldre (1990)   80

Phone: 34 878109

Château de Tremblay, 78490 Montfort l'Amaury
West of Versailles, off the N12 at Tremblay

Holes	9 Par 36 3080m.
Visitors	Welcome. Course closed Thursday in winter
Fees	FFr140–210
Facilities	Bar and restaurant; driving range; short course
Pro	François Berthet

Golf de la Vaucouleurs (1986)   81

Phone: 34 876229

78910 Civry-la-Forêt
Just west of Orvilliers

Holes	18 Par 73 6298m.
	18 Par 70 5638m.
Visitors	Welcome. Courses closed Wednesday in winter
Fees	FFr200–350
Facilities	Bar and restaurant; driving range
Pro	Raymond Marro

The two courses have contrasting characters. The River (the longer course) is a typical parkland design which takes you through woodland on rolling fairways and with a good number of water hazards. The shorter course is very similar to a links, with thick rough and excellent bunkers, including some of grass.

Golf de Villennes-sur-Seine (1984)   82

Phone: 39 753000

Rte d'Orgeval, 78670 Villennes-sur-Seine
West of Poissy at Villennes

Holes	18 Par 70 5665m.
Visitors	Welcome
Fees	FFr100–200
Facilities	Bar and restaurant; driving range; short course
Pro	Olivier Jaray

Golf des Yvelines (1990)　　　83

Phone: 34 864889

Château de la Couharde, 78940 La Queue-lez-Yveline

North of Montfort, off the N12 at La Queue

Holes	18 Par 72 6344m.
Visitors	Welcome
Fees	FFr200–330
Facilities	Bar and restaurant; driving range; short course
Pro	J P Chardonnet

Alsace & Franche Comté

Golf d'Ammerschwihr (1990)　　　84

Phone: 89 471730

Rte des Trois Epis, 68770 Ammerschwihr

North west of Colmar at Ammerschwihr

Holes	18 Par 71 5795m.
Visitors	Welcome
Fees	FFr160–200
Facilities	Bar and restaurant; driving range; short course
Pro	Denis Racine

Golf de Besançon (1968)　　　85

Phone: 81 557354

Le Chevillotte, 25620 Mamirolle

East of Besançon, off the D104

Holes	18 Par 72 6070m.
Visitors	Welcome. Course closed November to Feb
Fees	FFr170–220
Facilities	Bar and restaurant; driving range
Pro	M Millhouse

This course is an excellent test of the golfer's skills, as it takes you along well-wooded fairways, occasionally interrupted by streams. Several dog-leg holes add to the fun of the golf here.

Golf Club du Château de Bournel (1991)　　86

Phone: 81 860010

25680 Cubry

North east of Rougemont at Cubry

Holes	18 Par 72 5984m.
Visitors	Welcome
Fees	FFr200–300
Facilities	Bar and restaurant closed Tuesday; driving range
Pro	Laurent Etchenic

Golf de Kempferhof (1988)　　　87

Phone: 88 987272

351 Rue du Moulin, 67115 Plobsheim

South of Strasbourg, off the D468 at Plobsheim

Holes	18 Par 72 5980m.
Visitors	Welcome
Fees	FFr300–400
Facilities:	Bar and restaurant closed Tuesday; driving range
Pro	Pierre Pasquier

This is another creation of the American designer, Robert Von Hagge, in the grounds of a fine château. Lines of stately trees and masses of water form the basis of the course, enlivened by Von Hagge's penchant for splashing oddly-shaped bunkers here and there and for constructing humps and hollows around the greens. It is great entertainment.

Golf de la Largue (1988)　　　88

Phone: 89 247111

68580 Mooslargue

South of Attkirch/west of Ferrette at Mooslargue

Holes	18 Par 72 6250m.
Visitors	Welcome
Fees	FFr200–300
Facilities	Bar and restaurant; driving range

Golf de Luxeuil-Bellevue (1991)　　89

Phone: 84 958200

Genevrey, 70240 Saulx

South of Luxeuil-les-Bains off the N57

Holes	9 Par 36 3053m.
Visitors	Welcome. Course closed December to Feb
Fees	FFr100–120
Facilities	Bar and restaurant; practice ground
Pro	Robert Le Souder

Golf du Mont St Jean (1991)　　　90

Phone: 84 600971

39220 Les Rousses

On the north east side of Les Rousses

Holes	18 Par 72 6125m.
Visitors	Welcome. Course closed December to April
Fees	FFr150–240
Facilities	Bar and restaurant; driving range
Pro	Michel Suaz

Golf de Prunevelle (1930)   **91**

Phone: 81 981177

Ferme des Petits-Bans, 25420 Dampierre sur le Doube

South west of Montbéliard, off the D126 at Dampierre

Holes	18 Par 73 6238m.
Visitors	Welcome. Course closed December to Feb
Fees	FFr200–250
Facilities	Bar and restaurant; driving range
Pro	Harry Smith

Great vistas of mountains, the Vosges on one side and the Juras on the other, await the golfer at this excellent holiday course. The fairways are wide but there are some steep slopes to walk.

Golf du Rhin (1969)   **92**

Phone: 89 261676

Ile du Rhin, 68490 Chalampé

East of Mulhouse, off the D39. On an island in the middle of the Rhine near Chalampé

Holes	18 Par 72 6400m.
Visitors	Welcome. Course closed Monday
Fees	FFr150–250
Facilities	Bar and restaurant; driving range
Pro	Tony Price

Golf de Rougemont-le-Château (1990)   **93**

Phone: 84 237474

Ferme Goetz, Rte de Masevaux, 90100 Rougemont

North east of Belfort at Rougemont

Holes	18 Par 72 6000m.
Visitors	Welcome
Fees	FFr175–250
Facilities	Bar and restaurant; driving range
Pro	Lionel Burnet

Golf Les Rousses (du Rochat) (1987)   **94**

Phone: 84 600625

Le Rochat, 39220 Les Rousses

Just to the north east of Les Rousses

Holes	18 Par 70 5301m.
Visitors	Welcome. Course closed October to March
Fees	FFr160–230
Facilities	Bar and restaurant; driving range; short course
Pro	Gino Prudentino

Golf Club de Strasbourg (1934)   **95**

Phone: 88 661722

Rte du Rhin, 67400 Illkirch-Graffenstaden

South of Strasbourg, off the D468

Holes	3 loops of 9 **Blanc:** Par 35 2930m; **Rouge:** Par 36 2963m; **Bleu:** Par 37 3208m.
Visitors	Welcome on weekdays. Course closed Tuesday
Fees	FFr200
Facilities	Bar and restaurant; driving range
Pro	Mike Homer

Golf du Val d'Amour (1989)   **96**

Phone: 84 710423

Parcey, 39100 Dôle

South of Dôle, off the D405 at Parcey

Holes	9 Par 35 2717m.
Visitors	Welcome
Fees	FFr100–120
Facilities	Bar and restaurant; driving range
Pro	Fabien Dendyan

Golf du Val de Sorne (1988)   **97**

Phone: 84 430480

Vernantois, 39570 Lons-le-Saunier

Just south of Lons-le-Saunier, off the D117 at Vernantois

Holes	14 Par 54 4922m.
Visitors	Welcome
Fees	FFr120–180
Facilities	Bar and restaurant; driving range
Pro	Juan Ayala

Golf de la Wantzenau (1991)   **98**

Phone: 88 963773

Domaine du Golf, D301, 67610 La Wantzenau

North of Strasbourg at Le Wantzenau, off the D302

Holes	18 Par 72 6300m.
Visitors	Welcome
Fees	FFr210–300
Facilities	Bar and restaurant; driving range
Pro	Olivier Sabourin

Lorraine & Champagne-Ardennes

Golf de l'Abbaye des Sept Fontaines (1989)   99
Phone: 24 377727

Fagnon, 08090 Charleville-Mézières

South west of Charleville-Mézières, off the D3

Holes	9 Par 36 2875m.
Visitors	Welcome
Fees	FFr120–170
Facilities	Bar and restaurant closed Tuesday; driving range

Located in the Ardennes forest, the abbey has had a remarkable history. It was built in 1129, mostly destroyed during the Revolution, was restored and later became the family home of de Gaulle's wife, Yvonne Vendroux. The château is now the clubhouse for the charming parkland 9 hole course; a further 9 holes are at the planning stage.

Golf d'Arc-en-Barrois (1988)   100
Phone: 25 035114

52210 Arc-en-Barrois

South of Arc-en-Barrois; the club is signposted

Holes	9 Par 36 3089m.
Visitors	Welcome
Fees	FFr130–190
Facilities	Bar; driving range
Pro	Christian Arnut

Golf des Ardennes (1989)   101
Phone: 24 356465

Les Poursaudes, Villers-le-Tilleul, 08430 Poix-Terron

South of Charleville-Mézières, near Poix Tierron

Holes	9 Par 36 2816m.
Visitors	Welcome
Fees	FFr100–150
Facilities	Bar; driving range
Pro	Bruno Victoire

La Cordelière has one of the most fascinating clubhouses in the world, a château once owned by Count Chandon, of the notable Champagne house. The course runs partly through woodland and partly through open country. There is plenty of water about, especially at the short 8th hole.

Golf de Bitche (1987)   102
Phone: 87 961530

Rue des Prés, 57230 Bitche

Just east of Bitche, off the N62

Holes	18 Par 72 6082m.
	9 Par 34 2625m.
Visitors	Welcome
Fees	FFr140–250
Facilities	Bar and restaurant closed Tuesday in winter; driving range; tennis
Pro	Denys Taylor

The course lies on the hillside of Kindelberg and gives the golfer fine views over the surrounding countryside. It is a hilly course with several water hazards and notable for its charming woodland.

Golf de Combles en Barrois (1947)   103
Phone: 29 451603

55000 Combes-en-Barrois

South of Bar-le-Duc, off the D185

Holes	9 Par 33 2309m.
Visitors	Welcome
Fees	FFr120–150
Facilities	Bar and restaurant closed Thursday; driving range
Pro	Dany Mory

Golf de la Cordelière (1958)   104
Phone: 25 401876

Château de la Cordelière, 10210 Chaource

Just north east of Chaource, off the D443

Holes	18 Par 72 6154m.
Visitors	Welcome. Course closed Tuesday
Fees	FFr180–250
Facilities	Bar and restaurant closed Tuesday; practice ground
Pro	Maurice Vian

Golf de la Forêt d'Orient (1990)   105
Phone: 25 463778

Rouilly-Sacey, 10220 Piney

East of Troyes, off the D960

Holes	18 Par 71 6085m.
Visitors	Welcome
Fees	FFr160–200
Facilities	Driving range

Golf de la Grande Romanie (1988)   106
Phone: 26 666469

51460 Courtisols

North east of Châlons-sur-Marne, near the junction of the N3/D394 (towards Reims)

Holes	18 Par 72 6570m.
Visitors	Welcome

Fees   FFr200–250
Facilities   Bar and restaurant; driving range
Pro   Alexandre Macheprot

Golfclub des Images d'Epinal (1985)   107
Phone: 29 346597
Rue du Merle Blanc, 88001 Epinal
On the east side of Epinal
Holes   18 Par 70 5315m.
Visitors   Welcome
Fees   FFr100
Facilities   Bar; driving range
Pro   Valerie Cuny

Golf de Madine (1985)   108
Phone: 29 895600
Nonsard, 55210 Vigneulles
7 km south of Vigneulles
Holes   9 Par 36 3062m.
Visitors   Welcome
Fees   FFr70–100
Facilities   Bar and restaurant; driving range;
              short course; tennis

Golf de Metz-Chérisey (1988)   109
Phone: 87 527018
Château de Chérisey, 57420 Verny
South of Metz, off the D913 at Pournoy-la-Grasse
Holes   18 Par 73 6172m.
Visitors   Welcome
Fees   FFr100–200
Facilities   Bar and restaurant closed Tuesday;
              driving range; tennis
Pro   Joe Higgins

Golf de Nancy-Aingeray (1964)   110
Phone: 83 245387
54460 Liverdun
North west of Nancy, off the D90 near Aingeray
Holes   18 Par 69 5525m.
Visitors   Welcome
Fees   FFr200–300
Facilities   Bar and restaurant closed Monday;
              driving range

The course is charmingly scenic as it wanders
through delightful woodland. Although it is
short it has some testing holes: the short 12th
through an intimidating avenue of trees and the
dog-leg 13th, with its difficult second shot. It is a
lovely spot.

Golf de Reims-Champagne (1928)   111
Phone: 26 036519
Château des Dames-de-France, 51390 Gueux
West of Reims at Gueux
Holes   18 Par 72 6046m.
Visitors   Welcome
Fees   FFr200–300
Facilities   Bar and restaurant; driving range
Pro   Phillip Harisson

Golf de St Walfroy (1990)   112
Phone: 24 226485
08370 Margut
Just south east of Margut, off the D44
Holes   9 Par 33 2450m.
Visitors   Welcome. Course closed Monday
Fees   FFr100–200
Facilities   Bar and restaurant

Golf du Technopole de Metz (1990)   113
Phone: 87 203311
Rue Félix Savart, 57070 Metz Technopole 2000
On the east side of Metz; follow the signs to
Technopole 2000
Holes   18 Par 71 5774m.
Visitors   Welcome
Fees   FFr100–200
Facilities   Bar and restaurant closed Monday;
              driving range
Pro   Gerard Romain

Golf de la Vitarderie (1988)   114
Phone: 26 582509
Chemin de la Bourdonnerie, 51700 Dormans
Just south of Dormans, off the D41
Holes   18 Par 72 5969m.
Visitors   Welcome. Course closed Monday am.
Fees   FFr120–160
Facilities   Bar and restaurant; driving range

Golf de Vittel (1905/1989)   115
Phone: 29 081880
88804 Vittel
On the north side of Vittel; head for the
hippodrome and the club is signposted
Holes   18 Par 72 6326m (Mont St Jean)
              18 Par 72 6100m (Peuplin)
Visitors   Welcome
Fees   FFr200–250
Facilities   Bar and restaurant; driving range;
              compact course; swimming pool;
              tennis; squash
Pro   D Mory

Bourgogne

Golf d'Autun (1990)   116
Phone: 85 520928
Le Plan d'Eau du Vallon, 71400 Autun
East of Autun, off the N80

Holes	9 Par 33 2216m.
Visitors	Welcome
Fees	FFr100
Facilities	Restaurant; driving range; swimming pool; tennis
Pro	Brian Radcliffe

Golf d'Azy (1990)   117
Phone: 86 585000
Parc du Château, 58270 St Bénin d'Azy
East of Nevers, off the D978 near St Bénin

Holes	18 Par 73 6257m.
Visitors	Welcome
Fees	FFr150–200
Facilities	Bar and retaurant; driving range
Pro	E Didier

Golf de Beaune (1990)   118
Phone: 80 241029
Levernois, 21200 Beaune
South east of Beaune, off the D970 at Levernois

Holes	18 Par 72 6484m.
Visitors	Welcome
Fees	FFr140–200
Facilities	Bar and restaurant; driving range; short course
Pro	Jean Claude Brosse

Golf du Cap Vert (1990)   119
Phone: 80 466900
Parc du Cap Vert, 21800 Quétigny
East of Dijon, off the D108 at Quétigny

Holes	9 Par 35 2905m.
Visitors	Welcome
Fees	FFr130–150
Facilities	Bar and restaurant; driving range
Pro	Henri Bailly

Golf Club du Château de Chailly (1990)   120
Phone: 80 908961
Château de Chailly, 21320 Pouilly-en-Auxois
West of Pouilly, off the D977 bis

Holes	18 Par 72 6146m.
Visitors	Welcome
Fees	FFr350
Facilities	Bar and restaurant; driving range; swimming pool; tennis
Pro	J P Variclier

A visit to see the beguiling 16th century Château de Chailly, with its beautiful lake, is rewarding enough; it is now a renowned hotel. But the golf course is also rewarding; the fairways roll gently along, with the occasional stream or pond to add to the interest.

Golf Public de Châlon-sur-Saône (1979)   121
Phone: 85 934965
Parc de Loisirs St Nicolas, 73180 Chatenoy-en-Brese
On the east side of Châlon-sur-Saône

Holes	18 Par 71 5859m.
Visitors	Welcome (public course)
Fees	FFr135
Facilities	Bar and restaurant; driving range; tennis
Pro	Joel Vezin

Golf de Clairis (1973)   122
Phone: 86 863390
Domaine de Clairis, 89150 Savigny-sur-Clairis
South west of Sens, off the N60 in the Bois de Bléry

Holes	18 Par 72 5829m.
Visitors	Welcome. Course closed Wednesday in winter
Fees	FFr100–200
Facilities	Bar and restaurant; driving range

Golf de Dijon-Bourgogne (1972)   123
Phone: 80 357110
Bois des Norges, 21490 Norges-la-Ville
North of Dijon, off the N74 at Norges

Holes	18 Par 72 6179m.
Visitors	Welcome
Fees	FFr190–250
Facilities	Bar and restaurant; driving range; swimming pool; tennis
Pro	Jean Lamaison

Golf de la Fredière (1990)   **124**
Phone: 85 252740
Céron, 71110 Marcigny
West of Marcigny, off the D990 at Ceron
Holes	18 Par 65 4592m.
Visitors	Welcome
Fees	FFr130–180
Facilities	Bar and restaurant closed Wednesday; driving range; swimming pool
Pro	Gilles Charmat

Golf de Nevers (1969)   **125**
Phone: 86 581830
58470 Magny-Cours
South of Nevers, off the N7 at Magny
Holes	18 Par 71 5665m.
Visitors	Welcome
Fees	FFr120–180
Facilities	Bar and restaurant closed Wednesday; driving range
Pro	Pierre Raguet

Golf de Roncemay (1991)   **126**
Phone: 86 736987
Chassy, 89110 Aillant/Tholon
South of Jigney and Aillant, off the D955 at Roncenay
Holes	18 Par 72 6400m.
Visitors	Welcome on weekdays
Fees	FFr230
Facilities	Bar and restaurant; driving range
Pro	Jean Claude Iturrioz

Golf de Salives (1990)   **127**
Phone: 80 756645
Larçon, 21580 Salives
Salives is about 60 km north west of Dijon, and the club is west of Salives at Larcon
Holes	9 Par 36 2896m.
Visitors	Welcome
Fees	FFr100–200
Facilities	Bar and restaurant; driving range

Golf du Château de la Salle (1989)   **128**
Phone: 85 360971
71260 Lugny
North of Mâcon off the A6/N6, near Clissé at La Salle
Holes	18 Par 71 6024m.
Visitors	Welcome
Fees	FFr180–250
Facilities	Bar and restaurant; driving range; tennis
Pro	Emmanuel Ducret

Golf du Château de Tanlay (1989)   **129**
Phone: 86 757292
Par du Château, 89430 Tanlay
East of Tonnerre, off the D965 at Tanlay
Holes	9 Par 35 2618m.
Visitors	Welcome. Course closed Tuesday
Fees	FFr90–120
Facilities	Bar and restaurant; driving range
Pro	Luc Guiraud

SOUTH-WEST FRANCE

Poitou-Charentes

Golf du Cognac (1988)   1
Phone: 45 321817
St Brice, 16100 Cognac
East of Cognac, off the N41 at La Maurie
Holes   18 Par 72 6142m.
Visitors   Welcome. Course closed Tuesday in winter
Fees   FFr180–220
Facilities Bar and restaurant; driving range; tennis
Pro   Jean Marc Lecuona

Built on the banks of the Charente river and alongside the Martell family home, this course was financed by the brandy makers and expense was not spared. Jean Garaialde did the design and it is a long and demanding lay-out over undulating, well-wooded terrain. The greens are narrow and difficult and it adds up to a real golfing challenge. There is a big practice range and four practice holes. It is well worth a visit.

Golfclub du Connetable (1986)   2
Phone: 49 862021
86270 La Roche Posay, Parc du Connétable
On the west side of La Roche Posay
Holes   18 Par 72 5840m.
Visitors   Welcome. Course closed Tuesday in winter
Fees   FFr160–220
Facilities Bar and restaurant; driving range; swimming pool; tennis
Pro   Emmanuel Rider

Golf du Haut Poitou (1987)   3
Phone: 49 625362
Parc de Loisirs de St Cyr, 86130 Jaunay Clan
North of Poitiers, off the N10. Follow the signs to the Parc de Loisirs
Holes   18 Par 73 6590m.
Visitors   Welcome
Fees   FFr160–190
Facilities Bar and restaurant closed Tuesday in winter; driving range; short course; tennis; sailing
Pro   David Maxwell

Golf de l'Hirondelle (1955)   4
Phone: 45 611694
Champ Fleuri, 16000 Angoulême
Just south of Angoulême, off the D104
Holes   9 Par 33 2285m.
Visitors   Welcome. Course closed Tuesday
Fees   FFr100–140
Facilities Bar and restaurant; driving range
Pro   Guy Pena

Loudun Golf Club (1985)   5
Phone: 49 987806
Roiffé 86120 Les Trois Moutiers
North of Loudun, off the D147 at St Hilaire
Holes   18 Par 72 6280m.
Visitors   Welcome. Course closed Tuesday in winter
Fees   FFr160–220
Facilities Bar and restaurant; driving range; tennis
Pro   Deeone Sheen

Golf de Mignaloux-Beauvoir (1990)   6
Phone: 49 467027
86800 St Julien-l'Ars
South east of Poitiers at Mignaloux-Beauvoir (off the N145)
Holes   18 Par 71 6036m.
Visitors   Welcome
Fees   FFr150–210
Facilities Bar and restaurant; driving range; swimming pool; tennis
Pro   B Demeestere

Golf Club Niortais (1985)   7
Phone: 49 090141
Chemin du Grand Ormeau, 79000 Niort-Romagné
Just south of Niort, off the N150 (the turn is at the hippodrome)
Holes   15 Par 71 5991m.
Visitors   Welcome
Fees   FFr120–150
Facilities Bar and restaurant; driving range
Pro   Frederic Dufresne

Golf d'Oléron (1988)   8

Phone: 46 471159

La Vieille Perrotine, 17310 St Pierre d'Oléron

North east of St Pierre d'Oléron at Boyarville

Holes	9 Par 35 2700m.
Visitors	Welcome. Course closed Thursday in winter
Fees	FFr100–150
Facilities	Bar; driving range
Pro	Veronique Heniau

Golf du Petit Chêne (1987)   9

Phone: 49 632833

79310 Mazières en Gatine

Just south of Mazières, off the D743

Holes	18 Par 72 6015m.
Visitors	Welcome (public course)
Fees	FFr150–200
Facilities	Bar and restaurant; driving range
Pro	Patrick Grassin

Golf de la Prée Rochelle (1989)   10

Phone: 42 560221

17137 Marsily

North of La Rochelle at Nieul-sur-Mer

Holes	18 Par 72 6012m.
Visitors	Welcome
Fees	FFr130–220
Facilities	Bar and restaurant; driving range; tennis
Pro	Philippe Tourtrol

Golf de la Prèze (1990)   11

Phone: 45 232474

Ecuras, 16220 Montbron

North east of Montbron, off the D16

Holes	9 Par 36 3160m.
Visitors	Welcome
Fees	FFr120–200
Facilities	Bar and restaurant; driving range; swimming pool; tennis
Pro	Gilles Delvallade

Golf de Royan (Côte de Beauté) (1977)   12

Phone: 46 231624

17420 Saint-Palais

North west of Royan

Holes	18 Par 71 6013m.
Visitors	Welcome. Course closed Tuesday in winter
Fees	FFr170–230
Facilities	Bar and restaurant; driving range

This is a very entertaining design; the course runs through thickly wooded countryside but, since it is near the sea, it also incorporates sand dunes. Elevated tees and greens and several dog-legs add to the fun, and the views are splendid; especially of the ocean from the par 3 14th hole. It is a tough course, with some long carries needed from the tee, and the 18th is a wonderful hole, its small green guarded by a lake.

Golf de Saintes (1954)   13

Phone: 46 742761

Fontcouverte, 17100 Saintes

Just north east of Saintes, off the N150 at St Hilaire

Holes	18 Par 68 4985m.
Visitors	Welcome (public course). Closed Monday
Fees	FFr50–100
Facilities	Bar and restaurant; driving range

Golf de Trousse Chemise (1990)   14

Phone: 46 296937

Rte de la Levée Verte, 17880 Les Portes en Ré

On the north west point of the Ile de Ré

Holes	9 Par 35 2600m.
Visitors	Welcome
Fees	FFr100–200
Facilities	Bar and restaurant; driving range

Auvergne & Limousin

Golfclub des Avenelles (1986)   15

Phone: 70 200095

Toulon-sur-Allier, 03400 Yzeure

South east of Moulins, off the N7 at Toulon-sur-Allier

Holes	9 Par 34 2560m.
Visitors	Welcome. Course closed Tuesday
Fees	FFr100–140
Facilities	Bar and restaurant; driving range
Pro	Nathalie Cacot

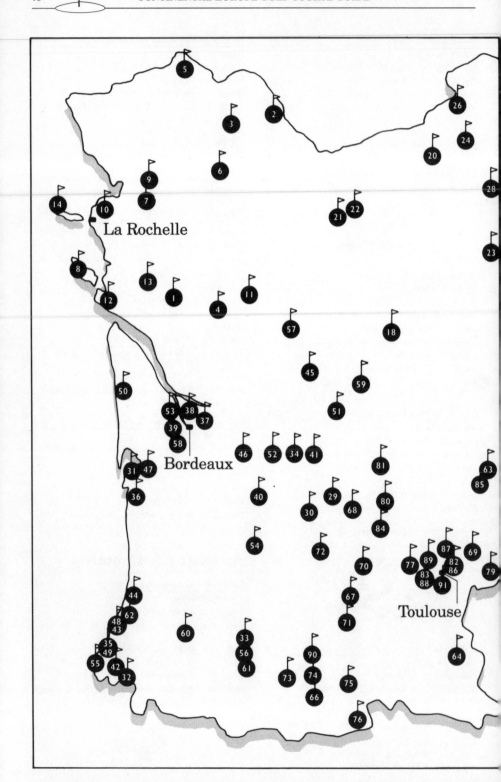

La Rochelle

Bordeaux

Toulouse

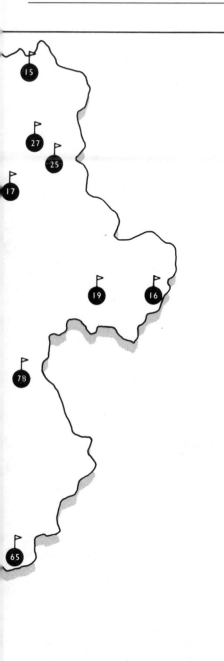

**FRANCE
SOUTH-WEST**

Golf de Chambon-sur-Lignon (1987)   16

Phone: 71 592810

Beaujeu, 43400 Le Chambon

South east of Le Chambon sur Lignon, off the D155

Holes	9 Par 36 3034m.
Visitors	Welcome. Course closed Tuesday except July/August
Fees	FFr120–170
Facilities	Bar and restaurant; practice ground
Pro	Richard Guidetti

Golf de Charade (1985)   17

Phone: 73 357309

Village de Charade, 63130 Royat

West of Clermont-Ferrand; follow the signs to Royat

Holes	9 Par 32 2217m.
Visitors	Welcome
Fees	FFr125–150
Facilities	Bar and restaurant; driving range
Pro	Daniel Roumand

Golf du Coiroux (1974)   18

Phone: 55 272566

Aubazine, 19190 Beynat

East of Brive, off the N89 at Aubazine

Holes	18 Par 70 5400m.
Visitors	Welcome (public course)
Fees	FFr120–200
Facilities	Bar and restaurant; driving range
Pro	J F Encuentra

Golf du Cros du Loup (1991)   19

Phone: 71 091777

Sénilhac, Ceyssac-La-Roche, 43000 Le Puy

Just west of Le Puy, on the D111

Holes	9 Par 36 3044m.
Visitors	Welcome. Course closed Tuesday
Fees	FFr100–150
Facilities	Bar and restaurant; driving range
Pro	Thierry Bastide

Golf de la Jonchère (1989)   20

Phone: 55 622305

Montgrenier, 23230 Gouzon

Off N145 at Gouzon

Holes	18 Par 71 5898m.
Visitors	Welcome. Course closed Tuesday in winter
Fees	FFr140–180
Facilities	Bar and restaurant; driving range
Pro	Pascal Isambert

Golf Municipal de Limoges (1976)   21

Phone: 55 302102

St Lazare, Ave du Golf, 87000 Limoges

Just south of Limoges off the N20

Holes	18 Par 72 6222m.
Visitors	Welcome. Course closed January to April
Fees	FFr90
Facilities	Bar and restaurant; driving range; swimming pool; tennis
Pro	Ives Saubaber

Golf de la Porcelaine (1988)   22

Phone: 55 311069

Célicroux, 87350 Panazol

East of Limoges, off the D941

Holes	18 Par 72 6048m.
Visitors	Welcome. Course closed Tuesday in winter
Fees	FFr150–200
Facilities	Bar and restaurant; driving range
Pro	Pierre Signeux

Golf du Rigolet (Mont-Dore) (1928)   23

Phone: 73 650079

63240 Le Mont-Dore

West of Mont-Dore, off the D213

Holes	9 Par 34 2115m.
Visitors	Welcome. Course closed October to April
Fees	FFr100–200
Facilities	Bar and restaurant

Golf de Ste Agathe (1988)   24

Phone: 70 032177

Villebret, 03310 Néris-les-Bains

South east of Montluçon, off the N144

Holes	9 Par 35 2524m.
Visitors	Welcome
Fees	FFr120–170
Facilities	Bar; driving range
Pro	Gilles Ostier

Golf de Thiers (1990)   25

Phone: 73 80149

Parc de Loisirs Iloa, Courty, 63300 Thiers

North west of Thiers, off the D906

Holes	9 Par 36 3380m.
Visitors	Welcome. Course closed Tuesday
Fees	FFr100–200
Facilities	Bar and restaurant; driving range
Pro	Nathalie Planchin

Golf du Val-de-Cher (1975)   26

Phone: 70 067115

03190 Nassigny

North of Montluçon at Nassigny

Holes	18 Par 69 5900m.
Visitors	Welcome
Fees	FFr100–200
Facilities	Bar and restaurant; driving range

Sporting Club de Vichy (1907)   27

Phone: 70 323911

Allée Baugnies, 03700 Bellerive-sur-Allier

On the south west side of Vichy, at Bellerive

Holes	18 Par 70 5463m.
Visitors	Welcome. Course closed Tuesday
Fees	FFr230–300
Facilities	Bar and restaurant; driving range
Pro	Christian Roumaud

Golf Club de Volcans (1984)   28

Phone: 73 621551

La Bruyère des Moines, 63870 Orcines

West of Clermont-Ferrand, off the D941 at Orcines

Holes	18 Par 72 6242m.
Visitors	Welcome. Course closed Tuesday in winter
Fees	FFr200–250
Facilities	Bar and restaurant; practice ground; short course
Pro	Lucien Roux

The course, about 3000 feet above sea level, is built on volcanic land and Le Puy de Dome looms over it. The views are magnificent and so is the course. The fairways, fringed by firs and heather, are wide and inviting and it is a proper test for any golfer, of whatever standard. It is maintained in superb condition and is relatively quiet.

Aquitaine

Golf Club d'Agen Bon-Encontre (1982)   **29**
Phone: 53 969578
Rte de St Ferréol, 47240 Bon-Encontre
Just east of Agen, off the N113 at Bon-Encontre
Holes   9 Par 35 2880m.
Visitors   Welcome
Fees   FFr100–200
Facilities   Bar and restaurant; driving range

Golf d'Albret (1989)   **30**
Phone: 53 655369
Le Pusocq, 47239 Barbaste
North west of Nérac, off the D655 beyond
Barbaste
Holes   18 Par 72 5927m.
Visitors   Welcome
Fees   FFr120–150
Facilities   Bar and restaurant; driving range
Pro   Veronique Heniau

Club d'Arcachon (1952)   **31**
Phone: 56 544400
35 Bd d'Arcachon, 33270 La Teste de Buch
South of Arcachon off the D217 at La Teste
Holes   18 Par 71 5934m.
Visitors   Welcome. Course closed Wednesday
in winter
Fees   FFr165–280
Facilities   Bar and restaurant; driving range
Pro   Frantz du Beau
The course was deisgned by Cecil Blandford and
is a reasonable test of golf over undulating
fairways lined with pine trees. The long 2nd
hole, a par 3, downhill to a difficult green is a
testing hole and there are many water hazards
to avoid during the second half.

Golf d'Arcangues (1990)   **32**
Phone: 59 431056
Argelous, 64200 Arcangues
South of Biarritz, off the D755 at Arcangues
Holes   18 Par 72 6092m.
Visitors   Welcome. Course closed Tuesday in
winter
Fees   FFr200–300
Facilities   Bar and restaurant; driving range
Pro   Olivier Leglise

Golf d'Artiguelouve (1986)   **33**
Phone: 59 830929
64230 Lescar, Domaine St Michel
North west of Pau, off the D501 near Artiguelove
Holes   18 Par 71 6063m.
Visitors   Welcome
Fees   FFr170–200
Facilities   Bar and restaurant; driving range;
swimming pool; tennis and squash
Pro   Alain Lopez

Golf Club de Barthe (1989)   **34**
Phone: 53 888331
47380 Tombeboeuf
East of Marmande, of the D124 near Tombeboeuf
Holes   9 Par 36 2775m.
Visitors   Welcome
Fees   FFr70
Facilities   Bar; driving range

Golf de Biarritz (1888)   **35**
Phone: 59 037180
Le Phare, Ave Edith Cavell, 64200 Biarritz
At Le Phare, close to the centre of Biarritz
Holes   18 Par 69 5379m.
Visitors   Welcome, but must book. Course
closed Tuesday in winter
Fees   FFr200–300
Facilities   Bar and restaurant; driving range
Pro   Richard Simpson
After Pau, this is the second oldest club in
France and was founded by the Hambro family,
who employed the American architect, Willie
Dunn (he built Shinnecock Hills) to design the
course. Biarritz is by no means long but the
trees and some testing short holes impose their
own difficulties, as do the breezes off the sea.

Golf de Biscarosse (1989)   **36**
Phone: 58 828893
Rte d'Ispe, 40600 Biscarosse
North of Biscarosse, off the D305
Holes   18 Par 68 5200m.
Visitors   Welcome
Fees   FFr150–250
Facilities   Bar; driving range
Pro   Pedro Navarro

Golf de Bordeaux Cameyrac (1972)   37

Phone: 56 729679

33450 St Sulpice Cameyrac

East of Bordeaux, off the N89 at Cameyrac

Holes	18 Par 72 5972m.
Visitors	Welcome
Fees	FFr160–250
Facilities	Bar and restaurant; driving range; short course; swimming pool; tennis
Pro	Veronique Bouneau

Golf Municipal de Bordeaux-Lac (1976)   38

Phone: 56 509272

Ave de Pernon, 33300 Bordeaux

North of Bordeaux near Pont des Religieuses

Holes	2 x 18 Par 72 6154/6159m.
Visitors	Welcome (public course). Course closed Tuesday
Fees	FFr160–180
Facilities	Bar and restaurant; driving range
Pro	Jean Delgado

Golf Bordelais (1905)   39

Phone: 56 285604

Domaine de Kater, Ave d'Eysines, 33200 Bordeaux

On the north west of Bordeaux, near the hippodrome

Holes	18 Par 67 4753m.
Visitors	Welcome
Fees	FFr170
Facilities	Bar and restaurant; driving range
Pro	Monique Saubader

Golf de Casteljaloux (1989)   40

Phone: 53 935160

Rte de Mont-de-Marsan, 47700 Casteljaloux

South west of Casteljaloux off the D933

Holes	18 Par 72 5916m.
Visitors	Welcome
Fees	FFr150–220
Facilities	Bar and restaurant; driving range
Pro	François Pommerol

Golf de Castelnaud (1987)   41

Phone: 53 017464

Le Menuisière, 47290 Castelnaud de Gratecambe

North of Villeneuve-sur-Lot, off the N21

Holes	18 Par 72 6322m.
Visitors	Welcome
Fees	FFr140–200
Facilities	Bar and restaurant; driving range; short course; swimming pool; tennis
Pro	Catherine Arsac

Golf de Chantaco (1928)   42

Phone: 59 261422

Rte d'Ascain, 64500 St Jean de Luz

Just south east of St Jean de Luz, off the D918

Holes	18 Par 70 5722m.
Visitors	Welcome. Course closed Tuesday in winter
Fees	FFr240–420
Facilities	Bar and restaurant; driving range; tennis
Pro	Jean Claude Harismendy

The famous golf architect, Harry Colt (of Le Touquet and Sunningdale fame) designed the course at the behest of the Lacoste family. It is a charming parkland course threaded through delightful woodland, and an occasional stream will enliven your round.

Golf de Chiberta (1927)   43

Phone: 59 638320

104 Bd des Plages, 64600 Anglet

Just north of Biarritz on the coast road

Holes	18 Par 71 5650m.
Visitors	Welcome, but must book. Course closed Thursday
Fees	FFr200–300
Facilities	Bar and restaurant; driving range; swimming pool; tennis
Pro	Pierre Dufourg

This is one of Tom Simpson's courses and is a charming mix of woodland and links; accuracy is at a premium here if you are to avoid the various hazards. It is a popular club and you must book ahead in the summer months.

Golf de la Côte d'Argent (1989)   44

Phone: 58 485465
40660 Moliets
On the coast at Moliets-Plage

Holes	18 Par 72 6127m.
Visitors	Welcome
Fees	FFr200–300
Facilities	Bar and restaurant; driving range; short course; swimming pool; tennis; archery
Pro	Frank Ducousso

This is a golf resort built in the pine forests alongside the Atlantic ocean. Robert Trent Jones has constructed a really tough course which wends its way through the pine trees, with gorse bushes ever ready to trap your ball in the rough, with the added attraction, near the end of the round, of a run of holes through the dunes.

Golf de la Croix de Mortemart (1989)   45

Phone: 53 032755
St-Félix-de-Reillac, 24260 Le Bugue
North of Le Bugue, off the D710

Holes	18 Par 72 6222m.
Visitors	Welcome
Fees	FFr150–250
Facilities	Bar and restaurant; driving range

Golf des Graves et du Sauternais (1989)   46

Phone: 56 622543
33210 Langon
Just east of Langon near St Pardon de Conques

Holes	18 Par 72 5850m.
Visitors	Welcome. Course closed Tuesday in winter
Fees	FFr100–130
Facilities	Bar and restaurant; driving range
Pro	Gilles De Maugras

Golf de Gujan Mestras (1990)   47

Phone: 56 668636
Rte de Sanguinet, 33470 Gujan-Mestras
Near Arcachon at Gujan

Holes	18 Par 72 6625m.
	9 Par 35 2630m.
Visitors	Welcome
Fees	FFr200–270
Facilities	Bar and restaurant; driving range
Pro	Christian Chabrier

Water, water, everywhere at this delightful and imaginative course near Arcachon. The greens of the 3rd and 5th holes seem to rise, like mirages, from the waves. It's enough to unnerve any golfer, but it's a lovely setting among the pine trees, even if the ferns and gorse and the huge bunkers make any wayward shots more difficult to retrieve.

Golf d'Hossegor (1927)   48

Phone: 58 435699
Ave du Golf, 40150 Hossegor
On the east side of Hossegor

Holes	18 Par 71 6004m.
Visitors	Welcome. Course closed Tuesday in winter
Fees	FFr200–300
Facilities	Bar and restaurant; driving range
Pro	Réné Darrieumerlon

You might think you were on a traditional Surrey course when you play Hossegor, with its flat fairways, heather and avenues of trees. There are many dog-leg holes and the par 3s are superb. Such is its quality that it has been the venue for many amateur tournaments.

Golf d'Ilbarritz (1987)   49

Phone: 59 237465
Ave Reine Victoria, 64210 Bidart
Just south of Biarritz, off the D911 on the coast

Holes	9 Par 32 2185m.
Visitors	Welcome (public course). Closed Monday in winter
Fees	FFr140
Facilities	Bar and restaurant; driving range
Pro	Philippe Mendiburu

This is a golf practice centre, modelled on American and Japanese lines. There are 14 practice areas where you can try to improve every aspect of your game.

Golf International de Lacanau (1980)   50

Phone: 56 032560
33680 Lacanau-Océan
Just east of Lacanau-Océan; follow the signs on the D6

Holes	18 Par 72 5932m.
Visitors	Welcome
Fees	FFr150–230
Facilities	Bar and restaurant; driving range
Pro	Jean Louis Pega

This is very much a golf resort, with an hotel and apartments for rent. All sorts of sporting activities are available nearby including tennis, squash, board sailing and surfing. The golf course, designed by John Harris, is pretty good, too. It was cut through the pine forests and has several lakes. Beware that it gets very busy in August.

Golf de Lolivarie (1985)   51

Phone: 53 302269

La Croix Sagelat, 24170 Belvès

Just north of Belvès at Sagelat

Holes	9 Par 35 2200m.
Visitors	Welcome. Course closed Tuesday except July/August
Fees	FFr100–120
Facilities	Bar and restaurant; driving range; pitch & putt course

Golf de Marmande (1987)   52

Phone: 53 208760

Carpette, 47200 Marmande

South east of Marmande off the N113

Holes	9 Par 36 2667m.
Visitors	Welcome. Course closed Tuesday
Fees	FFr90–120
Facilities	Bar and restaurant; driving range; tennis
Pro	Veronique Heniau

Golf du Médoc (1988)   53

Phone: 56 720110

Chemin de Courmateau, Louens, 33290 Blanquefort

North west of Bordeaux, off the D1 at Louens

Holes	18 Par 72 6316m (Le Château)
	18 Par 72 6281m (Les Vignes)
Visitors	Welcome. Course closed Wednesday
Fees	FFr200–300
Facilities	Bar and restaurant; driving range

The original Médoc course is highly rated and is reminiscent of some Scottish courses with generous fairways negated by its length, the deep rough and a good supply of bunkers. The newer course runs through the pine forests, with many dog-leg holes. Since this is claret country each hole is sponsored by a local château, whose products will soothe you after your round.

Golfclub de Mont-de-Marsan (1978)   54

Phone: 58 756305

40090 Saint-Avit

North east of Mont-de-Marsan, off the D932

Holes	9 Par 34 2503m.
Visitors	Welcome
Fees	FFr120–150
Facilities	Bar and restaurant; driving range
Pro	M Beaufranc

Golf de la Nivelle (1907)   55

Phone: 59 471899

Place William Sharp, 64500 Ciboure

Just to the south of St Jean de Luz

Holes	18 Par 70 5587m.
Visitors	Welcome. Course closed Thursday
Fees	FFr220–320
Facilities	Bar and restaurant; driving range; tennis
Pro	Jean Palli

Golf de Pau (1856)   56

Phone: 59 320233

Rue du Golf, 64140 Pau Billère

On the south west side of Pau

Holes	18 Par 69 5389m.
Visitors	Welcome
Fees	FFr200–250
Facilities	Bar and restaurant closed Monday; driving range
Pro	Armand Harismendy

The oldest course on the European continent, the Pau club was founded by British officers at the instigation of the Duke of Hamilton and has remained under the influence of the British throughout its history. It is said that, up to 1935, the membership was composed only of the British. The course, below the town by the river, is fairly flat but is protected by its many trees and punishing rough. It is a charming course and the clubhouse has some wonderful paintings and trophies.

Golf Public de Périgueux (1981)   57

Phone: 53 530235

Domaine de Saltgourde, 24430 Marsac

Just west of Périgueux, off the D710

Holes	18 Par 72 5860m.
Visitors	Welcome (public course)
Fees	FFr180
Facilities	Bar and restaurant closed Tuesday; driving range
Pro	Eric Smith

Golf de Pessac (1989) **58**

Phone: 56 362447

Rue de la Princesse, 33600 Pessac
On the south west side of Bordeaux close to exit
13 of the ringroad (N250 to Arcachon)

Holes	3 loops of 9 Par 36 (all) 3023/3100/ 3142m.
Visitors	Welcome
Fees	FFr220–270
Facilities	Bar and restaurant; driving range
Pro	Christian Chatrier

Built on the edge of the Landes forest, the
courses are lined with pine trees and water is a
perpetual threat to the golfer. If water doesn't
get your ball one of the eccentrically shaped
bunkers, splashed across the fairways with wit
and cunning, will. It's a lovely landscape and a
fine test of golf.

Golf Club de Rochebois (1989) **59**

Phone: 53 281801

Rte de Montfort, Vitrac, 24200 Sarlat
South of Sarlat, off the D703 near Vitrac

Holes	9 Par 36 2992m.
Visitors	Welcome. Course closed Tuesday in winter
Fees	FFr180–220
Facilities	Bar and restaurant; driving range; swimming pool
Pro	Crawford Campbell

Golf de Salies-de-Béarn (1987) **60**

Phone: 59 383759

Rte d'Orthez, 64270 Salies-de-Béarn
Just north east of Salies, off the D933

Holes	9 Par 31 2060m.
Visitors	Welcome
Fees	FFr100–120
Facilities	Bar and restaurant; driving range; swimming pool; tennis
Pro	M Castaigne

Scottish Golf d'Aubertin (1987) **61**

Phone: 59 827373

64290 Aubertin
South west of Pau near Aubertin

Holes	18 Par 66 4700m.
Visitors	Welcome
Fees	FFr100–120
Facilities	Bar and restaurant; driving range; swimming pool; tennis

Golf de Seignosse (1989) **62**

Phone: 58 431732

Carrefour Boncau, 40510 Seignosse
North east of Hossegor at Seignosse

Holes	18 Par 72 6124m.
Visitors	Welcome
Fees	FFr200–300
Facilities	Bar and restaurant closed Wednesday; driving range
Pro	Michel Tapia

The Seignosse course has rapidly gained a
reputation as one of the most beautiful in
France; designed by Robert Von Hagge, it is
very much the flagship of Golf Espace. The
fairways swoop and plunge through the wooded
terrain of splendid oaks and straight pines. From
the elevated tees there are wonderful views of
the rolling fairways, some designed as dog-legs
and many with water hazards. It is great
entertainment and is a course that Jose Maria
Olazabal plays for fun.

Midi-Pyrénées

Golf d'Albi (Lasbordes) (1989) **63**

Phone: 63 549807

Château de Lasbordes, 81000 Albi
Just west of Albi at Lasbourdes

Holes	18 Par 72 6255m.
Visitors	Welcome. Course closed Tuesday
Fees	FFr150–200
Facilities	Bar and restaurant; driving range
Pro	Francis Mayes

Golf Club de l'Ariège (1985) **64**

Phone: 61 645678

Unjat, 09240 la Bastide-de-Sérou
Just east of la Bastide de Sérou, on the D211 at
Unjat

Holes	18 Par 71 5949m.
Visitors	Welcome
Fees	FFr120–200
Facilities	Bar and restaurant; driving range; 6 short holes; tennis

Golf de la Barouge (1955)   65

Phone: 63 610672
Pont de l'Arm, 81660 Mazamet
Just north of Mazamet, off the D112

Holes	18 Par 70 5628m.
Visitors	Welcome
Fees	FFr180–220
Facilities	Bar and restaurant closed Tuesday; driving range
Pro	Didier Charria

The original nine holes were laid down by Mackenzie Ross and the second nine were added by Fred Hawtree. It is a charming, archetypal parkland course by the Thore river.

Golf de la Bigorre (1992)   66

Phone: 62 910620
Pouzac, 65200 Bagneres de Bigorre
Close to Bagneres, off the D26

Holes	18 Par 72 5909m.
Visitors	Welcome
Fees	FFr150–200
Facilities	Practice ground
Pro	Jean Paul Hontas

Golf d'Embats (1990)   67

Phone: 62 052080
Rte de Montesquieu, 32000 Auch
West of Auch, off the D943

Holes	18 Par 65 4815m.
Visitors	Welcome
Fees	FFr130–150
Facilities	Restaurant; driving range
Pro	Jean Paul Douvier

Golfclub d'Espalais (1986)   68

Phone: 63 290456
82400 Valence d'Agen
Just south of Valence d'Agen, off the D12

Holes	9 Par 35 2570m.
Visitors	Welcome
Fees	FFr150
Facilities	Bar and restaurant; driving range; swimming pool; tennis

Golf des Etangs de Fiac (1987)   69

Phone: 63 706470
81500 Lavaur
East of Lavaur, off the D112 near Viterbel

Holes	18 Par 71 5725m.
Visitors	Welcome
Fees	FFr190–260
Facilities	Bar and restaurant closed Tuesday; driving range; swimming
Pro	J Lynch

Golf de Fleurance (1989)   70

Phone: 62 062626
Lassale, 32500 Fleurance
South of Fleurance off the N21

Holes	9 Par 36 2908m.
Visitors	Welcome
Fees	FFr100–140
Facilities	Bar and restaurant; driving range; squash
Pro	Gerard Camlong

Golf de Gascogne (1989)   71

Phone: 62 660310
32140 Masseube
Just south of Masseube off the D929

Holes	9 Par 36 3027m.
Visitors	Welcome
Fees	FFr100–120
Facilities	Bar and restaurant; driving range; short course

Golf de Guinlet (1991)   72

Phone: 62 098084
32800 Eauze
North east of Eauze, off the D29

Holes	18 Par 71 5535m.
Visitors	Welcome
Fees	FFr150–200
Facilities	Bar and restaurant; driving range; swimming pool; tennis
Pro	Jean Marc Douvier

Golf du Lac de Lourdes (1988)   73

Phone: 62 420206
Le Lac, 65100 Lourdes
Just west of Lourdes by the lake

Holes	18 Par 72 5700m.
Visitors	Welcome
Fees	FFr160–200
Facilities	Bar and restaurant; driving range
Pro	Frederic Martin

Golf Municipal de Laloubère (1983)   **74**

Phone: 62 961114

Hippodrome de Laloubère

South of Tarbes, off the D935 (the course is in the middle of the race track)

Holes	9 Par 36 3135m.
Visitors	Welcome. Course closed on racing days
Fees	Ffr100–200
Facilities	Bar and restaurant

Golf de Lannemezan (1962)   **75**

Phone: 62 980101

La Demi Lune, 65300 Lannemezan

Just south of Lannemezan, off the D929

Holes	18 Par 71 5920m.
Visitors	Welcome
Fees	FFr150–200
Facilities	Bar and restaurant closed Wednesday; driving range
Pro	Robert Lasserre

Golf de Luchon (1908)   **76**

Phone: 61 790327

Rte de Montauban, 31110 Luchon

Just east of Luchon

Holes	9 Par 33 2400m.
Visitors	Welcome
Fees	FFr130–160
Facilities	Bar and restaurant; driving range
Pro	Roger Picabea

Golf les Martines (1986)   **77**

Phone: 62 072712

Rte de Ste Livrade, 32600 L'Isle Jourdain

West of Toulouse. Off the N124 north of L'Isle Jourdain

Holes	9 Par 35 2835m.
Visitors	Welcome
Fees	FFr100–160
Facilities	Bar and restaurant; driving range; swimming pool; tennis
Pro	Olivier Allard

Golf de Mezeyrac (1988)   **78**

Phone: 65 444141

Soulages-Bonneval, 12210 Laguiole

West of Laguiole off the D541 at Mezeyrac

Holes	9 Par 34 2630m.
Visitors	Welcome. Course closed December to March
Fees	FFr100–150
Facilities	Bar and restaurant; driving range; tennis
Pro	Pascal Vincent

Golfclub de la Montagne Noire (1990)   **79**

Phone: 63 503533

Les Montagnols, St-Affrique-les-Montagnes, 81290 Labruguière

South of Castres at St Affrique

Holes	18 Par 72 6375m.
Visitors	Welcome
Fees	FFr100–200
Facilities	Bar and restaurant; driving range; short course; swimming pool; tennis

Country Golf Club de Montauban (1990)   **80**

Phone: 63 313540

Les Aiguillons, D959, 82000 Montauban

Between Montauban and Molières, off the D959

Holes	9 Par 36 2900m.
Visitors	Welcome
Fees	FFr200–300
Facilities	Bar and restaurant; driving range

Golf des Roucous (Sauveterre) (1987)   **81**

Phone: 63 958370

82110 Sauveterre

Nearly 40 km north of Montauban, off the D19 near Sauveterre

Holes	9 Par 35 2622m.
Visitors	Welcome
Fees	FFr150
Facilities	Bar and restaurant; driving range; swimming pool; tennis
Pro	Gerard Camlong

Golf Saint Gabriel (1989)   **82**

Phone: 61 841665

Lieu dit Castie, 31850 Montrabé

Just east of Toulouse off the D112 near Montrabé

Holes	12 Par 46 3458m.
Visitors	Welcome
Fees	FFr100–150
Facilities	Bar and restaurant; driving range; swimming pool
Pro	Jean Marc Sauvage

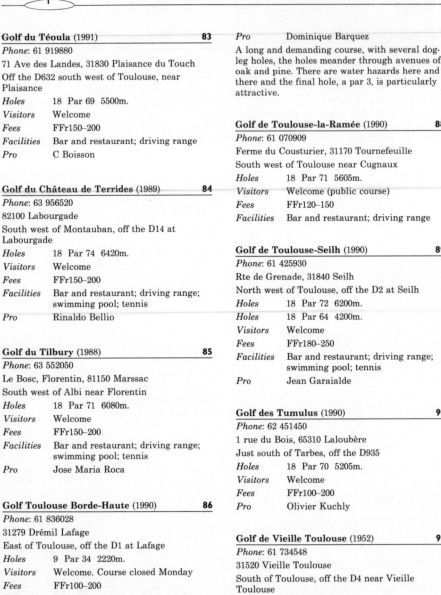

Golf du Téoula (1991)   83

Phone: 61 919880
71 Ave des Landes, 31830 Plaisance du Touch
Off the D632 south west of Toulouse, near Plaisance

Holes	18 Par 69 5500m.
Visitors	Welcome
Fees	FFr150–200
Facilities	Bar and restaurant; driving range
Pro	C Boisson

Golf du Château de Terrides (1989)   84

Phone: 63 956520
82100 Labourgade
South west of Montauban, off the D14 at Labourgade

Holes	18 Par 74 6420m.
Visitors	Welcome
Fees	FFr150–200
Facilities	Bar and restaurant; driving range; swimming pool; tennis
Pro	Rinaldo Bellio

Golf du Tilbury (1988)   85

Phone: 63 552050
Le Bosc, Florentin, 81150 Marssac
South west of Albi near Florentin

Holes	18 Par 71 6080m.
Visitors	Welcome
Fees	FFr150–200
Facilities	Bar and restaurant; driving range; swimming pool; tennis
Pro	Jose Maria Roca

Golf Toulouse Borde-Haute (1990)   86

Phone: 61 836028
31279 Drémil Lafage
East of Toulouse, off the D1 at Lafage

Holes	9 Par 34 2220m.
Visitors	Welcome. Course closed Monday
Fees	FFr100–200
Facilities	Bar and restaurant; driving range; swimming pool
Pro	Thierry Grenier

Golf de Toulouse Palmola (1974)   87

Phone: 61 842450
31680 Buzet sur Tarn
North east of Toulouse, off the N88 at Buzet

Holes	18 Par 72 6200m.
Visitors	Welcome. Course closed Tuesday
Fees	FFr200–350
Facilities	Bar and restaurant; driving range; swimming pool; tennis

Pro	Dominique Barquez

A long and demanding course, with several dog-leg holes, the holes meander through avenues of oak and pine. There are water hazards here and there and the final hole, a par 3, is particularly attractive.

Golf de Toulouse-la-Ramée (1990)   88

Phone: 61 070909
Ferme du Cousturier, 31170 Tournefeuille
South west of Toulouse near Cugnaux

Holes	18 Par 71 5605m.
Visitors	Welcome (public course)
Fees	FFr120–150
Facilities	Bar and restaurant; driving range

Golf de Toulouse-Seilh (1990)   89

Phone: 61 425930
Rte de Grenade, 31840 Seilh
North west of Toulouse, off the D2 at Seilh

Holes	18 Par 72 6200m.
Holes	18 Par 64 4200m.
Visitors	Welcome
Fees	FFr180–250
Facilities	Bar and restaurant; driving range; swimming pool; tennis
Pro	Jean Garaialde

Golf des Tumulus (1990)   90

Phone: 62 451450
1 rue du Bois, 65310 Laloubère
Just south of Tarbes, off the D935

Holes	18 Par 70 5205m.
Visitors	Welcome
Fees	FFr100–200
Pro	Olivier Kuchly

Golf de Vieille Toulouse (1952)   91

Phone: 61 734548
31520 Vieille Toulouse
South of Toulouse, off the D4 near Vieille Toulouse

Holes	18 Par 71 5444m.
Visitors	Welcome. Course closed Tuesday
Fees	FFr200–250
Facilities	Bar and restaurant; driving range
Pro	Richard Olalainty

SOUTH-EAST FRANCE

Rhone-Alpes

Golfclub d'Aix-les-Bains (1913)   I

Phone: 79 612335

Ave du Golf, 73100 Aix-les-Bains

On the south side of Aix-les-Bains

Holes	18 Par 71 5597m.
Visitors	Welcome
Fees	FFr190–280
Facilities	Bar and restaurant; driving range
Pro	J Lambie

Aix is one of the oldest courses in France, in the celebrated spa town which was de rigueur for the smart set in the early years of the century. This is a delightful holiday course which, despite its relative shortness, poses some problems; notably at the long 2nd hole, uphill to a tiny green, and at two tough short holes (6th and 9th).

Golf Club d'Albon (1990)   2

Phone: 75 030390

Château de Senaud, 26140 St Rambert d'Albon

South of St Rambert d'Albon, near St Vallier

Holes	18 Par 72 6108m.
Visitors	Welcome
Fees	FFr180–250
Facilities	Bar and restaurant; driving range; short course; swimming pool; tennis
Pro	Gilles Crochat

In the heart of the Rhône wine country the club offers an array of facilities in addition to golf; even the children have their own play chalet. The great château looms over the course, whose fairways dip and roll through the woods, with the numerous streams and ponds threatening your every shot.

Golf des Arcs (1982)   3

Phone: 79 074395

73700 Bourg St Maurice

Southwest of Les Arcs in Arc 1800

Holes	18 Par 67 4854m.
Visitors	Welcome. Course closed from end-September to end-June
Fees	FFr150–200
Facilities	Bar and restaurant; driving range; swimming pool; tennis
Pro	Andre Leclercq

Golf Club du Beaujolais (1991)   4

Phone: 74 670444

Domaine de Chiel, 69480 Lucenay

North west of Lyon, near Anse

Holes	9 Par 36 2935m.
Visitors	Welcome
Fees	FFr110–170
Facilities	Bar and restaurant; driving range
Pro	Claude Soules

Golf de Bossey (1983)   5

Phone: 50 437525

Châteay de Crévin, 74160 St Julien-en-Genevois

East of St Julien, at Bossey

Holes	18 Par 71 6022m.
Visitors	Welcome, but must book. Course closed December to mid-March
Fees	FFr300
Facilities	Bar and restaurant; driving range; swimming pool; tennis and squash
Pro	Daniel Danevin

This hilly course is a real challenge for any golfer, with a premium put on accuracy and sensible tactics. It was designed by Robert Trent Jones and the problems of the steeply sloping terrain are compounded by his familiar mélange of water hazards, huge bunkers and tricky greens. The course sits in the lee of Mont Saleve and the scenery is wonderful.

Golf de Bouvent (1990)   6

Phone: 74 228206

Parc des Loisirs de Bouvent, 01100 Bourg-en-Bresse

On the east side of Bourg-en-Bresse; head for Parc de Bouvent

Holes	9 Par 36 3150m.
Visitors	Welcome
Fees	FFr50–100
Facilities	Bar and restaurant

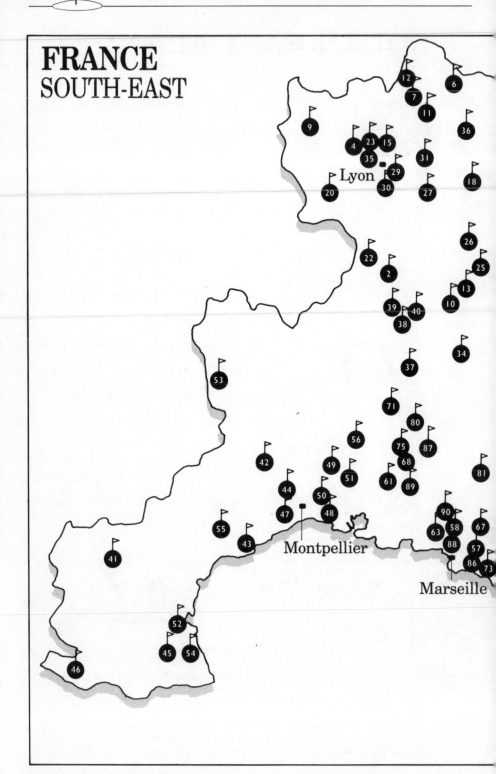

FRANCE
SOUTH-EAST

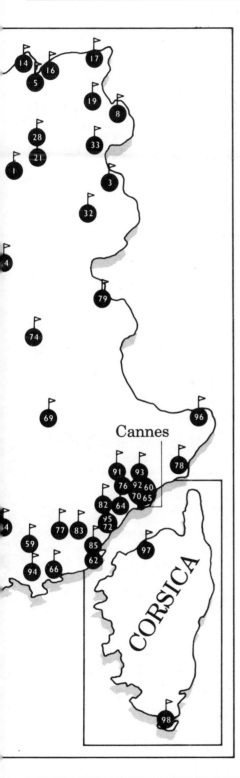

Cannes

CORSICA

Golf de la Bresse (1990)   7

Phone: 74 514209

Domaine de Mary, 01400 Condessiat

South west of Bourg-en-Bresse at Condessiat

Holes	18 Par 72 6217m.
Visitors	Welcome
Fees	FFr250
Facilities	Bar and restaurant; driving range

Club de Chamonix (1982)   8

Phone: 50 530628

74400 Les Praz de Chamonix

Just north of Chamonix, off the N506

Holes	18 Par 72 6087m.
Visitors	Welcome. Course closed November to April
Fees	FFr200–250
Facilities	Bar and restaurant; driving range
Pro	J C Bonnaz

The celebrated winter sports resort of Chamonix has a golf course which is something of an oddity – not surprisingly since it was designed by Robert Trent Jones. Under the towering heights of Mont Blanc, it is rather flat and might have been flown in from Florida. It shows Jones's inevitable penchant for small plateau greens of bizarre shape, protected by huge bunkers and streams. Never mind, the views are magnificent.

Golf de Champlong-Villeret (1985)   9

Phone: 77 697060

Domaine de Champlong, 42300 Roanne

South west of Roanne, off the D53 at Champlong

Holes	9 Par 31 2000m.
Visitors	Welcome. Course closed Tuesday in winter
Fees	FFr130–160
Facilities	Driving range; tennis
Pro	Bruno Letanter

Golf La Chapelle en Vercors (1985)   10

Phone: 75 481162

Quartier Les Baumes, 26420 La Chapelle en Vercors

Just south of La Chapelle

Holes	9 Par 32 2300m.
Visitors	Welcome. Course closed November to April
Fees	FFr75–100
Facilities	Bar and restaurant; tennis

Golf du Clou (1985)   11

Phone: 74 981965

01330 Villars-les-Dombes

Just south of Villars-les-Dombes, off the N83

Holes	18 Par 67 5000m.
Visitors	Welcome
Fees	FFr140–180
Facilities	Bar and restaurant; driving range; short course
Pro	J P Selliez

If you have strong nerves and great accuracy with your irons, you should visit Golf du Clou, whose course is built around a large lake. There are numerous carries over water and several of the greens are mischievously built on the lake itself; most notably the 16th (185 metres) and the 17th (191 metres).

Golf de la Commanderie (1964)   12

Phone: 85 304412

01290 Lamusse Crottet

East of Maçon, off the N79

Holes	18 Par 70 5600m.
Visitors	Welcome. Course closed Tuesday
Fees	FFr150–200
Facilities	Bar and restaurant; driving range
Pro	Philip Wakeford

Golf de Corrençon-en-Vercors (1988)   13

Phone: 76 958042

38250 Villars-de-Lans

South of Villars-de-Lans at Correncon

Holes	18 Par 72 5520m.
Visitors	Welcome
Fees	FFr180–250
Facilities	Bar and restaurant; driving range; short course
Pro	Hubert Courtessi

Golf de Divonne (1931)   14

Phone: 50 403411

01220 Divonne-les-Bains

Just west of Divonne, off the D984c

Holes	18 Par 72 6035m.
Visitors	Welcome
Fees	FFr250–500
Facilities	Bar and restaurant closed Tuesday; driving range; tennis
Pro	Michel Alsuguren

The course was re-designed by Donald Harradine in 1963 and more changes were made ten years later. The situation, in the foothills of the Juras, is a delight. The golfer has views over Lake Geneva and to Mont Blanc and the Alps. It is an excellent and testing course.

Golf Club de la Dombes (1986)   15

Phone: 78 918484

01390 Mionnay

North of Lyon, off the N83 near Mionnay

Holes	18 Par 71 6030m.
Visitors	Welcome
Fees	FFr150–250
Facilities	Bar and restaurant closed Monday; driving range; swimming pool; tennis
Pro	Jacques Visseaux

Golf Club d'Esery (1988)   16

Phone: 50 365870

Chemin Verne, 74930 Esery

Holes	18 Par 72 6350m.
Visitors	Welcome during the week. Course closed Monday & December to March
Fees	FFr280
Facilities	Bar and restaurant; swimming pool
Pro	J Noailly

The centrepiece of the club is the 14th century manor house which is now the clubhouse and from the terrace you have a grand view of the Arve valley and the mountains. The course is fairly open but very challenging, partly due to the many water hazards presented by criss-cross streams and by ponds

Royal Golf Club Evian (1904/1990)   17

Phone: 50 268500

Rive sud du Lac Léman, 74500 Evian

Just to the south west of Evian

Holes	18 Par 72 6006m.
Visitors	Welcome. Course closed mid-December to February
Fees	FFr200–400
Facilities	Bar and restaurant; driving range; swimming pools; tennis; archery
Pro	Jean Marc Bochaton

Occasionally a golf course is set in such beautiful surroundings that the degree of golfing challenge becomes almost secondary; Killarney in Ireland and Banff Springs in Canada are two prime examples. The Royal Club Evian provides another – not that the challenge at any of the three is less than considerable! Situated close to Mont Blanc on the French shores of Lake Geneva, Evian has an almost fairytale ambience and quality abounds in this unique spa resort. The golf course has recently been reshaped by American architect Cabell Robinson and now, aside from the views, large, dazzling bunkers are the most dominant feature. Extensive practice facilities are available and there are priority tee times for guests at the famous hotel, which was refurbished a few years ago.

Golf de Faverges-de-la-Tour (1987) 18
Phone: 74 974252
38110 Faverges-de-la-Tour
North east of La Tour-du-Pin, off the N516 at Faverges
Holes	9 Par 34 2612m.
Visitors	Welcome
Fees	FFr120–150
Facilities	Bar and restaurant; driving range; swimming pool; tennis
Pro	Didier Bissieres

Golf de Flaine-les-Carroz (1990) 19
Phone: 50 908544
74300 Flaine
South east of Cluses, near Flaine off the D106
Holes	18 Par 65 3690m.
Visitors	Welcome. Course closed November to May
Fees	FFr180
Facilities	Bar and restaurant; driving range; swimming pool; tennis
Pro	Patrick Lacroix

Golf du Forez (1986) 20
Phone: 77 308685
Domaine de Presles, Craintilleux, 42210 Montrond-les-Bains
South west of Montrond-les-Bains, near Sury
Holes	18 Par 70 5672m.
Visitors	Welcome
Fees	FFr150–200
Facilities	Bar; driving range
Pro	Jean Arbide

Golf de Giez (1991) 21
Phone: 50 444841
74210 Giez
West of Faverges at Giez
Holes	18 Par 70 5950m.
	9 Par 33 2450m.
Visitors	Welcome
Fees	FFr300
Facilities	Bar and restaurant; driving range

Golf de Gourdan (1988) 22
Phone: 75 670384
07430 Saint Clair
North of Annonay, off the N82
Holes	18 Par 71 6000m.
Visitors	Welcome
Fees	FFr120–230
Facilities	Bar and restaurant closed Wednesday; driving range
Pro	Patrick Blanc

Golf du Gouverneur (1991) 23
Phone: 72 264034
Château du Breuil, 01390 Monthieux
North of Lyon off the A6
Holes	18 Par 72 6477m.
	18 Par 72 5959m.
Visitors	Welcome
Fees	FFr200–250
Facilities	Bar and restaurant; practice ground

Golf Club de Grenoble 'Les Alberges' (1921) 24
Phone: 76 890347
Vaulnaveys Le Haut, 38410 Uriage
South east of Grenoble, off the D524 at Uriage
Holes	9 Par 33 2005m.
Visitors	Welcome
Fees	FFr140–180
Facilities	Bar and restaurant; driving range
Pro	Patrick Beauregard

Golf Club de Grenoble 'Bresson' (1989) 25
Phone: 76 736500
Rte de Montavie, 38320 Eybens
South of Grenoble, off the D5 at Bresson
Holes	18 Par 72 6343m.
Visitors	Welcome
Fees	FFr230–330
Facilities	Bar and restaurant; driving range
Pro	Alain Paligot

These two courses are part of the same club. The original nine hole course was later augmented with a design by Robert Trent Jones Jnr. The course sweeps and bobs through woodland and is scattered with water hazards and the eccentric bunker shapes which are the Jones trademark.

Golf Club de Grenoble 'St Quentin' (1988)   26
Phone: 76 936728
St Quentin-en-Isère, 38210 Tullins
North west of Grenoble, off the N532 near St
Quentin

Holes	18 Par 73 6260m.
Visitors	Welcome
Fees	FFr200–300
Facilities	Bar and restaurant

Golf de l'Isle d'Abeau (1987)   27
Phone: 74 432884
Le Rival, 38300 Bourgoin-Jallieu
North west of Bourgoin-Jallieu, off the N6 at
L'Isle d'Ablay

Holes	9 Par 35 3050m.
Visitors	Welcome. Course closed Tuesday
Fees	FFr100–150
Facilities	Driving range
Pro	D Duffeur

Golf du Lac d'Annecy (1953)   28
Phone: 50 601289
Echarvines, 74290 Talloires
South east of Annecy, off the D909

Holes	18 Par 69 5016m.
Visitors	Welcome. Course closed Tuesday, and from December to March
Fees	FFr185–250
Facilities	Bar and restaurant; driving range
Pro	John Wilson

The course is relatively short but is laid out over
the hilly terrain of the Roc de Chère plateau and
has some difficult approaches to tight greens. It
is worth a visit for the views alone, wonderful
vistas of mountains and lakes, in particular the
beautiful Lac d'Annecy.

Golf de Lyon-Chassieu (1989)   29
Phone: 78 309477
Route de Lyon, 69680 Chassieu
East of Lyon at Chassieu

Holes	18 Par 70 5941m.
Visitors	Welcome
Fees	FFr160–220
Facilities	Bar and restaurant; driving range
Pro	D Gauchon

Golf de Lyon-Verger (1977)   30
Phone: 78 028420
69360 St Symphorien d'Ozon
South of Lyon, off the A7 at Solaize

Holes	18 Par 70 5577m.
Visitors	Welcome
Fees	FFr170–250
Facilities	Bar and restaurant closed Friday; driving range
Pro	Hubert Sauzet

Golf de Lyon-Villete d'Anthon (1965)   31
Phone: 78 311133
38230 Villette d'Anthon
East of Lyon at Villette d'Anthon

Holes	18 Par 72 6727m.
	18 Par 72 6185m.
Visitors	Welcome. Courses closed Tuesday
Fees	FFr200–300
Facilities	Bar and restaurant; practice ground

Golf de Méribel (1990)   32
Phone: 79 005267
73550 Méribel-Altiport
Just to the north of Méribel

Holes	18 Par 70 5319m.
Visitors	Welcome. Course closed November to May
Fees	FFr200–250
Facilities	Driving range; swimming pool; tennis
Pro	Didier Aubin

Golf du Mont d'Arbois (1922/1964)   33
Phone: 50 212979
Le Mont d'Arbois, 74120 Megève
On the east side of Megève

Holes	18 Par 72 6130m.
Visitors	Welcome. Course closed December to May
Fees	FFr200–300
Facilities	Bar and restaurant; driving range; tennis
Pro	Guido Parodi

This is a real curiosity, way up near the top of
the Mont d'Arbois, with its clubhouse part of a
ski-lift station. The fairways become ski runs in
winter and it is just as popular with golfers in
August. The club was founded by a Rothschild
and designed by Henry Cotton.

Golf du Pilhon (1987)   **34**

Phone: 75 214675

Val Maravel, 26310 Luc en Diois

Southeast of Luc en Diois, off the D150 at Val Maravel

Holes	9 Par 32 2200m.
Visitors	Welcome (public course)
Fees	FFr40–60
Facilities	Bar; driving range; pitch & putt course

Golf de Salvagny (1988)   **35**

Phone: 78 488360

100 Rue des Granges, 69890 La Tour de Salvagny

West of Lyon off the N7 at La Tour

Holes	18 Par 72 6185m.
Visitors	Welcome
Fees	FFr200–270
Facilities	Bar and restaurant; driving range; short course
Pro	Michel Oltz

Golf Club de la Sorelle (1990)   **36**

Phone: 74 354727

Domaine de Gravagueux, 01320 Villete-sur-Ain

West of Amberieu en Bugey, off the A42

Holes	18 Par 72 6100m.
Visitors	Welcome
Fees	FFr140
Facilities	Bar and restaurant closed Monday; practice ground
Pro	Thierry Merle

Golf de la Valdaine (1989)   **37**

Phone: 75 018666

Château le Monard, 26740 Montboucher/Jabron

East of Montélimar at Montboucher

Holes	18 Par 71 5625m.
Visitors	Welcome
Fees	FFr170–260
Facilities	Bar and restaurant; driving range

Golf de Valence le Bourget (1988)   **38**

Phone: 75 594171

26120 Montmeyran-Chabeuil

South east of Valence, off the D538a near Montmeyran

Holes	12 Par 43 3035m.
Visitors	Welcome. Course closed Tuesday
Fees	FFr80–110
Facilities	Bar and restaurant; driving range

Golf de Valence-Chânalets (1989)   **39**

Phone: 75 831623

26500 Buorg-lès-Valence

Just north of Valence, off the D67 to Chateauneuf

Holes	9 Par 35 2771m.
Visitors	Welcome
Fees	FFr100–120
Facilities	Bar and restaurant; driving range
Pro	Raphael Leroux

Golf de Valence-St Didier (1984)   **40**

Phone: 75 596701

St Didier de Charpey, 26300 Bourg de Péage

East of Valence, off the D119 at St Didier

Holes	18 Par 71 5807m.
Visitors	Welcome
Fees	FFr170–230
Facilities	Bar and restaurant; driving range
Pro	Philippe Rousseau

Languedoc-Roussillon

Golf d'Auriac (1988)   **41**

Phone: 68 725730

Rte de St Hilaire, 11000 Carcassone

Just south of Carcassone at Auriac

Holes	9 Par 36 3009m.
Visitors	Welcome
Fees	FFr160–200
Facilities	Bar and restaurant; driving range; swimming pool; tennis
Pro	Jean Pierre Basurco

Golf de Bombequiols (1987)   **42**

Phone: 67 737267

St André de Buèges, 34190 Ganges

South of Ganges, off the D108 at St André

Holes	9 Par 35 2765m.
Visitors	Welcome
Fees	FFr100–200
Facilities	Bar and restaurant; driving range

Golf du Cap d'Agde (1989)   43

Phone: 67 265440

Rue de Volvire de Brassac, 34300 Cap d'Agde

In Cap d'Agde; follow the signs

Holes	18 Par 72 6300m.
Visitors	Welcome
Fees	FFr225–275
Facilities	Bar and restaurant; driving range; short course
Pro	Xavier Bernard

By the sea at Cap d'Agde this course has plenty of links character with scrub and sand dunes awaiting an inaccurate shot, albeit the fairways are generous. The old fort looms over you as you tackle the intimidating par 5 2nd hole with its subtly sloping green. Both halves of the course finish severely, and the 18th green is defended by two deep bunkers.

Golf de Coulondres (1986)   44

Phone: 67 841375

34980 St Gely du Fesc

North east of Montpellier, off the D986 at St Gely

Holes	18 Par 72 6174375m.
Visitors	Welcome
Fees	FFr200–240
Facilities	Bar and restaurant; driving range; short course; swimming pool
Pro	Olivier Mono

Golf de Falgos (1992)   45

Phone: 68 395142

BP 9, 66260 Saint Laurent de Cerdans

South west of Perpignan, off the D3

Holes	18 Par 70 5671m.
Visitors	Welcome
Fees	FFr160–200
Facilities	Bar and restaurant; practice ground; swimming pool; horseriding

Golf de Font-Romeu (1987)   46

Phone: 68 301078

Ave Jean-Paul, 66120 Font-Romeu

In the centre of Font-Romeu

Holes	9 Par 34 2500m.
Visitors	Welcome
Fees	FFr130–160
Facilities	Bar and restaurant; driving range; tennis and squash
Pro	Jacques Bories

Golf Club de Fontcaude (1991)   47

Phone: 67 033430

BP 56 Domaine de Fontcaude, 34990 Juvignac

West of Montpellier at Juvignac

Holes	18 Par 72 6292m.
Visitors	Welcome
Fees	FFr190–260
Facilities	Bar and restaurant; practice ground; short course; swimming pool
Pro	Bruno Tancogne

Golf de la Grande Motte (1987)   48

Phone: 67 560500

34280 La Grande Motte

In La Grande Motte

Holes	18 Par 72 6161m.
Visitors	Welcome
Fees	FFr200–260
Facilities	Bar and restaurant; driving range; compact course and short course; tennis
Pro	P Porquier

Some twelve miles east of Montpellier, in the famous reclaimed marshlands of the Camargue, Robert Trent Jones has sculpted a classic, if typical, piece of FLorida and planted it in the south of France. The trees, the bunkering, the ubiquitous water hazards and, perhaps most importantly, the high quality conditioning bear all the hallmarks of golf in America's Sunshine State. Golf de la Grande Motte annually plays host to the European Tour Qualifying School; a course certain therefore to sort the men from the boys.

Golf des Hauts de Nimes (1989)   49

Phone: 66 233333

Rte de Sauve, Vacquerolles, 30900 Nimes

Just west of Nimes, off the D999

Holes	18 Par 72 6300m.
Visitors	Welcome
Fees	FFr160–200
Facilities	Bar and restaurant; driving range

Golf Club de Massane (1988) **50**

Phone: 67 872096

34670 Baillauges

East of Montpellier, off the N113 at Baillauges

Holes	18 Par 72 6375m.
Visitors	Welcome
Fees	FFr200–260
Facilities	Bar and restaurant; driving range; swimming pool; tennis
Pro	Nicolas Armand

Golf Club de Nimes Campagne (1968) **51**

Phone: 66 701737

Rte de St Gilles, 30000 Nimes

South of Nimes, off the D42

Holes	18 Par 72 6135m.
Visitors	Welcome. Course closed Tuesday
Fees	FFr200–220
Facilities	Bar and restaurant; driving range; swimming pool; tennis
Pro	Tito Lassalle

Close to the delightful town of Nimes, the clubhouse was formed from an elegant 19th century building which was formerly inhabited by a religious order. The course hosted the World Under 25 Championship in 1979 when Bernhard Langer won his first important tournament by the extraordinary margin of 17 strokes. Unless you can hit the ball like Langer it is far from a pushover, but a genuine test of a golfer's skills, not surprisingly since it was designed by Donald Harradine. There are some really severe holes including the par 3 16th; and the two long holes on the second nine, the 13th and the 18th, are especially challenging.

Golf de la Pinède (1986) **52**

Phone: 68 407040

8 rue Raoul-Calas, 11370 Leucate

In Leucate

Holes	9 Par 34 2340m.
Visitors	Welcome
Fees	FFr 100–200
Facilities	Bar and restaurant; driving range

Golf du Sabot (1991) **53**

Phone: 66 328400

48500 La Canourgue

South east of La Canourgue, off the D998

Holes	9 Par 33 2325m.
Visitors	Welcome. Course closed January
Fees	FFr150
Facilities	Bar and restaurant; driving range; swimming pool; tennis

Golf de St Cyprien (1976) **54**

Phone: 68 210171

66750 St Cyprien-Plage

Just north of St Cyprien-Plage

Holes	18 Par 73 6480m.
	9 Par 35 2724m.
Visitors	Welcome
Fees	FFr200–500
Facilities	Bar and restaurant; driving range; swimming pool; tennis
Pro	Patrick Lacroix

St Cyprien was developed as a golf resort, with an hotel and plenty of apartments. Graham Marsh lent his name to the design of the course, which is built on reclaimed marshland (no pun intended). Naturally there are many water hazards and the prevalence of brisk winds, added to the links character of one of the loops, makes it similar to some British seaside courses. The views of the Pyrenees and of the sea add to its appeal.

Golf de St Thomas Béziers (1986) **55**

Phone: 57 986201

Rte de Pézénas, 34290 Servian

North east of Béziers, off the N113

Holes	9 Par 36 2950m.
Visitors	Welcome
Fees	FFr50–100
Facilities	Bar and restaurant; driving range

Golf d'Uzès (1991) **56**

Phone: 66 224003

Pont des Charrettes, Mas de la Place, 30700 Uzès

Just south of Uzès

Holes	9 Par 36 2953m.
Visitors	Welcome
Fees	FFr120
Facilities	Bar and restaurant; driving range; swimming pool
Pro	Kristen Nygard

Provence – Alpes – Côte d'Azur

Golf International d'Allauch (1988) **57**

Phone: 91 050039

Domaine de Fontvieille, Rte des 4-Saisons, 13190 Allauch

East of Marseille, off the D2 near Les Camoins

Holes	18 Par 72 5800m.
Visitors	Welcome
Fees	FFr100–200
Facilities	Bar and restaurant; driving range; swimming pool; tennis; horseriding

Golf Club Aix-Marseille (1935)   58

Phone: 42 242041

Domaine de Riquetti, 13290 Les Milles
South of Aix, off the D9 near Les Milles

Holes	18 Par 72 6291m.
Visitors	Welcome. Course closed Thursday
Fees	FFr220–400
Facilities	Bar and restaurant; driving range
Pro	Roger Cotton

Golf Club Barbaroux (1989)   59

Phone: 94 590743

Rte de Cabasse, 83170 Brignoles
Just east of Brignoles, off the D79

Holes	18 Par 72 6124m.
Visitors	Must book
Fees	FFr300–400
Facilities	Bar and restaurant; driving range; tennis
Pro	Paul Delanzo

This course will appeal to the extrovert in any golfer; you can go for your shots and achieve minor miracles, but the punishments if you fail are severe. It was designed by Pete Dye, of Crooked Stick and Kiawah Island fame, and is an extraordinary mélange of styles. There are holes straight from Florida with masses of water; huge greens, alongside steep ravines; and some of the terrain has even been re-designed to look like a links. It is certainly dramatic and will repay a prolonged visit.

Golf de la Bastide du Roy (Biot) (1930)   60

Phone: 93 650848

06410 Biot
North west of Antibes in Biot

Holes	18 Par 70 5064m.
Visitors	Welcome
Fees	FFr200–240
Facilities	Bar and restaurant; driving range
Pro	Lucien Autiero

Golf des Baux de Provence (1989)   61

Phone: 90 543702

Domaine de Manville, 13520 Les Baux-en-Provence
In Les Baux

Holes	9 Par 36 2812m.
Visitors	Welcome
Fees	FFr150–200
Facilities	Bar and restaurant; driving range

Golf du Beauvallon (1990)   62

Phone: 94 961698

Bd des Collines, 83120 Ste Maxime
Between Ste Maxime and St Tropez at Beauvallon

Holes	9 Par 34 2504m.
Visitors	Welcome
Fees	FFr200–300
Facilities	Bar and restaurant; driving range
Pro	Hugues Siboulet

Golf de Cabriès-Calas (1989)   63

Phone: 42 225862

13480 Calas
South east of Aix, off the D9 near Calas

Holes	18 Par 72 5980m.
Visitors	Welcome
Fees	FFr130–150
Facilities	Bar and restaurant; driving range; short course
Pro	Laurent du Bouexic

Golf de Cannes Mandelieu (1891/1966)   64

Phone: 93 495539

Rte du Golf, 06210 Mandelieu
West of Cannes and close to La Napoule

Holes	18 Par 71 5676m.
Visitors	Welcome. Course closed Tuesday
Fees	FFr260–300
Facilities	Bar and restaurant; driving range; short course
Pro	Roger Damiano

Created originally by the Grand Duke Michael of Russia, who is said to have played a handy game off a handicap of 70, the course was re-designed by Harry Colt. The holes wind their way through avenues of umbrella pines over quite flat ground, which is cut in two by the Siagne river. This entails the use of a ferry from green to tee on two occasions. It is a difficult course where a Women's European Tour event was staged in 1991.

Cannes Mougins Country Club (1978)   65

Phone: 93 757913

175 Rte d'Antibes, 06250 Mougins
North of Cannes, off the D35

Holes	18 Par 72 6263m.
Visitors	Welcome
Fees	FFr300–350
Facilities	Bar and restaurant closed Monday; driving range
Pro	Michel Damiano

Set in wooded hills close to the picturesque hill village of Mougins and inland from Cannes, Cannes Mougins is now a regular venue on the PGA European Tour. Stretching to over 6200 metres (6849 yards) with a number of testing tee shots, it is a challenging par 72 from the back tees. The course has a severe start – a 410 metre par 4 running beside a stream and 201 metre par 3 to an elevated green – but an even tougher finish with the 389 metre 17th hole, played to a green directly behind a pond about 30 metres across. There is an attractive and well-equipped clubhouse – a converted olive mill – which offers a full range of catering except on Mondays.

Golf de Cavalière (1991) 66
Phone: 94 711007
Cavalière, 83980 Le Lavandou
East of Le Lavandou, on the coast at Cavalière
Holes   18 Par 69 5368m.
Visitors   Welcome
Fees   FFr200–300
Facilities Bar and restaurant; driving range; swimming pool; tennis

Golf de Château-l'Arc (1985) 67
Phone: 42 532838
Rousset-sur-Arc, 13790 Fuveau
South east of Aix at Les Michels (D57a)
Holes   18 Par 72 6300m.
Visitors   Welcome, but must book
Fees   FFr250–350
Facilities Bar and restaurant; driving range; swimming pool; tennis
Pro   Eric Follet

Golf Club de Châteaublanc (1988) 68
Phone: 90 333908
Les Plans, 84310 Morières-lès-Avignon
East of Avignon, off the N7 near the airport
Holes   18 Par 72 6161.
Visitors   Welcome
Fees   FFr170–220
Facilities Bar and restaurant closed Tuesday; driving range; short course
Pro   Eric Rossary

Golf de Digne (1990) 69
Phone: 92 323838
St Pierre-de-Gaubert, 04000 Digne
South of Digne, off the N85 and D12
Holes   18 Par 73 5910m.
Visitors   Welcome (public course)
Fees   FFr140–220
Facilities Bar and restaurant; driving range; swimming pool; tennis
Pro   Philippe Pee

Golf du Domaine de St Donat (1991) 70
Phone: 93 995760
La Paoute, 188 Rte de Cannes, 06130 Plan-de-Grasse
South east of Grasse, off the D209 near Mouans-Sartoux
Holes   18 Par 71 5950m.
Visitors   Welcome
Fees   FFr100–200
Facilities Bar and restaurant; driving range; swimming pool; tennis

Golf de la Drome Provencale (1990) 71
Phone: 75 985703
Clansayes, 26130 St Paul Trois Châteaux
South of Montelimar, off the A7 towards Grignan
Holes   9 Par 35 2435m.
Visitors   Welcome
Fees   FFr125
Facilities Bar and restaurant; practice ground

Golf de l'Estérel (1989) 72
Phone: 94 824748
Ave du Golf, 83700 Valescure
North of St Raphael, near Valescure
Holes   18 Par 71 5921m.
Visitors   Welcome
Fees   FFr250–300
Facilities Bar and restaurant; driving range; short course; swimming pool; tennis
Pro   G Alexandre

Within two years of its opening in 1989 the Robert Trent Jones course at Esterel was considered good enough to stage the 1991 Mediterranean Open, one of the most prestigious events on the PGA European Tour. Esterel has been described as the 'new jewel of the Riviera', a course carved out of a dramatic landscape deep in the heart of a glorious pine forest. Water hazards are prominent at Esterel, several of the greens are multi-tiered and all of them are quick. One professional described the greens as 'elephant's graveyards' and five have been dug up since then. At the short 15th, destined perhaps to become the most celebrated hole, the golfer must carry a vast water filled chasm and then land, oh so deftly, on a small heavily contoured putting surface. It is an exacting course and certainly not one for the faint-hearted.

Golf de Frégate (1992)   73
Phone: 42 085959
St Cyr-Bandol
Just north west of Bandol, off the D559
Holes   18 Par 72 6225m.
Visitors Welcome
Fees   FFr100–200
Facilities Bar and restaurant; driving range;
            short course

Golf Public de Gap Bayard (1989)   74
Phone: 92 501683
Centre d'Oxygénation, 05000 Gap
North of Gap, off the N85 at Col Bayard
Holes   18 Par 72 6041m.
Visitors Welcome. Course closed mid-
            November to mid-May
Fees   FFr150–200
Facilities Bar and restaurant; driving range;
            tennis
Pro   Olivier Rougeot
The views will soothe your mind on this
delightful holiday course; each hole seems to
show a different aspect of the Ecrin Chain or
Val de Durance. They happily call a game here a
'golf walk' and, as you stroll through the larches
and pines and enjoy the scenery, you will
probably agree.

Golf du Grand Avignon (1989)   75
Phone: 90 314994
Les Chênes Verts, 84270 Védène
North east of Avignon, off the D6 near Védène
Holes   18 Par 71 6027m.
Visitors Welcome
Fees   FFr200–250
Facilities Bar and restaurant; driving range;
            short course
Pro   Stephanie Lanfranchi

Golf de la Grande Bastide (1990)   76
Phone: 93 777008
Chemin des Pichelines, 06740 Châteauneuf de
Grasse
Just east of Grasse, off the D2085 near Opio
Holes   18 Par 72 6105m.
Visitors Welcome
Fees   FFr240–300
Facilities Bar and restaurant; driving range
Pro   Stephane Damiano
The course, opened in 1991, is set in an
attractive valley overlooked by two typical
Provençal hill villages. The designer, Cabel
Robinson, worked with Robert Trent Jones and
the course bears many of his mentor's hallmarks:
contoured fairways and greens, a plethora of
bunkers and plenty of water. The most

challenging hole is the 350 metre 15th where a
small lake to the left of the fairway places a
premium on an accurate tee shot, while more
water running along the right of the fairway
makes for a difficult second shot into the green.

Golf de Lou Roucas (1991)   77
Rte de Bagnols-en-Forêt (D47), 83920 La Motte
South east of Draguignan, off the D54 at La
Motte
Holes   18 Par 72 6300m.
Visitors Welcome
Fees   FFr100–200
Facilities Bar and restaurant; driving range

Golf de Monte Carlo (1911)   78
Phone: 93 410911
La Turbie, 06320 Cap d'Ail
North of Monte Carlo off the D22
Holes   18 Par 71 5667m.
Visitors Must book
Fees   FFr350–450
Facilities Bar and restaurant closed Monday
            in winter; driving range
Pro   F Ruffien-Meray
The Monte Carlo Golf Club, founded in 1911 and
with a fine clubhouse of the same era, is one of
the oldest on the Riviera. Built on a steep
hillside over 860 metres above sea level, it offers
some splendid views over the Mediterranean and
the surrounding mountains. The European Tour
professionals, who play a regular summer
tournament at Monte Carlo, produce some
spectacular scoring over this short course (Ian
Woosnam holds the course record with a 60) but
the average player will need to avoid wayward
shots especially from the tee. A hole to
remember is the short 14th where from the tee
you can see Monte Carlo several hundred metres
below. Gary Player called it one of the best
courses 'of its kind' in the world.

Golf de Montgenèvre (1986)   79
Phone: 92 219423
Rte d'Italie, 05100 Montgenèvre
North east of Briançon, off the N94 at
Montgenèvre
Holes   9 Par 37 3080m.
Visitors Welcome
Fees   FFr50–100
Facilities Bar and restaurant; driving range

Golf du Moulin (1992) 80

Phone: 90 343404

Rte de Camaret, 84100 Orange

North east of Orange, off the D975

Holes	9 Par 34 2200m.
Visitors	Welcome. Course closed Tuesday
Fees	FFr100–200
Facilities	Bar and restaurant; driving range
Pro	Frederic Monreal

Golf de Pierrevert (1992) 81

Phone: 92 721719

Domaine de la Grande-Gardette, 04860 Pierrevert

South west of Manosque at Pierrevert

Holes	18 Par 72 6000m.
Visitors	Welcome
Fees	FFr160–220
Facilities	Bar and restaurant; driving range
Pro	J P Ruffier-Meray

Riviera Golf Club (1991) 82

Phone: 97 976767

Ave des Amazones, 06230 Mandelieu-la-Napoule

West of Cannes at Mandelieu

Holes	18 Par 72 5736
Visitors	Welcome
Fees	FFr250–300
Facilities	Bar and restaurant; driving range
Pro	C Termat

Golf de Roquebrune sur Argens (1989) 83

Phone: 94 829291

Domaine des Planes, D7, 83520 Roquebrune sur Argens

West of Fréjus, off the D7 at Roquebrune

Holes	18 Par 71 6030m.
Visitors	Welcome
Fees	FFr220
Facilities	Bar and restaurant; driving range
Pro	Pascal Halek

In the rugged and beautiful setting of the foothills of the Maures, this is an interesting course which runs through the pines, oaks, oleanders and mimosas. It is quite hilly with some stiff climbs up to the elevated tees, from where you will be rewarded with spectacular views of the Alpes-Maritimes on one side and of the Gulf of St Tropez on the other.

Golf de la Ste Baume (1988) 84

Phone: 94 786012

83860 Nans-les-Pins

Just north of Nans-les-Pins, off the N560

Holes	18 Par 72 6167m.
Visitors	Welcome
Fees	FFr170–250
Facilities	Bar and restaurant; driving range; swimming pool; tennis
Pro	Bruno Lacroix

Golf de Sainte-Maxime (1991) 85

Phone: 94 492660

Rte du Débarquement, La Nartelle, 83120 Sainte-Maxime

North of Ste Maxime, off the D98 near La Nartelle

Holes	18 Par 71 6123m.
Visitors	Welcome
Fees	FFr230–260
Facilities	Bar and restaurant closed Tuesday in winter; driving range
Pro	Mark Wallace

This is a hilly and demanding course which will test both your legs and your repertoire of shots. A bonus is the breath-taking view across the Gulf of St Tropez. At least you can take advantage of the funicular railway which will carry you up to the 11th tee and the drop from the 17th tee to the green will give most people vertigo.

Golf de la Salette (1989) 86

Phone: 91 271216

Impasse des Vaudrans, 13011 La Valentine

East of Marseille, off the A50 at La Valentine

Holes	18 Par 72 5820m.
Visitors	Welcome. Course closed Tuesday
Fees	FFr230–350
Facilities	Bar and restaurant; driving range; swimming pool; tennis
Pro	Anthony Moerdik

Golf de Saumane (1989)   87

Phone: 90 202082

Domaine de Goult, 84800 Saumane
East of Avignon, off the D938 at Saumane

Holes	18 Par 72 6200m.
Visitors	Welcome
Fees	FFr100–200
Facilities	Bar and restaurant; driving range; short course

Golf de Septèmes (1991)   88

Phone: 91 962859

Domaine de Freyguières, Rte de la Télévision, 13240 Septèmes-les-Vallons
North of Marseille, off the N8 at Septèmes

Holes	9 Par 31 3100m.
Visitors	Welcome
Fees	FFr90–120
Facilities	Bar and restaurant; driving range; swimming pool; tennis
Pro	Jerome Gantois

Golf de Servanes (Mouriès) (1989)   89

Phone: 90 475995

Chemin du Mas-Neuf, 13890 Mouriès
West of Salon-de-Provence, off the D5 at Mouriès

Holes	18 Par 72 6100m.
Visitors	Welcome
Fees	FFr200–250
Facilities	Bar and restaurant; driving range
Pro	Alain Brioland

Set Golf International (1991)   90

Phone: 42 641182

Le Pey Blanc, Chemin de Granet, 13090 Aix en Provence
On the north west side of Aix, off the N7 at Célony

Holes	9 Par 36 2660m.
Visitors	Welcome
Fees	FFr150–200
Facilities	Bar and restaurant; driving range; swimming pool; tennis and squash
Pro	Patrick Cotton

Golf et Country Club de Taulane (1992)   91

Phone: 93 603130

Domaine du Château de Taulane, 83840 La Martre
North west of Grasse, off the N85

Holes	18 Par 72 6269m.
Visitors	Welcome. Course closed mid-November to March
Fees	FFr280–380
Facilities	Bar and restaurant; practice ground; swimming pool
Pro	Max Vitte

Golf du Val Martin (1988)   92

Phone: 93 420798

Domaine de Val Martin, 06560 Valbonne
12 km north of Cannes

Holes	9 Par 35 2370m.
Visitors	Welcome
Fees	FFr100–200

Golf de Valbonne (Opio) (1966)   93

Phone: 93 420008

06560 Valbonne
North of Cannes, off the D3 at Valbonne

Holes	18 Par 72 5892m.
Visitors	Welcome
Fees	FFr300–370
Facilities	Bar and restaurant; driving range; swimming pool; tennis
Pro	John Norsworthy

Close to the attractive mediaeval village of Valbonne, Golf Opio Valbonne lies in attractive wooded hills with some spectacular views to the lower Alps. The par of 72 is not too demanding although accurate driving is needed on a number of holes. The character of the two halves is quite distinct; the shortish first nine runs through hilly country but the longer second nine is much more open. The most demanding hole is the par 4 7th – a 419 metre dog-leg. The golf course is part of a complex which includes a three-star hotel and an attractive bar/restaurant.

Golf de Valcros (1964)   94

Phone: 94 668102

83250 La Londe-Les Maures
East of Hyères, off the N98 at La Londe

Holes	18 Par 70 5272m.
Visitors	Welcome
Fees	FFr180–250
Facilities	Bar and restaurant; driving range; swimming pool; tennis
Pro	Jean Pierre Charpenez

Golf de Valescure (1895)   **95**

Phone: 94 824046

Rue du Golf, 83700 Valescure/St Raphael

Just north of St Raphael, near Valescure

Holes	18 Par 68 5067m.
Visitors	Welcome, but must book
Fees	FFr240–280
Facilities	Bar and restaurant; driving range; swimming pool; tennis and squash; archery
Pro	Emile Cougourdan

Golf de Viévola (1978)   **96**

Phone: 93 046102

Domaine de Viévola, 06430 Tende

Off the N204, north of Tende

Holes	9 Par 32 2004m.
Visitors	Welcome. Course closed Thursday except July/August and from December to March
Fees	FFr160–220
Facilities	Bar and restaurant; driving range; tennis;
Pro	Nuccio Giordano

Corsica

Golf de Spano (1989)   **97**

Phone: 95 607552

Cocody Village, Commune de Lumio, 20260 Calvi

North east of Calvi, off the N197 at Lumio

Holes	9 Par 32 2120m.
Visitors	Welcome
Fees	FFr140–200
Facilities	Bar and restaurant; driving range; swimming pool; tennis

Golf de Spérone (1990)   **98**

Phone: 95 731713

Domaine de Spérone, 20169 Bonifacio

East of Bonifacio, on the coast at Pianterella

Holes	18 Par 72 6130m.
Visitors	Welcome, but must book
Fees	FFr330–400
Facilities	Bar and restaurant; driving range
Pro	Philippe Allain

On the southern tip of the island of Corsica, the course has a magnificent situation on the clifftops. Designed by Trent Jones it has already received great critical acclaim.

GERMANY

THE successes of Bernhard Langer, winner of the US Masters Championship in 1985 and many times a Ryder Cup player, have been one of the reasons for a great awakening of German interest in golf.

Thirty years ago golf was a socially exclusive game, played by rich Germans and by foreigners. In 1960 there were no more than about fifty courses, and the number increased during the following two decades to roughly 150 courses. But the number has increased at an extremely rapid rate during the last dozen years or so and there are now over 300 in Germany. The rate of growth shows little sign of diminishing since there are at least another sixty courses in various stages of development.

It should be mentioned that a high proportion (well over one third) of the German courses comprise nine holes.

The country does not seem to be a particularly popular destination for a golfing holiday and yet both Hamburg and Munich would offer excellent bases for such a holiday with many fine courses within reach, such as Feldafing and Falkenstein. There are many other great courses such as the Frankfurter and the magnificent Club Zur Vahr, which is considered to be one of the best championship courses in Europe.

The standards of course maintenance and of clubhouse facilities are very high in Germany, which may be some consolation to British tourists who, at the end of 1992, contemplated an exchange rate of less than 2.5 marks to the pound.

Unit of currency: Deutschmark
Rate of exchange (approx. at 1.1.93): DM2.50–£1
International dialling code: (010 49)

NORTHERN GERMANY

Aachener Golfclub (1927)

Phone: 0241 12501

Schurzelter Str 300, 5100 Aachen-Seffent

North west of Aachen off the A4. Head for Lautensburg and then towards Seffent

Holes   18 Par 72 6063m.

Visitors   Welcome, but must book from April to October

Fees   DM50–70

Facilities   Bar and restaurant; practice ground

Pro   Wim van Mook

The fairways run through lines of trees; if you are off line you will lose a shot but will usually find your ball. The main difficulty is provided by the greens, which are mostly elevated and well-protected by bunkers.

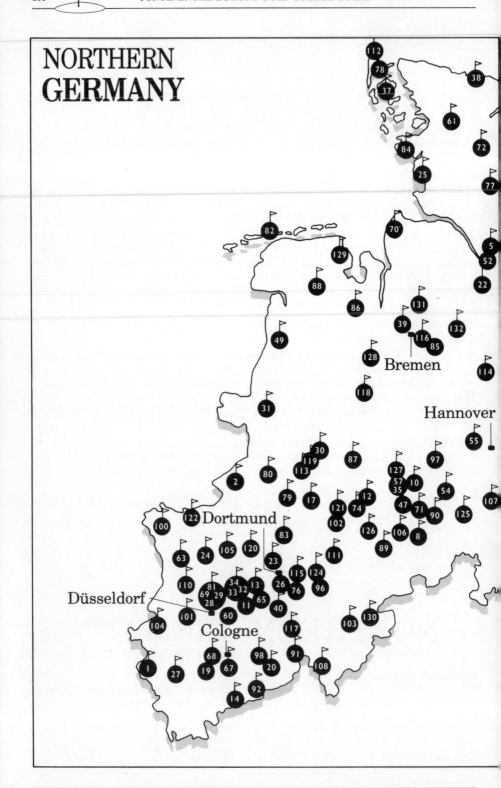

NORTHERN GERMANY

Bremen

Hannover

Dortmund

Düsseldorf

Cologne

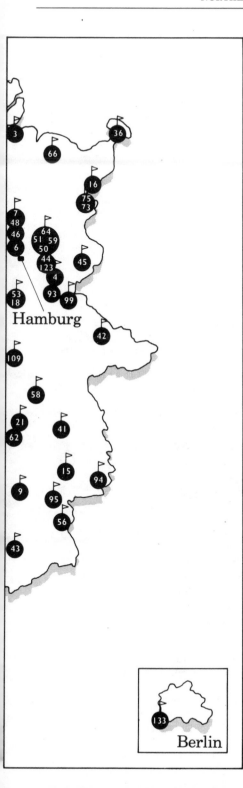

Hamburg

Berlin

GC Ahaus (1987)　　　　　　　　　**2**

Phone: 02567 405

Schmäinghook 36, 4422 Ahaus-Alstätte
North west of Ahaus off the K22 between
Alstätte and Ottenstein

Holes	18 Par 72 6180m.
Visitors	Welcome
Fees	DM50–80
Facilities	Bar and restaurant; practice ground
Pro	Graham Glasgow

GC Altenhof (1971)　　　　　　　　**3**

Phone: 04351 41227

Schloss Altenhof, 2330 Eckernförde
Just south west of Eckernförde off the B76

Holes	18 Par 72 6071m.
Visitors	Welcome, but must book
Fees	DM40–60
Facilities	Bar and restaurant; practice ground; swimming pool
Pro	N Robinson

GC Am Sachsenwald (1988)　　　　**4**

Phone: 04104 6120

Am Riesenbett, 2055 Dassendorf
East of Reinbek off the B207, through
Dassendorf towards Aumühle then Riesenbett

Holes	18 Par 72 6118m.
Visitors	Welcome
Fees	DM50–60
Facilities	Bar and restaurant; practice ground; short course
Pro	Malcolm Grogan

GC An der Pinnau (1982)　　　　　**5**

Phone: 04106 81800

Pinnebergerstr 81a, 2085 Quickborn-Renzel
North west of Hamburg off the A7. Take the exit
to Quickborn and head for Pinneberg and Renzel

Holes	18 Par 74 6493m.
Visitors	Welcome, but must book
Fees	DM45–60
Facilities	Bar and restaurant; practice ground
Pro	S Arrowsmith

GC Auf der Wendlohe (1964)   **6**

Phone: 040 5505014

Oldesloer Str 251, 2000 Hamburg 61 – Schnelsen

North of Hamburg off the E7 at exit Hamburg–
Schnelsen–N; head for Garstedt on the B432

Holes	18 Par 72 6050m.
	9 Par 36 3080m.
Visitors	Welcome weekdays; at weekends with members only
Fees	DM50
Facilities	Bar and restaurant closed Monday; practice ground
Pro	Glyn Jones

GC Bad Bramstedt (1975)   **7**

Phone: 04192 3444

Ochsenweg 38, 2357 Bad Bramstedt

South of Bad Bramstedt towards Hamburg

Holes	9 Par 35 2863m.
Visitors	Welcome
Fees	DM35–45
Facilities	Bar and restaurant; practice ground
Pro	D Lewis

Bad Driburg GC (1976)   **8**

Phone: 05253 842500

Am Kurpark, 3490 Bad Driburg

North of Bad Driburg towards Bad Pyrmont

Holes	9 Par 36 3053m.
Visitors	Welcome
Fees	DM30–35
Facilities	Bar and restaurant; practice ground; swimming pool; tennis
Pro	R Issitt

GC Bad Salzdetfurth-Hildesheim (1972)   **9**

Phone: 05063 1516

3202 Bad Salzdetfurth, Wesseln, In der Bünte

South of Hildesheim off the A7. Take the
Salzgitter exit and head for Wendhausen and
Wesseln on the B243

Holes	9 Par 36 3105m.
Visitors	Welcome, but must book
Fees	DM25–30
Facilities	Bar and restaurant; practice ground
Pro	W Müller

GC Bad Salzuflen (1956)   **10**

Phone: 05222 10773

Am Schwaghof, 4902 Bad Salzuflen

Just north of Bad Salzuflen, off the A2 at the
Exter exit

Holes	18 Par 72 6163m.
Visitors	Welcome, but must book. Course closed January
Fees	DM50–60
Facilities	Bar and restaurant; practice ground
Pro	J Paterson

This is quite an exclusive club with excellent
facilities and a splendid course. There is a hill in
its centre and the holes run around it and over
it and this inevitably adds to the difficulties. The
first half runs through the woods and the course
opens out a little more during the second half.
The short 17th is immensely difficult, with a
carry of 220 metres uphill to a double-tiered
green.

GC Bergisch Land (1928)   **11**

Phone: 02053 7177

Siebeneickerstr 386, 5600 Wuppertal

North of Wuppertal off the A46. Take the
Wuppertal/Katernberg exit, and go towards
Neviges

Holes	18 Par 71 5920m.
Visitors	Welcome on weekdays; introduction only at weekends
Fees	DM65–80
Facilities	Bar and restaurant closed Monday in winter; practice ground
Pro	Johannes Bauerdick

Bielefelder GC (1977)   **12**

Phone: 0521 105103

Dornberger Str 377, 4800 Bielefeld-Hoberge 1

West of Bielefeld off the A2

Holes	18 Par 72 6056m.
Visitors	Welcome, but must book
Fees	DM35–45
Facilities	Bar and restaurant; practice ground
Pro	H Kahre

GC Bochum (1982)   **13**

Phone: 0234 799832

Im Mailand 127, 4630 Bochum/Stiepel

South of Bochum in Stiepel

Holes	18 Par 68 5300m.
Visitors	Welcome, but must book
Fees	DM50–60
Facilities	Bar and restaurant; practice ground
Pro	M Neumann

GC Bonn-Godesberg in Wachtberg (1960) **14**
Phone: 0228 344003
Landgrabenweg, 5307 Wachtberg/Oberbachem
South of Bonn at Oberbachem, 4km from Bad Godesberg

Holes	18 Par 71 5857m.
Visitors	Welcome, but must book
Fees	DM50–70
Facilities	Bar and restaurant; practice ground
Pro	K Riechart

GC Braunschweig (1926) **15**
Phone: 0531 691369
Schwarzkopfstr 10, 3300 Braunschweig
South of Braunschweig off the B248

Holes	18 Par 71 5893m.
Visitors	Welcome, but must book
Fees	DM40–50
Facilities	Bar and restaurant; practice ground
Pro	R Wiseman

GC Brodauer Mühle (1989) **16**
Phone: 04561 8140
Baumallee 14, 2430 Gut Beusloe
North east of Neustadt in Beusloe off the B501 through Ostseeheilbad Grömitz

Holes	9 Par 36 3027m.
Visitors	Welcome
Fees	DM25–35
Facilities	Bar and restaurant; practice ground; tennis

GC Brückhausen Everswinkel-Alverskirchen (1989) **17**
Phone: 02582 227
Holling 4, 4416 Everswinkel 2
East of Münster near Everswinkel

Holes	9 Par 36 3043m.
Visitors	Welcome
Fees	DM50
Facilities	Bar and restaurant under construction 1992
Pro	Karel Scopovy

GC Buchholz-Nordheide (1985) **18**
Phone: 04181 36200
An der Rehm 25, 2110 Buchholz
South of Buchholz, off the A1 at the Dibberson exit

Holes	18 Par 71 6130m.
Visitors	Welcome weekdays; at weekends only with member
Fees	DM60
Facilities	Bar and restaurant; practice ground
Pro	Frank Hamdorf

Golf Burg Konradsheim (1988) **19**
Phone: 02235 76094
Frenzenstrasse 148a, 5042 Erftstadt-Konradsheim
North of Erftstadt towards Konradsheim

Holes	9 Par 36 3074m.
Visitors	Welcome
Fees	DM60–70
Facilities	Bar and restaurant; practice ground
Pro	H Ranft

GC Burg Overbach Much (1984) **20**
Phone: 02245 5550
Burg Overbach, 5203 Much
In Much

Holes	18 Par 72 6056m.
Visitors	Welcome, but must book. Course closed January to March
Fees	DM50–70
Facilities	Bar and restaurant; practice ground
Pro	R Hauser

Burgdorfer Golfclub (1970) **21**
Phone: 05085 7144
Waldstr 15, 3167 Burgdorf-Ehlershausen
North east of Hannover via the B3 through Celle towards Ehlershausen

Holes	18 Par 74 6426m
Visitors	Welcome, but must book
Fees	DM40–60
Facilities	Bar and restaurant; practice ground
Pro	L Theeuwen

GC Buxtehude (1982)   22

Phone: 04161 81333
Zum Lehmfeld 1, 2150 Buxtehude
Just south of Buxtehude off the A1

Holes	18 Par 74 6505m.
Visitors	Welcome weekdays and weekends before 9.30 am
Fees	DM60–80
Facilities	Bar and restaurant closed Monday and January/February; practice ground
Pro	Mike Fitton

GC Castrop-Rauxel in Frohlinde (1989)   23

Phone: 02305 62027
Dortmunder Strasse 383, 4620 Castrop-Rauxel
Just east of Castrop-Rauxel off the A45 at exit Dortmund-Marten

Holes	18 Par 72 6146m.
Visitors	Welcome
Fees	DM55–80
Facilities	Bar and restaurant; practice ground
Pro	S Maharaj

GC Dinslaken-Hünxer Wald (1982)   24

Phone: 02858 6480
Hardtbergweg (Messenhof), 4224 Hünxe
North of Dinslaken off the A3 at Dinslaken-N; head for Kirchhellen and Hünxe

Holes	9 Par 35 2978m.
Visitors	Welcome, but must book
Fees	DM35–50
Facilities	Bar and restaurant; practice ground

GC Dithmarschen (1984)   25

Phone: 04843 6300
Dorfstrasse 11, 2242 Warwerort b/Büsum, in Spieicherkoog
14km south west of Heide via the B203 through Büsum to Warwerort

Holes	9 Par 36 2642m.
Visitors	Welcome
Fees	DM25–35
Facilities	Bar and restaurant; practice ground; swimming pool
Pro	P Clark

Dortmunder GC (1956)   26

Phone: 0231 774133
Reichsmarkstr 12, 4600 Dortmund
South of Dortmund, on the B234 to Aplerdeck

Holes	18 Par 72 6174m.
Visitors	Welcome, but must book
Fees	DM40–50
Facilities	Bar and restaurant; practice ground
Pro	V Knötnschild

If you have the urge to open your shoulders and give your ball a big hit, this is the course to visit. It is a big and open course, with very few trees; the main hazards are provided by water.

GC Düren (1978)   27

Phone: 02421 67278
Trierbachweg 32, 5160 Düren-Gürzenich
West of Düren, through Mariaweiler and towards Schevenhütte

Holes	9 Par 35 2843m.
Visitors	Welcome except Monday and Saturday; course closed December to February
Fees	DM50
Facilities	Bar and restaurant closed Monday, Thursday and Friday; practice ground
Pro	Hans Gross

GC Düsseldorf-Hösel (1984)   28

Phone: 02102 68629
In den Höfen 32, 4030 Ratingen 6 (Hösel)
North east of Düsseldorf off Autobahn 3. Take the Breitscheid exit along the 227 towards Velbert

Holes	18 Par 72 6169m.
Visitors	By reservation; weekends only with member
Fees	DM50–70
Facilities	Bar and restaurant; practice ground
Pro	Martyn Robinson

This is a long and undulating course with some tough driving holes, especially on the dog-leg holes, most notably the 7th, 11th and 15th. There are some mischievously located fairway bunkers and several plateau greens.

Düsseldorfer GC (1961) 29

Phone: 02102 81092

Rittergut Rommeljans, 4030 Ratingen

North east of Düsseldorf off the A3 towards Ratingen

Holes	18 Par 71 5886m.
Visitors	Welcome Tuesday-Friday. Course closed January/February
Fees	DM60–90
Facilities	Bar and restaurant
Pro	Uli Knappman

Hawtree designed the course and it is a hard test for all types of golfer. The fairways are narrow and the greens are sizeable and well-bunkered; and there are plenty of water hazards to be avoided. The course calls for that blend of power and accuracy which is so elusive.

GC Dütetal (1983) 30

Phone: 05404 5296

Wersener Str 17, 4531 Lotte

West of Osnabrück off the A1 through Westerhappeln towards Lotte

Holes	9 Par 35 2687m.
Visitors	Welcome
Fees	DM36–50
Facilities	Bar and restaurant; practice ground

GC Emstal (1978) 31

Phone: 0591 63837

Lookenstrasse 25, 4450 Lingen/Ems, Altenlingen-Beversundern

Just north west of Lingen off the B70

Holes	9 Par 35 2660m.
Visitors	Welcome
Fees	DM30–40
Facilities	Bar and restaurant; practice ground; swimming pool; tennis
Pro	D Bryan

Essener GC Haus Oefte (1959) 32

Phone: 02054 83911

Laupendahler Landstr, 4300 Essen-Kettwig 18

South of Essen on the B224 towards Heidhausen; turn after Werden

Holes	18 Par 72 6137m.
Visitors	Welcome
Fees	DM50–80
Facilities	Bar and restaurant; practice ground
Pro	R Sommer

Essen-Heidhausen GC (1970) 33

Phone: 0201 404111

Preutenborbeckstr 36, 4300 Essen 16

South of Essen on the B224 towards Velbert

Holes	18 Par 71 5937m.
Visitors	Welcome, but must book
Fees	DM35–50
Facilities	Bar and restaurant; practice ground
Pro	G Kothe

Golfriege des Etuf (1962) 34

Phone: 0201 441426

Frh-v-Stein-str 92a, 4300 Essen-Hügel

South of Essen off the B224 towards Essen-Werden; head for Balderney See

Holes	9 Par 32 2228m.
Visitors	Welcome
Fees	DM35–45
Facilities	Bar and restaurant
Pro	Diana Franz

Int GC Exter (Golfpark Heerhof) (1984) 35

Phone: 05228 7507

Finnebachstr 31, 4900 Herford

10km east of Herford

Holes	9 Par 36 3066m.
Visitors	Welcome (public course)
Fees	DM30–40
Facilities	Bar and restaurant; practice ground
Pro	M Spray

GC Fehmarn (1990) 36

Phone: 04371 5653

Kämmerweg 1, 2448 Burg auf Fehmarn

On Fehmarn island, south west of Burg, off the E47

Holes	9 Par 33 2316m.
Visitors	Welcome
Fees	DM40–50
Facilities	Bar and restaurant; practice ground
Pro	T Thatford

GC Föhr (1966) 37
Phone: 04681 3277
Golfplatz, 2270 Nieblum auf Föhr
On Föhr island, just south west of the airport of Wyk

Holes	18 Par 72 6045m.
Visitors	Welcome
Fees	DM45–55
Facilities	Bar and restaurant; practice ground
Pro	A Assmus

Förde GC Glücksburg (1972) 38
Phone: 04631 2547
2391 Glücksburg-Bockholm
North east of Flensburg off the A7, through Glücksburg

Holes	9 Par 36 3036m.
Visitors	Welcome, but must book
Fees	DM30–40
Facilities	Bar and restaurant; practice ground
Pro	D Ohle

Garlstedter Heide GC (1905) 39
Phone: 04795 417
Am Golfplatz 10, 2861 Garlstedt
North of Bremen off the B6 to Garlstedt

Holes	18 Par 75 6435m.
Visitors	Welcome on weekdays but must book; weekends by introduction only
Fees	DM60–70
Facilities	Bar and restaurant; practice ground
Pro	H Weber

The course was laid out on 220 acres of thick forest on the Garlstedter Heath by Bernard von Limburger. The huge pine trees seem to compress the fairways and such was the brilliance of the design, with many dog-legs and six holes of over 500 yards, that a mere 24 bunkers were required. Both power and accuracy are needed off the tees in order to put the ball in position to attack the green. Many professionals judge it to be one of the toughest courses in Europe, including Neil Coles who won the German Open here in 1971.

GC Gelstern (1988) 40
Phone: 02351 56460
5885 Schalksmühle-Gelstern 2
Just north of Lüdenscheid towards Schalksmühle

Holes	9 Par 36 3034m.
Visitors	Welcome. Course closed December to March
Fees	DM 25–50
Facilities	Bar and restaurant; practice ground
Pro	P Koerber

GC Gifhorn (1982) 41
Phone: 05371 52888
3170 Gifhorn
North of Braunschweig off the B188 to Hanover; head for Wilsche

Holes	9 Par 36 3130m.
Visitors	Welcome
Fees	DM30–40
Facilities	Bar and restaurant; practice ground; swimming pool
Pro	N Coombs

GC an der Göhrde (1968) 42
Phone: 05863 556
3139 Zernien Braasche
West of Dannenberg via the B191 to Zernien, then Braasche

Holes	9 Par 36 3058m.
Visitors	Welcome
Fees	DM30–40
Facilities	Bar and restaurant; practice ground
Pro	G Gilligan

GC Göttingen (1969) 43
Phone: 05551 61915
Schloss Levershausen, 3410 Nottheim 1
North of Göttingen via the B3 to Südheim, then Levershausen

Holes	18 Par 72 6040m.
Visitors	Welcome, but must book
Fees	DM40–50
Facilities	Bar and restaurant;
Pro	W Kreuzer

GC Groszensee (1984) 44
Phone: 04154 6473
Hamburgerstr 17, 2077 Groszensee
South east of Ahrensburg off the B435 to Schwarzenkate

Holes	9 Par 36 3100m.
Visitors	Welcome
Fees	DM30–45
Pro	Gary Milliner

GC Gut Grambek (1982) 45

Phone: 04542 4627
Schlossstrasse 21, 2411 Grambek/Mölln
South of Mölln off the B207 to Gut Grambek

Holes	18 Par 71 6029m.
Visitors	Welcome, but must book at weekends
Fees	DM50–70
Facilities	Bar and restaurant closed Monday; practice ground
Pro	Clive Smailes

GC Gut Kaden (1984) 46

Phone: 04193 1421
Kadener Str 9, 2081 Alveslohe
North west of Norderstedt off the A7, at Alverslohe

Holes	18 Par 72 6076m.
Visitors	Welcome weekdays; weekends with member only
Fees	DM50
Facilities	Bar and restaurant;
Pro	W Mych

GC Gut Ottenhausen zu Lage (1985) 47

Phone: 05232 66829
Ottenhauser Str 100, 4937 Lage/Lippe
South of Lage off the A2. Take the Lage/
Detmold exit and head for Lage/Pivitsheide

Holes	18 Par 72 6226m.
Visitors	Welcome
Fees	DM30–40
Facilities	Bar and restaurant closed Monday; practice ground
Pro	Daniel Chisholm

GC Gut Waldorf (1969) 48

Phone: 04194 383
2359 Kisdorferwohld, Kisdorf
North west of Hamburg off the A7 and B433 at Kisdorf

Holes	18 Par 72 6073m.
Visitors	Welcome on weekdays; weekends with member only
Fees	DM50–60
Facilities	Bar and restaurant closed Monday and November to March; practice ground
Pro	Timothy Parker

GC Gutshof Papenburg-Aschendorf (1987) 49

Phone: 04961 74811
Gutshofstrasse 141, 2990 Papenburg-Aschendorf
South of Papenburg off the B401

Holes	9 Par 36 3072m.
Visitors	Welcome
Fees	DM30–40
Facilities	Bar and restaurant; practice ground
Pro	Alec Bickerdike

GC Hamburg-Ahrensburg (1966) 50

Phone: 04102 51309
Am Haidschlag 45, 2070 Ahrensburg
North east of Hamburg off the A1, through Ahrensburg to Haidschlag

Holes	18 Par 70 5719m.
Visitors	Welcome on weekdays
Fees	DM40–60
Facilities	Bar and restaurant; practice ground
Pro	Jochen Strüver

The course was originally designed by Bernard von Limburger but alterations were made by Robert Trent Jones in 1977. It is certainly testing as it runs through avenues of trees with several sharp dog-leg holes. Water comes into play and especially at the short 11th where you must carry your ball over the Bredenbeker lake and at the 12th where you must clear the lake off the tee.

GC Hamburg-Walddörfer (1960) 51

Phone: 040 6051337
Schevenbarg, 2075 Ammersbek
20km north east of Hamburg off Route 75

Holes	18 Par 73 6154m.
Visitors	Welcome weekdays, weekends with member
Fees	DM50–60
Facilities	Bar and restaurant closed Monday; practice ground; 9 hole pitch & putt; swimming pool; tennis
Pro	Gerry Bennett

Walddörfer is quite a long course and its difficulties lie in the narrow fairways which are cut through trees. Its challenge lies in the first dozen holes or so, since the course then opens out over flat terrain. The clubhouse facilities are excellent.

Hamburger GC (Falkenstein) (1905)   52

Phone: 040 812177

In den Bargen 59, 2000 Hamburg 55

West of Hamburg via the B431 through Osdorf to
Blankenese and Rissen

Holes	18 Par 71 5925m.
Visitors	On weekends by introduction
Fees	DM45–60
Facilities	Bar and restaurant; practice ground
Pro	A Mazza

One of Germany's most distinguished courses,
Falkenstein was designed by Colt, Alison and
Morrison and changes were later made by
Bernard von Limburger. No two fairways are
adjacent and each hole has its own distinct
character as they wind their way through the
heather and trees. It is a very long course, which
demands both power and accuracy if the golfer
is to make any headway and the greens are large
and difficult. The second hole is a real tiger, as
is the 17th with masses of heather to carry off
the tee and more to negotiate near the green. It
is a fine and very enjoyable course.

Hamburger GC in der Lüneberger Heide (1957)   53

Phone: 04105 2331

2105 Seevetal 1, Am Golfplatz 24

South of Hamburg. Take the Hittfeld exit off the
A1 and head for Natenbergweg

Holes	18 Par 70 5685m.
Visitors	Welcome weekdays, weekends with members
Fees	DM50–60
Facilities	Bar and restaurant closed January/ February; swimming pool; tennis; horse riding
Pro	J Grombein

This is a challenging course especially over the
first half with its narrow fairways which run
through woodland. The second nine are more
open but run over hilly terrain and the finishing
holes are severe. The short 16th hole runs up a
hill to a green surrounded by trees and from the
tee the golfer can see only the top of the flag
and the edge of the green. The 17th hole, at over
400 yards, is another test, a dog-leg with an
elevated green, and the 18th has an out of
bounds area on the left. It is a fine course which
is always in superb condition.

Hamelner G & CC (Schloss Schwöbber) (1985)   54

Phone: 05154 2004

Schloss Schwöbber, 3258 Aerzen

South west of Hameln off the B83

Holes	18 Par 72 6056m.
Holes	18 Par 60 3450m.
Visitors	Welcome
Fees	DM40–90
Facilities	Bar and restaurant; practice ground; swimming pool; tennis; horseriding; fishing
Pro	Richard Lewington

Hannover GC (1923)   55

Phone: 05137 73068

Am Blauen See, 3008 Garbsen 1

West of Hannover off the A2. Take the Garbsen
exit and head for Herrnhausen and Blauen See

Holes	18 Par 71 5855m.
Visitors	Welcome
Fees	DM35–50
Facilities	Bar and restaurant; practice ground
Pro	H Koch

Hannover is a beautifully designed course with
each hole running in isolation through the
pines. After a quiet start the course shows its
teeth as the holes get longer and much nar-
rower. It is a popular and very welcoming club
with a very large practice area. The course is
situated alongside a lake which is the venue for
many kinds of water sports.

GC Harz (1969)   56

Phone: 05322 6737

107 Am Breitenberg, 3388 Bad Harzburg

On the south west side of Bad Harzburg, via the
B82 and B6 from the A7

Holes	9 Par 35 2781m.
Visitors	Welcome
Fees	DM30–40
Facilities	Bar and restaurant; practice ground
Pro	M Spence

GC Herford (1984)   57

Phone: 05228 7434

Heideholz 8, 4973 Vlotho-Exter

North east of Herford near Lindemanns
Windmill

Holes	9 Par 36 3092m.
Visitors	Welcome
Fees	DM30–40
Facilities	Bar and restaurant; practice ground
Pro	G Pilkington

GC Herzogstadt Celle (1986) 58
Phone: 05086 395
Beukenbusch 1, 4200 Celle/Garssen
North east of Celle off the B191; after Alvern
head for Garssen
Holes   18 Par 71 5934m.
Visitors   Welcome, but must book
Fees   DM30–40
Facilities   Bar and restaurant;
Pro   W Knowles

GC Hoisdorf (1977) 59
Phone: 04107 7831
2073 Lütjensee, Hofbornbek-Hoisdorf
North east of Hamburg off the A1; head for
Lütjensee and Siekerberg
Holes   18 Par 71 6010m.
Visitors   Welcome, but must book
Fees   DM50–60
Facilities   Bar and restaurant; practice ground
Pro   M Stewart

GC Hubbelrath (1961) 60
Phone: 02104 72178
Bergische Landstr 700, 4000 Düsseldorf
East of Düsseldorf, via the B7 towards
Mettmann
Holes   18 Par 72 6042m.
Visitors   Welcome, but must book
Fees   DM70–100
Facilities   Bar and restaurant; practice ground;
            short course; swimming pool
Pro   G Danz
This was the scene of the 1992 German Open,
won by Vijay Singh with a remarkable score of
26 under par. Lesser mortals will also enjoy this
rolling parkland course with its profusion of
trees. There are some very tight driving holes
and tricky greens, especially the 18th where you
must try to assess the huge slopes.

GC Husumer Bucht (1990) 61
Phone: 04841 72238
Schwesing-Hohlacker, 2250 Husum
East of Husum off the B201
Holes   9 Par 36 3059m.
Visitors   Welcome
Fees   DM35–50
Facilities   Bar and restaurant closed Monday;
            practice ground
Pro   Rolf Kebbel

GC Isernhagen (1983) 62
Phone: 05139 2998
Auf Gut Lohne, 3004 Isernhagen 5
North east of Hanover; off the B3 at Gut Lohne
Holes   18 Par 73 6334m.
Visitors   Welcome, but must book
Fees   DM40–60
Facilities   Bar and restaurant; practice ground
Pro   U Bruns

Issum-Niederhein GC (1973) 63
Phone: 02935 3626
Pauenweg 68, 4174 Issum
East of Issum off the A57 at the Alpen exit
Holes   18 Par 71 5862m.
Visitors   Welcome weekdays; weekends before
            10am
Fees   DM70–80
Facilities   Bar and restaurant
Pro   Steven Tomkinson

GC Jersbek (1986) 64
Phone: 04532 23555
Oberteicherweg, 2072 Gut Jersbek
North west of Bargteheide off the B75, towards
Jersbek
Holes   18 Par 71 6029m.
Visitors   Welcome, but must book
Fees   DM50–70
Facilities   Bar and restaurant; practice ground

GC Juliana (1978) 65
Phone: 0202 647070
Frielinghausen 1, 4322 Sprockhövel 1
North of Wuppertal off the A46 near exit
Wuppertal-Oberbarmen
Holes   18 Par 71 5744m.
Visitors   Welcome
Fees   DM40–50
Facilities   Bar and restaurant; practice ground
Pro   G Hillier

GC Kitzeberg (1902) 66
Phone: 0431 23404
2305 Heikendorf, Kitzeberg
North west of Kiel off the B76 and via the B502
through Laboe and Mönkeberg
Holes   9 Par 35 2835m.
Visitors   Welcome
Fees   DM30–40
Facilities   Bar and restaurant
Pro   N Sumner

Köln-Marienburger GC (1949)   **67**
Phone: 0221 384793
Schillingsrotter Weg, 5000 Köln 51
In Cologne, on the south side of the city
Holes	9 Par 36 3075m.
Visitors	Welcome, but must book
Fees	DM50–60
Facilities	Bar and restaurant; practice ground
Pro	H Becker

GC Köln-Refrath (1906)   **68**
Phone: 02204 63114
Golfplatz 2, 5060 Bergisch Gladbach
West of Köln off the B55; follow signs to
Eissporthalle
Holes	18 Par 72 6045m.
Visitors	Welcome, but must book
Fees	DM50–70
Facilities	Bar and restaurant; practice ground
Pro	K Marx

The course sits in a charming stretch of
woodland, the Königsforst, and the fairways run
through avenues of trees. There are several dog-
leg holes, which require accuracy off the tee,
and the water hazards add to the fun.

Krefelder GC (1930)   **69**
Phone: 02151 570071
Eltweg 2, 4150 Krefeld-Linn
In East Krefeld
Holes	18 Par 72 6040m.
Visitors	Welcome, but must book
Fees	DM80–100
Facilities	Bar and restaurant; practice ground
Pro	R Tillmanns

The club began its life with nine holes and then
moved to a new location in 1940. It is an
extremely demanding course which twists and
turns over fairly open terrain, although the
winds can cause real problems. There are many
dog-leg holes which demand great accuracy from
the tee since the landing areas are restricted.
The German Open has been played here many
times and has produced distinguished winners
such as Bobby Locke, Bernard Hunt, Roberto de
Vicenzo and Donald Swaelens.

Küsten-GC Klint (1979)   **70**
Phone: 04723 2737
Rosenhof 25, 2190 Nordseebad Cuxhaven
South west of Cuxhaven off the A27, between
Cuxhaven and Oxstedt
Holes	18 Par 72 6059m.
Visitors	Welcome
Fees	DM40–50
Facilities	Bar and restaurant; practice ground
Pro	Edmund Kranz

Lippischer GC Blomberg-Cappel (1981)   **71**
Phone: 05236 459
Huxollweg, 4933 Blomberg-Cappel
West of Blomberg off the B1
Holes	18 Par 72 6110m.
Visitors	Welcome, but must book. Course closed December to March
Fees	DM40–50
Facilities	Bar and restaurant; practice ground
Pro	R Lauermann

GC Lohersand (1957)   **72**
Phone: 04336 3333
Am Golfplatz, 2371 Sorgbrück
North west of Rendsburg via the B77 through
Schleswig
Holes	9 Par 36 3020m.
Visitors	Welcome
Fees	DM30–40
Facilities	Bar and restaurant; practice ground
Pro	K Waldon

Lübeck-Travemünder GC (1921)   **73**
Phone: 04502 74018
Kowitzberg 41, 2400 Lübeck-Travemünde
North east of Lübeck off the B76 at Travemünde
Holes	18 Par 72 6071m.
Visitors	Welcome
Fees	DM50–70
Facilities	Bar and restaurant; practice ground
Pro	A Varley

Travemünde is a pleasant Baltic resort of old
houses and has a beach. The course is ideal for
holiday golfers, since it presents few real
difficulties and there are some good views of the
sea.

GC Marienfeld (1988)   **74**
Phone: 05247 8880
In der Remse 27, 4834 Marienfeld
Just south east of Harsewinkel, off the B513
towards Marienfeld
Holes	9 Par 36 3033m.
Visitors	Welcome
Fees	DM35–45
Facilities	Bar and restaurant; practice ground; swimming pool; tennis
Pro	L Plesse

GC Maritim Timmendorferstrand (1973)   **75**

Phone: 04503 5152

Am Golfplatz 3, 2408 Timmendorferstrand

North east of Lübeck off the A1 at exit Ratekau

Holes	18 Par 72 6095m.
	18 Par 61 3755m.
Visitors	Welcome, but must book
Fees	DM50–80
Facilities	Bar and restaurant; practice ground
Pro	Rainer Hinz

The course is situated at a popular resort on the Baltic coast, just over forty miles from Hamburg. There are all kinds of sporting facilities nearby and the main Maritim Course is quite a challenge, with several dog-leg holes and water hazards. The short course is also good fun.

Märkischer GC Hagen (1965)   **76**

Phone: 02334 51778

Tiefendorfer Str 48, 5800 Hagen 1 (Berchum)

5km north east of Hagen at Berchum

Holes	9 Par 36 3057m.
Visitors	Welcome, but must book
Fees	DM25–40
Facilities	Bar and restaurant
Pro	D Giese

Mittelholsteinischer GC Aukrug (1969)   **77**

Phone: 04873 595

Zum Glasberg 9, 2356 Aukrug/Bargfeld

West of Neumünster via the B430 through Hohenwestedt

Holes	18 Par 72 6117m.
Visitors	Welcome, but must book
Fees	DM50–70
Facilities	Bar and restaurant; practice ground
Pro	R Denton

GC Morsum auf Sylt (1989)   **78**

Phone: 04654 387

Zum Wäldchen, 2280 Klein-Morsum

South east of Sylt island in Klein-Morsum

Holes	9 Par 36 3055m.
Visitors	Welcome
Fees	DM50–70
Facilities	Bar and restaurant; practice ground

GC Münster-Wilkinghege (1965)   **79**

Phone: 0251 211201

Steinfürter Str 448, 4400 Münster

North west of Münster off the A1 at exit Munster-Nord

Holes	18 Par 71 5955m.
Visitors	Welcome, but must book
Fees	DM50–70
Facilities	Bar and restaurant; practice ground
Pro	C Westerman

GC Münsterland (1950)   **80**

Phone: 02551 5178

Bagno, 4430 Steinfurt 1

North west of Steinfurt off the A1

Holes	9 Par 33 2480m.
Visitors	Welcome. Course closed December to February
Fees	DM30–40
Facilities	Bar and restaurant; practice ground
Pro	C Leader

Niederrheinischer GC (1956)   **81**

Phone: 0203 721469

Grossenbaumer Allee 240, 4100 Duisburg

South of Duisburg off the A3

Holes	9 Par 36 3045m.
Visitors	Introduction only at weekends
Fees	DM40–60
Facilities	Bar and restaurant; practice ground
Pro	J Dennison

GC Norderney (1956)   **82**

Phone: 04932 680

Karl Riegerweg, 2982 Norderney

On Norderney island, and a few kilometres east of Norderney

Holes	9 Par 36 2946m.
Visitors	Welcome
Fees	DM26–30
Facilities	Bar and restaurant; practice ground
Pro	R Bremer

GC Nordkirchen (1978)   83

Phone: 02596 3005

Golfplatz 6, 4717 Nordkirchen

North of Nordkirchen off the B58

Holes	18 Par 71 5900m.
Visitors	Welcome. Course closed mid-December to mid-March
Fees	DM40–50
Facilities	Bar and restaurant closed Monday
Pro	Andreas Rössler

Nordsee GC St Peter-Ording (1971)   84

Phone: 04863 3545

Zum Böhler Strand 16, 2252 St Peter-Ording

On the North Sea coast, off the B202; south east of St Peter-Ording in St Peter-Böhl

Holes	9 Par 36 2931m.
Visitors	Welcome
Fees	DM30–40
Facilities	Bar and restaurant; practice ground
Pro	Paul Robeson

GC Oberneuland (1990)   85

Phone: 0421 259321

H Badenweg 25, 2800 Bremen

8km east of Bremen off the A27

Holes	9 Par 33 2470m.
Visitors	Welcome
Fees	DM36–50
Facilities	Bar and restaurant; tennis

Oldenburgischer GC (1964)   86

Phone: 04402 7240

Auf dem Golfplatz, 2902 Rastede/Wemkendorf

North west of Oldenburg via the B69 towards Rastede and Wemkendorf

Holes	18 Par 72 6087m.
Visitors	Welcome
Fees	DM30–40
Facilities	Bar and restaurant; practice ground
Pro	J Walter

Osnabrücker GC (1955)   87

Phone: 05402 636

Am Golfplatz 3, 4516 Bissendorf/Jeggen

East of Osnabrück off the A30. Take the Bissendorf exit and head for Schledehausen and Jeggen

Holes	18 Par 71 5881m.
Visitors	Welcome, but must book
Fees	DM40–60
Facilities	Bar and restaurant; practice ground
Pro	H Theeuwen

GC Ostfriesland (1980)   88

Phone: 04944 3040

Fliederstr 1, 2964 Wiesmoor/Hinrichsfehn

Just south of Wiesmoor via the B75 towards Remels, and then Blauer Fasan

Holes	18 Par 73 6265m.
Visitors	Welcome, but must book
Fees	DM40–50
Facilities	Bar and restaurant; practice ground; swimming pool; tennis
Pro	S Parry

GC Paderborn Land (1983)   89

Phone: 05258 6498

Glockenpohl, 4796 Salzkotten-Thüle

West of Paderborn through Salzkotten to Thüle

Holes	9 Par 34 2758m.
Visitors	Welcome
Fees	DM20–30
Facilities	Bar and restaurant; practice ground
Pro	G Schurr

Pyrmonter Golfclub (1964)   90

Phone: 05281 8196

Auf dem Winzenberg 2, 4927 Lügde

Take the B1 or B83 to Lügde (near Bad Pyrmont), and then follow signs to Sonnenhof for 2km

Holes	9 Par 35 2860m.
Visitors	Welcome, but must book at weekends
Fees	DM40–50
Facilities	Bar and restaurant; practice ground
Pro	William Murray

GC Reichshof (1991)   91

Phone: 02297 7131

5226 Reichshof-Hassel

Near the Reichshof-Eckenhagen exit off the A4

Holes	9 Par 36 3033m.
Visitors	Welcome
Fees	DM35–50
Facilities	Bar and restaurant; practice ground

GC Rhein-Sieg (1971)   **92**
Phone: 02242 6501
Haus Dürresbach, 5202 Hennef
South of Hennef towards Söven

Holes	18 Par 72 6070m.
Visitors	Welcome, but must book
Fees	DM50–60
Facilities	Bar and restaurant; practice ground
Pro	H Knopp

St Dionys Golfclub (1972)   **93**
Phone: 04133 6277
Widukindweg, 2123 St Dionys
South of Hamburg via the B4 to Winsen,
through Wittorf towards Barum

Holes	18 Par 72 6225m.
Visitors	Welcome
Fees	DM60–80
Facilities	Bar and restaurant; practice ground
Pro	K Mahl

This is an excellent and entertaining course;
ideal for a relaxing holiday game since there is
hardly any rough. St Dionys is laid out over flat
heathland which is made attractive by the
masses of pines and firs which line the fairways.

GC St Lorenz Schöningen (1990)   **94**
Phone: 05352 1697
Klostergut St Lorenz, 3338 Schöningen
South of Helmstedt via the B244 through
Schöningen towards Königslutter

Holes	9 Par 37 3289m.
Visitors	Welcome, but must book
Fees	DM30–40
Facilities	Bar and restaurant; practice ground
Pro	C Lindup

GC Salzgitter Liebenburg (1985)   **95**
Phone: 05341 37376
Sportpark Mahnerberg, 3320 Salzgitter Bad 51
South of Salzgitter towards Mahnerberg

Holes	9 Par 37 3031m.
Visitors	Welcome. Course closed December to February
Fees	DM35–45
Facilities	Bar and restaurant closed Monday; practice ground; tennis and squash
Pro	Gerhard Dyck

Sauerland GC (Neheim-Hüsten) (1958)   **96**
Phone: 02932 31546
Zum Golfplatz, 5760 Arnsberg 1
North west of Arnsberg, off the A44

Holes	9 Par 35 2937m.
Visitors	Welcome
Fees	DM30–35
Facilities	Bar and restaurant; practice ground
Pro	T Croft

GC Schaumburg (1988)   **97**
Phone:05724 4670
3063 Obernkirchen, Röserheide
Off the A2 at the Bad Eilsen exit to
Obernkirchen

Holes	9 Par 37 2941m.
Visitors	Welcome, but must book
Fees	DM40–50
Facilities	Bar and restaurant; practice ground

GC Schloss Georghausen (1962)   **98**
Phone: 02207 4938
Georghausen 8, 5253 Lindlar-Hommerich
South west of Lindlar, near Obersteeg

Holes	18 Par 72 6045m.
Visitors	Welcome, but must book
Fees	DM45–60
Facilities	Bar and restaurant; practice ground
Pro	G Kessler

GC Schloss Lüdersburg (1985)   **99**
Phone: 04153 6112
2127 Lüdersburg bei Lüneburg
North east of Lüneberg. Go through Lüdersburg
towards Echem on the B209

Holes	18 Par 73 6180m.
Visitors	Welcome
Fees	DM50–70
Facilities	Bar and restaurant; practice ground; short course

The club lies to the south east of Hamburg in
delightful countryside not far from the River
Elbe. At the centre of the club is an 18th century
manor house, a remarkable baroque building, in
which you can rent an apartment. The course
itself is all charm as it wends its way through
avenues of mature trees. The challenge is
increased markedly by the amount of water that
must be crossed; it affects the play of almost
every hole. On the 5th, 11th, 13th (with an island
green) and 14th holes, it is a particular menace.

Land-Golfclub Schloss Moyland (1986)   100

Phone: 02821 60896

Moyländer Allee 1, 4194 Bedburg-Hau/Moyland
South west of Kleve off the B57

Holes	9 Par 36 2863m.
Visitors	Welcome, but must book
Fees	DM40–60
Facilities	Bar and restaurant; practice ground; tennis
Pro	G Morris

GC Schloss Myllendonk (1965)   101

Phone: 02161 641049

Myllendonker Str 113, 4052 Korschenbroich 1
Just east of Mönchengladbach off the A52

Holes	18 Par 72 6120m.
Visitors	Welcome Tuesday to Friday and must book
Fees	DM50–70
Facilities	Bar and restaurant closed Monday; practice ground
Pro	Gerrit Kerkman

GC Schloss Vornholz (1987)   102

Phone: 02587 464

Langenbreede 8, 4722 Ennigerloh-Ostenfelde
North east of Ennigerloh through Ostenfelde to
Sportpark Votnholz

Holes	9 Par 36 3026m.
Visitors	Welcome
Fees	DM 36–50
Facilities	Bar and restaurant; swimming pool; tennis

GC Schmallenberg (1988)   103

Phone: 02972 5034

5948 Schmallenberg
East of Schmallenberg off the B55 towards
Winkhausen

Holes	18 Par 72
Visitors	Welcome. Course closed December to March
Fees	DM 40–60
Facilities	Bar and restaurant

Schmitzhof-Wegberg GC (1975)   104

Phone: 02436 479

5144 Wegberg-Schmitzhof
West of Mönchengladbach through Rickeltath
towards Merbek/Arsbeck

Holes	18 Par 72 6310m.
Visitors	Welcome, but must book
Fees	DM30–50
Facilities	Bar and restaurant; practice ground; short course
Pro	E Theeuwen

GC Schwarze Heide (1986)   105

Phone: 02045 82488

Gahlener Str 44, 4250 Bottrop-Kirchhellen
North of Bottrop off the A31. Take the Bottrop/
Feldhausen exit to Kirchhellen, then to Gahlen/
Schermbeck

Holes	9 Par 36 3036m.
Visitors	Welcome weekdays; weekends with member only
Fees	DM60
Facilities	Bar and restaurant closed Monday; practice ground
Pro	Siegfried Vollrath

Sennelager (British Army) GC (1973)   106

Phone: 05252 53794

Senne 1, 4792 Bad Lippspringe
9km east of Paderborn off the B1

Holes	18 Par 73 5835m.
Holes	9 Par 34 2607m.
Visitors	Welcome on weekdays; after 2pm weekends
Fees	DM38–48
Facilities	Bar and restaurant; practice ground

GC Sieben-Berge (GC Rheden) (1964/83)   107

Phone: 05182 2680

Schlossstr. 3211 Rheden
Just south of Gronau via the B3 through Elze
and Gronau to Rheden

Holes	9 Par 36 3035m.
Visitors	Welcome, but must book
Fees	DM30–40
Facilities	Bar and restaurant; practice ground; tennis
Pro	J Dunford

Siegen-Olpe GC (1966)   108

Phone: 02762 7589

Ottfingen, 5963 Wenden 4

West of Siegen off the A45. Take the
Freudenberg exit towards Rothemühle

Holes	9 Par 35 2862m.
Visitors	Welcome
Fees	DM30–35
Facilities	Bar and restaurant; practice ground
Pro	K Hahn

Soltau Golfclub (1982)   109

Phone: 05191 14077

Golfplatz Hof Loh, 3040 Soltau/Tetendorf

Just south of Soltau via the B3 to Tetendorf

Holes	18 Par 73 6224m.
Visitors	Welcome
Fees	DM45–60
Facilities	Bar and restaurant; practice ground; short course
Pro	Stefanie Müller-Lampertz

GC Stadtwald (1985)   110

Phone: 02151 594663

Hüttenallee 188/Rennbahn Stadtwald, 4150
Krefeld

In north Krefeld off the A57 at the Krefeld-
Gartenstadt exit

Holes	9 Par 34 2553m.
Visitors	Welcome after 11am. Course closed during horseraces and on Monday
Fees	DM40–60
Facilities	Bar and restaurant
Pro	John Little

This is an interesting nine hole course which
has been built inside the perimeter of the race
course. It is flat and the hazards include not
only water but also the hedges and jumps of the
race course.

GC Stahlberg im Lippetal (1975)   111

Phone: 02527 8191

Ebbecke 14, 4775 Lippetal/Lippborg

North west of Soest, off the A2

Holes	9 Par 36 3075m.
Visitors	Welcome
Fees	DM30–35
Facilities	Bar and restaurant closed Monday; practice ground
Pro	W Lemmens

GC Sylt (1986)   112

Phone: 04651 45311

2283 Wenningstedt

On Sylt island, north of Westerland through
Wenningstedt towards Braderup

Holes	18 Par 72 6200m.
Visitors	Welcome
Fees	DM70–80
Facilities	Bar and restaurant; practice ground
Pro	G Clark

GC Tecklenburger Land (1971)   113

Phone: 05455 1035

Wallen/Lienen 1, 4542 Tecklenburg

Just west of Tecklenburg

Holes	9 Par 36 3080m.
Visitors	Welcome, but must book. Course closed Mondays.
Fees	FM40–60
Facilities	Bar and restaurant; practice ground
Pro	J Laarman

GC Tietlingen (1979)   114

Phone: 05162 3889

Tietlingen 6c, 3032 Fallingbostel 1

East of Walsrode off the A7. Take the
Fallingbostel exit and go through Tietlingen
towards Hertman-Löns-Grab

Holes	9 Par 36 3021m.
Visitors	Welcome but must book; weekends with member only
Fees	DM35–40
Facilities	Bar and restaurant; practice ground
Pro	W McVey

GC Unna-Fröndenberg (1988)   115

Phone: 02373 70060

Schwarzer Weg, 5758 Fröndenberg

Just south of Unna off the A443/B233

Holes	18 Par 72 6177m.
Visitors	Welcome with some restrictions
Fees	DM36–50
Facilities	Bar and restaurant; practice ground; short course
Pro	Joep Weijers

Club zur Vahr (1905)   **116**

Phone: 0421 230041

Bgm Spitta-Allee 34, 2800 Bremen 41

East of Bremen off the A27 at the Bremen-Vahr exit to Vahr

Holes	9 Par 36 2931m (twinned with Garlstedt GC)
Visitors	Welcome; weekends by introduction only
Fees	DM40–50
Facilities	Bar and restaurant; practice ground
Pro	H Weber

GC Varmert (1976)   **117**

Phone: 02269 7299

5883 Kierspe-Varmert

West of Kierspe off the B237 towards Rönsahl

Holes	9 Par 36 3024m.
Visitors	Welcome, but must book
Fees	DM35–50
Facilities	Bar and restaurant; practice ground
Pro	G Thomas

GC Vechta-Welpe (1990)   **118**

Phone: 04441 5539

Welpe 5, 2848 Vechta

60km south west of Bremen, via the M1 and B69

Holes	18 Par 72 6143m.
Visitors	Welcome
Fees	DM30–40
Facilities	Bar and restaurant; practice ground
Pro	Thomas Lloyd

Velper GC (1981)   **119**

Phone: 05456 419

Heinr. Hensiekstr 1, Birkenhof, 4535 Westerkappeln-Velpe

West of Osnabrück off the A30. Take the Westerkappeln exit towards Tecklenburg

Holes	9 Par 35 2891m.
Visitors	Welcome
Fees	DM20–30
Facilities	Bar and restaurant; practice ground
Pro	S Walker

Vestischer GC Recklinghausen (1974)   **120**

Phone: 02361 26520

Bockholter Str 475, 4350 Recklinghausen

North west of Recklinghausen near Loemühle airport

Holes	18 Par 72 6111m.
Visitors	Welcome
Fees	DM35–50
Facilities	Bar and restaurant; practice ground
Pro	U Lechtermann

Warendorfer GC An der Ems (1987)   **121**

Phone: 02586 1792

Vohren 41, 4410 Warendorf

Just east of Warendorf off the B64 towards Sassenberg

Holes	9 Par 36 3080m.
Visitors	Welcome
Fees	DM30–50
Facilities	Bar and restaurant; practice ground
Pro	K Phillips

GC Wasserburg-Anholt (1972)   **122**

Phone: 02874 3444

Am Schloss 3, 4294 Isselburg-Anholt

10km west of Bocholt off the A3 via the B67 through Rees-Loom towards Killingen and Anholt

Holes	18 Par 72 6141m.
Visitors	Welcome, but must book. Closed December to March
Fees	DM35–60
Facilities	Bar and restaurant;
Pro	F di Matteo

GC Wentorf Reinbeker (1901)   **123**

Phone: 040 7202141

Golfstr 2, 2057 Wentorf

South east of Hamburg off the B5 and B207

Holes	18 Par 70 5686m.
Visitors	Welcome; weekends with member only
Fees	DM50–60
Facilities	Bar and restaurant; practice ground
Pro	J Galbraith

Golf Club Werl (1973)   **124**

Phone: 02922 2522

Unnaer Strasse 23, 4760 Werl

South of Werl off the B63 towards the NATO complex

Holes	9 Par 33 2320m.
Visitors	Must book. Course closed December to February
Fees	DM25–30
Facilities	Bar and restaurant; practice ground
Pro	A Grandison

GC Weserbergland Polle (1982) **125**
Phone: 05535 270
3453 Polle, Weissenfelder Mühle
North west of Holzminden off the B83 near Polle

Holes	18 Par 72 6114m.
Visitors	Welcome
Fees	DM40–50
Facilities	Bar and restaurant; practice ground
Pro	N Savazal

Westfälischer GC Gütersloh (1968) **126**
Phone: 05244 2340
Gütersloher Str 127, 4835 Rietberg 2
South east of Gütersloh towards Rietberg

Holes	18 Par 72 6135m.
Visitors	Welcome, but must book
Fees	DM50–70
Facilities	Bar and restaurant; practice ground
Pro	Dirk Randolff

GC Widukind-Land (1987) **127**
Phone: 05228 7050
Auf dem Stickdorn 65, 4972 Löhne Wittel
West of Bad Oeynhausen off the A2, towards
Löhne

Holes	12 (played as 18) Par 73 6243m.
Visitors	Welcome, but must book
Fees	DM 30–50
Facilities	Bar and restaurant closed January/ February
Pro	Peter Koenig

GC Wildeshausen (1978) **128**
Phone: 04431 1232
Glanerstrasse, 2878 Wildeshausen
North west of Wildeshausen off the B213

Holes	9 Par 36 3040m.
Visitors	Welcome; weekends with member only
Fees	DM20–30
Facilities	Bar and restaurant; practice ground
Pro	R Foster

GC Wilhelmshaven (1980) **129**
Phone: 04421 42242
Raffineriestr, 2940 Wilhelmshaven
8km north of Wilhelmshaven towards Hooksiel
and Vosslapp

Holes	9 Par 36 3298m.
Visitors	Welcome, but must book
Fees	DM30–40
Facilities	Bar and restaurant; practice ground; swimming pool
Pro	D Sanders

GC Winterberg (1961) **130**
Phone: 02981 1770
In der Büre, 5788 Winterberg
Just north west of Winterberg off the B480

Holes	9 Par 35 2840m.
Visitors	Welcome. Course closed November to March
Fees	DM30–50
Facilities	Bar and restaurant
Pro	I Clegg

GC Worpswede (1974) **131**
Phone: 04763 7313
2864 Vollersode, Gielermühlen-Vollersode
North of Worpswede off the B74 through
Giehlermühle towards Steden

Holes	18 Par 71 5865m.
Visitors	Welcome
Fees	DM50–60
Facilities	Bar and restaurant; practice ground
Pro	D MacLauchlan

GC Wümme (1986) **132**
Phone: 04263 3352
Hof Emmen Westerholz, 2723 Scheeseel
Just north of Rotenburg off the B75 towards
Abbendorf

Holes	9 Par 36 3071m.
Visitors	Welcome, but must book
Fees	DM30–40
Facilities	Bar and restaurant closed Monday
Pro	Kenton Wright

Berlin

Berlin-Wannsee GC (1895) **133**
Phone: 030 8055075
Am Stölpchenweg, 1000 Berlin 39
South west of Berlin via the A15 through
Nikolassee to Wannsee

Holes	9 Par 35 2845m.
Visitors	Welcome
Fees	DM30–40
Facilities	Bar and restaurant
Pro	U Tapperthofen

In the 1930s the German Amateur Championship
was held here and was won by Henry Longhurst.
It is a miracle that the club survived the
depredations of the Cold War but it is still there
on the outskirts of Berlin and amounts to an
interesting and well-balanced parkland course.

SOUTHERN GERMANY

Allgäuer Golf- und Landclub (1984) 1
Phone: 08332 1310
Hofgut Boschach, 8942 Ottobeuren
Just south of Ottobeuren towards Eldern

Holes	18 Par 72 6125m.
Visitors	Welcome. Course closed November to April
Fees	DM50–70
Facilities	Bar and restaurant; practice ground
Pro	M Chesters

GC Altötting-Burghausen Schloss Piesing (1988) 2
Phone: 08678 7001
Piesing 2, 8261 Haiming
To the north east of Burghausen towards Haiming

Holes	18 Par 69 5081m.
Visitors	Welcome
Fees	DM50–60
Facilities	Bar and restaurant closed Monday; practice ground
Pro	Horst Rosenkranz

The stylish old castle sits at the hub of this club, which has plans to extend its course during 1993. It is a very attractive parkland course where the main hazards are presented by a stream and several lakes; there are many lovely trees on the course.

GC Ansbach (1960) 3
Phone: 09803 262
Hotel Schloss Colmberg, 8801 Colmberg
15km north west of Ansbach, via Neunstetten and Colmberg

Holes	9 Par 33 2380m.
Visitors	Welcome. Course closed December to March
Fees	DM40
Facilities	Bar and restaurant; practice ground
Pro	M Woodhouse

Aschaffenburger GC (1980) 4
Phone: 06024 7140
Am Heigenberg 30, 8759 Hösbach/Feldkahl
North of Aschaffenburg off the A3. Take the Hösbach exit towards Mömbris

Holes	9 Par 34 2500m.
Visitors	Welcome except Wednesday pm and Thursday pm
Fees	DM50–60
Facilities	Bar and restaurant closed Monday; practice ground
Pro	Mark Richardson

GC Augsburg (1959) 5
Phone: 08234 5621
Engelshofer Str 2, 8903 Bobingen-Burgwalden
South west of Augsburg off the B17N to Burgwalden

Holes	18 Par 71 5833m.
Visitors	Welcome. Closed December to April
Fees	DM50–70
Facilities	Bar and restaurant; practice ground
Pro	P Ries

On the outskirts of the renowned medieval city of Augsburg, this is a difficult course on which to score well. It is laid out over quite hilly ground, with narrow fairways and many water hazards and therefore puts a premium on accuracy and sensible tactics.

GC Bad Herrenalb-Bernbach (1968) 6
Phone: 07083 8898
Berbacherstr, 7506 Bad Herrenalb
East of Baden-Baden off the B462 towards Gernsbach; turn to Bad Herrenalb

Holes	9 Par 34 2610m.
Visitors	Welcome
Fees	DM40–50
Facilities	Bar and restaurant; practice ground
Pro	P Congreve

Bad Kissingen GC (1911) 7

Phone: 0971 3608

Euerdorferstr 11, 8730 Bad Kissingen
Just south of Bad Kissingen off the B287
towards Hammelburg

Holes	18 Par 70 5680m.
Visitors	Welcome, but must book at weekends. Course closed December to March
Fees	DM50–60
Facilities	Bar and restaurant; practice ground
Pro	Ian Dibb

This relatively short course is great fun because
of the River Saale which runs right through it.
It affects the play on most of the holes and is a
particular problem on the 3rd, 11th, 15th and
17th holes where it runs all the way alongside
the fairways.

GC Bad Liebenzell (1989) 8

Phone: 07052 1574

Golfplatz 3, 7263 Bad Liebenzell
Just north east of Bad Liebenzell off the B295

Holes	18 Par 7235 6119m.
Visitors	Welcome
Fees	DM50–70
Facilities	Bar and restaurant
Pro	Werner Linnenfelser

GC Bad Mergentheim (1971) 9

Phone: 07931 7579

Erlenbachtal 36, 6990 Bad Mergentheim
East of Bad Mergentheim off the B290 towards
Iggerseim and Erlenbachtal

Holes	9 Par 32 2115m.
Visitors	Welcome. Course closed December to February
Fees	DM35–45
Facilities	Bar and restaurant; practice ground
Pro	H Laird

GC Bad Nauheim (1956) 10

Phone: 06032 2153

Am Golfplatz, 6350 Bad Nauheim
In north Bad Nauheim

Holes	9 Par 34 2720m.
Visitors	Welcome. Course closed December to February
Fees	DM40–50
Facilities	Bar and restaurant; practice ground
Pro	B Raschke

GC Bad Neuenahr-Ahrweiler (1979) 11

Phone: 02641 2325

Remagenerweg, 5483 Bad Neuenahr-Ahrweiler
East of Bad Neuenahr off the B266 near
Lohrsdorf

Holes	18 Par 72 6075m.
Visitors	Welcome, but must book
Fees	DM50–75
Facilities	Bar and restaurant; practice ground; tennis; horseriding
Pro	M Nickel

GC Bad Tölz (1983) 12

Phone: 08041 9994

Strass 124, 8170 Wackersberg/Bad Tölz
Just west of Bad Tölz

Holes	9 Par 36 2942m.
Visitors	Welcome on weekdays, at weekends with member. Course closed November to April
Fees	DM40
Facilities	Bar and restaurant
Pro	Stephen Rohrsetzer

A charming nine hole course which is nearly
1000 feet up in the mountains. The views of the
woods and the steepling terrain are delightful
and there are many other courses within a 30
mile radius of Bad Tölz.

GC Bad Wörishofen (1978) 13

Phone: 08346 777

Schlingenerstr 27, 8951 Rieden
South east of Bad Wörishofen through Rieden

Holes	18 Par 71 5952m.
Visitors	Welcome (public course). Course closed December to March
Fees	DM50–70
Facilities	Bar and restaurant; practice ground
Pro	M Seidel

GC Bad Wildungen (1930) 14

Phone: 05621 2260

Talquellenweg, 3590 Bad Wildungen
In south Bad Wildungen

Holes	9 Par 35 2835m.
Visitors	Welcome
Fees	DM35–45
Facilities	Bar and restaurant; practice ground
Pro	A Stein

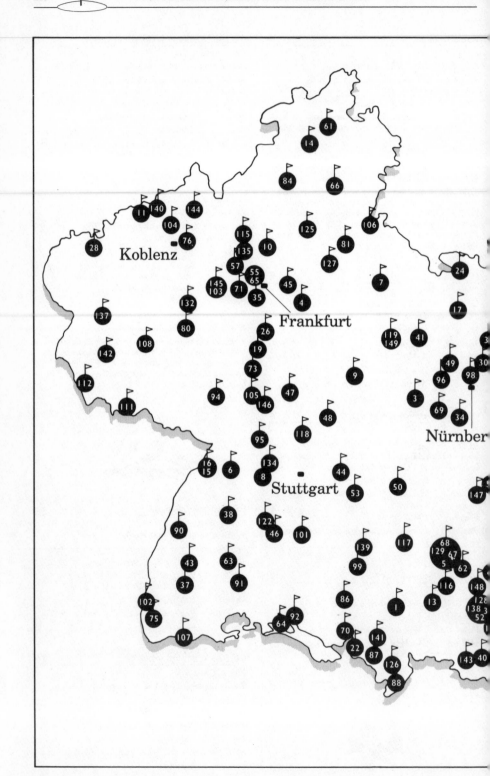

Koblenz

Frankfurt

Nürnber

Stuttgart

SOUTHERN GERMANY

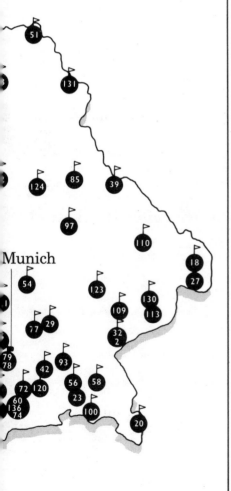

GC Baden-Baden (1901) 15

Phone: 07221 23579

Fremersbergstr 127, 7570 Baden-Baden

West of Baden-Baden off the A5

Holes	18 Par 64 4413m.
Visitors	Welcome. Course closed December to February
Fees	DM65–90
Facilities	Bar and restaurant closed Monday; practice ground
Pro	Erich Totzke

Baden-Hills Golf & Curling Club (1982) 16

Phone: 07221 682339

7550 Rastatt

North west of Baden-Baden towards Hugelsheim on the B36

Holes	18 Par 71 5672m.
Visitors	Welcome, but must book
Fees	DM20–30
Facilities	Bar and restaurant; practice ground
Pro	R Walker

GC Bamberg (1973) 17

Phone: 09547 1524

Gut Leimershof, 8613 Breitengüssbach

North east of Bamberg via the B173, to Gut Leimershof

Holes	18 Par 72 6175m.
Visitors	Welcome. Course closed December to March
Fees	DM40–60
Facilities	Bar and restaurant; practice ground
Pro	P Godefroy

Golf und Landclub Bayerwald (1970) 18

Phone: 08581 1040

Frauenwaldstrasse 2, 8392 Waldkirchen

Just south east of Waldkirchen off the B12

Holes	9 Par 36 3021m.
Visitors	Welcome (public course). Closed November to April
Fees	DM35–45
Facilities	Bar and restaurant; practice ground
Pro	S Case

GC Bensheim (1989) 19

Phone: 06251 67731
Ausserhalb 56, 6150 Bensheim 1
South of Bensheim off the B47

Holes	9 Par 36 3105m.
Visitors	Welcome
Fees	DM50–70
Facilities	Bar and restaurant; practice ground

GC Berchtesgaden (1955) 20

Phone: 08652 2100
Obersalzberg, 8240 Berchtesgaden
Just east of Berchtesgaden at Obersalzburg

Holes	9 Par 34 2567m.
Visitors	Welcome. Course closed December to April
Fees	DM40–60
Facilities	Bar and restaurant; practice ground

GC Beuerberg (1982) 21

Phone: 08179 617
Gut Sterz, 8196 Beuerberg
North of Penzberg through Sterz

Holes	18 Par 73 6036m.
Visitors	Welcome on weekdays. Course closed January to April
Fees	DM80
Facilities	Bar and restaurant; practice ground
Pro	Andy Hahn

GC Bodensee-Weissensberg (1986) 22

Phone: 08389 89190
Lampertsweiler 51, 8995 Weissensberg
Just north of Lindau via the B12 to Kempten

Holes	18 Par 71 6112m.
Visitors	Welcome. Course closed January
Fees	DM70–90
Facilities	Bar and restaurant; practice ground
Pro	C Potts

Chiemsee GC Prien (1961) 23

Phone: 08051 62215
8210 Prien-Bauernberg
Just south of Prien

Holes	9 Par 36 2956m.
Visitors	Welcome. Course closed December to April
Fees	DM40–50
Facilities	Bar and restaurant; practice ground
Pro	R Krause

GC Coburg Schloss Tambach (1981) 24

Phone: 09567 1212
Schloss Tambach, 8636 Weitramsdorf
West of Coburg towards Schweinefurt

Holes	9 Par 36 3080m.
Visitors	Welcome. Clubhouse closed December to March
Fees	DM40–50
Facilities	Bar and restaurant closed Monday and December to March; practice ground
Pro	David Entwhistle

GC Dachau (1965) 25

Phone: 08131 10879
an der Flosslände, 8060 Dachau
North of München via the B304 to Dachau-East

Holes	9 Par 36 2960m.
Visitors	Welcome, but must book. Course closed December to April
Fees	DM40–60
Facilities	Bar and restaurant; practice ground

GC Darmstadt-Traisa (1973) 26

Phone: 06151 146543
Dippelshof, 6109 Mühltal-Traisa
South east of Darmstadt at Traisa

Holes	9 Par 33 2514m.
Visitors	Welcome
Fees	DM50–65
Facilities	Bar and restaurant; practice ground
Pro	N Coles

Donau Golfclub Rassbach (1989) 27

Phone: 08501 1313
Rassbach 8, 8391 Thyrnau bei Passau
North east of Passau off the B388 between Kellberg and Hauzenberg

Holes	18 Par 72 6097m.
Visitors	Welcome. Course closed December to January
Fees	DM40–50
Facilities	Bar and restaurant; practice ground
Pro	Phil Leech

Donau is a pretty tough customer, laid out over very undulating ground and with a number of dog-leg holes which counsel accuracy from the tee. There are lots of water hazards, too, and they affect more than half the holes.

GC Eifel (1979) **28**
Phone: 06593 1241
Kölner Strasse, 5533 Hilleheim-Berndorf
Just north east of Hilleshiem off the B421
towards Berndorf
Holes   9 Par 36 3090m.
Visitors   Welcome, except Sunday
Fees   DM35–70
Facilities   Bar and restaurant closed Tuesday;
            practice ground
Pro   Colin Gess

GC Erding-Grünbach (1973) **29**
Phone: 08122 6465
Am Kellerberg, 8059 Grünbach-Erding
East of Erding in Grünbach
Holes   18 Par 72 6158m.
Visitors   Welcome. Course closed December to
            March
Fees   DM50–70
Facilities   Bar and restaurant; practice ground
Pro   E Dimmitt

GC Erlangen (1977) **30**
Phone: 09126 5040
Am Schleinhof, 8524 Kleinsendlbach
East of Erlangen off the B2
Holes   9 Par 32 2166m.
Visitors   Welcome. Course closed December to
            March
Fees   DM30–40
Facilities   Bar and restaurant; practice ground
Pro   W Hachey

GC Eschenried (1984) **31**
Phone: 08131 3238
Kurfürstenweg 10, 8066 Eschenried
North west of München at Eschenried
Holes   18 Par 72 6088m.
Visitors   Welcome
Fees   DM60–80
Facilities   Bar and restaurant closed Monday;
            practice ground; tennis
Pro   Adrian Parish
The course runs through a nature reserve and
has some lovely old trees. Many water hazards,
some very large and oddly-shaped bunkers and
marshy areas just off the fairways make the
course interesting and quite difficult.

GC Falkenhof (1985) **32**
Phone: 08678 8996
Falkenhof 1, 8261 Marktl/Inn-Oberpising
North of Burghausen off the B12 at exit Marktl
Holes   9 Par 36 2956m.
Visitors   Welcome. Course closed December to
            February
Fees   DM50
Facilities   Bar and restaurant; practice ground
Pro   Robert McNeilly

GC Feldafing (1926) **33**
Phone: 08157 7005
Tutzingerstr 15, 8133 Feldafing
In Feldafing
Holes   18 Par 71 5708m.
Visitors   Welcome on weekdays. Course closed
            December to March
Fees   DM60
Facilities   Bar and restaurant; practice ground;
            short course
Pro   T Flossman
Feldafing is one of Germany's oldest golf courses
and one of its most splendidly situated. Welcome
to golf in Bavaria! Feldafing enjoys an idyllic
location nestling peacefully beside Lake
Starnberg, once the playground of Bavarian
nobility. With the not-so-distant mountains
providing a magnificent backcloth, it is difficult
to believe that Munich is only 20 miles to the
north east. By modern standards Feldafing is not
a long course but there are several tricky holes
and each of the par 3s is potentially a card
wrecker.

GC Franken Abenberg (1988) **34**
Phone 09178 5541
Am Golfplatz 19, 8549 Abenberg
South west of Schwabach off the A6. Take the
Schwabach exit towards Abenberg
Holes   18 Par 72 6127m.
Visitors   Welcome
Fees   DM60–80
Facilities   Bar and restaurant; practice ground
Pro   J Twigg

Frankfurter Golf Club (1913)   35

Phone: 069 6662318

Golfstr 41, 6000 Frankfurt am Main 71

In south Frankfurt 6km from the castle, near the airport

Holes	18 Par 71 5860m.
Visitors	Welcome, but must book
Fees	DM75–95
Facilities	Bar and restaurant; practice ground
Pro	H Strüver

Designed by Harry Colt, Frankfurter GC is rated as one of Germany's best courses and has staged the German Open on many occasions; both Tony Jacklin and Seve Ballesteros have won the championship here. It is a stern test where golfers must use every club in the bag. The fairways run through thick forest and the 11 par 4s average around 430 yards; the greens are sizeable and very well-defended by bunkers.

GC Fränkische Schweiz (1972)   36

Phone: 09194 4827

Kanndorf 8, 8553 Ebermannstadt

Just east of Ebermannstadt at Kanndorf

Holes	18 Par 72 6050m.
Visitors	Welcome. Course closed November to March
Fees	DM350–70
Facilities	Bar and restaurant; practice ground
Pro	David Blakeman

Freiburger GC (1970)   37

Phone: 07661 5569

Krüttweg, 7815 Kirchzarten

East of Freiburg off the B31 towards Titisee; turn at Littenweiler to Kappel

Holes	18 Par 72 6068m.
Visitors	Welcome
Fees	DM50–60
Facilities	Bar and restaurant; practice ground
Pro	P Weggenmann

Freudenstadt GC (1928)   38

Phone: 07441 3060

Hohenrieder Strasse, 7290 Freudenstadt

In the south east of Freudenstadt off the B28

Holes	9 Par 35 2930m.
Visitors	Welcome
Fees	DM55
Facilities	Bar and restaurant; practice ground
Pro	Stephen Ramsden

GC Furth im Wald (1982)   39

Phone: 09973 1240

Voithenberg 1, 8492 Furth im Wald

Just north west of Furth im Wald towards Voithenberg

Holes	9 Par 35 2952m.
Visitors	Welcome. Course closed December to April
Fees	DM30–40
Facilities	Bar and restaurant; practice ground
Pro	I Stewart

Garmisch-Partenkirchen GC (1928)   40

Phone: 08824 8344

Gut Buchwies, 8106 Oberau

North east of Garmisch off the A95, towards Buchwies in Oberau

Holes	18 Par 72 6050m.
Visitors	Welcome. By introduction only at weekends. Course closed November to April
Fees	DM65–80
Facilities	Bar and restaurant; practice ground
Pro	A Hagl

GC Geiselwind im Steigerwald (1987)   41

Phone: 09556 1777

Friedrichstrasse 10, 8614 Geiselwind

Just north of Geiselwind

Holes	18 Par 73 6365m.
Visitors	Welcome. Course closed November to February
Fees	DM40–60
Facilities	Bar and restaurant; practice ground

GC Grafing-Oberelkofen (1982)   42

Phone: 08092 3701

Hochreiterhof 7, 8018 Grafing-Oberelkofen

Just south of Grafing

Holes	9 Par 36 2937m.
Visitors	Welcome. Course closed December to March
Fees	DM45–60
Facilities	Bar and restaurant; practice ground
Pro	K Sparkes

GC Gütermann Gutach (1924)   **43**
Phone: 07681 21346
Golfstrasse, 7809 Gutach/Breisgau
North east of Frieburg off the B294 in Gutach
Holes   9 Par 34 2630m.
Visitors   Welcome. Course closed December to March
Fees   DM40–60
Facilities Bar and restaurant; practice ground
Pro   D Pugh

GC Haghof (1983)   **44**
Phone: 07182 3040
Alfdorf 2, 7077 Aldorf/Haghof
South of Welzheim at Haghof
Holes   9 Par 35 2932m.
Visitors   Welcome weekdays
Fees   DM40
Facilities Bar and restaurant; practice ground
Pro   B Reilly

Hanau Golfclub (1959)   **45**
Phone: 06181 82071
Wilhelmsbader Allee 32, 6450 Hanau-Wilhelmsbad
East of Frankfurt at Wilhelmsbad
Holes   18 Par 72 6192m.
Visitors   Welcome weekdays
Fees   DM60–80
Facilities Bar and restaurant closed Monday; practice ground
Pro   Martin Day

GC Hechingen-Hohenzollern (1955)   **46**
Phone: 07471 2600
7450 Hechingen, Hagelwasen
Just west of Hechingen; turn off at the Fasanengarten/Weilheim sign in Hechingen
Holes   9 Par 35 5708m.
Visitors   Welcome weekdays. Course closed November to April
Fees   DM35
Facilities Bar and restaurant; practice ground
Pro   K Schieban

GC Heidelberg-Lobenfeld (1968)   **47**
Phone: 06226 40490
Biddersbacherhof, 6921 Lobbach-Lobenfeld
East of Heidelberg via the B292, through Aglasterhausen
Holes   18 Par 72 6235m.
Visitors   Welcome. Course closed November to March
Fees   DM50–70
Facilities Bar and restaurant; practice ground
Pro   G Illingworth

GC Heilbronn-Hohenlohe (1964)   **48**
Phone: 07941 62801
7111 Öhringen-Friedrichsruhe
North east of Heilbronn off the A6. Take the Öhringen exit towards Zweiflingen/Friedrichsruhe
Holes   18 Par 71 6116m.
Visitors   Welcome; by introduction only at weekends. Course closed November to April
Fees   DM50–70
Facilities Bar and restaurant; practice ground
Pro   B Amara

GC Herzogenaurach (1967)   **49**
Phone: 09132 83628
8522 Herzogenaurach
North east of Herzogenaurach off the A3 at the Herzo-Base (US base course)
Holes   9 Par 36 3108m.
Visitors   By introduction only
Fees   DM25–35
Facilities Bar and restaurant; practice ground

GC Hochstatt-Härtsfeld-Reis (1981)   **50**
Phone: 07326 7979
Hofgut Hochstatt, 7086 Neresheim
North east of Heidenheim off the B466, head for Dischingen after Neresheim
Holes   9 Par 36 3085m.
Visitors   Welcome. Course closed November to March
Fees   DM25–30
Facilities Bar and restaurant; practice ground
Pro   P Smith

GC Hof (1985)   51

Phone: 09281 43749

Gattendorf, 8671 Hof-Haidt

North east of Hof via the B173 through Haidt

Holes	9 Par 36 3105m.
Visitors	Welcome. Course closed December to April
Fees	DM45–60
Facilities	Bar and restaurant; practice ground
Pro	Ladislav Bartunek

Golf Club Hohenpähl (1988)   52

Phone: 08808 1330

Gut Hochschloss, 8121 Pähl

40km south east of Munich, and north east of Pähl off the B2 towards Weilheim

Holes	18 Par 71 6073m.
Visitors	Welcome weekdays; weekends with member. Course closed December to March
Fees	DM60–80
Facilities	Bar and restaurant closed Monday; practice ground
Pro	John Bradley

GC Hohenstaufen (1959)   53

Phone: 07162 27171

Unter dem Ramsberg, 7322 Donzdorf

East of Göppingen in Donzdorf

Holes	9 Par 36 3120m.
Visitors	Welcome. Course closed December to March
Fees	DM35–45
Facilities	Bar and restaurant; practice ground
Pro	R Miller

Golf und Landclub Holledau (1986)   54

Phone: 08756 1700

Weihern 3, 8301 Rudelzhausen

South of Mainburg in Au

Holes	18 Par 72 6105m.
Visitors	Welcome. Course closed December to March
Fees	DM50–70
Facilities	Bar and restaurant; practice ground; short course
Pro	T Paterson

Homburger GC (1899)   55

Phone: 06172 38808

Saalburgchaussee 2a, 6380 Bad Homburg

West of Bad Homburg off the A661 at Oberürsel-West. Go towards Usingen/Saalburg on the B456

Holes	10 Par 34 2652m.
Visitors	Welcome, but must book
Fees	DM30–50
Facilities	Bar and restaurant;
Pro	F Tauber

GC Höslwang im Chiemgau (1975)   56

Phone: 08075 714

8201 Höslwang/Chiemgau Gut Kronberg

North of Bad Endorf at Gut Kronberg

Holes	9 Par 35 6210m.
Visitors	Welcome. Course closed December to April
Fees	DM35–70
Facilities	Bar and restaurant closed Tuesday; practice ground
Pro	Francesco Carli

GC Idstein-Wörsdorf Gut Henriettenthal (1989)   57

Phone: 06126 8866

Am Nassen Berg, 6270 Idstein

North of Idstein off the A3. Take the Idstein exit towards Wörsdorf/Henriettenthal

Holes	18 Par 72
Visitors	Welcome, but must book
Fees	DM50–70
Facilities	Bar and restaurant; practice ground

GC Im Chiemgau (1982)   58

Phone: 08669 7557

Kötzing 1, 8224 Chieming-Hart

North of Chieming through Sordermoning to Hart/Knesing

Holes	18 Par 72 6070m.
Visitors	Welcome. Course closed December to April
Fees	DM45–70
Facilities	Bar and restaurant; practice ground; short course
Pro	G Thomson

GC Ingolstadt (1977)   59
Phone: 0841 85778
Gerolfingerstr, 8070 Ingolstadt-Spitzelmühle
Just west of Ingolstadt towards Friedrichshofen
and Klinikum
Holes   9 Par 35 3009m.
Visitors   Welcome. Course closed December to
             March
Fees   DM5–700
Facilities   Bar and restaurant; practice ground
Pro   J Pugh

GC Isarwinkel (1985)   60
Phone: 08041 3210
Flint Kaserne, 8170 Bad Tölz
East of Bad Tölz in the grounds of the US base
Holes   9 Par 32 2113m.
Visitors   Welcome. Course closed December to
             March
Fees   DM20–30
Facilities   Bar and restaurant; practice ground

GC Kassel-Wilhelmshöhe (1958)   61
Phone: 0561 33509
Am Ehlener Kreuz, 3500 Kassel
5km west of Kassel in the 'Habichtswald'
Holes   18 Par 70 5675m.
Visitors   Welcome. Course closed December to
             March
Fees   DM40–60
Facilities   Bar and restaurant; practice ground
Pro   P Smith

GC Königsbrunn (1986)   62
Phone: 08231 31153
Benzstrasse 25, 8901 Königsbrunn
South of Augsburg near Mering
Holes   9 Par 33 1923m.
Visitors   Welcome. Course closed December to
             March
Fees   DM25–35
Facilities   Bar and restaurant; practice ground

Golf and Countryclub Königsfeld (1990) 63
Phone: 07725 7159
7744 Königsfeld/Martinsweiler
North of Königsfeld off the A81
Holes   18 Par 70 6130m.
Visitors   Welcome. Course closed December to
             March
Fees   DM36–50
Facilities   Bar and restaurant; practice ground;
             swimming pool; tennis

Konstanz GC (1965)   64
Phone: 07533 5124
Kargegg 1, 7753 Allensbach 3, Langenrain
North west of Konstanz. After Allensbach head
for Langenrain
Holes   18 Par 72 6100m.
Visitors   Welcome
Fees   DM50–70
Facilities   Bar and restaurant; practice ground
Pro   M Bingger

Kronberg GC (1954)   65
Phone: 06173 1426
Schloss Friedrichshof, 6242 Kronberg
North west of Frankfurt off the B455
Holes   18 Par 68 5365m.
Visitors   Introduction only at weekends
Fees   DM50–70
Facilities   Bar and restaurant; practice ground
Pro   A Schilling
The great attraction of this course is its location
in the grounds which surround a beautiful
castle, which you can see from many of the
fairways. It is quite a short and hilly course with
some excellent par 4s, many of them designed as
dog-legs.

Kurhessischer GC Oberaula (1988)   66
Phone: 06628 1573
Am Golfplatz, 6435 Oberaula-Hausen
West of Bad Hersfeld off the A7 at Oberaula
Holes   18 Par 72 6100m.
Visitors   Welcome, but must book
Fees   DM50–70
Facilities   Bar and restaurant; practice ground

GC Auf dem Lechfeld Königsbrunn (1984)   67

Phone: 08231 32637
Föllstrasse 32a, 8901 Königsbrunn
South of Augsburg off the B17 at exit
Königsbrunn-Nord

Holes	9 Par 36 2891m.
Visitors	Welcome. Course closed November to March
Fees	DM35–50
Facilities	Bar and restaurant; practice ground
Pro	D Johnson

GC Leitershofen (1982)   68

Phone: 0821 434919
Deuringerstr, 8901 Stadtbergen/Augsburg
Just south west of Augsburg

Holes	9 Par 36 3090m.
Visitors	Welcome. Course closed December to April
Fees	DM25–30
Facilities	Bar and restaurant; practice ground
Pro	P Garnier-Bradley

GC Lichtenau-Weickershof (1980)   69

Phone: 09827 6907
Weickershof 1, 8814 Lichtenau
East of Ansbach through Lichtenau

Holes	18 Par 72 6070m.
Visitors	Welcome
Fees	DM50–70
Facilities	Bar and restaurant; practice ground
Pro	F Piater

GC Lindau-Bad Schachen (1954)   70

Phone: 08382 78090
Am Schönbühl, 8990 Lindau/Bodensee
Just north of Lindau

Holes	18 Par 70 5690m.
Visitors	Welcome
Fees	DM60–80
Facilities	Bar and restaurant; practice ground
Pro	R Richardson

GC Main-Taunus (1979)   71

Phone: 06122 52550
Auf der Heide, 6200 Wiesbaden-Delkenheim
East of Wiesbaden near Delkenheim

Holes	18 Par 72 6044m.
Visitors	Welcome
Fees	DM70–90
Facilities	Bar and restaurant; practice ground
Pro	D Howard

GC Mangfalltal (1987)   72

Phone: 08063 6300
Oed 1, 8152 Feldkirchen-Westerham
North of Feldkirchen towards Glonn

Holes	9 Par 35 2956m.
Visitors	Welcome. Course closed November to March
Fees	DM40–55
Facilities	Bar and restaurant; practice ground
Pro	R Birch

Mannheim-Viernheim GC (1970)   73

Phone: 06204 78737
Alte Mannheimer Str, 6806 Viernheim
North east of Mannheim

Holes	9 Par 36 3125m.
Visitors	Welcome weekdays; at weekends with member. Course closed Monday
Fees	DM50–60
Facilities	Bar and restaurant; practice ground
Pro	Clive Jenkins

GC Margarethenhof/Tegernsee (1982)   74

Phone: 08022 74031
Gut Steinberg, 8184 Gmund am Tegernsee
West of Gmund towards Bad Tölz on the B472;
then head for Marienstein

Holes	18 Par 72 6010m.
Visitors	Welcome. Course closed December to April
Fees	DM40–60
Facilities	Bar and restaurant; practice ground
Pro	F Bernardi

GC Markgräflerland (1984) 75

Phone: 07626 6609

Am Siedlungshof, Villa Umbach, 7842 Kandern
Just west of Kandern

Holes	9 Par 36 3051m.
Visitors	Welcome, but must book
Fees	DM40–60
Facilities	Bar and restaurant; practice ground
Pro	I Martin

Mittelrheinischer GC Bad Ems (1928) 76

Phone: 02603 6541

Denzerheide, 4527 Bad Ems
Just north of Bad Ems in the Nassau Nature
Park

Holes	18 Par 72 6050m.
Visitors	Welcome. Closed December to March
Fees	DM50–75
Facilities	Bar and restaurant; practice ground
Pro	J Dixon

Bad Ems was the main venue for the German Open before World War II and Henry Cotton won the 1939 championship here. It is located on the Denzerheide hills above the city and from the undulating fairways there are fine views over the Eifel and the Taunus. The second half is the less severe part of the course and the 18th is a delightful finishing hole. The clubhouse has accommodation.

GC München-Nord Eichenried (1989) 77

Phone: 08123 1005

Münchener Strasse 55, 8059 Eichenried
North east of München at Eichenried

Holes	18 Par 73 6125m.
Visitors	Welcome on weekdays; at weekends with member. Course closed December to January
Fees	DM70–90
Facilities	Bar and restaurant; indoor practice ground
Pro	Graham Stewart

Münchener GC Strasslach (1910) 78

Phone: 08170 450

Tölzerstrasse, 8021 Strasslach
South of München through Pullach to Strasslach

Holes	18 Par 72 6066m.
Visitors	Welcome, but must book
Fees	DM70–90
Facilities	Bar and restaurant; practice ground
Pro	A Castillo-Fernandez

This is an ideal holiday course since it is by no means exacting, with wide fairways laid out over rolling terrain. The views of the Bavarian Alps are delightful.

Münchener GC Thalkirchen (1910) 79

Phone: 089 7231304

Zentralländstr 40, 8000 München
In München head for Tierpark Hellabrun at Thalkirchen

Holes	9 Par 34 2528m.
Visitors	Welcome. Course closed December to March
Fees	DM70
Facilities	Bar and restaurant; practice ground

GC Nahetal (1971) 80

Phone: 06708 3755

Drei Buchen, 6550 Kreuznah
Just southwest of Bad Münster, on the B379 opposite the exit to Schloss Ebernburg

Holes	18 Par 72 6075m.
Visitors	Welcome, but must book
Fees	DM40–60
Facilities	Bar and restaurant; practice ground
Pro	H Goerke

GC Neuhof (1989) 81

Phone: 06102 37010

Hofgut Neuhof, 6072 Dreieich
Just south of Frankfurt via the A661 to Dreieich

Holes	18 Par 72 5995m.
Visitors	Welcome weekdays. Course closed January/February
Fees	DM70–90
Facilities	Bar and restaurant closed Monday; practice ground
Pro	Gerd Petermann-Casanova

GC Neumarkt (1988) 82

Phone: 09186 1574

Ruppertslohe 18, 8451 Lauterhofen
North east of Neumarkt off the A6 at exit Alfeld; head for Lauterhofen

Holes	9 Par 36 3030m.
Visitors	Welcome. Course closed December to February
Fees	DM40–50
Facilities	Bar and restaurant closed Monday; practice ground
Pro	Scott Jobson

GC Oberfranken (1965)   83

Phone: 09228 1022

Petershof 1, 8656 Thurnau

15km north west of Bayreuth via the B505 to Thurnau

Holes	18 Par 72 6152m.
Visitors	Welcome. Course closed December to March
Fees	DM40–60
Facilities	Bar and restaurant; practice ground
Pro	A Parker

Oberhessischer GC (1973)   84

Phone: 06427 8558

Maximilianenhof, 3553 Cölbe-Bernsdorf

North east of Marburg. In Cöoble-Bernsdorf turn for Reddehausen

Holes	9 Par 36 3050m.
Visitors	Welcome
Fees	DM30–50
Facilities	Bar and restaurant closed Monday; practice ground
Pro	Trevor Rigby

GC Oberpfälzer Wald (1977)   85

Phone: 09439 466

Oedengrup, 8461 Kemnath bb/Fuhrn, Neunburg vorm Wald

West of Neunburg in Kemnath bei Fuhrn

Holes	18 Par 72 6060m.
Visitors	Welcome (public course). Closed December to April
Fees	DM40–50
Facilities	Bar and restaurant; practice ground
Pro	D Holloway

GC Oberschwaben-Bad Waldsee (1969)   86

Phone: 07524 5900

Fürstl Hofgut Hopfenweiler, 7967 Bad Waldsee

On the north east side of Bad Waldsee

Holes	18 Par 72 6148m.
Visitors	Welcome. Course closed December to February
Fees	DM55–75
Facilities	Bar and restaurant; practice ground
Pro	Thomas Schinnenburg

GC Oberstaufen-Steibis (1987)   87

Phone: 08386 8529

In der Au 5, 8974 Oberstaufen-Steibis

South of Oberstaufen towards the Hochgratbahn/Steibis

Holes	9 Par 36 3065m.
Visitors	Welcome. Course closed November to March
Fees	DM45–60
Facilities	Bar and restaurant; practice ground
Pro	K Vince

Oberstdorf GC (1961)   88

Phone: 08322 2895

Gebrgoibe 1, 8980 Oberstdorf

Just south of Oberstdorf towards Flugschanze

Holes	9 Par 35 2782m.
Visitors	Welcome. Course closed November to May
Fees	DM40–55
Facilities	Bar and restaurant; practice ground
Pro	B Rowe

GC Olching (1979)   89

Phone: 08142 3240

Feurstr 89, 8037 Olching

West of München at Olching

Holes	18 Par 72 6094m.
Visitors	Welcome, but must book at weekends
Fees	DM65–80
Facilities	Bar and restaurant; practice ground
Pro	J Arnold

GC Ortenau (1979)   90

Phone: 07821 7721

Im Gereut 8, 7630 Lahr-Reichenbach

Just east of Lahr, via the B415 to Reichenbach

Holes	9 Par 36 5490m.
Visitors	Welcome. Course closed December to March
Fees	DM30–40
Facilities	Bar and restaurant; practice ground
Pro	A Hochgürtel

GC Oschberghof (1976) **91**
Phone: 0771 84525
Golfplatz 1, 7710 Donaueschingen
Just north east of Donaueschingen off the A81
Holes 18 Par 74 6570m.
Visitors Welcome. Course closed December to March
Fees DM70–110
Facilities Bar and restaurant; practice ground; swimming pool
Pro T Gerhardt

Golfclub Owingen-Überlingen (1989) **92**
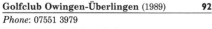
Phone: 07551 3979
Hofgut Lugenhof, 7776 Owingen
Near Lake Constance (Bodensee) at Uberlingen off the B31
Holes 18 Par 72 6138m.
Visitors Welcome
Fees DM50–70
Facilities Bar and restaurant closed Monday; practice ground
Pro R Newsome

GC Pfaffing-Wasserburger Land (1989) **93**
Phone: 08076 1718
Köckmühle, 8098 Pfaffing
On the outskirts of Pfaffing
Holes 18 Par 72 6120m.
Visitors Welcome
Fees DM50–70
Facilities Bar and restaurant; practice ground

GC Pfalz (1975) **94**
Phone: 06327 2973
Postfach 22, 6730 Neustadt
South east of Neustadt off the B39 towards Speyer
Holes 18 Par 72 6090m.
Visitors Welcome, but must book
Fees DM60–90
Facilities Bar and restaurant; practice ground
Pro Mike Hayes
Although rather flat the course is laid out through heavily wooded terrain and offers an excellent challenge to any golfer. There are several dog-leg holes, water hazards and some well-placed bunkers, both around the greens and on the fairways.

GC Pforzheim Karlshäuser Hof (1987) **95**
Phone: 07237 9100
Karlshäuser Weg, 7531 Ölbronn-Dürrn
North east of Pforzheim off the B294 at Dürrn
Holes 18 Par 72 6050m.
Visitors Welcome
Fees DM50–75
Facilities Bar and restaurant closed Monday; practice ground
Pro Paul Sierocinski

GC Puschendorf in Franken (1989) **96**
Phone: 09101 7552
Forstweg 2, 8501 Puschendorf
South west of Herzogenaurach through Langenzenn to Kirchfenbach/Puschendorf
Holes 9 Par 36 2965m.
Visitors Welcome
Fees DM50–70
Facilities Bar and restaurant; practice ground

Golf- und Landclub Regensburg (1968) **97**
Phone: 09403 505
Jagdschloss Thiergarten, 8411 Altenthann
East of Regensburg off the A3. Take the exit to Neutraumbling, and head for Donaustauf/ Walhalla and Sulzbach/Lichtenwald
Holes 18 Par 71 5785m.
Visitors Welcome weekdays, at weekend with member. Course closed November to March
Fees DM50–75
Facilities Bar and restaurant; practice ground
Pro Russel Maw
An elegant clubhouse sits at the hub of this well-established course, which was cut through dense forest. Although not long, the many trees, the occasional water hazard and several dog-leg holes make Regensburg an interesting challenge.

GC am Reichswald (1960) **98**
Phone: 0911 305730
N-Kraftshof, 8500 Nürnburg 14
10km north of Nürnburg off the B4 towards Kraftshof
Holes 18 Par 72 6193m.
Visitors Welcome. Course closed January to March
Fees DM60–80
Facilities Bar and restaurant; practice ground
Pro J Gornert

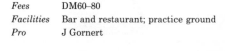

GC Reischenhof (1991) 99

Phone: 07353 1732

Reischenhof, 7959 Wain

South east of Laupheim via the B30 to Schwendi/Wain

Holes	9 Par 36 3144m.
Visitors	Welcome. Course closed Monday
Fees	DM45–60
Facilities	Bar and restaurant; practice ground
Pro	H Francis

GC Reit im Winkl (1985) 100

Phone: 08640 8216

Rathausplatz 1, 8216 Reit im Winkl

West of Reit im Winkl towards Birnbach

Holes	9 Par 35 2559m.
Visitors	Welcome. Course closed November to April
Fees	DM40–60
Facilities	Bar and restaurant; practice ground
Pro	S Mühlbauer

GC Reutlingen-Sonnenbühl (1989) 101

Phone: 07128 2018

Im Zerg, 7419 Sonnenbühl-Undingen

South of Reutlingen via the B312 to Pfullingen, then Sonnenbühe-Undingen and Erpfingen

Holes	18 Par 72 6040m.
Visitors	Welcome. Course closed December to March
Fees	DM50–70
Facilities	Bar and restaurant; practice ground

Rhein-Golf-Club Badenweiler (1971) 102

Phone: 03389 260786

7847 Badenweiler

West of Badenweiler, just over the border in France

Holes	18 Par 72 6362m.
Visitors	Welcome
Fees	DM60–90
Facilities	Bar and restaurant; practice ground
Pro	T Price

GC Rhein-Main (US GC Rheinblick) (1977) 103

Phone: 0611 373014

Weisser Weg, 6200 Wiesbaden-Frauenstein

West of Wiesbaden in Rheinblick

Holes	18 Par 72 5966m.
Visitors	Introduction required
Fees	DM40–60
Facilities	Bar and restaurant; practice ground
Pro	R White

GC Rhein-Wied (1990) 104

Phone: 02622 83523

Gut Burghof, 5450 Neuwied 22

North east of Neuwied off the N42 at exit Heimbach-Weis

Holes	9 Par 36 3018m.
Visitors	Welcome
Fees	DM35–45
Facilities	Bar and restaurant closed Monday; practice ground

Golfclub Rheintal (1971) 105

Phone: 06202 53767

6836 Oftersheim

South west of Heidelberg, towards Oftersheim, then Walldorf

Holes	18 Par 72 5840m.
Visitors	Introduction only (US Army course)
Fees	DM30–50
Facilities	Bar and restaurant; practice ground
Pro	A Winkler

GC Rhön (1971) 106

Phone: 06657 1334

Am Golfplatz, 6417 Hofbieber

East of Fulda via the B458 to Hofbieber

Holes	18 Par 70 5675m.
Visitors	Welcome. Course closed December to March
Fees	DM40–50
Facilities	Bar and restaurant; practice ground
Pro	N Staples

GC Rickenbach (1980) 107

Phone: 07765 88830

Henneman 7, 7884 Richenbach

North of Bad Säckingen off the B34

Holes	9 Par 34 2749m.
Visitors	Welcome. Course closed December to March
Fees	DM40–60
Facilities	Bar and restaurant; practice ground; swimming pool; tennis
Pro	C Dew

Rolling Hills GC (1986) 108

Phone: 06851 5156

6587 Baumholder

On the south west side of Baumholder

Holes	9 Par 36 2732m.
Visitors	Welcome
Fees	DM25–35
Facilities	Bar and restaurant; practice ground

Rottaler Golf & Countryclub (1972) 109

Phone: 08561 2861

8341 Postmünster- Kaismühle

West of Pfarrkirchen off the B388 towards Postmünster

Holes	18 Par 72 6105m.
Visitors	Welcome (public course). Closed December to March
Fees	DM40–50
Facilities	Bar and restaurant; practice ground
Pro	R Porter

Golf- und Landclub Rusel (1981) 110

Phone: 09920 911

Werststrasse 17, 8360 Deggendorf

North east of Deggendorf towards Regen

Holes	9 Par 36 3035m.
Visitors	Welcome. Course closed December to May
Fees	DM50–70
Facilities	Bar and restaurant; practice ground; short course
Pro	J Taylor

GC Saar-Pfalz Katharinenhof (1982) 111

Phone: 06843 8797

Gersheim-Rubenheim

South of Blieskastel via the B423; head for Ehlingen/Erfweiler near Assweiler

Holes	9 Par 36 3056m.
Visitors	Welcome
Fees	DM40–50
Facilities	Bar and restaurant; practice ground
Pro	H Stocks

GC Saarbrücken (1961) 112

Phone: 06837 401

Oberlimbergerweg, 6634 Wallerfangen-Gisingen

West of Saarlouis off the B406 towards Gisingen

Holes	18 Par 72 6231m.
Visitors	Welcome. Course closed January
Fees	DM45–65
Facilities	Bar and restaurant; practice ground
Pro	F Le Chevalier

GC Sagmühle (1983) 113

Phone: 08532 2038

Schwaim 52, 8394 Bad Griesbach

Just south of Bad Griesbach via the B388 to Schwaim

Holes	18 Par 72 6218m.
Visitors	Welcome. Course closed December to March
Fees	DM60
Facilities	Bar and restaurant; practice ground
Pro	M Probst

St Eurach Land- und Golfclub (1973) 114

Phone: 08801 1332

Eurach 8, 8127 Iffeldorf

North west of Penzberg, and 4km west off A95 at Iffeldorf

Holes	18 Par 71 5888m.
Visitors	Welcome midweek. Course closed November to mid-April
Fees	DM100
Facilities	Bar and restaurant; swimming pool; tennis
Pro	Wolfgang John

The views from the fairways of this course in the Alpine approaches are worth the price of the green fee (well, just about). All around are wooded slopes and distant peaks and the course itself is a lovely walk through lines of trees. It is an entertaining course with many water hazards to avoid.

GC Schloss Braunfels (1970)   115

Phone: 06442 4530

Homburger Hof, 6333 Braunfels

Just west of Braunfels

Holes	18 Par 73 6288m.
Visitors	Welcome on weekdays
Fees	DM60–90
Facilities	Bar and restaurant; practice ground
Pro	Derek McLellan

GC Schloss Igling (1991)   116

Phone: 08248 1003

Schloss Stuben, 8939 Igling

On the outskirts of Igling

Holes	9 Par 35 2682m.
Visitors	Welcome. Course closed mid-November to March
Fees	DM50–70
Facilities	Bar and restaurant closed Monday; practice ground
Pro	John Wilkinson

GC Schloss Klingenburg Günzburg (1980) 117

Phone: 08225 3030

8876 Jettingen-Scheppach

South east of Günzburg off the A8 at the Burgan exit to Jettingen/Schönenberg

Holes	18 Par 72 6065m.
Visitors	Welcome
Fees	DM60–90
Facilities	Bar and restaurant; practice ground
Pro	H Besser

GC Schloss Liebenstein (1982)   118

Phone: 07133 16019

Schloss Liebenstein, 7129 Neckarwestheim

South of Heilbronn

Holes	18 Par 72 5869m.
Visitors	Welcome
Fees	DM50–70
Facilities	Bar and restaurant; practice ground
Pro	W Kretschy

GC Schloss Mainsondheim (1988)   119

Phone: 09324 4656

Schlossweg 1, 8716 Mainsondheim

North of Kitzingen off the A3 at the Kitzingen exit

Holes	9 Par 36 3020m.
Visitors	Welcome
Fees	DM40–50
Facilities	Bar and restaurant; practice ground
Pro	Harry Bannerman

GC Schloss Maxlrain (1988)   120

Phone: 08061 1403

Aiblinger Strasse 1, 8201 Tuntenhausen

35 mins from Munich via the Salzburg autobahn. Exit at Bad Aibling, and go on 3km beyond Aibling

Holes	18 Par 72 6076m.
Visitors	Welcome
Fees	DM60–80
Facilities	Bar and restaurant closed Monday; practice ground; short course
Pro	Richard Foster

This relatively new course has been hewn through heavy woodland and the lines of trees and several water hazards are its main difficulties. There are several dog-leg holes (the 5th and the 14th turn at right angles) which call for straight driving and caution.

GC Schloss Reichertshausen (1986)   121

Phone: 08441 7004

Schlossstrasse 7, 8069 Reichertshausen

South of Pfaffenhofen in Reichertshausen

Holes	9 Par 36 2944m.
Visitors	Welcome. Course closed November to March
Fees	DM40–60
Facilities	Bar and restaurant; practice ground
Pro	P Walker

GC Schloss Weitenburg (1984)   122

Phone: 07472 8061

Sommerhalde 9, 7245 Starzach-Sulzau

South west of Rottenburg. After Weitingen follow signs to Schloss Weitenburg

Holes	18 Par 72 6089m.
Visitors	Welcome
Fees	DM30–70
Facilities	Bar and restaurant; practice ground; short course
Pro	D Creamer

Golfclub Schlossberg Grünbach (1985) **123**
Phone: 08734 7035
Grünbach, 8386 Reisbach
North east of Reisbach to Grunbach, then
Schlossberg
Holes 18 Par 72 6053m.
Visitors Welcome. Course closed November
to March
Fees DM35–45
Facilities Bar and restaurant; practice ground
Pro P Haworth

Golf- und Landclub Schmidmühlen (1969) **124**
Phone: 09474 701
Am Theilberg 1, 8456 Schmidmühlen
North west of Burglengenfeld off the A93
Holes 9 Par 36 2727m.
Visitors Welcome. Course closed December to
March
Fees DM30–40
Facilities Bar and restaurant; practice ground
Pro A Emanuell

GC Schotten (1972) **125**
Phone: 06044 1375
Lindenstr 5, 6479 Schotten-Eschenrod
East of Schotten off the B455 and B276 towards
Gedern
Holes 9 Par 32 2165m.
Visitors Welcome.
Fees DM30–50
Facilities Bar and restaurant closed November
to April; short course
Pro Günter Kleffel

GC Sonnenalp (1976) **126**
Phone: 08321 7276
Hotel Sonnenalp, 8972 Ofterschwang
Just south west of Sonthofen off the B19
Holes 18 Par 72 6038m.
Visitors Welcome. Course closed December to
April
Fees DM70–85
Facilities Bar and restaurant; practice ground
Pro B Kennedy

GC Spessart (1972) **127**
Phone: 06056 3594
Alsberg a.d.H, 6483 Bad Soden-Salmünster
Just east of Bad Soden off the A66
Holes 18 Par 72 6039m.
Visitors Must book.
Fees DM50–70
Facilities Bar and restaurant; practice ground
Pro S Walker

GC Starnberg (1987) **128**
Phone: 08151 12157
Uneringer Strasse, 8130 Starnberg/Hadorf
West of Starnberg through Hadorf
Holes 18 Par 71 5970m.
Visitors Welcome, but must book. Course
closed mid-November to mid-March
Fees DM60–80
Facilities Bar and restaurant; practice ground
Pro Christoph Killian

GC Stauden am Weiherhof (1988) **129**
Phone: 08238 3727
Weiherhof, 8901 Gessertshausen
South west of Augsburg via the B300 to
Gessertshausen, then towards Fischach and
Weierhof
Holes 9 Par 32 2086m.
Visitors Welcome. Course closed December to
March
Fees DM25–35
Facilities Bar and restaurant; practice ground;
tennis

Steigenberger Golf-Resort Bad Griesbach
(1987) **130**
Phone: 08532 7418
Kurallee 1, 8394 Bad Griesbach
28km south west of Passau off the M3 at exit
Passau-West or Pocking
Holes 18 Par 72 6218m.
18 Par 72 5884m.
18 Par 71 5744m.
Visitors Welcome, but must book
Fees DM50–70
Facilities Bar and restaurant; practice ground;
short courses; swimming pool; tennis
Pro John O'Flynn and 28 teaching pros.
Bad Griesbach is the training course of the
German Golf Association and is an extraordinary place with its three golf courses of 18 holes
and two nine hole courses. By 1995 there will be
three more golf courses, designed by Bernhard
Langer, and another nine hole course. There is
every type of practice facility including a driving
range with nearly 200 bays (the Golfodrom).
There are plenty of excellent hotels in the area
and shuttle-buses take the golfers to and from
the course.

GC Stiftland (1982)   **131**
Phone: 09638 1271
Ernestgrün 35, 8591 Neualbenreuth
East of Waldsassen towards Neualbenreuth
Holes   9 Par 3 6 3056m.
Visitors   Welcome. Course closed December to
             April
Fees   DM30–40
Facilities Bar and restaurant; practice ground
Pro   P Dunn

GC Stromberg-Schindeldorf (1989)   **132**
Phone: 06724 1035
Am Südhang 1a, 6534 Stromberg-Schindeldorf
Just north of Stromberg
Holes   18 Par 72 6012m.
Visitors   Welcome, but must book (public
             course)
Fees   DM40–60
Facilities Bar and restaurant; practice ground;
             swimming pool; tennis

Stuttgarter GC Neckartal (1974)   **133**
Phone 07141 89150
975 Aldinger Str, 7140 Ludwigsburg-Pattonville
Take the B27 to the north of Stuttgart. Take the
exit at Remseck/Pattonville
Holes   18 Par 73 6310m.
Visitors   Welcome. Course closed Monday
Fees   DM50-75
Facilities Bar and restaurant closed Monday;
             practice ground

Stuttgarter GC Solitude (1927)   **134**
Phone: 07044 6909
7256 Mönsheim
North west of Stuttgart at Mönsheim
Holes   18 Par 72 6065m.
Visitors   Welcome, but must book
Fees   DM70
Facilities Bar and restaurant; practice ground
Pro   F Lengsfield
This is a splendid course laid out over gentle
hills with some surrounding forest. The fairways
are generous and the difficulty of the course lies
in the thick rough and the well-positioned
bunkers. The 12th hole, which has a lake by the
green, is formidable and so is the short 8th.

GC Taunus (1983)   **135**
Phone: 06083 1883
Merzhäuser Landstr, 6395 Weilrod-Altweilnau
Southeast of Weilrod near Atweilnau
Holes   18 Par 72 5881m.
Visitors   Welcome
Fees   DM45–65
Facilities Bar and restaurant; practice ground
Pro   B Weber

Tegernseer GC Bad Wiessee (1958)   **136**
Phone: 08022 8769
Robognerhof, 8182 Bad Wiessee
North west of Bad Wiessee via the B318
Holes   18 Par 70 5501m.
Visitors   Welcome. Course closed December to
             March
Fees   DM70–90
Facilities Bar and restaurant; practice ground
Pro   V Knörnschild

GC Trier-Mosel (1977)   **137**
Phone: 06507 4374
5559 Ensch-Birkenheck
North east of Trier off the A1. Take the
Schweich exit, head for Hetzerad, Bekond and
Thönich
Holes   9 Par 36 3050m.
Visitors   Welcome
Fees   DM30–50
Facilities Bar and restaurant; practice ground;
             short course
Pro   H Goerke

Golfclub Tutzing (1983)   **138**
Phone: 08158 3600
8132 Tutzing-Deixlfurt
Just west of Tutzing
Holes   18 Par 72 6159m.
Visitors   Welcome. Course closed December to
             April
Fees   DM60–80
Facilities Bar and restaurant; practice ground
Pro   D Hennings
This is a long course built on fairly flat
farmland. The fairways are lush and holding and
there are some very challenging long holes, with
several blind shots to be negotiated. There is a
splendid Alpine style clubhouse.

GC Ulm (1963)   139

Phone: 07306 2102

Wochenauer Hof, 7901 Illerieden

South of Ulm between Illerbirchberg and
Illerrieden

Holes	14 Par 72 6073m.
Visitors	Welcome of weekdays. By introduction only at weekends
Fees	DM50–70
Facilities	Bar and restaurant; practice ground
Pro	M Emery

GC Waldbrunnen (1983)   140

Phone: 02645 15621

Brunnenstr 7, 5469 Windhagen-Rederscheid

East of Windhagen; follow signs to Dorint
Waldbrunnen

Holes	9 Par 33 2408m.
Visitors	Welcome, but must book
Fees	DM40–55
Facilities	Bar and restaurant; practice ground
Pro	J Nixon

Golfclub Waldegg-Wiggensbach (1982)   141

Phone: 08370 733

Hof Waldegg, 8961 Wiggensbach/Oberallgau

Just west of Wiggensbach near the Swiss/
Austrian border

Holes	18 Par 65 4757m.
Visitors	Welcome. Course closed November to April
Fees	DM40–50
Facilities	Bar and restaurant; practice ground
Pro	J Taylor

GC Weiherhof-Nunkirchen (1990)   142

Phone: 06874 588

Weiherhof Golfplatz, 6648 Nunkirchen-Wadern

Take the Nonnweiler exit off the A1 and go
towards Wadern and Nunkirchen

Holes	9 Par 36 2880m.
Visitors	Welcome
Fees	DM30
Facilities	Bar and restaurant; practice ground; swimming pool
Pro	Hugh Hamilton

Land und Golfclub Werdenfels (1973)   143

Phone: 08821 2473

Schwaigwang, 8100 Garmisch-Partenkirchen

Just north of Garmisch-Partenkirchen (US
course)

Holes	9 Par 36 3274m.
Visitors	Welcome. Course closed November to March
Fees	DM40–60
Facilities	Bar and restaurant; practice ground

Golfclub Westerwald (1979)   144

Phone: 02666 8220

Postfach 1231, Alexanderring 9, 5238
Hachenburg

South of Hackenburg off the B8 to Steinen; turn
at Dreifelden

Holes	9 Par 36 3020m.
Visitors	Welcome weekdays
Fees	DM45
Facilities	Bar and restaurant
Pro	Hermann Labonte

Wiesbadener GC (1893)   145

Phone: 0611 460238

Chaussehaus 17, 6200 Wiesbaden

North west of Wiesbaden towards Schlangenbad

Holes	9 Par 34 2655m.
Visitors	Welcome
Fees	DM50–70
Facilities	Bar and restaurant closed Monday and mid-December to February; practice ground
Pro	Gerry Cox

This is one of the oldest clubs in Germany; it
was founded in 1893 although the course was not
built until 1911. It is a truly delightful course
laid out over hilly ground in the lee of the
Taurus mountains. Fine old trees abound and
the stream which meanders through the course
adds to its charm.

GC Wiesloch-Hohenhardter Hof (1983)   146

Phone: 06222 72081

Hohenhardter Hof, 6908 Wiesloch/Baiertal

Just east of Wiesloch off the A6

Holes	18 Par 72 6080m.
Visitors	Welcome
Fees	DM30–40
Facilities	Bar and restaurant; practice ground
Pro	H Rübman

Wittelsbacher GC Rohrenfeld-Neuburg (1988)

147

Phone: 08431 44118

Gut Rohrenfeld, 8858 Neuburg 2/Donau

East of Neuburg near Rohrenfeld

Holes	18 Par 72 6065m
Visitors	Welcome
Fees	DM70–90
Facilities	Bar and restaurant; practice ground
Pro	Gerhard Koenig

Clumps of trees, scattered hither and thither, enliven this course, which twists and turns over fairly level country. There are a few water hazards but the main problems are presented by the many dog-leg holes, which demand accuracy from the tee. One novel feature, for a German course, is the double green which is shared by the 1st and 15th holes.

GC Wörthsee (1982)   148

Phone: 08152 3872

Gut Schluifeld 8031 Wörthsee

West of München via the B12 to Lindau; head for Wessling

Holes	18 Par 71 5915m.
Visitors	Welcome. Course closed December to March
Fees	DM60–90
Facilities	Bar and restaurant; practice ground
Pro	J Mills

GC Würzburg-Kitzingen (1950)   149

Phone: 09321 4956

Geschäftsstelle Schustergasse 3, 8700 Würzburg

In Kitzingen at the Larson Barracks (US Army grounds)

Holes	9 Par 36 3325m.
Visitors	Welcome Tuesday to Friday and some weekends
Fees	US$25 (payment in dollars)
Facilities	Bar and restaurant; practice ground
Pro	Trevor Pearman

GREECE

A S THE Honorary Secretary of the Hellenic Golf Federation ruefully wrote: '300 days of sun and we have only four courses.' It seems strange that golf has hardly been developed in Greece, although the National Tourist Organisation is hoping to build a few more courses in the near future. However, the existing courses are all well worth a visit, especially Glyfada, even if it is next door to Athens airport.

Unit of currency: Drachma
Rate of exchange (approx. at 1.1.93): Gdr320–£1
International dialling code: (010 30)

Corfu Golf Club (1971)   1

Phone: 30 661 94220
PO Box 71, Ropa Valley, Ermones Beach
West of Corfu at Ermones beach

Holes	18 Par 72 6300m.
Visitors	Welcome. Course closed November to March
Fees	Gdr6–10,000
Facilities	Bar and restaurant; practice ground
Pro	David Crawley

Glyfada Golf Club (1967)   2

Phone: 01 8946820
PO Box 7016, 16610 Glyfada
South of Athens at Glyfada

Holes	18 Par 72 6198m
Visitors	Welcome
Fees	Gdr6–10,000
Facilities	Bar and restaurant; practice ground
Pro	J Sotiropoulos

Near the airport on a stretch of land between the Saronic Gulf and the slopes of Mount Imitos, this tough and entertaining course was laid down by Donald Haradine, who used the massed ranks of umbrella pines to defend every hole. He added several dog-legs and fast greens to the mixture to produce a course which will challenge the most accomplished of golfers.

Afandu Golf Club (1973)   3

Phone: 0241 27306
PO Box 47, 85100 Rhodes
South of Rhodes at Afandu

Holes	18 Par 72 6060m.
Visitors	Welcome
Fees	Gdr3600
Facilities	Bar and restaurant; practice ground
Pro	Basili Anastasiou

Port Carras Golf Club (1979)   4

Phone: 0375 71381
Porto Carras, Halkidiki
At Porto Carras; about 100km south east of Thessaloniki on the Sithonian peninsula

Holes	18 Par 72 6086m.
Visitors	Welcome
Fees	Gdr4–10,000
Facilities	Bar and restaurant
Pro	P Andrade

ITALY

NEW golf courses have been relatively slow to appear in Italy in recent years; only a dozen or so have opened for play since 1988. One of the major problems, an abiding one in Europe, is the difficulty of obtaining planning consent; and the trend seen in Spain and Portugal of building large holiday complexes with golf courses has not found much favour in Italy. However, around 50 courses are in various stages of development.

The country has many well-established courses; nearly 20 were built before World War II, most of them during the 1920s. They include Menaggio, Roma, Milano, Venezia and Villa d'Este. Several of them have certainly stood the test of time and are still ranked among the best in Europe. This especially can be said of the beautiful course of Villa d'Este, and newer courses such as Trent Jones's design at Pevero in Sardinia, Biella and Olgiata maintain the reputation of Italian golf.

The majority of the Italian courses are located in the north and the lakes would make a splendid base for a golfing holiday, or any kind of holiday for that matter. Visitors are generally very welcome at Italian clubs, where the facilities are excellent. A point should, however, be made about the cost of living in Italy; inflation is a severe problem and it is an expensive country in which to take a holiday.

Unit of currency: Lira
Rate of exchange (approx. at 1.1.93): IL2100–£1
International dialling code: (010 39)

Adriatic Golfclub Cervia (1987)   **1**

Phone: 0544 992786

Via Ielenia Gora, 48016 Cervia-Milano Marittima
Just north of Cervia off the S16

Holes	18 Par 72 6246m.
Visitors	Welcome. Course closed Monday and October to March
Fees	IL50–75,000
Facilities	Bar and restaurant; driving range
Pro	Roberto Paris

Cervia is a holiday resort with good beaches, water sports and tennis and can now offer an interesting golf course designed by Marco Croze. Surrounded by pine forests the course has two big lakes which come into play on the second half and the architect has tried to give some of the characteristics of a links to the opening nine holes.

Golfclub Albarella (1972)   **2**

Phone: 0426 67124

Isola de Albarella, 45010 Rosolina
On Albarella island, off the S443 and south of Chioggia

Holes	18 Par 72 6065m.
Visitors	Welcome. Course closed Tuesday
Fees	IL50,000
Facilities	Bar and restaurant; driving range; swimming pool; tennis
Pro	Fabrizio Sintich

About thirty miles to the south of Venice, the course sits at the mouth of the River Po. The Italian Open of 1986, which was won by David Feherty, was held here and it has the true calibre of a championship course.

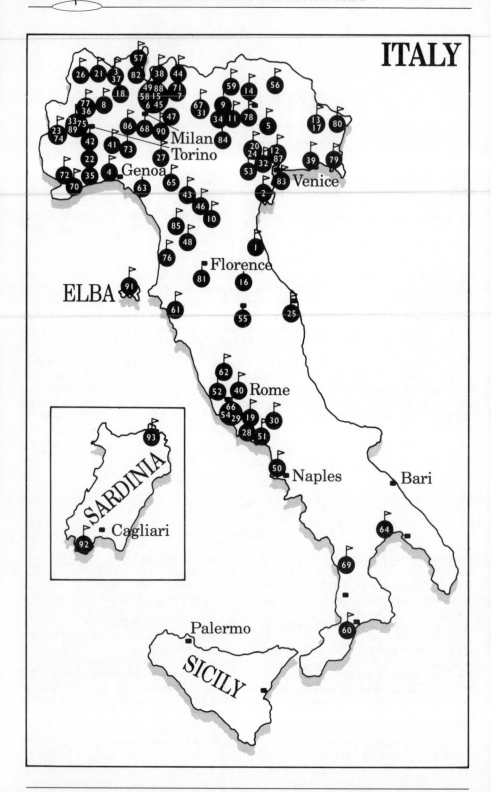

Golf Alpino di Stresa (1925)   3

Phone: 0323 20101

Viale Panorama 49, 28040 Vezzo

To the south west of Stresa near Lake Maggiore

Holes	9 Par 34 2675m.
Visitors	Welcome. Course closed Tuesday
Fees	IL50,000
Facilities	Bar and restaurant
Pro	Giacomo Pasquale

Golfclub Arenzano della Pineta (1969)   4

Phone; 010 9111817

Piazza del Golf 3, 16011 Arenzano

Just west of Arenzano

Holes	9 Par 36 2445m.
Visitors	Welcome but must book at weekends. Course closed Tuesday and in October
Fees	IL50–70,000
Facilities	Bar and restaurant; practice ground; tennis
Pro	Adriano Mori

Asiago Golf Club (1967)   5

Phone: 0424 462721

Via Meltar 2, 36012 Asiago

Just east of Asiago

Holes	9 Par 35 2948m
Visitors	Welcome. Course closed November-May
Fees	IL50–75,000
Facilities	Bar and restaurant; practice ground

Barlassina Country Club (1956)   6

Phone: 0362 560621

Via Privata Golf 42, 20030 Birago di Camnago

North of Milano, off the S35 near Seveso

Holes	18 Par 72 6053m.
Visitors	Welcome, but must book. Members only on Sunday. Course closed Monday
Fees	IL80–120,000
Facilities	Bar and restaurant; practice ground; swimming pool; tennis
Pro	Nando Randina

The course was built by a group of wealthy folk from Milan as part of a private club and still retains its exclusive ambience. It is a pleasant parkland course which meanders through pines, birches, poplars and oaks, the fairways occasionally broken by small streams, and is an eminently relaxing holiday course.

Golfclub Bergamo l'Albenza (1961)   7

Phone: 035 640028

12 Via Longoni, 24030 Almenno San Bartolomeo

North west of Bergamo, off the S342

Holes	3 x 9 Par 36 (all) 3098/3100/2962m.
Visitors	Welcome on weekdays only. Course closed Monday
Fees	IL60–100,000
Facilities	Bar and restaurant; practice ground
Pro	Marlo Rendina

The first 18 holes were laid down by Henry Cotton and, true to his philosophy, add up to an honest test for any golfer: the challenges and the penalties are clearly apparent and take the form of narrow fairways fringed by beautiful trees, and well-protected greens. The use of dog-leg holes, the ubiquitous pine trees and water hazards add to the difficulties and the 14th hole is a notable challenge. The clubhouse is superb and so is the scenery.

Golfclub Biella Le Betulle (1958)   8

Phone: 015 679151

Reg Valcarozza, 13050 Magnano

South west of Biella off the S338 near Zubiera

Holes	18 Par 73 6427m.
Visitors	Welcome. Course closed Monday, December to March
Fees	IL50–75,000
Facilities	Bar and restaurant
Pro	Agostino Reale

Long and uncompromising, this is one of the best courses in Italy. Designed by John Morrison it was carved through a forest of silver birches and oaks, its difficulties made the more severe by water hazards, well-situated bunkers, hillocks and hollows.

Bogliaco Golfclub (1912)   9

Phone: 0365 643006

25080 Bogliaco Lago di Garda

North east of Brescia and just north of Gardone

Holes	9 Par 34 2572m.
Visitors	Welcome. Course closed Tuesday
Fees	IL40–60,000
Facilities	Bar and restaurant; practice ground; swimming pool
Pro	T Luciano

Bologna Golf Club (1959)　　　　10

Phone: 051 969100
Via Sabatini 69, 40050 Monte San Pietro
West of Bologna near Monte San Pietro

Holes	18 Par 72 6171m.
Visitors	Welcome. Course closed Monday
Fees	IL50–75,000
Facilities	Bar and restaurant; practice ground; swimming pool; tennis
Pro	Bruno Ghezzo

Henry Cotton built this course in 1959 and gave his usual challenge to the golfer, in that the penalties for a poor shot are clearly on show. It is a delightful course with superb views of the Apennines, and the fairways wend their charming way through avenues of pines, oaks and cypress trees. There are some severe holes, including the very long dog-leg 5th hole.

Ca'degli Ulivi Golfclub (1991)　　　　11

Phone: 045 7256463
37010 Marciaga Castion di Costermano
Just north of Garda near the lake

Holes	18 Par 72 6000m.
Visitors	Welcome. Course closed Monday
Fees	IL80–100,000
Facilities	Bar and restaurant; practice ground; short course; swimming pool; tennis
Pro	George Kromichal

This new course has a magnificent clubhouse on a hill and from its windows and terraces there are views of the whole golf course. If your game is off-colour you might be advised to stay there since this is a course where any inaccuracies are ruthlessly punished. A good lunch with a bottle of the local wine and a knock around the short course is a welcome option.

Ca'della Nave Golf Club (1986)　　　　12

Phone: 041 5401555
Piazza della Vttoria 14, 30030 Martellago
North west of Venice At Martellago

Holes	18 Par 72 6040m.
Visitors	Welcome. Course closed Tuesday
Fees	IL80–100,000
Facilities	Bar and restaurant; practice ground; short course; swimming pool; tennis
Pro	Peter O'Connor

Cansiglio Golfclub (1958)　　　　13

Phone: 0438 585398
Pian del Cansiglio, 31029 Vittorio Veneto
North east of Vittorio Veneto at Pian del Cansiglio

Holes	9 Par 35 2869m.
Visitors	Welcome. Course closed November to April
Fees	IL45–60,000
Facilities	Bar and restaurant; practice ground
Pro	Ugo Scafa

Campo Carlo Magno Golfclub (1922)　　　　14

Phone: 0465 41003
38084 Madonna di Campiglio
North west of Trento at Maddona di Campiglio

Holes	9 Par 35 2300m.
Visitors	Welcome. Course closed October to June
Fees	IL20–50,000
Facilities	Bar and restaurant; practice ground
Pro	Alberto Silva

Carimate Golfclub (1962)　　　　15

Phone: 031 790226
2 Via Airoldi, 22060 Carimate
South east of Como off the A9 at Carimate

Holes	18 Par 71 5982m.
Visitors	Must book at weekends. Course closed Monday and end-December to end-January
Fees	IL60–90,000
Facilities	Bar and restaurant; practice ground; swimming pool; tennis
Pro	Emilio Songia

Golfclub Casentino (1988)　　　　16

Phone: 0575 520167
52014 Poppi, Loc Palazoo
North of Arezzo off the S71 near Poppi

Holes	9 Par 36 2775m.
Visitors	Welcome. Course closed Tuesday
Fees	IL50,000
Facilities	Bar and restaurant; practice ground
Pro	Alessandro Pissilli

Golfclub Castel d'Aviano (1990) 17
Phone: 0434 652305
Via Montello 57, Castello, 33081 Aviano
North west of Pordenone near Aviaro

Holes	9 Par 36 2879m.
Visitors	Welcome. Course closed Tuesday
Fees	IL50,000
Facilities	Bar and restaurant; practice ground; tennis
Pro	Stefano Pietrobono

Golfclub Castelconturbia (1984) 18
Phone: 0322 832093
Via Suno, 28010 Agrate Conturbia
North of Novara, off the S32 near Agrate

Holes	3 x 9 Par 36 (all) 2862/2900/3080m.
Visitors	Welcome on weekdays only. Course closed Monday
Fees	IL70–110,000
Facilities	Bar and restaurant; practice ground; swimming pool; tennis
Pro	A Angelini

The views of distant mountains from the fairways of this fine course are magnificent. Many of the professionals who played the 1991 Italian Open probably raised their eyes heavenwards since only half a dozen of them managed to break par. It does not seem a difficult course since the fairways are reasonably open and it is not long. But the greens are very difficult and demand an accurate placement of the approach shots. It is a very searching test of any golfer's skills.

Castelgandolfo Golfclub (1987) 19
Phone: 06 9312301
Via di S Spirito 13, 00040 Castelgandolfo
South east of Rome, off the S7 near Albano

Holes	18 Par 72 6025m.
Visitors	Welcome, but by introduction only at weekends. Course closed Monday
Fees	IL80–100,000
Facilities	Bar and restaurant; practice ground; swimming pool; tennis
Pro	Augusto Venier

Golfclub Castello della Montecchia (1990) 20
Phone: 049 8055550
Via Montecchia, 35030 Selvazzano
West of Padova at Selvazzano

Holes	18 Par 72 6255m.
	9 Par 36 3010m.
Visitors	Welcome. Course closed Monday
Fees	IL80–100,000
Facilities	Bar and restaurant; practice ground; swimming pool; tennis
Pro	Renzo Trentin

Cervino GC (1955) 21
Phone: 0166 949131
Cervinia Breuil 11021
North east of Aosta near Breuil-Cervinia

Holes	9 Par 34 2523m.
Visitors	Welcome. Course closed October to June
Fees	IL50–75,000
Facilities	Bar; practice ground
Pro	Luca Cantarella

This is the highest course in Italy at 6500 feet, with the famous Matterhorn towering above. The views are superb and the ball flies flatteringly farther in the thinner air.

GC Cherasco (Le Chiocciole) (1983) 22
Phone: 0172 48772
Fraschetta, Cascina Roma, 12062 Cherasco
South west of Alba, off the A6 at Cherasco

Holes	18 Par 72 5863m.
Visitors	Introduction only on weekends and in July/August. Closed Tuesdays and December to February
Fees	IL80–100,000
Facilities	Bar and restaurant; practice ground; tennis
Pro	Vincenzo Pelle

Claviere GC (1927) 23
Phone: 011 2398346
10050 Claviere
East of Briançon, off the S24 at Claviere

Holes	9 Par 32 2325m.
Visitors	Welcome. Closed November-May
Fees	IL20–50,000
Facilities	Bar and restaurant; practice ground
Pro	Lucio Merlino

Golfclub Colli Berici (1991)   24

Phone: 0444 601780

Strada Monti Communali, 36040 Brendola

10km south of Vicenza near Brendola

Holes	9 Par 35 2840m.
Visitors	Welcome. Course closed Monday
Fees	IL50,000
Facilities	Bar and restaurant; practice ground; swimming pool
Pro	Antonello Ballarin

Conero Golfclub Sirolo (1987)   25

Phone: 071 7360613

Via Betellico 6, 60020 Sirolo

South of Ancona off the A14 at Sirolo

Holes	18 Par 72 6185m.
Visitors	Welcome. Course closed Monday
Fees	IL50,000
Facilities	Bar and restaurant; practice ground; short course; swimming pool; tennis
Pro	M G Allende

GC Courmayeur et Grandes Jorasses (1963) 26

Phone: 0165 89103

Courmayeur 11013

Just to the north east of Courmayeur

Holes	9 Par 35 2686m.
Visitors	Welcome. Course closed October to June
Fees	IL50,000
Facilities	Bar and restaurant; driving range
Pro	Augusto Venier

Croara Golf Club (1977)   27

Phone: 0523 977105

29010 Croara di Gazzola

South west of Piacenza, off the S45

Holes	18 Par 72 6065m.
Visitors	Welcome. Course closed Tuesday and January
Fees	IL50,000
Facilities	Bar and restaurant; practice ground; swimming pool; tennis
Pro	Guiseppe Turrini

Circolo del Golf Eucalyptus (1988)   28

Phone: 06 926252

Via Cogna 3/5, 04011 Campo di Carne, Aprilia

Between Latina and Roma at Aprilia

Holes	9 Par 37 3167m.
Visitors	Welcome. Course closed Tuesday
Fees	IL35–40,000
Facilities	Bar and restaurant; practice ground; swimming pool; tennis
Pro	Mario Napoleoni

Golf Club Fioranello (1979)   29

Phone: 06 7138291

00040 Santa Maria delle Mole

South east of Rome off the S7 at Santa Maria

Holes	18 Par 70 5388m.
Visitors	Welcome. Course closed Wednesday
Fees	IL50,000
Facilities	Bar and restaurant; practice ground; swimming pool
Pro	Romolo Croce

Fiuggi Golf Club (1926)   30

Phone: 0775 55250

Superstrada Anticolana 1, 03015 Fiuggi Fonte

Just south of Fiuggi

Holes	9 Par 35 2848m.
Visitors	Must book on weekends. Course closed Tuesday in winter
Fees	IL20–50,000
Facilities	Bar and restaurant; practice ground; swimming pool; tennis
Pro	Gaetano Macciocchi

Golfclub Franciacorta (1986) 31
Phone: 030 984167
Loc Castagnola, 25040 Nigoline di Corte Franca
North of Rovato at Nigoline
Holes   18 Par 72 6060m.
Visitors   Welcome. Course closed Tuesday
Fees   IL50–75,000
Facilities   Bar and restaurant; practice ground; short course; swimming pool; tennis
Pro   Romolo Napleoni
The result of a collaboration between Pete Dye (of Kiawah Island fame) and Marco Croze, this is an archetypal American design. Water threatens you all the way over the first dozen holes and the greens are vast and undulating. Dye's trademark of timber on the faces of bunkers and around the greens is much in evidence and it all adds up to a fearsome attack on any golfer's nerves and skill.

Frassanelle Golfclub (1988) 32
Phone: 049 9910477
35030 Frassanelle di Rovolon
Between Padova and Venezia, near Bastia
Holes   18 Par 72 6120m.
Visitors   Welcome. Course closed Tuesday
Fees   IL50–70,000
Facilities   Bar and restaurant
Pro   Fiorigi Girardi

Golfclub Le Fronde (1975) 33
Phone: 011 938053
Via Sant'Agostino 68, 10051 Avigliana
West of Torino, off the S25 near Avigliana
Holes   18 Par 72 6077m.
Visitors   Welcome. Course closed Mondays and January/February
Fees   IL60–75,000
Facilities   Bar and restaurant; practice ground; swimming pool
Pro   Michele Rolando
The main difficulties of this course are presented by the thick woodland which fringes the fairways and any inaccuracies are punished. Other problems are caused by the strong winds which sometimes afflict the course which is laid out on the slopes of Mount Cuneo. The views are superb, of the Susa Valley and the mountains.

Gardagolf Golfclub (1985) 34
Phone: 0365 674707
Via Angelo Omodeo 2, 25080 Soiana Del Lago
South of Salo, off the S572
Holes   18 Par 72 6505m.
9 Par 35 2415m.
Visitors   Welcome. Course closed Monday in winter
Fees   IL60–80,000
Facilities   Bar and restaurant; practice ground; swimming pool; tennis
Pro   Franco Maestroni
The course was designed by Donald Steel and the club offers a good range of sporting activities. The courses are situated in superb terrain which stretches around the hills of Polpenazze and there are views of the old fortress of Manerba and of Lake Garda. The fairways wind through lines of olive and cypress trees and ancient oaks and present a varying and interesting challenge.

Garlenda Golf Club (1965) 35
Phone: 0182 580012
Via del Golf 7, 17030 Garlenda
North of Alassio at Garlenda
Holes   18 Par 71 5964m.
Visitors   Welcome. Course closed Wednesday except July/August
Fees   IL50–75,000
Facilities   Bar and restaurant; practice ground; swimming pool; tennis
Pro   Franco Zanini
Tucked away to the north of Alassio, the course was laid out on three different levels by John Harris. Many of the holes lie in the valley but you must also climb up through the vineyards and pines to higher ground. The trees demand accuracy, especially from the tees, and a river bed (usually dry) adds to the fun, especially at the short 13th, where you must knock your ball over it to the green. It is a delightful place, a real haven away from the tourist spots.

Golfclub I Roveri (1924/1971) 36
Phone: 011 923571
Rotta Cerbiatta 24, 10070 Fiano
North of Torino beyond Venaria
Holes   18 Par 72 6128m.
9 Par 36 3107m.
Visitors   Welcome. Course closed Monday and December to February
Fees   IL80–100,000
Facilities   Bar and restaurant; practice ground
Pro   Marcello Vinzi

Golfclub des Iles Borromées (1987) **37**

Phone: 0323 30243

28010 Brovello Carpugnino, Motta Rossa

Just south of Stresa off the S33

Holes	18 Par 72 6455m.
Visitors	Welcome. Course closed Monday and December to March
Fees	IL50,000
Facilities	Bar and restaurant; practice ground
Pro	G Canonica

Lanzo Golf Club (1962) **38**

Phone: 031 840169

22024 Lanzo d'Intelvi

North of Como, off the S340 near Argegno

Holes	9 Par 34 2450m.
Visitors	Welcome. Course closed Monday and October to February
Fees	IL30–50,000
Facilities	Bar and restaurant; practice ground

Golf Club Lignano (1991) **39**

Phone: 0431 428025

Via della Bonifica 3, 33054 Lignano Sabbiadoro

Near the centre of Lignano

Holes	18 Par 72 6280m.
Visitors	Welcome. Course closed Tuesday in winter
Fees	IL65,000
Facilities	Bar and restaurant; practice ground; swimming pool; tennis
Pro	Fortunato Ghezzo

Marco Simone Golf Club (1990) **40**

Phone: 0774 571311

Via Palombarese, 00012 Guidonia

North of Rome at Guidonia

Holes	18 Par 72 6407m.
Visitors	Welcome
Fees	IL50,000
Facilities	Bar and restaurant; short course

Margara Golfclub (1975) **41**

Phone: 0131 778555

Via Tenuta Margara 25, 15043 Fubine

West of Alessandria off the A21 at Fubine

Holes	18 Par 72 6045m.
Visitors	Welcome. Course closed Monday and December to January
Fees	IL50,000
Facilities	Bar and restaurant; practice ground; swimming pool; tennis
Pro	Guiseppe Sita

GC La Margherita (1989) **42**

Phone: 011 9795113

Strada Pralorma 29, Carmagnola

West of Asti, near Pralormo

Holes	18 Par 72 6278m.
Visitors	Welcome. Course closed Tuesday and January to February
Fees	IL50,000
Facilities	Bar and restaurant; swimming pool
Pro	Aldo Cameran

Golf Matilde di Canossa (1987) **43**

Phone: 0522 371295

Via Casinazzo 1, 42100 S Bartolomeo

Just south west of Reggio Emilia, off the A1

Holes	18 Par 72 6326m.
Visitors	Welcome
Fees	IL50,000
Facilities	Bar and restaurant closed Monday; practice ground
Pro	Liguorino De Gori

Menaggio & Cadenabbia Golfclub (1907) **44**

Phone: 0344 32103

Via Golf 12, 22010 Grandola e Uniti

Just south west of Menaggio

Holes	18 Par 69 5277m.
Visitors	Welcome, but must book. Course closed Tuesday, and December to February
Fees	IL70–90,000
Facilities	Bar and restaurant; practice ground
Pro	Delfino Gerolamo

This is the second oldest club in Italy and sits in the beautiful countryside of the Val Menaggio on the Lake Como shore. It was founded by a wealthy Englishman called Wyatt and later re-designed by John Harris. The hilly terrain and narrow, undulating fairways ensure that it is a testing course and the views are magnificent. There is also a notable golfing library in the clubhouse.

Milano Golfclub (1928)   45

Phone: 039 303081

Via dei Mulini 7, 20052 Parco di Monza
North of Milano and Monza. Head for the Parco
di Monza

Holes	18 Par 72 6414m.
	9 Par 36 2976m.
Visitors	Welcome, but must book at weekends. Course closed in August
Fees	IL80–100,000
Facilities	Bar and restaurant closed Monday; practice ground; swimming pool
Pro	G Grappasonni

The park was once owned by the now defunct
Italian royal family and it makes a superb
setting for one of the country's best courses. The
original design was by an Englishman called
Blandford and the course was re-modelled in the
Sixties and augmented by a further loop of nine
holes. The Italian Open has been staged here on
several occasions.

Modena Golf & Country Club (1987)   46

Phone: 059 553482

Via Vandelli 22a, 41050 Colombaro di Formigine
South of Modena between Formigine and
Maranello

Holes	18 Par 72 5785m.
Visitors	Welcome
Fees	IL100,000
Facilities	Bar and restaurant; practice ground; swimming poo; tennis
Pro	Nicola Carrera

Molinetto Golfclub (1982)   47

Phone: 02 92105128

SS Padana Sup 11, 200063 Cernusco Sul Naviglio
East of Milano, off the S11. Head for Cernusco

Holes	18 Par 72 6021m.
Visitors	Welcome during the week only. Course closed Monday
Fees	IL70,000
Facilities	Bar and restaurant; practice ground; swimming pool; tennis courts
Pro	Fernando Perini

This is quite a flat course but is a good test for
any golfer by dint of its narrow fairways and the
prevalence of water, which affects the play on
half the holes. It is part of a thriving country
club with many tennis courts (some indoor), and
an Olympic-sized swimming pool. The practice
ground is floodlit.

Montecatini Golf (1985)   48

Phone: 0572 62218

Via dei Brogi Loc Pievaccia, 51015 Monsummano
Terme
South east of Montecatini at Monsummano

Holes	18 Par 72 5932m.
Visitors	Welcome. Course closed Tuesday
Fees	IL50,000
Facilities	Bar and restaurant; practice ground
Pro	Mauro Ravinetto

Golfclub Monticello (1975)   49

Phone: 01 928055

Via Volta 4, 22070 Cassina Rizzardi
South west of Como, off the A9 near Fino
Mornasco

Holes	2 x 18 Par 72 6028/6365m.
Visitors	Members only at weekends. Course closed Monday
Fees	IL50–80,000
Facilities	Bar and restaurant; practice ground; swimming pool; tennis
Pro	Alberto Croce

As the venue for the Italian Open on many
occasions there is no doubt about the pedigree of
this course and you can tread in the footsteps of
such champions as Billy Casper, Brian Barnes
and Greg Norman, who holds the course record.
It is one of the few clubs in Italy with two
courses, which are both excellent challenges for
golfers of any standard. Hundreds of thousands
of trees, two lakes and the high-crested hills in
the background make golf here a most enjoyable
experience.

Circolo Golf Napoli (1968)   50

Phone: 081 5264296

Via Campiglione 11, 80072 Arco Felice
West of Napoli on the coast at Arco Felice

Holes	9 Par 35 2940m.
Visitors	By introduction only. Course closed Monday and Tuesday
Fees	IL40,000
Facilities	Bar and restaurant; practice ground; tennis
Pro	Cesirio Croce

Golf Club Nettuno (1989)   51

Phone: 06 9819419

Via della Campana, 00048 Nettuno
West of Latina at Nettuno

Holes	18 Par 72 6260m.
Visitors	Welcome. Course closed Wednesday
Fees	IL50,000
Facilities	Bar and restaurant; practice ground
Pro	Marco Luzzi

Olgiata Golf Club (1961)   **52**

Phone: 06 3789141

Largo Olgiata 15, 00123 Roma

North west of Rome, off the S2 near La Storta

Holes	18 Par 72 6185m.
	9 Par 34 2968m.
Visitors	By introduction only. Course closed Monday
Fees	IL50–80,000
Facilities	Bar and restaurant; practice ground; swimming pool
Pro	Ugo Grappasonni

The course was designed by C K Cotton and has an impeccable pedigree since it has been the venue for both the Eisenhower Trophy and the World Cup. It is a splendid parkland course with arrays of oaks and elms to threaten any wayward shots and the start is as unrelenting as the finish, where two par 5 holes often take their toll.

Padova Golfclub (1966)   **53**

Phone: 049 9130078

35030 Valsanzibio di Galzignano

South of Padova, off the A13 near Battaglia Terme

Holes	18 Par 72 6053m.
Visitors	Welcome. Course closed Monday and January
Fees	IL50–80,000
Facilities	Bar and restaurant; practice ground; swimming pool; tennis
Pro	Paolo Bernardini

Golf Club Parco de'Medici (1989)   **54**

Phone: 06 6553477

Autostrada Roma-Fiumicino km 4.5, 00148 Roma

On the south west side of Rome, off the A12

Holes	18 Par 72 6164m.
Visitors	Welcome. Course closed Tuesday
Fees	IL80,000
Facilities	Bar and restaurant; practice ground; short course; swimming pool; tennis
Pro	Roberto Terrinoni

Perugia Golf Club (1960/91)   **55**

Phone: 075 5172204

06074 Santa Sabina-Ellera

South west of Perugia near Ellera

Holes	18 Par 71 5560m.
Visitors	Welcome. Course closed Monday
Fees	IL40–50,000
Facilities	Bar and restaurant; practice ground
Pro	Barlozzo Antonelli

Golfclub Petersberg (1989)   **56**

Phone: 0471 6553477

Steinacherhof, 39040 Petersberg/Monte S Pietro

South of Bolzano, off the S48. Head for Monte S Pietro

Holes	9 Par 34 2550m.
Visitors	Welcome on weekdays only. Course closed November to April
Fees	IL50,000
Facilities	Bar and restaurant closed Tuesday; practice ground
Pro	Christopher Mawdsley

Piandisole GC (1966)   **57**

Phone: 0323 47100

Via alla Pineta 1, 28057 Premeno

North east of Verbania

Holes	9 Par 34 2512m.
Visitors	Welcome. Course closed December-March
Fees	IL50,000
Facilities	Bar and restaurant; practice ground
Pro	Paolo Ammirati

Golfclub La Pinetina Di Carbonate (1971)   **58**

Phone: 031 933202

Via al Golf 4, 22070 Appiano Gentile

South west of Como at Appiano

Holes	18 Par 71 6035m.
Visitors	Welcome. Course closed Tuesday
Fees	IL50–75,000
Facilities	Bar and restaurant; practice ground; swimming pool; tennis
Pro	Marcello Barzan

Ponte di Legno Golfclub (1985)   **59**

Phone: 0364 900306

Ponte di Legno, Brescia

At Ponte di Legno (north of Brescia)

Holes	9 Par 34 2409m.
Visitors	Welcome. Course closed October to June
Fees	IL30,000
Facilities	Bar and restaurant; practice ground
Pro	Emilio Ros

Golf Club Porto d'Orra (1977)   60

Phone: 0961 791045
88063 Catanzaro Lido
East of Catanzaro on the S106 along the coast

Holes	9 Par 35 2843m.
Visitors	Welcome. Course closed Monday
Fees	IL30–50,000
Facilities	Bar and restaurant; practice ground
Pro	Toribio Sanchez

Golfclub Punta Ala (1964)   61

Phone: 0564 922121
Via del Golf 1, 58040 Punta Ala
In Punta Ala (on the coast opposite Elba)

Holes	18 Par 72 6213m.
Visitors	Welcome
Fees	IL40–70,000
Facilities	Bar and restaurant; practice ground
Pro	Jeffrey Hall

This is one of Italy's best courses, whose fairways wind and roll through the pine trees. Each hole has its own distinct character in its tree-lined cocoon, and there are occasional glimpses of the sea. It is an excellent design and has the advantage of being close to the sandy beaches of the west coast.

Le Querce Golf Club (1987)   62

Phone: 0761 68374
S2 Cassia, 01036 Nepi-Sutri
South of Viterbo, off the S2 at Sutri

Holes	18 Par 72 6433m.
Visitors	Welcome. Course closed Wednesday
Fees	IL40–70,000
Facilities	Bar and restaurant; practice ground

Rapallo Golf Club (1930)   63

Phone: 0185 261777
Via Mameli 377, 16035 Rapallo
Just west of Rapallo

Holes	18 Par 70 5694m.
Visitors	Must book on weekends. Course closed Tuesday
Fees	IL80–100,000
Facilities	Bar and restaurant; practice ground; tennis
Pro	Manuel Caressa

Laid out alongside the River Boate this is not an especially long course but demands accuracy and some modest tactics if you are to score well. Offsprings from the main river cause the problems, aided by some stately trees, dog-leg holes and well-protected greens. It is a lot of fun.

Golfclub Riva Dei Tessali (1971)   64

Phone: 099 6439251
Castellaneta, 74025 Marina di Ginosa
West of Taranto, off the S106 at Riva dei Tessali

Holes	18 Par 71 5960m.
Visitors	Welcome. Course closed Tuesday in winter
Fees	IL50,000
Facilities	Bar and restaurant; practice ground; swimming pool; tennis
Pro	Bruno Cozenza

Golf Club La Rocca (1985)   65

Phone: 0521 834037
Via Campi 8, 43038 Sala Baganza
Just to the south west of Parma at Sala Baganza

Holes	18 Par 72 6103m.
Visitors	Welcome. Course closed Monday, and January to March
Fees	IL50,000
Facilities	Bar and restaurant; practice ground
Pro	Alfiero Pellegrini

Golf Club Roma (1903)   66

Phone: 06 7803407
Via dell'Acquasanta 3, Via Appia Nuova 716A, 00178 Roma
On the south side of Rome, off the S7

Holes	18 Par 71 5854m.
Visitors	By introduction only. Closed Monday
Fees	IL80–100,000
Facilities	Bar and restaurant; practice ground; swimming pool
Pro	Pietro Manca

This is the senior Italian course and lies within the boundaries of Rome itself; from the wide fairways you can see many landmarks including the Appian Way. It is a formidable course, especially from the back tees, by dint of the various streams which meander across the terrain and the fast, sloping greens; the 17th is a particularly difficult hole. The first Italian Championship was held here in 1906 and was won by Denys Scott, an Englishman.

Golfclub La Rossera (1972)   67

Phone: 035 838600
Via Montebello 4, 24060 Chiuduno
East of Bergamo, off the A4 at Chiuduno

Holes	9 Par 35 2640m.
Visitors	Welcome. Course closed Tuesday
Fees	IL40–60,000
Facilities	Bar and restaurant; practice ground
Pro	Gary Watson

Golf Pubblico Le Rovedine (1978)   68

Phone: 02 57602730
Via C Mars, 20090 Noverasco di Opera
South of Milano. Take the S412 off the ring road

Holes	18 Par 72 6205m.
Visitors	Welcome. Course closed Monday
Fees	IL50,000
Facilities	Bar and restaurant; practice ground; swimming pool; tennis
Pro	Joe Messana

San Michele Golfclub (1985)   69

Phone: 0982 91012
Loc Bosco 8/9, 87022 Cetraro
Just north of Cetraro on the coast

Holes	9 Par 31 2600m.
Visitors	Welcome
Fees	IL50,000
Facilities	Bar and restaurant; driving range
Pro	Luis Gallardo

Golfclub Sanremo degli Ulivi (1928)   70

Phone: 0184 557093
Via Campo Golf 59, 18038 San Remo
On the north west side of San Remo

Holes	18 Par 67 5230m.
Visitors	Welcome. Course closed Tuesday
Fees	IL50–75,000
Facilities	Bar and restaurant; practice ground
Pro	Mario Bianco

Golfclub Royal Sant'Anna (1978)   71

Phone: 0341 577551
22040 Annone di Brianza
Just south east of Lecco

Holes	9 Par 35 2930m.
Visitors	Welcome. Course closed Tuesday
Fees	IL80,000
Facilities	Bar and restaurant; practice ground; swimming pool; tennis
Pro	Lorenzo Brambilla

Golfclub Santa Croce (1991)   72

Phone: 0171 387041
Fraz Mellana, 12012 Boves
South of Cuneo, at Boves

Holes	18 Par 72 6050m.
Visitors	Welcome. Course closed Tuesday and December to March
Fees	IL50–70,000
Facilities	Bar and restaurant; practice ground; swimming pool
Pro	Giorgio Colombatto

Golfclub La Serra (1972)   73

Phone: 0131 954778
Via Astigliano 42, 15049 Valenza
Just north of Alessandria off the S494

Holes	9 Par 36 2823m.
Visitors	Welcome. Course closed December to February
Fees	IL35–50,000
Facilities	Bar and restaurant; practice ground; swimming pool; tennis
Pro	Domenico Caputo

Golf Sestrieres (1932)   74

Phone: 0122 76243
Piazza Agnelli 4, 10058 Sestriere
Just south of Sestriere off the S23

Holes	18 Par 67 4598m.
Visitors	Welcome. Course closed October to June
Fees	IL50–75,000
Facilities	Bar and restaurant; practice ground
Pro	Marcello Vinzi

Stupinigi GC (1972)   75

Phone: 011 343975
Corse Unione Sovietica 506, 10135 Torino
On the south west side of Torino, off the S23

Holes	9 Par 33 2175m.
Visitors	Welcome. Course closed Monday and August
Fees	IL50,000
Facilities	Bar and restaurant; practice ground
Pro	Franco Luzi

Tirrenia Golf Club (1968)　　76

Phone: 050 37518

Viale San Guido, 56018 Tirrenia

South west of Piza, off the A12 at Tirrenia

Holes	9 Par 36 3065m.
Visitors	Welcome. Course closed Tuesday
Fees	IL50,000
Facilities	Bar and restaurant
Pro	Massimo Mulas

Torino GC (1956)　　77

Phone: 011 9235440

Via Grange 137, 10070 Fiano Torinese

North of Torino near Fiano

Holes	2 x 18 Par 72 6216/6211m.
Visitors	Welcome. Course closed Monday and January/February
Fees	IL80–100,000
Facilities	Bar and restaurant; practice ground; swimming pool
Pro	O Bolognesi

The club started its life with nine holes laid out by John Morrison and a further nine were later added by John Harris in 1975. There is an American look to the course with its water hazards and large undulating greens and the 12th, a double dog-leg hole, is a notable test. The fourth nine holes were laid out by the Italian architect Marco Croze in 1986.

Trentino Golf Folgaria (1987)　　78

Phone: 0461 981682

38057 Pergine

South of Trento near Folgaria

Holes	9 Par 35 2582m.
Visitors	Welcome. Course closed November to April
Fees	IL50,000
Facilities	Bar and restaurant; practice ground
Pro	Malcolm Harrison

Trieste Golf Club (1971)　　79

Phone: 040 226159

Via Padriciano 80, 34012 Trieste

Just north east of Trieste

Holes	9 Par 36 3010m.
Visitors	Welcome. Course closed Tuesday
Fees	IL20–50,000
Facilities	Bar and restaurant; practice ground; tennis
Pro	Ezio Pavan

Udine Golf Club (1971)　　80

Phone: 0432 800418

1 Via dei Faggi, 33034 Fagagna-Villaverde

North west of Udine, off the S464

Holes	9 Par 36 2944m.
Visitors	Welcome. Course closed Tuesday
Fees	IL50,000
Facilities	Bar and restaurant; practice ground
Pro	Luciano Tavarini

Ugolino Golf Club (1943)　　81

Phone: 055 2301009

Via Chiantigiana 3, 50015 Grassina

South of Firenze off the S222

Holes	18 Par 70 5741m.
Visitors	Welcome. Closed Monday
Fees	IL50–75,000
Facilities	Bar and restaurant; practice ground; swimming pool; tennis
Pro	Franco Rosi

The course is situated in delightful countryside and runs through hilly terrain which is strewn with olive trees, umbrella pines and cypress trees. It is a short course but the 4th and 8th holes, which are laid through claustrophobic avenues of trees, are particularly fine and the finish is quite demanding. Ugolino is the home course of one of Italy's best golfers, Baldovino Dassu.

Varese Golfclub (1934)　　82

Phone: 0332 229302

Via Vitt Veneto 32, 21020 Luvinate

West of Varese, off the S394

Holes	18 Par 71 5942m.
Visitors	Must book. Course closed Monday
Fees	IL50–75,000
Facilities	Bar and restaurant; practice ground
Pro	Silvano Abbiati

The course lies between the mountains and the lakes, several of which can be seen from the fairways, including Varese and Maggiore. One of the most remarkable views, across forest and water to distant mountains, comes from the 10th tee. It is a challenging course, on which Peter Alliss won the Italian Open in 1958. The clubhouse was once a 12th century monastery and is an extraordinarily charming building.

Venezia Golfclub (1928)   **83**
Phone: 041 731015
Via del Forte, 30011 Alberoni
On the Lido di Venezia near Alberoni
Holes   18 Par 72 6199m.
Visitors   Welcome but must book. Course closed Monday
Fees   IL80–100,000
Facilities   Bar and restaurant; practice ground
Pro   Regan O'Rourke

A distinct links atmosphere prevails at this course, mainly because it was built on sand dunes at the southern end of the Lido island, amid the waters of the Adriatic. In addition, there are lots of trees to compound the golfer's problems and the challenge presented by the course is firmly stated by the difficult short 5th hole, which is followed by a very tough par 5. Further challenging par 5s ensue with the 8th, a tiger at nearly 600 yards with water on the left side, and the 11th which also has menacing water hazards. It is a testing course where the 1974 Italian Open, won by Peter Oosterhuis, was held.

Verona Golfclub (1962)   **84**
Phone: 045 510060
Ca'del Sale 15, 37066 Sommacampagna
West of Verona at Sommacampagna
Holes   18 Par 72 6037m.
Visitors   Welcome. Course closed Tuesday
Fees   IL50,000
Facilities   Bar and restaurant; practice ground; tennis
Pro   Eugenio Ridolfi

Versilia Golf Club (1988)   **85**
Phone: 0584 881574
Via della Sipe 40, 55045 Pietrasnata (LU)
Off the A12 west of Lucca and just south of Pietrasanta
Holes   18 Par 72 5115m.
Visitors   Welcome
Fees   IL70,000
Facilities   Bar and restaurant; practice ground; swimming pool; tennis
Pro   Angelo Croce

This is very much a holiday course in a popular tourist area and the casual visitor should avoid August when there are many competitions. The main interest of the course is the use of water, which affects your play on more than half the holes. The course is short and flat, but has the advantage, if there are non-golfers in your party, of an excellent swimming pool, tennis court and a good restaurant.

Golfclub Vigevano Santa Martretta (1974)   **86**
Phone: 0381 346628
Via Chitola 49, 27029 Vigevano
On the south east side of Vigevano, of the S494
Holes   9 Par 36 2978m.
Visitors   Welcome. Course closed Monday
Fees   IL20–50,000
Facilities   Bar and restaurant; practice ground
Pro   Giovanni Veronelli

Villa Condulmer Golf Club (1961)   **87**
Phone: 041 457062
Via della Croce 3, 31021 Zerman di Mogliano
North west of Venice at Mogliano Veneto
Holes   18 Par 71 5905m.
Visitors   Welcome. Course closed Monday
Fees   IL50,000
Facilities   Bar and restaurant; practice ground; tennis
Pro   Ugo Scafa

Villa d'Este Golfclub (1926)   **88**
Phone: 031 200200
Via per Cantu 13, 22030 Montorfano
South east of Como at Montorfano
Holes   18 Par 71 5787m.
Visitors   Must book. Course closed January
Fees   IL70–100,000
Facilities   Bar and restaurant closed Monday; practice ground
Pro   Giancarlo Frigerio

Twenty miles north of Milan, five miles from Lake Como and adjacent to the shores of pretty Lake Montorfano is the magnificent layout at Villa d'Este. It is undoubtedly one of the top five courses in Italy (it was ranked 28th in Europe by Golf World magazine in 1991). Always beautifully maintained, the fairways wend their way around a dense forest of pines, chestnuts and firs. Particularly noteworthy are the six par 3 holes which frequently require six different club selections. All in all Villa d'Este offers a classic examination of mature parkland golf.

Vinovo Golfclub (1985)   **89**
Phone: 011 9653880
Via Stupinigi 182, 10048 Vinovo
Just southwest of Torino, off the S23 near the hippodrome
Holes   9 Par 32 2082m.
Visitors   Welcome. Course closed Monday
Fees   IL25–35,000
Facilities   Bar and restaurant; practice ground
Pro   S Fiammengo

Golfclub Zoate (1984)   **90**
Phone: 02 90632183
Via Verdi 6, 20067 Zoate di Tribiano
South east of Milano at Tribiano
Holes   18 Par 72 6122m.
Visitors   Welcome. Course closed Monday
Fees   IL 50–75,000
Facilities Bar and restaurant; swimming pool;
             tennis
Pro   Stefano Zerega

The club has twice hosted the Italian Open,
which was won by Baldovino Dassu in 1976 and
Mark James in 1982. It is an excellent course
whose difficulties are enhanced by the water
hazards and tricky plateau greens.

Elba

Elba Golfclub dell'Acquabona (1971)   **91**
Phone: 0565 940066
57037 Portoferraio Elba
To the south east of Portoferraio on Elba
Holes   9 Par 34 2572m.
Visitors   Welcome. Course closed Monday in
             winter
Fees   IL50,000
Facilities Bar and restaurant; swimming pool
Pro   Giovanni Ciprandi

Sardinia

Golfclub Is Molas (1975)   **92**
Phone: 070 9241013
09010 Pula, Sardinia
South of Cagliari in S. Margharita
Holes   18 Par 72 6383m.
Visitors   Welcome
Fees   IL50–75,000
Facilities Bar and restaurant; practice ground;
             swimming pool; tennis
Pro   Pastillo Arcangel

Pevero Golfclub Costa Smeralda (1972)   **93**
Phone: 0789 96210
097020 Porto Cervo, Costa Smeralda, Sardinia
Just south of Porto Cervo
Holes   18 Par 72 6168m.
Visitors   Welcome, but must book. Course
             closed Tuesday
Fees   IL55–100,000
Facilities Bar and restaurant; practice ground;
             swimming pool
Pro   Luciano Cau

Robert Trent Jones has designed many extraordinary courses in many countries but some critics
consider Pevero to be his masterpiece. It was
originally commissioned by the Aga Khan and
perhaps the biggest wonder is that Pevero exists
at all given the nature of the landscape out of
which it was carved, blasted and in other ways
created. The land in question is the dramatic,
wild scrubland and jagged, rocky coastline of
Sardinia's Costa Smeralda region. The design of
Pevero stands as a monument to Trent Jones at
his most daring with several of the holes
affording sudden sweeping views of distant
mountains and of the vivid turquoise sea.

THE NETHERLANDS

G OLF historians have put up persuasive evidence that an embryonic form of the game was played as early at 1297 in Holland. The arguments presented by the scholarly Steven van Hengel in 'Early Golf' are enough to make any Scotsman blanch.

It is surprising, therefore, that it is only in the last decade that a spectacular growth in enthusiasm for the game has occurred in the Netherlands; and the entrepreneurs have made a determined effort to satisfy the surging demand. In the last seven years over 50 golf courses have been built to bring the number up to around 130; roughly one third of these are 9 hole courses.

It must be said that many of the newer courses offer fairly basic facilities, but they are ideal places for people to learn the game.

In contrast some of the older Dutch courses are among the finest in Europe. First, a great triumvirate of links courses lies in a line, starting with The Hague and going northwards to Noordwijk and Kennemer. They bear comparison with any rivals and represent magnificently stern tests of golf. In comparison there are the gentler charms of the Golf Cub De Pan on the outskirts of Utrecht, of the Eindhoven Club, and of De Haar, with its fairy tale castle.

The Netherlands is a rewarding place for any golfer and is easily accessible from Britain on the cross-Channel ferries. The Dutch people usually speak excellent English and tee times can be booked without any difficulty. There is a remarkably good system of motorways in the country and from a base such as Amsterdam, Utrecht or The Hague, a golfer can choose to play on some memorable courses.

Unit of currency: Dutch florin (or Guilder)
Rate of exchange (approx. at 1.1.93): Dfl 2.70–£1
International dialling code: (010 31)

Golfclub Almeerderhout (1987)	I

Phone: 03240 21818

Watersnipweg 19-21 1341AA Almere

East of Amsterdam off the A6; take the N27 exit and in Zeewolde turn left for the club

Holes	18 Par 72 5896m.
Visitors	Welcome
Fees	Dfl50–70
Facilities	Bar and restaurant; driving range; par 3 course
Pro	Ryan Tolmeyer

Amsterdamse Golf Club (1990)	2

Phone: 02907 7866

Bauduinlaan 35, 1165 NE Halfweg

Off the N5 west of Amsterdam. Take the exit to Spaarnwoude, head for Houtrak-Ruirgoord and then turn into Bauduinlaan

Holes	18 Par 72 5927m.
Visitors	Must book
Fees	Dfl50–75
Facilities	Bar and restaurant; pitch & putt
Pro	Nigel Lancaster

THE NETHERLANDS

Alkmaar

Amsterdam

The Hague

Utrecht

Rotterdam

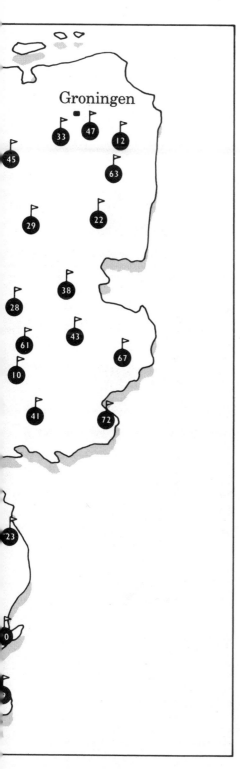

Groningen

Golfclub Amsterdam Old Course (1934) 3

Phone: 020 6043650

Zwartelaantje 4, 1099 CE Amsterdam

South east of Amsterdam off the Utrecht road
(A2). Take the Diemen/ Duivendrecht exit (S211)
and then first left after sign 'Amsterdam-Zuid-
Oost'; take two more left turns to the club

Holes	9 Par 35 2632m.
Visitors	Must book
Fees	Dfl75–90
Facilities	Bar and restaurant closed Monday; practice ground
Pro	Nigel Lancaster

Anderstein Golf Club (1986) 4

Phone: 03433 1330

Woudenbergseweg 13a, 3953 ME Maarsbergen

On the N226 near junction with E35 at Maarn

Holes	18 Par 72 6037m.
Visitors	Pm only; or at weekends with a member
Fees	Dfl40/60
Facilities	Bar/restaurant closed Monday in winter; practice ground; 5 practice holes
Pro	Mauk de Booy

The course, which opened in 1986, has two
distinct characteristics. Some of the holes on the
first half were built on the polderland (reclaimed
land) and water is one of the primary hazards, as
it is on many other holes. The rest of the course
threads its way through the forest and there are
some very tight holes where accuracy is
essential from the tee. The 18th hole is a very
interesting double dogleg through towering trees
to a three-tiered green. It is a busy club and non-
members can only play in the afternoons (you
must book ahead).

Golf Club de Berendonck (1985) 5

Phone: 08894 20039

Weg door de Berendonck 40, 6603 LP Wijchen

Off the A50 between Arnhem and Oss. Take the
Nijmegen/Venlo turn (A73)

Holes	18 Par 71 5928m.
Visitors	Must book
Fees	Dfl25–35
Facilities	Bar and restaurant: driving range
Pro	Andrew Allen

Golfcentrum Best (1988)   6

Phone: 04998 91443

Golflaan 1, 5683 RZ Best

Off the A2 north west of Eindhoven. After the canal turn right for Bataweg then left for the club

Holes	18 Par 72 5935m.
Visitors	Must book
Fees	Dfl60–80
Facilities	Bar and restaurant; driving range
Pro	H Dieben

Golfclub Broekpolder (1981)   7

Phone: 010 474 8140

Watersportweg 100, 3138 HD Vlaardingen

West of Rotterdam off the A20. Take the Vlaardingen West exit

Holes	18 Par 72 6048m.
Visitors	Must book
Fees	Dfl60–90
Facilities	Bar and restaurant closed Monday in winter; driving range
Pro	J Hage

The course, designed by Frank Pennink on land reclaimed from the sea (polderland), opened for play over ten years ago. It is very flat but good use is made of water hazards and the greens are quick.

Golfclub Brugse Vaart (1988)   8

Phone: 01170 53410

Brugse Vart 10, 4501 NE Oostburg

Off the N58 south of Oostburg

Holes	9 Par 35 2708m.
Visitors	Welcome
Fees	Dfl50–70
Facilities	Bar; driving range
Pro	Olivier Buysse

Openbare Golf Brunssummerheide (1985)   9

Phone: 045 270968

Rimburgerweg 51, 6445 PA Brunssum

Take Brunssum exit off the A2 Eindhoven to Heerlen road. The club is a few km south east of the town

Holes	18 Par 71 5457m.
Visitors	Welcome
Fees	Dfl40–60
Facilities	Bar and restaurant; driving range; pitch and putt course
Pro	Dick Kuysters

Golfclub de Breuninkhof (1990)   10

Phone: 05716 1955

Breuninkhofweg, Bussloo

Off the A1 east of Amersfoort; take the N345 Zutphen exit. Follow sign to Deventer/Wilp (not Bussloo)

Holes	9 Par 36 3062m.
Visitors	Welcome
Fees	Dfl30–45
Facilities	Bar and restaurant closed Monday; practice ground
Pro	Bee Baboe

Golf & Country Club Cappelle aan den Ijssel (1977)   11

Phone: 45 30559

's Gravenweg 311, 2900 AS Capelle a/d Ijssel

East of Rotterdam; head for Capelle

Holes	18 Par 69 5217m.
Visitors	Welcome
Fees	Dfl45/75
Facilities	Bar and restaurant
Pro	Frans Willem Castien

Golfbaan de Compagnie (1990)   12

Phone: 05987 25272

Sportpark de Langeleegte, Ontspanningsweg, Veendam

About 3km west of Veendam (off the N33)

Holes	9 Par 36 3085m.
Visitors	Welcome
Fees	Dfl40–50
Facilities	Bar; driving range (both closed on Monday)
Pro	Pim van den Toorn

Crayestein Golf (1988)   13

Phone: 078 211221

Baanhoekweg 50, 3313 LP Dordrecht

East of Dordrecht off the A15. Take the Papendrecht exit, then signs to de Staart

Holes	18 Par 71 5754m.
Visitors	Welcome
Fees	Dfl40–50
Facilities	Bar and restaurant; practice ground
Pro	Henk en Kees Kuijsters

Golfclub Cromstrijen (1989)   14

Phone: 01865 4455

Veerweg 26, 3281 LX Numansdorp

Take Numansdorp exit off the A29 Rotterdam-Zierikzee; turn right to Hollandsch Diep

Holes	18 Par 72 6135m.
Visitors	Welcome
Fees	Dfl40–80
Facilities	Bar and restaurant closed Monday; driving range; 9 hole short course
Pro	Martin Shoulder

Golf & Countryclub Crossmoor (1986)   15

Phone: 04950 18438

Laurabosweg 6-8, 6006 VR Weert

South east of Eindhoven off the A2; take the exit for Parklaan-Diesterbaan

Holes	18 Par 72 6052m.
Visitors	Welcome
Fees	Dfl50–95
Facilities	Bar and restaurant; driving range
Pro	Rudi Brown

Domburgsche Golfclub (1914)   16

Phone: 01188 1573

Schelpweg 26, 4357 BP Domburg

North west of Middelburg exit off the A58. Head for Domburg; the club is on the edge of the village

Holes	9 Par 35 2549m.
Visitors	Welcome
Fees	Dfl50–60
Facilities	Bar and restaurant
Pro	L Verberne

Golfclub De Dommel (1928)   17

Phone: 04105 12316

Zegenwerp 12, 5271 NC St Michielsgestel

Off the N2 north of Eindhoven; take the turn to St Michielsgestel and then to Schijndel

Holes	12 Par 70 5562m.
Visitors	Welcome
Fees	Dfl35–80
Facilities	Bar and restaurant closed Monday; practice ground
Pro	M J Groenendaal

This attractive parkland course, with its profusion of mature trees, was designed by Harry Colt in the late 1920s. It has an unusual layout of 12 holes, some with different tees, to make up a full course of 18 holes. Water affects the play on several holes.

Golf & Country Club Edda Huzid (1989)   18

Phone: 03429 1661

Hunnenweg 16, 3781 NN Voorthuizen

The course is just east of Voorthuizen, off the N344

Holes	9 Par 36 3074m.
Visitors	Welcome
Fees	Dfl30–55
Facilities	Bar and restaurant; driving range
Pro	Bob Hesselman

Edese Golfclub (1978)   19

Phone: 08308 21985

Sportcenter Papendal, Sportlaan 1, 6816 VE Arnhem

West of Arnhem off the N224; take the turn for Papendal

Holes	18 Par 72 6075m.
Visitors	Welcome
Fees	Dfl30–60
Facilities	Bar and restaurant closed Monday
Pro	Kees Borst

Eindhovensche Golfclub (1930)   20

Phone: 04902 14816

Eindhovenseweg 300, 5553 VB Valkenswaard

South of Eindhoven off the N69; turn left 3km south of Waalre

Holes	18 Par 70 5918m.
Visitors	Welcome
Fees	Dfl45–90
Facilities	Bar and restaurant closed Monday; driving range
Pro	G Jeurissen

The course was started at the instigation of Dr A F Philips, the brother of the founder of the great electrical company. It was designed by Harry Colt and opened for play in 1930. It resembles many of the courses in Surrey, as its fairways snake beguilingly between avenues of pines. The club has played host to many championships, including the Dutch Open.

Golfpark Flevoland (1989)   21

Phone: 03200 30077
Bosweg 1, 8200 AC Lelystad
Take the Lelystad-Noord exit off the A6
Amsterdam-Emmeloord, take road to Lelystad-
Haven and follow signs to the club

Holes	9 Par 36 2870m.
Visitors	Welcome
Fees	Dfl40–50
Facilities	Bar closed Monday; driving range
Pro	Rob van der Brink

Drentse Golfclub De Gelpenberg (1970)   22

Phone: 059117 1784
Gebbeveenweg 1, 7854 TD Aalden
West of Emmen off the N31; turn south for
Aalden

Holes	18 Par 70 5867m.
Visitors	Welcome
Fees	Dfl60–75
Facilities	Bar and restaurant; practice ground
Pro	WJNM Stevens

Golf-en Countryclub Geysteren (1974)   23

Phone: 04784 1809
Het Spekt 2, 5862 AZ Geysteren
Between Venray and Wansumn off the N270

Holes	18 Par 72 6063m.
Visitors	Welcome
Fees	Dfl40–90
Facilities	Bar and restuarant closed Monday in winter; driving range
Pro	LG van Mook

Golfclub Grevelingenhout (1988)   24

Phone: 01113 2650
Oudendijk 2, 4311 NA Bruinisse
Take the Zierikzee (N59) exit off the A29 from
Rotterdam. Turn right in Bruinisse for Aqua
Delta and then first left

Holes	18 Par 72 5965m.
Visitors	Must book
Fees	Dfl40–80
Facilities	Bar and restaurant closed Monday in winter; driving range; 9 hole short course
Pro	Koen Kroon

Haagsche Golf & Country Club (1893)   25

Phone: 01751 19251
Groot Haesebroekseweg 22, 2243 EC Wassenaar
Off the A44 at Wassenaar

Holes	18 Par 71 5674m.
Visitors	Must book in advance.
Fees	Dfl50–100
Facilities	Bar and restaurant; practice ground
Pro	A B Loesberg

The club dates back to the late 19th century but
the Germans destroyed it during World War II
and the present course was opened in 1947. It is
one of the stiffest tests of golf in Europe, a
wonderful links course laid out among plunging
fairways and with tight and undulating greens.
Severe trouble awaits any inaccurate shots:
willow scrub and buckthorn will trap your ball.
When the wind gets up, it is an intimidating
course for the most accomplished golfers:
novices should be warned. The Haagsche has
been the setting for the Dutch Open on many
occasions.

Golfclub De Haar (1974)   26

Phone: 03407 2860
Parkweg 5, 3451 RH Vleuten
North of Utrecht off the A2; take the Vleuten
exit and make for Harmelen and Woerdan

Holes	9 Par 36 2868m.
Visitors	Welcome
Fees	Dfl50–100
Facilities	Bar and restaurant closed Monday
Pro	Alistair Donald

The magnificent 16th century De Haar Castle
dominates the whole area and the course runs
through its grounds, by courtesy of the owner,
Baron Van Zuylen van Nijevelt. An eccentrically
shaped lake runs across several holes and the
course is worth a visit to see the extraordinary
variety of trees and vegetation - as well as the
great romantic castle.

Haarlemmermeersche Golfclub (1986)   27

Phone: 02508 1706
Cruquiusdijk 122, 2142 EV Vijfhuizen
South east of Haarlem off the N201. Head for
Vijfhuizen

Holes	9 Par 36 2938m.
Visitors	Welcome
Fees	Dfl35–45
Facilities	Bar and restaurant; driving range; pitch and putt course
Pro	H Peetoom

Hattemse Golf & Country Club (1930)   28

Phone: 05206 41285

Veenwal 11, 8051 AS Hattem

South west of Zwolle, between Hattem and Heerde

Holes	9 Par 34 2613m.
Visitors	Welcome
Fees	Dfl30–60
Facilities	Bar and restaurant closed Monday
Pro	HW Vaatjes

Golfclub Havelte (1986)   29

Phone: 05214 2200

Kolonieweg 2, 7971 RA Havelte

From Meppel go north on the N32; take the N371 through Havelte towards Uffelte

Holes	9 Par 36 3036m.
Visitors	Welcome
Fees	Dfl35–60
Facilities	Bar and restaurant
Pro	Henk Beekhof

Golf Club Herkenbosch (1992)   30

Phone: 04752 1458

Stationsweg 106, 6075 CD Herkenbosch

Take the N274 to the south of Roermond, and follow signs to Melick and then to Herkenbosch

Holes	18 Par 72 6120m.
Visitors	Welcome
Fees	Dfl70–90
Facilities	Bar and restaurant closed Monday; practice ground

Leender Golfclub Haviksoord (1977)   31

Phone: 04906 1818

Maarheezerweg-N 11, 5595 XG Leende

South of Eindhoven off the A2

Holes	9 Par 35 2898m.
Visitors	Welcome
Fees	Dfl25–35
Facilities	Bar and restaurant; driving range
Pro	Flip Klok

Hilversumsche Golf Club (1910)   32

Phone: 035 857 060

Soestdijkerstraatweg 172, 1213 XJ Hilversum

South-east of Hilversum. On the N201 near the junction with the A27

Holes	18 Par 71 5859m.
Visitors	Must book. Members only at weekends.
Fees	Dfl60–90
Facilities	Bar and restaurant; practice ground
Pro	Martin Morbey

The club was founded in the early years of this century and has held the Dutch Open on several occasions. The course was carved out of the forests; its fairways are lined with mature trees and sit on flat, sandy soil.

Golf Club Holthuizen-Roden (1985)   33

Phone: 05908 15103

South west of Groningen; off the A7 take the exit for Leek and Roden (N372); turn left in Roden for Peize

Holes	9 Par 36 2743m.
Visitors	Welcome
Fees	Dfl55–65
Facilities	Bar and restaurant; driving range (both closed on Monday)
Pro	Daan Blok

Golfclub de Hooge Bergsche (1989)   34

Phone: 01892 20052

Rottebandreef 40, Hooge Bergse Bos, 2661 JK Bergschenhoek

North of Rotterdam off the A20

Holes	9 Par 35 2870m.
Visitors	Welcome
Fees	Dfl35–45
Facilities	Bar; driving range

Golf & Countryclub Hoenshuis (1986)   35

Phone: 045 753300

Heonsweg 17,6367 GM Voerendaal

Off the A79 between Maastrich and Heerlen

Holes	18 Par 72 6066m.
Visitors	Welcome
Fees	Dfl60–90
Facilities	Bar and restaurant; driving range
Pro	R Salmon

Golfbaan de Hoge Dijk (1991)   36
(Olympus Open Golfclub)
Phone: 002946 5373
Abcouderstraat 46, 1105 AA Amsterdam
South of Amsterdam off the A2. Take the A9,
marked for Amersfoort, and then the S111
towards Bullewijk. Turn left at the Academisch
Medish Centrum

Holes	9 Par 34 2498m.
Visitors	Welcome
Fees	Dfl35
Facilities	Bar (New clubhouse due to open at the end of 1993); driving range
Pro	C Broekhuijsen

Golfclub de Hoge Kleij (1985)   37
Phone: 033 616944
Appelweg 4, 3832 RK Leusden
East of Utrecht off the A28

Holes	18 Par 72 6080m.
Visitors	Must book
Fees	Dfl60–90
Facilities	Bar and restaurant closed Monday in winter; driving range
Pro	Tim Giles

Golf & Country Club Hooge Graven (1991) 38
Phone: 05291 51692
Hessenweg Oost 3a, 7735 KP Arrien
East of Ommen off the N34

Holes	9 Par 36 3100m.
Visitors	Welcome
Fees	Dfl50–70
Facilities	Bar; driving range
Pro	F Willems

Golfclub de Hooge Vorssel (1991)   39
Phone: 04124 1897
Slotenseweg 11, 5388 R Nistelrode
South of Oss off the A50; head for Heesch and
Nistelrode

Holes	9 Par 36 3018m.
Visitors	Welcome
Fees	Dfl100
Facilities	Bar; driving range; pitch and putt
Pro	Anthony Verbunt

Kennemer Golf & Country Club (1910)   40
Phone: 02507 12836
Kennemerweg 78, 2040 AB Zandvoort
Just off the N201 at Zandvoort

Holes	3 x 9 Par 72 2951m/2916m/2942m.
Visitors	Reserve in advance. Not Tuesday (Ladies Day) or Friday (visiting societies)
Fees	Dfl100
Facilities	Bar and restaurant closed Monday; practice ground
Pro	J Buchanan

The fine old thatched clubhouse gives command-
ing views of this marvellous, traditional links,
which was designed by Harry Colt and began
play in 1928. An extra loop of 9 holes was added
by Frank Pennink.

The holes wind through the sandhills in a
most beguiling way; the fairways are lined with
gorse bushes and small trees but are reasonably
generous in width, even if the bumps and
hollows rarely allow a level stance. It is a
magnificent seaside course, very challenging in
the wind and has been the venue of the Dutch
Open many times. Its clubhouse is full of interest
and includes a 17th century Dutch painting of
two young golfers.

Keppelse Golfclub (1926)   41
Phone: 08348 1416
Oude Zutphenseweg 15, Hoog-Keppel
North of Doetinchem, off the N317 at Laag
Keppel

Holes	9 Par 35 2680m.
Visitors	Welcome
Fees	Dfl30–65
Facilities	Bar
Pro	Hein Kaal

Golfclub Kleiburg (1974)   42
Phone: 01810 13330
Krabbeweg 9, 3231 NB Brielle
West of Rotterdam off the A15, and a few
kilometres east of Brielle

Holes	18 Par 72 6170m.
Visitors	Welcome
Fees	Dfl30–40
Facilities	Bar and restaurant; driving range
Pro	Wim Coudijs

Golfclub de Koepel (1983) **43**

Phone: 05496 76150

Rijssensestraat 172, 7642 NN Wierden

Off the N344 south of Wierden

Holes	9 Par 35 2863m.
Visitors	Welcome
Fees	Df160–80
Facilities	Bar and restaurant closed Monday; driving range
Pro	Andrew Young

Golf Club Kralingen (1931) **44**

Phone: 010 4522283

Kralingseweg 200, 3062 CG Rotterdam

In Rotterdam-East, off the A16. Head for Kralingen and the club is after the lake

Holes	9 Par 32 2428m.
Visitors	Welcome
Fees	Df125–30
Facilities	Bar and restaurant; driving range
Pro	Richard Heykant

Golf & Country Club Lauswolt (1965) **45**

Phone: 05126 2594

Van Harinxmaweg 8a, 9244 CJ Beetsterzwaag

North east of Heerenveen; turn towards Beetsterzwang

Holes	9 Par 36 2969m.
Fees	Df160–80
Facilities	Bar
Pro	John Too

Golfclub Nieuwegein Benson Lodge (1985) **46**

Phone: 03402 40769

Blokhoeve 7, 3438 KC Nieuwegein

South of Utrecht off the A12; take the Nieuwegein/Houten exit

Holes	9 Par 34 2348m.
Visitors	Welcome
Fees	Df135–50
Facilities	Bar and restaurant; driving range
Pro	R Visser

Noord Nederlandse Golf & Country Club (1950) **47**

Phone: 05906 2004

Pollselaan 5, 9756 CJ Glimmen

South of Groningen, off the A28; take the Glimmen exit and head for Zuidlaren

Holes	18 Par 70 5677m.
Visitors	Welcome
Fees	Df140–70
Facilities	Bar and restaurant; driving range
Pro	Kees Visser

De Noordhollandse Golfclub (1982) **48**

Phone: 072 156807

Sluispolderweg 6, 1817 BM Alkmaar

Off the A9, north of Alkmaar

Holes	9 Par 36 3098m.
Visitors	Welcome
Fees	Df150–100
Facilities	Bar and restaurant; practice ground
Pro	Philip Horn

Noordwijkse Golfclub (1915) **49**

Phone: 02523 73761

Randweg 25, 2204 AL Noordwijk

7km north of Noordwijk off the A44

Holes	18 Par 72 5868m.
Visitors	Must book. Cannot play between 12 and 3pm weekdays, nor after 8am at weekends (except with a member).
Fees	Df1100
Facilities	Bar and restaurant closed Monday in winter; practice ground; 4 practice holes
Pro	Tom O'Mahoney

There is a panoramic view of what awaits you on this magnificent course from the elevated first tee and from the windows of the bar and the restaurant on the top floor of the clubhouse. When the wind blows, as it usually does, less doughty golfers might choose the comforts of the bar. Noordwijk is a classic links, which offers a daunting test of golf on its roller-coaster fairways which snake between the dunes. A few holes during the first half are cut through forest but the majority are shaped through the sandhills. Noordwijk has been the venue for the Dutch Open on many occasions.

Nunspeetse Golf & Country Club (1988) **50**

Phone: 03412 58034

Plesmanlaan 30, 8072 PT Nunspeet

Off the A28 south west of Zwolle and just to the east of Nunspeet

Holes	3 loops of 9 Par 36; all approx. 3050m.
Visitors	Must book
Fees	Df165–85
Facilities	Bar and restaurant; driving range

Oosterhoutse Golf Club (1985)   51

Phone: 01620 58759
Dukaatstraat 21, 4903 RN Oosterhout
North of Breda off the A27; take the exit to
Oosterhout-Zuid

Holes	18 Par 72 6010m.
Visitors	Can play only with a club member
Fees	Dfl35–60
Facilities	Bar and restaurant; driving range
Pro	Kees Renders

Golfclub Oude Maas (1975)   52

Phone: 01890 18058
Veerweg 2a, 3161 EX Rhoon
South west of Rotterdam, off the A15; take the
Rhoon exit

Holes	18 Par 70 5354m.
Visitors	Must book
Fees	Dfl30–50
Facilities	Bar and restaurant closed Monday in winter; driving range
Pro	Rinus Goor

Golfclub Ouden Rhijn (1991)   53

Phone: 03406 21661
Zandweg 206, 3454 HE De Meern
Off the A12, west of Utrecht; follow signs for
Vleuten

Holes	9 Par 34 2455m.
Visitors	Welcome
Fees	Dfl30
Facilities	Bar: driving range
Pro	H T Herrema

Utrechse Golf Club De Pan (1894)   54

Phone: 03404 56427
Amersfoortseweg 1, 3735 LJ Bosch en Duin
East of Utrecht at Bosch en Duin sign

Holes	18 Par 72 5702m.
Visitors	Must book
Fees	Dfl60–90
Facilities	Bar/restaurant closed Monday in winter; practice ground
Pro	Cees Dorrestein

This is the second oldest course in Holland
(after the Haagsche) and will have its centenary
in 1994. It was designed by Harry Colt and is a
delightful course with its well-kept fairways
meandering through a heavily wooded landscape. The course, as befits one which has been
the scene of the Dutch Open on several
occasions, is an exacting one, especially during
the second nine when intelligent play from the
tee is required. It is a delightful lay-out and its
design has similarities to other great courses
such as the Berkshire and Hardelot in Northern
France.

Golfclub de Purmerend (1989)   55

Phone: 02990 44646
Westerweg 50, 1445 AD Purmerend
North of Amsterdam off the N247

Holes	18 Par 72 5782m.
Visitors	Must book
Fees	Dfl70–80
Facilities	Bar and restaurant; practice ground, swimming pool
Pro	Nigel Clarke

Golfclub Reymerswael (1986)   56

Phone: 02235 1265
Grensweg 21, 4411 ST Rilland-Bath
Off the A58, south west of Bergen op Zoom; take
the Rilland/Bath exit and go south

Holes	9 Par 36 2993m.
Visitors	Welcome
Fees	Dfl40–50
Facilities	Bar; driving range
Pro	Jan Kuysters

Golfclub Het Rijk van Nijmegen (1987)   57

Phone: 08891 76644
Postweg 17, 6561 KJ Groesbeek
South east of Nijmegen on the Groesbeek road

Holes	18 Par 72 6114m; 2 other loops of 9 (2083m and 2412m).
Visitors	Must book
Fees	Dfl45–80
Facilities	Bar and restaurant (restaurant closed Monday and Tuesday); driving range; pitch and putt course
Pro	Brian Gee

Rijswijk Golfclub (1989)   58

Phone: 070 3954864
Delftweg 58, 2289 AL Rijswijk
South east of The Hague off the A4

Holes	18 Par 71 5708m.
Visitors	Welcome
Fees	Dfl45–50
Facilities	Bar and restaurant; driving range
Pro	John Woof

Rosendaelsche Golfclub (1895)   **59**

Phone: 085 421438

Apeldoornseweg 450, 6816 SN Arnhem

North of Arnhem, off the A12

Holes	18 Par 72 6057m.
Visitors	Must book
Fees	Dfl50–80
Facilities	Bar and restaurant; practice ground
Pro	JGM Dorrestein

The club was founded in 1895 and is one of the oldest in the Netherlands; it moved to its present location in the early years of the century. The course is distinguished by the great variety of trees which enliven the surroundings and put a premium on accurate striking: pines and firs, birch, American oak and maple, beeches and many others.

Wassenaarse Golfclub Rozenstein (1984)   **60**

Phone: 01751 17846

Hoge Klei 1, 2242 XZ Wassenaar

North of The Hague, off the A44

Holes	9 Par 36 3035m.
Visitors	Welcome
Fees	Dfl30–70
Facilities	Bar and restaurant; driving range; 6 short holes
Pro	G B Janmaat

Sallandsche Golfclub De Hoek (1934)   **61**

Phone: 05709 3269

Golfweg 2, 7431 PR Diepenveen

Off the N46 north of Deventer. Head for Diepenveen

Holes	18 Par 72 5894m.
Visitors	Must book
Fees	Dfl50–90
Facilities	Bar and restaurant; practice ground
Pro	Johnny Balvert

Golfclub De Schoot (1973)   **62**

Phone: 04138 73011

Schootsedijk 18, 5491 TD St Oedenrode

Off the N265 north of Eindhoven, close to St Oedenrode

Holes	9 Par 35 2630m.
Visitors	Welcome
Fees	Dfl30–35
Facilities	Bar and restaurant; driving range
Pro	Fred Mol

Golfclub de Semslanden (1986)   **63**

Phone: 05999 65353

Nieuwe Dijk 1, 9514 BX Gasselternijveen

North east of Gasselte off the N34

Holes	9 Par 36 3029m.
Visitors	Welcome
Fees	DFl35–50
Facilities	Bar and restaurant closed on Monday; practice ground
Pro	P L Vermeer

Golfclub Spaarnwoude (1977)   **64**

Phone: 023 385599

Het Hoge Land 8, 1981 LT Velsen

Off the A9 north of Haarlem. Take the Velsen exit

Holes	18 Par 72 5868m.
	9 Par 34 2687m.
Visitors	Welcome
Fees	Dfl30
Facilities	Bar and restaurant; practice ground; 18 holes for beginners; 12 pitch and putt holes
Pro	Ad Wessels

Part of a park of 75 000 acres created from low-lying land, this is one of the busiest golf complexes in Europe. There are 27 holes laid out among trees and with water hazards affecting many of them; in addition there is an 18 hole par 3 course and 12 pitch-and-putt holes. The complex has absolutely no frills, and is aimed mainly at novice golfers, so you must be patient on the main golf course.

Golf & Country Club De Tongelreep (1984) **65**

Phone: 040 520962

Velddoornweg 2, 5644 SZ Eindhoven

On the west side of Eindhoven. Take the Waalre exit off the E34; in Waalre take first right 3 times for the club

Holes	9 Par 35 2634m.
Visitors	Must book
Fees	Dfl40–50
Facilities	Bar and restaurant; driving range; 5 practice holes
Pro	J Stevens

Noordbrabantse Golfclub Toxandria (1928) **66**

Phone: 01611 2201

Veenstraat 89, 5124 NC Molenschot

East of Breda off the A16 or A27. Head for Rijen and then for Molenschot

Holes	18 Par 70 5760m.
Visitors	Must book
Fees	Dfl60–90
Facilities	Bar and restaurant; driving range
Pro	Ray Leach

This delightful course wends its way through a landscape of ancient trees and was designed by Harry Colt and opened in 1930; it was updated by Frank Pennink. The challenges of the various holes are subtly varied and from the clubhouse you have fine views of the course.

Twentsche Golfclub (1926) **67**

Phone: 074 912773

Enschedesestraat 381, 7552 CV Hengelo

On the west side of Enschede, near the university

Holes	9 Par 34 2681m.
Visitors	Welcome
Fees	Dfl30–50
Facilities	Bar and restaurant; driving range
Pro	Wiljan van Mook

Burggolf Vegilinbosschen (1990) **68**

Phone: 05138 96111

Legemeersterweg 16-18, 8527 DS Legemeer (bij St Nicolaasga)

Off the A50 north of Lemmer. Take the St Nicolaasga exit, turn right to Langweer, right to the club

Holes	18 Par 72 5765m.
Visitors	Must book
Fees	Dfl50–70
Facilities	Bar and restaurant closed Monday in winter; practice ground
Pro	S Moore

Golfclub Veldzijde (1992) **69**

Phone: 02979 81143

Bovendijk 41, 3648 NP Wilnis

South west of Amsterdam off the N201; head for Wilnis (N212)

Holes	9 Par 34 2580m.
Visitors	Welcome
Fees	Dfl25–40
Facilities	Bar closed Mondays
Pro	Jacques Belvert

Veluwse Golfclub (1957) **70**

Phone: 05769 1275

Nr 57, 7346 AC Hoog Soeren

Off the N344, north west of Apeldoorn

Holes	9 Par 35 2852m.
Visitors	Welcome
Fees	Dfl35–65
Facilities	Bar
Pro	Alan Gibson

Golfbaan Waterland (1992) **71**

Phone: 020 6343506

Buikslotermeerdijk 141, 1027 AC Amsterdam

Off the A10 ringroad; take the Volendam exit after the IJ tunnel

Holes	9 Par 36 2765m.
Visitors	Welcome
Fees	DFl 25–35
Facilities	Bar and restaurant; practice ground

Golf & Country Club Winterswijk (1990) **72**

Phone: 05430 62293

Henxel 33, 7113 RG Winterswijk

North east of Winterswijk off the N319; head for Vreden

Holes	9 Par 36 2961m.
Visitors	Welcome
Fees	Dfl30–60
Facilities	Bar and restaurant; driving range
Pro	Focko Nauta

Burggolf Westerpark (1985) **73**

Phone: 079 517283

Heuvelweg 3, 2716 DZ Zoetermeer

East of The Hague, off the A12. Take the exit for Nootdorp and follow signs for Westerpark

Holes	9 Par 35 2822m.
Visitors	Must book
Fees	Dfl35–45
Facilities	Bar and restaurant closed Monday in winter; practice ground
Pro	Richard Paul

Westfriese Golfclub (1988) **74**

Phone: 02286 3444

Zittend 19, 1617 KS Westwoud

Take the Hoorn (N302) exit off the A7 north of Amsterdam. Turn left to Westwoud

Holes	9 Par 36 2840m.
Visitors	Must book
Fees	Dfl50–70
Facilities	Bar; restaurant closed Monday & Tuesday; practice ground
Pro	Peter Ackerley

Golf Club Wittem (1956) **75**

Phone: 04455 2370

Dalbissenweg 22, 6281 NC Mechelen
East of Maastricht, off the N278; head for
Landsrade

Holes	9 Par 36 2933m.
Visitors	Welcome
Fees	Dfl40–60
Facilities	Bar and restaurant

Golf Club De Woeste Kop (1984) **76**

Phone: 01155 4467

Justassweg 4, 4571 NB Axel
South of Axel, off the N253

Holes	9 Par 34 2729m.
Visitors	Welcome
Fees	Dfl50–70
Facilities	Bar open pm; practice ground
Pro	R Watkins

Golf Wouwse Plantage (1973) **77**

Phone: 01657 9593

Zoomvlietweg 66, 4725 TD Wouwse Plantage
Off the A58 east of Bergen op Zoom; follow
Zoomvlietweg south

Holes	18 Par 72 5865m.
Visitors	Welcome
Fees	Dfl35–60
Facilities	Bar and restaurant; driving range
Pro	Phil Helsby

Zaanse Golf Club (1987) **78**

Phone: 02990 32806

Zuiderweg 68, 1456 NH Wijde Wormer
Off the A7 north of Amsterdam; take the Zaanse
Schans exit

Holes	9 Par 35 2641m.
Visitors	Welcome
Fees	Dfl30–40
Facilities	Bar and restaurant; driving range
Pro	Craig Deane

Golfclub Zeegersloot (1984) **79**

Phone: 01720 74567

Kromme Aarweg 5, 2403 NB Alphen a/d Rijn
Off the N207 at Alphen

Holes	18 Par 70 5183m.
Visitors	Welcome
Fees	Dfl35–45
Facilities	Bar and restaurant closed Monday; practice ground; 9 hole short course
Pro	Svenn Muts

Golfclub Zeewolde (1987) **80**

Phone: 03242 2103

Golflaan 1, Zeewolde
Take the Hilversum (N27) exit off the A6
Amsterdam-Almere, left to N305 to Zeewolde

Holes	18 Par 70 5954m.
Visitors	Welcome
Fees	Dfl45–60
Facilities	Bar and restaurant; driving range; 9 hole short course
Pro	Peter van Wijk

Zuid Limburgse Golf & Country Club (1956) **81**

Phone: 04455 1397

Dalbissenweg 22, 6281 NC Mechelen
East of Maastricht off the N278. Follow the
signs to Gulpen and then Landsrade. The club is
signposted

Holes	18 Par 71 5924m.
Visitors	Welcome
Fees	Dfl50–75
Facilities	Bar and restaurant closed Monday in winter; practice ground
Pro	Andrew Horsman

NORWAY

INTEREST in golf has grown strongly in Norway during the last few years, partly due to the influence of neighbouring Sweden, where the game has recently expanded at a furious rate.

But there are still only around twenty courses in Norway, and only half of them offer the full 18 holes. Just a handful of new clubs have been opened in the past few years, and aspiring golf course builders have to conquer severe opposition both from farmers and environmentalists.

Many of the existing courses are closed during the winter months, and the best known of them are Oslo, the oldest course in Norway, Bergen, Stavanger and Trondheim. The celebrated Midnight Cup is held at the latter club.

Whereas the level of green fees in Norway is eminently reasonable (from £10 to £20), the cost of living is very high. British golfers will neither be amused by the cost of a beer or a bottle of wine, nor by the charges for hotel rooms.

Unit of currency: Norwegian Krone
Rate of exchange (approx. at 1.1.93): NKr10–£1
International dialling code: (010 47)

Arendal og Omega Golf Club (1986)   **1**

Phone: 041 60524

Nes Verk, 4934 Nesgrenda

Off the E18 north west of Kristiansand; follow the R415 to Hovde and the club is signposted

Holes	9 Par 36 2970m.
Visitors	Welcome. Course closed November to mid-April
Fees	NKr130
Facilities	Driving range
Pro	Geoff Dixon

Bergen Golf Club (1937)   **2**

Phone: 05 182077

PO Box 470, 5001 Bergen

Around 10km north of Bergen

Holes	9 Par 33 2230m.
Visitors	Welcome
Fees	Nkr150
Facilities	Bar and restaurant; driving range
Pro	Steve Norris

This is a testing course, not least for the golfer's stamina as he negotiates the very hilly terrain. There is an unusual start, with two short holes (which might remind some readers of the Church Stretton course in Shropshire, which was designed by James Braid). There are streams, valleys and ravines, and very tight greens on this interesting course, which is surrounded by mountains.

NORWAY

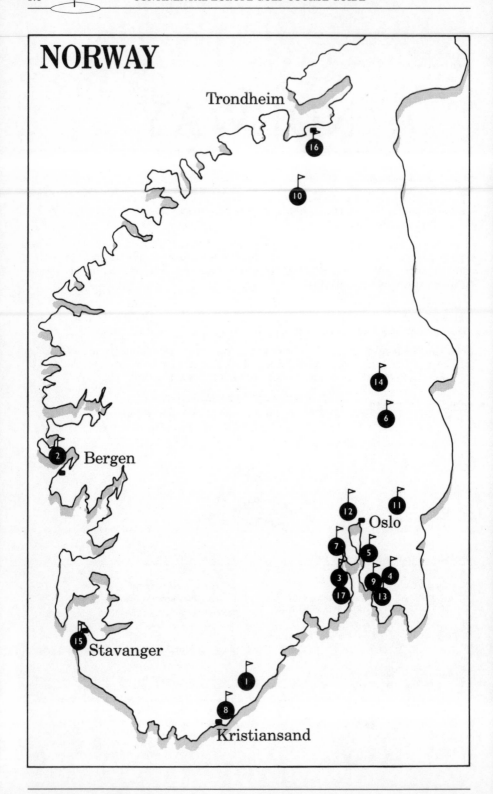

Trondheim

Bergen

Oslo

Stavanger

Kristiansand

Borre Golf Club (1989)   **3**

Phone: 33 73079

Semb Hovedgard, 3190 Horten

Off the E18 south west of Oslo between Borre
and Horten

Holes	18 Par 73 5779m.
Visitors	Welcome. Course closed December to March
Fees	NKr200
Facilities	Bar and restaurant; practice ground
Pro	Johan Tanum

This recently opened course was designed by the
Swedish architect, Tommy Nordstrom, on
undulating farmland. The mature trees, rolling
terrain and water hazards make an interesting
challenge in lovely countryside.

Borregaard Golf Club (1927)   **4**

Phone 09 157401

PO Box 348, 1701 Sarpsborg

Just north of Sarpsborg

Holes	9 Par 32 2203m.
Visitors	Welcome. Course closed mid-November to mid-April
Fees	NKr120
Facilities	Bar and restaurant; driving range
Pro	Fraser Mudie

Drobak Golf Club (1992)   **5**

Phone: 09 931680

Belsjoveien 50, Drobak

Off the E6 south of Oslo; at Drobak roundabout
follow signs to the club

Holes	18 Par 70 5340m.
Visitors	Welcome. Course closed October to April
Fees	NKr200
Facilities	Bar and restaurant; practice ground
Pro	Howard Riendeau

Hedmark Golf Club (1980)   **6**

Phone: 064 13588

Boks 71, 2401 Elverum

North of Oslo at Elverum (E6 and R24)

Holes	18 Par 72 5851m.
Visitors	Welcome. Course closed mid-October to April
Fees	NKr150
Facilities	Driving range
Pro	Keith Dudman

Kjekstad Golfclub (1976)   **7**

Phone: 03 285850

PO Box 201, 3430 Royken

East of Drammen off the R282 at Royken

Holes	18 Par 67 4744m.
Visitors	Welcome. Course closed October to April
Fees	NKr150–200
Facilities	Bar and restaurant; practice ground
Pro	Douglas Craig

Kristiansand Golfclub (1973)   **8**

Phone: 042 45863

Korsvik, Randesund, Box 31, 4601 Kristiansand

East of Kristiansaid off the E18 and R401

Holes	9 Par 36 2485m.
Visitors	Welcome. Course closed November to April
Fees	NKr100
Facilities	Bar and restaurant; driving range
Pro	David Brough

Onsoy Golf Club (1987)   **9**

Phone: 09 333555

Box 458, 1601 Fredrikstad

South of Oslo near Frederikstad (E6 and R110)

Holes	18 Par 72 6000m.
Visitors	Welcome. Course closed November to March
Fees	NKr200
Facilities	Bar and restaurant; driving range

Oppdal Golf Club (1988)   **10**

Phone: 074 22510

PO Box 19, 7341 Oppdal

In Oppdal wintersports resort

Holes	9 Par 36 2950m.
Visitors	Welcome. Course closed October to May
Fees	NKr100–200
Facilities	Bar and restaurant; driving range

Oppegard Golf Club (1985)   **11**

Phone: 02 991875

PO Box 137, 1412 Sofiemyr

Just to the south of Kolbotn

Holes	9 Par 36 2775m.
Visitors	Welcome. Course closed November to April
Fees	NKr150–200
Facilities	Bar and restaurant; driving range
Pro	David Lloyd

Oslo Golfclub (1924) **12**

Phone: 02 504402

Bogstad, 0757 Oslo-7

9 km west of Oslo; follow signs to Bogstad Camping

Holes	18 Par 72 6000m.
Visitors	Welcome before 2pm on weekdays, and after 2pm at weekends. Course closed November to April
Fees	NKr250–300
Facilities	Bar and restaurant; practice ground
Pro	Stephen Newey

The oldest course in Norway has Lake Bogstad on two sides, which adds to the charm of this undulating parkland course. From the back tees it is a long haul at nearly 6800 yards and the short third at around 240 yards will test any golfer.

Skjeberg Golf Club (1986) **13**

Phone: 09 166310

PO Box 3014, Kurland, 1701 Sarpsborg

South of Oslo, off the E6 near Sarpsborg

Holes	18 Par 72 5581m.
Visitors	Welcome. Course closed November to April
Fees	NKr130–150
Facilities	Bar and restaurant; driving range

Sorknes Golf Club (1990) **14**

Phone: 064 40041

Sorknes Gard, 2450 Rena

Off the R3 at Rena

Holes	9 Par 36 2840m.
Visitors	Welcome. Course closed November to May
Fees	NKr100–150
Facilities	Driving range

Stavanger Golfclub (1956) **15**

Phone: 04 557025

Longebakke 45, 4042 Hafrsfjord

Just west of Stavanger off the E18

Holes	18 Par 70 5508m.
Visitors	Welcome
Fees	NKr150–200
Facilities	Restaurant; driving range
Pro	Raymond Lees

Superb views of the Stokka lakes await the players of this excellent course, its fairways cut through thick pine forest. Accuracy is required here and the pedigree of the course was acknowledged when the European Ladies Team Championship was played here a few years ago.

Trondheim Golfclub (1950) **16**

Phone: 07 531885

Sommersaeter, Box 169, 7001 Trondheim

Just to the north of Trondheim

Holes	9 Par 36 2766m.
Visitors	Welcome. Course closed November to April
Fees	NKr120
Facilities	Bar and restaurant; driving range
Pro	Tom Vollan

This is a fascinating course where the golfers are blessed with dazzling sights across the old capital of Norway and of the Trondheim fjord. The different tees which are used for the second nine holes make this course an interesting test, as the holes wind through the forest, along the hills and by the water.

The Midnight Cup is played here every year and begins at midnight on Midsummer's Day; the golfers' capacity to withstand draughts of akavit is as important as their playing skills.

Vestfold Golfclub (1958) **17**

Phone: 033 65655

PO Box 64, 3101 Tonsberg

8km S of Tonsberg off the E18

Holes	18 Par 73 5860m.
Visitors	Welcome
Fees	NKr120–180
Facilities	Driving range
Pro	George Beal

PORTUGAL

G OLF was established in Portugal by the British, when a band of wine shippers laid out nine holes at Oporto in 1890. It is the second oldest golf club in Europe. The game in Portugal is still primarily the preserve of visitors from northern Europe, especially the British. Over the last two or three decades they have flocked to Portugal to play golf in the delightful winter sunshine.

The golf resorts of the Algarve were built specifically to satisfy the market for sunshine golf. Where Penina, Vale do Lobe and Quinta do Largo led, others have followed and no large scale residential holiday development is thought to be complete without its golf course.

This sort of development brought its own inherent problems. Golf courses were built to sell houses and apartments on the surrounding land and, with priority tee times and discounted green fees being offered to residents, the ordinary visiting golfer, especially during the boom times of the 1980s, was often made to feel unwelcome. He also learned that the green fees demanded were unacceptably high.

As we go to press, many of the green fees in Portugal are in the region of £40; and it must be stressed that these charges usually cover one round of golf only, not a day's golf. In comparison with many other parts of Europe, golf in Portugal has become very expensive – perhaps too expensive in these recessionary days. The visiting golfer should ensure that he has a golf and accommodation package which is priced at an acceptable level.

Unit of currency: Escudo
Rate of exchange (approx. at 1.1.93): Esc220–£1
International dialling code: (010 351)

Alto Golf Club (1991)

Phone: 081 459119

Apt 1, Alvor, 8500 Portimao
East of Portimao. Off the N125 at Alvor

Holes	18 Par 72 6125m.
Visitors	Welcome
Fees	Esc7600
Facilities	Bar and restaurant; practice ground
Pro	Robert Bridge

The course was opened in 1991 by the President of Portugal and was originally designed by the maestro of European golf, Henry Cotton. After Cotton's death the golf writer, Peter Dobereiner, undertook the task of building the course and he adhered strictly to Cotton's principles, one of the firmest of which was that golf courses should be fair tests for all golfers. Gimmickry has been avoided and the course is notable for its very large, undulating and immensely speedy greens. There are several tough holes, especially the 16th: at 660 yards from the back tee, it is rightly called 'O Gigante'.

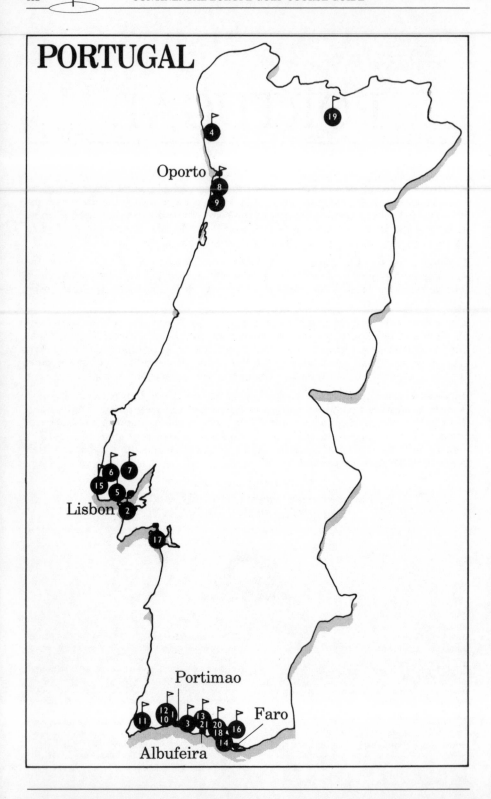

PORTUGAL

Oporto

Lisbon

Portimao

Faro

Albufeira

Aroeira Club de Campo de Portugal (1972) 2

Phone: 0351 2263244

Quinta da Aroeira, Fonte da Telha, 2825 Monte de Caparica

20 km south of Lisbon off the A2; on the Costa da Caparica at Aroeira

Holes	18 Par 72 6040m.
Visitors	Welcome
Fees	Esc5500
Facilities	Bar and restaurant; practice ground; riding centre
Pro	Joaquin Moura

Designed by Frank Pennink, the course was carved through the pine forests and hundreds of thousands of new trees were also planted. After the revolution of the early 1970s the course lay dormant and unused for a decade but is now back to its brilliant best, a secluded jewel which is, nevertheless, not far from Lisbon. With its trees, water hazards and many dog-leg holes, it is a rewarding and delightful test for all golfers.

Carvoeiro Golf & Country Club (1991) 3

Phone: 082 341794

Apt 245, 8401 Lagoa

West of Carvoeiro off the N125

Holes	18 Par 71 5871m.
Visitors	Must book
Fees	Esc7000
Facilities	Bar and restaurant; practice ground
Pro	R Gritter

Estela Golfclub (1986) 4

Phone: 052 685567

Rio Alto, Estela 4490, Povoa de Varzim

North of Oporto off the N13 at Estela

Holes	18 Par 72 6095m.
Visitors	Welcome
Fees	Esc4000–8000
Facilities	Bar and restaurant
Pro	Carlos Alberto

On the north-west coast, in the wine country not far from Oporto, the designers of the Estela course were faced with a stretch of archetypal links territory, a terrain of scrub and sand dunes alongside the sea that would not have looked out of place in Scotland. Nor would this golf course, a really challenging links with narrow fairways winding through those intimidating dunes; in proper links style the ball can be run up and on to the greens, which are very fast and have severe borrows. There are lovely views of the sea as you tackle this fine course, which has already been the venue for a European Tour event.

Estoril Palacio Golf Club (1945) 5

Phone: 01 26-80176

Av da Republica, 2765 Estoril

North of Estoril on the Sintra road

Holes	18 Par 69 5210m.
	9 Par 33 2350m.
Visitors	Must book
Fees	Esc5100–7000
Facilities	Bar and restaurant; driving range; swimming pool
Pro	J Rodrigues

Once the haunt of an array of deposed royalty from all corners of Europe, this course, designed by Mackenzie Ross, swoops and rolls through avenues of pine and eucalyptus trees. It has a wonderful setting between the peaks of the Sintra hills and the sea and offers terrific holiday golf.

International Golf Academy Estoril-Sol (1976) 6

Phone: 01 92 32461

Estrada de Lagoa Azul 3, Linho, 2765 Sintra

North of Estoril off the Sintra road

Holes	9 Par 34 2010m.
Visitors	Must book
Fees	Esc4500–7000
Facilities	Bar and restaurant; practice ground
Pro	M Gallagher

Lisbon Sports Club (1962) 7

Phone: 01 4310077

Casal da Carregueira, Belas, 2745 Queluz

West of Lisbon. At Queluz take the road to Belas

Holes	18 Par 68 5866m.
Visitors	Welcome on weekdays only
Fees	Esc5000
Facilities	Bar and restaurant; practice ground; swimming pool; tennis courts
Pro	Jose Baltazar

Miramar Golfclub (1934) 8

Phone: 02 7622067

Praia de Miramar, Av Sacadura Cabral, 4405 Valadares

South of Oporto off the N109

Holes	9 Par 33 2532m.
Visitors	Must book
Fees	Esc3000–5000
Facilities	Bar and restaurant; practice ground; swimming pool; tennis courts
Pro	Manuel Ribeiro

Oporto Golf Club (1890)   9

Phone: 02 722008

Pedreira, Silvalde, 4500 Espinho

18km south of Oporto, off the N109

Holes	18 Par 71 5668m.
Visitors	Must book
Fees	Esc5000–7000
Facilities	Bar and restaurant; practice ground
Pro	Carlos Agostinho

This is the oldest golf club in Portugal and one of the oldest in Europe. It was founded by a group of British wine shippers and moved to its present site in 1900. The course has been changed on various occasions over the years, most notably in the 1950s by Mackenzie Ross.

Palmares Golf Club (1975)   10

Phone: 082 72953

Meia Praia, 8600 Lagos

North east of Lagos; head for Meia Praia and follow the signs to the club

Holes	18 Par 71 5961m.
Visitors	Must book
Fees	Esc7300
Facilities	Bar and restaurant; practice ground
Pro	Luis Espadinha

The course, designed by Frank Pennink, has two separate styles, both links and parkland. The first hole drifts right down a long hill and introduces the player to the holes which run along the beach in typical links style. You then move inland and take up the challenge of the holes which run up and down the quietly undulating hills. The almond trees and shrubs are a delight during springtime and the views of the distant Monchique Hills and the Bay of Lagos are always impressive.

Parque da Floresta (1987)   11

Phone: 082 65333

Vila do Bispo, Budens

West of Lagos off the N125. The course is close to Salema and is signposted

Holes	18 Par 72 5888m.
Visitors	Welcome
Fees	Esc6000
Facilities	Bar and restaurant; practice ground
Pro	Peter Jones

The club is at the heart of a residential development above the fishing village of Salema, and is surrounded by a nature reserve. Pepe Gancedo, who also built Torrequebrada on the Costa del Sol, designed the course over

dauntingly hilly terrain. Narrow fairways with steep slopes, deep ravines and double-tiered plateau greens make the course a spectacular test. Some people call the course quirky and some call it dramatic and some use epithets which should not be seen in print; suffice it to say that it is not for the faint-hearted golfer, and some modifications have recently been made to ease its severity.

Penina Golf Club (1966)   12

Phone: 082 415415

PO Box 146, Penina Portimao

Between Portimao and Lagos, off the N125

Holes	18 Par 73 6054m (Championship). 9 Par 35 2842m (Monchique)
Visitors	Must book; hotel residents have priority
Fees	Esc5000–9500
Facilities	Bars and restaurants; practice ground; tennis courts; short course
Pro	Robin Liddle

This was the first of the Algarve golf projects, masterminded by the great champion Henry Cotton, who planted some 350000 trees on the unpromising flat and swampy terrain of Penina. The huge tees enable courses of varying lengths and difficulty to be set up, from a monstrous 7500 yards to a modest 5800. Cotton always believed in 'honest' courses, where the greens are fast and true and the punishment for a stray shot fits the crime. Penina is a great test for golfers of all levels of activity, from the professionals (the Portuguese Open has been played here many times) to the long handicap golfer. Holes such as the long 5th, the short 13th with its menacing lake and the uphill 18th will challenge and amuse any golfer.

Pine Cliffs Golf & Country Club (1990)   13

Phone: 089 50787

Pinhal do Concelho, Acoteias, 8200 Albufeira

Between Albufeira and Vilamoura off the N125

Holes	9 Par 34 2324m.
Visitors	By introduction only. Course reserved for Pine Cliffs and Hotel Sheraton residents
Fees	Esc6000
Facilities	Bar and restaurant; practice ground
Pro	D Ingram

Quinta do Lago Golfclub (1974)   14

Phone: 089 396 002

Almansil, 8100 Loule

South of Almansil in the Quinta do Lago estate

Holes	4 loops of 9: A Par 36 2860m; B Par 37 3172m; C Par 36 2945m; D Par 35 2697m.
Visitors	Must book
Fees	Esc10,000
Facilities	Bars and restaurants; practice ground; squash and tennis courts; horse riding
Pro	Domingos Silva

Many British golfers, especially during the 1970s, experienced their first taste of 'continental' golf, in warm weather and relaxed surroundings, at Quinta do Lago. The estate covers around 2000 acres and has an array of facilities including bars and restaurants, horse riding, tennis courts and water sports; and the four 9-hole courses are brilliantly conceived. Set in delightful countryside, the fairways meander between the umbrella pines and the many water hazards which make the course a tough but agreeable test of golf. On the beautifully springy and lush turf, the ball sits up and begs the player to hit it decisively into the superb greens. It is a wonderful place to play golf, and has hosted many professional tournaments.

Guia Quinta da Marinha Golf Course (1985) 15

Phone: 01 4869881

Quinta da Marinha, 2750 Cascais

West of Estoril at Cabo Raso

Holes	18 Par 71 5606m.
Visitors	Must book
Fees	Esc6000–8000
Facilities	Bar and restaurant; swimming pools; tennis courts
Pro	A Dantas

Designed by Trent Jones, the course shows many of his hallmarks; although the fairways are wide, bunkers and water hazards abound in the most eccentric positions. But the course is interesting and there are splendid views of the ocean.

Golf Club San Lorenzo (1988)   16

Phone: 089 396522

South of Almansil in the Quinta do Lago estate; follow the signs

Holes	18 Par 72 6238m.
Visitors	Must book. The hotel guests have priority
Fees	Esc12,500
Facilities	Bar and restaurant; practice ground
Pro	B Evans

The course is owned by the Forte Hotel group and it is difficult to book a time to play, since hotel guests have priority. The best plan is to stay either at the Dona Filipa or the Penina hotel and enjoy both San Lorenzo and Penina for the cost of a room.

San Lorenzo is a most attractive and demanding course, which is designed and maintained to the highest standards. After an amiable start through the umbrella pines, the course presents golfers with an increasingly stiff challenge. The 6th, 7th and 8th holes run along the beautiful Ria Formosa Estuary and the water menaces each shot. The 8th is especially tough as it weaves through bunkers and lakes. The finishing stretch is as severe as any, with plenty of water to erode a player's confidence. The 18th hole will tingle anyone's nerves; it demands a mid-iron of pinpoint accuracy to a small sloping green with water left, right, back and front.

Troia Golf Club (1979)   17

Phone: 065 44151

Torralta Troia, 2900 Setubal

South of Setubal on the Troia peninsula (N235.1)

Holes	18 Par 72 5874m.
Visitors	Must book
Fees	Esc5100–7000
Facilities	Bar and restaurant; practice ground
Pro	F Pina

This is another Trent Jones creation, built with links traditions in mind along a sand-bar with the Atlantic on one side. The fairways are narrow and scattered with many bunkers to add to the perils presented by the sand and scrub and the pine trees. The greens are small and burnished. It all adds up to a considerable golfing test.

Vale do Lobo Golf Club (1968)   18

Phone: 089 394444

Vale do Lobo, 8100 Loule

Southwest of Almansil; follow the signs to Vale de Lobo

Holes	3 x 9 Yellow: Par 36 2905m; Orange: Par 36 2753m; Green: Par 35 2532m.
Visitors	Must book
Fees	Esc10,000
Facilities	Bar and restaurant; driving range
Pro	David Harding

This is one of the senior Algarve courses, which was originally designed by Henry Cotton. The three loops of 9 holes run through undulating land bedecked with pines and skirted by sandy beaches. There are some wonderful holes here and every player remembers the wonderful par 3 seventh hole on the Yellow course, where you must carry your ball across the cliffs to the green. It is sad that the greed of the developers has entailed a positively claustrophobic encroachment of villas and apartments on to the edges of the course.

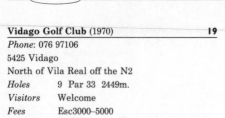

Vidago Golf Club (1970)   19

Phone: 076 97106

5425 Vidago

North of Vila Real off the N2

Holes	9 Par 33 2449m.
Visitors	Welcome
Fees	Esc3000–5000
Facilities	Bar and restaurant; swimming pool; tennis courts
Pro	Manuel Teixeira

Vila Sol Golf Club (1991)   20

Phone: 089 301296

8125 Quarteira

North east of Quarteira, just off the N396 towards Loule

Holes	18 Par 72 5880m.
Visitors	Must book
Fees	Esc10,000
Facilities	Bar and restaurant; practice ground
Pro	David Silva

This is one of the newest courses on the Algarve and was designed by Donald Steel, who cut the fairways through thick forests of pine. Narrow fairways, water hazards and small well-bunkered greens call for great accuracy and the long 6th hole is notable, not only for its views of the Loule mountains, but also for its difficulty; a lake mischievously interrupts the fairway. It is not a long course but is a most attractive one and was considered good enough to host the Portuguese Open of 1992.

Vilamoura Golf Club (1969)   21

Phone: 089 33652

Vilamoura, 8125 Quarteira

West of Faro, off the N125 at Vilamoura

Holes	Vilamoura 1: 18 Par 72 5995m. Vilamoura 2: 18 Par 72 5866m. Vilamoura 3: 27 Pinhal 2935m, Lago 2953m, Marina 3180m
Visitors	Must book in advance
Fees	Esc7000
Facilities	Bar and restaurant; practice ground
Pro	Joaquin Catarino/Manuel Pardal/ Abilio Coelho

The original course was designed by Frank Pennink and, with its undulating fairways ringed by mature trees, it has some of the character of a typical Surrey course; you can imagine yourself at Swinley Forest or the Berkshire. It is a very tough test, with four outstanding short holes. Vilamoura 2 (once called Dom Pedro and also designed by Pennink, with some additions by Trent Jones) is more open. The third course, designed by Joseph Lee, opened for play in 1991; it is notable for its generous fairways, but profuse bunkering and the presence of water on eight of the holes makes it a test of the golfer's accuracy.

SPAIN

THE package tourist boom of the Sixties and Seventies, when northern Europeans headed for the sun and fun of Spain, brought in its wake the golfing boom. Dozens of new courses were built especially on the Costa del Sol, and hundreds of thousands of golfers, especially the British, went to experience this new golfing idyll.

As the decade of the Eighties progressed, however, the attractions of Spain, both to ordinary holidaymakers and to golfers, withered. Over-development of the favoured resorts and its accompanying tawdriness drove many people away. On the golfing front too many courses were built, as in Portugal, as adjuncts to over-ambitious real estate projects. Priority tee times for residents and grossly over-priced green fees made holiday golfers feel unwelcome; so did the lousy service and the take-it-or-leave-it attitudes of those who staffed the golf clubs.

But the recent recession has in many cases wrought a change in these attitudes, especially on the Costa del Sol where the tough and enterprising mayor of Malaga, Jesus Gil, is trying hard to clean up the tourism act. Many Spanish golf courses, dependent on the income from visitors for their survival, have had to lower their prices radically to entice their customers back. It is noticeable how many clubs are now charging about £25 a round, when a few years ago the going rate was at least double. Visitors can reduce those fees by taking advantage of the many discounts that are on offer.

Despite the recession, the building of golf courses has picked up in Spain in the last five years; there are well over a hundred courses now in play and over thirty of them have been opened during that time.

Much of that activity has been concentrated on the Costa del Sol. The great courses such as Valderrama, Torrequebrada, Las Brisas and Sotogrande have been augmented by new courses such as La Cala, Monte Mayor and Alcaidesa. But the stretch of tourist country between Gibraltar and Malaga is not the only good golfing destination in Spain. Valencia has El Saler, rated by 'Golf World' as one of the best courses in Europe, and El Bosque; while Barcelona has El Prat, Mas Nou and Jose Maria Olazabal's extraordinary creation, Masia Bach. Nor should the northern coast be ignored with some fine courses near Santander and San Sebastian, including Pedrena and Neguri.

Unit of currency: Peseta
Rate of exchange (approx. at 1.1.93): Ptas175–£1
International dialling code: (010 34)

Oviedo

Bilbao

55 49 33 71
91 81

Vigo

19
72
79
85

90
56

Zaragoza

Salamanca

66

31 26
51 61 46 82
76 86
36 6

Madrid

59
88

Cordoba

Sevilla

8 74 75
57

28 18
47 58
2

Cádiz

89
68 50

COSTA DEL SOL

CANARY ISLANDS
LANZAROTE

107

110
108
109

105
106

GRAN
CANARIA

TENERIFE

SPAIN

16

27
52

53
40
21

1335
84

4169
60

78
22

Barcelona

964

42 20

1025
39

Valencia

67

73
2332

Alicante

62

87

38

BALEARIC ISLANDS
MENORCA

104

103

96

98
95

IBIZA

99
197 101
94

100

Palma

92
93

102

MALLORCA

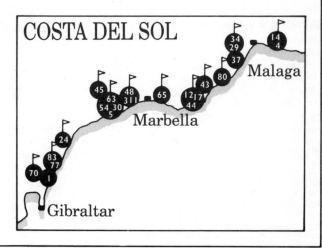

COSTA DEL SOL

34
29

14
4

37

80

Malaga

45

48
311

65

43

12 17

44

54 30
5

63

Marbella

24

83
77

70 I

Gibraltar

Alcaidesa Links Golf Course (1992)   1

Phone: 956 791040
C-nac 340km 126, San Roque, Cadiz
On the coast, 15 km from Gibraltar at San Roque
Holes   18 Par 72 5983m.
Visitors   Welcome, but must book
Fees   Ptas3500
Facilities Bar and restaurant; practice ground;
              swimming pool;
Pro   Stephen Field

The course, designed by Peter Alliss and Clive Clark, opened in 1992, and is being enthusiastically billed as the only links course on the Costa del Sol. It is certainly by the sea and runs in true Scottish and Lancashire links style through the dunes. There are fine views, especially of the nearby Rock of Gibraltar.

Golf Almerimar (1976)   2

Phone: 951 480234
04700 Urb Almerimar, El Ejido
South west of Almeria, off the D340 at Almerimar
Holes   18 Par 72 6111m.
Visitors   Welcome
Fees   Ptas7000
Facilities Bar and restaurant; practice ground;
              swimming pool; tennis
Pro   Juan Parron Cruz

Aloha Golf (1975)   3

Phone: 952 812388
Nueva Andalucia, 29600 Marbella
West of Marbella, close to Puerto Banus
Holes   18 Par 72 6261m.
Visitors   Book one day ahead
Fees   Ptas8000
Facilities Bar and restaurant; practice ground;
              swimming pool; tennis
Pro   Jose Luis Mangas

Añoreta Golf (1989)   4

Phone: 952 404000
Avda del Golf, 29730 Rincon del la Victoria
East of Malaga, off the N340 near Nerja
Holes   18 Par 72 6054m.
Visitors   Welcome
Fees   Ptas4000
Facilities Bar and restaurant; practice ground;
              swimming pool; tennis
Pro   J A Gomez

The first design by the Ryder Cup player Jose Maria Canizares, the course is reasonably flat, with generous fairways lined by elegant palm trees. But the many water hazards and the excellent bunkering make it a splendid test for any golfer.

Atalaya Park Golf & Country Club (1968)   5

Phone: 952 781894
29680 Estepona
Between Estepona and Marbella, off the N340
Holes   18 Par 73 6212m.
Visitors   Book in advance
Fees   Ptas 5000
Facilities Bar and restaurant; practice ground;
              tennis
Pro   Derek Strachan

This has been a familiar venue for visiting British golfers over the last two decades or so and is a very pleasant parkland course among the pine and eucalyptus trees. The elevated greens pose their problems; a second course will be open for play soon.

Centro Deportivo Barberan (1967)   6

Phone: 91 2188505
28043 Cuatro Vientos
South west of Madrid off the E90
Holes   9 Par 36 3064m.
Visitors   Welcome
Fees   Ptas3000
Facilities Bar and restaurant; practice ground

Club Deportivo La Barganiza (1982)   7

Phone: 985 742468
Apto 277, 33080 Oviedo
Between Oviedo and Gijon
Holes   18 Par 70 5298m.
Visitors   Welcome
Fees   Ptas5000–7000
Facilities Bar and restaurant; practice ground;
              swimming pool; tennis
Pro   Miguel Bellido

Club de Golf Bellavista (1976)   8

Phone: 955 319017
Ctra Huelva-Aljaraque, 21110 Aljaraque
West of Huelva near Aljaraque
Holes   9 Par 36 3126m.
Visitors   Welcome
Fees   Ptas3000
Facilities Bar and restaurant; practice ground;
              swimming pool; tennis and squash
Pro   Miguel Sanchez

Club de Bonmont-Terres Noves (1990) 9

Phone: 977 818100

Montroig del Camp

South west of Tarragona; after Cambrils head for Montroig

Holes	18 Par 72 6202m.
Visitors	Welcome
Fees	Ptas5500–7000
Facilities	Bar and restaurant; practice ground; swimming pool; tennis
Pro	Laurentino Blanco

Between the hills and the Mediterranean, the course was designed by Robert Trent Jones Jr, who did indeed move mountains and dig lakes in his efforts to introduce a piece of Florida to Spain. There are water hazards, bunkers galore, huge ravines and patches of rocks, bumps and hillocks. It is a severe test of anyone's golf, even the professionals, who played the Catalan Open here in 1991.

Club de Golf El Bosque (1975) 10

Phone: 96 1804142

Crta Godelleta km 4, 100, 46370 Chiva

West of Valencia, off the N111 at Chiva

Holes	18 Par 72 6367m.
Visitors	Welcome
Fees	Ptas5000
Facilities	Bar and restaurant; practice ground; swimming pool; tennis; horse riding
Pro	Alfonso Pinto

Designed by Robert Trent Jones the course was greatly modified in 1989 prior to the El Bosque Open in the following year. The fairways are generous and you will meet the familiar Trent Jones hallmarks of oddly positioned bunkers, water hazards and greens of bizarre shapes and rapid speeds. But it is good fun for the holiday golfer and is a testing enough course for the pros, too; the Mediterranean Open was held here last year.

Club de Golf Las Brisas (1968) 11

Phone: 952 810875

Nueva Andalucia, 29660 Marbella

West of Malaga, near Puerto Banus

Holes	18 Par 73 6198m.
Visitors	Must book
Fees	Ptas 9000
Facilities	Bar and restaurant; practice ground; swimming pool
Pro	Sebastian de Miguel

Las Brisas, which runs through a valley leading from the Sierra Blanca mountains to the sea, was Robert Trent Jones's second project in Spain and is as tough as they come. Avenues of trees, pine and eucalyptus, almond and fig, orange and palm, line the undulating fairways which are larded with enormous bunkers and made perilous by water hazards. The greens are

quick, with fierce runs and borrows. At the Spanish Open in 1987 Nick Faldo was the only player to break par. You have been warned.

La Cala Golf & Country Club (1991) 12

Phone: 952 345246

La Cala de Mijas, Mijas Corta

West of Fuengirola off the N340

Holes	2 x 18 Par 72 5960m/6160m.
Visitors	Welcome, but usually after 11.30am
Fees	Ptas5000
Facilities	Bar and restaurant; practice ground; short course; swimming pool; tennis and squash
Pro	Ricardo de Miguel

This new club has impeccable credentials in the shape of its course designer, Cabell Robinson, who worked for Trent Jones for many years. The first course, opened in 1991, is a splendid (if energy sapping) lay-out with immaculate fairways peppered with huge white bunkers and with very rapid undulating greens. The second course opened for play at the beginning of 1993.

Caldes International Golf (1991) 13

Phone: 93 8651897

Av Montbui 46, 80140 Caldes de Montbui

North of Barcelona at Caldez de Montbui

Holes	18 Par 72 6125m.
Visitors	Welcome
Fees	Ptas5000
Facilities	Bar and restaurant; practice ground

Club El Candado (1968) 14

Phone: 952 299340

Urban, El Candado, El Palo, Malaga

Just east of Malaga at El Palo

Holes	9 Par 34 2332m.
Visitors	Welcome
Fees	Ptas 5000
Facilities	Bar and restaurant; swimming pool; tennis
Pro	Manuel Lucas Rodriguez

Club de Golf de Castiello (1958) 15

Phone: 985 366313

Apto 161, 33080 Gijon

On the south east side of Gijon

Holes	18 Par 67 4814m.
Visitors	Welcome
Fees	Ptas7000
Facilities	Bar and restaurant; practice ground; swimming pool
Pro	Angel Sierra Canal

Real Club de Golf de Cerdanya (1929)   16

Phone: 972 881338

Apto 63, 17520 Puigcerda

On the border, just west of Puigcerda

Holes	18 Par 71 5856m.
Visitors	Welcome
Fees	Ptas5000
Facilities	Bar and restaurant; practice ground
Pro	Vicente Diaz

Close to the principality of Andorra, the course is about 3000 feet above sea level and is one of the oldest in Spain. Despite its altitude Cerdanya is no mountain tiger but more a quiet parkland course with its own distinctive ambience.

Golf El Chaparral (1992)   17

Phone: 3452 493800

Urb El Chaparral, 29648 Mijas Costa

West of Fuengirola off the N340

Holes	18 Par 72 5700m.
Visitors	Welcome
Fees	Ptas4000
Facilities	Bar and restaurant; practice ground
Pro	Juan Rosa Flores

The very busy Pepe Gancedo designed this new addition to the growing stock of courses on the Costa del Sol. It has the unusual format of six short holes, six par 4s and six long holes, like the Red course of the Berkshire. Its lush and rolling fairways run along the valley between wooded hills and the greens have some puzzling undulations. El Chaparral bodes well to be an excellent course.

Cortijo Grande Club de Golf (1976)   18

Phone: 951 479176

Cortijo Grande, Apt 2, 04639 Turre

North east of Almeria, near Turre and Mojacar

Holes	18 Par 72 6024m.
Visitors	Welcome
Fees	Ptas5000
Facilities	Bar and restaurant; practice ground

Golf Club de la Coruña (1962)   19

Phone: 981 285200

Apto 737, 15080 La Coruña

South of La Coruña, off the N550 at Arteijo

Holes	18 Par 72 6037m.
Visitors	Welcome
Fees	Ptas5000
Facilities	Bar and restaurant; practice ground; swimming pool; tennis
Pro	Jose Santiago

Club de Golf Costa de Azahar (1960)   20

Phone: 964 280979

Ctra Grao-Benicasim, El Grao de Castellon

North of Valencia; on the coast at El Grao

Holes	9 Par 35 2724m.
Visitors	Welcome
Fees	Ptas5000
Facilities	Bar and restaurant; practice ground; swimming pool; tennis
Pro	Amancio Sanchez

Golf de Costa Brava (1968)   21

Phone: 972 837150

17246 Sta Cristina de Aro, Gerona

Just inland from San Feliu, off the C250

Holes	18 Par 70 5445m.
Visitors	Welcome
Fees	Ptas4500–6700
Facilities	Bar and restaurant; practice ground; swimming pool; tennis; horse riding
Pro	Miguel Gil

Club de Golf Costa Dorada (1983)   22

Phone: 977 653361

Crta del Cattlar, km 3, 43080 Tarragona

Just north east of Tarragona, near Cattlar/Cruce

Holes	9 Par 36 2972m.
Visitors	Welcome
Fees	Ptas5000
Facilities	Bar and restaurant; practice ground; swimming pool; tennis
Pro	Francisco Jimenez

Club de Golf Don Cayo (1974)   23

Phone: 965 848046

Conde de Altea 49, Altea

Just north of Altea

Holes	9 Par 36 3078m.
Visitors	Welcome
Fees	Ptas5000
Facilities	Bar and restaurant; practice ground; swimming pool; tennis
Pro	Gregorio Sanz

La Duquesa Golf Club (1987)   24

Phone: 952 890425

Urb El Hacho, 29691 Manilva

West of Estepona off the N340

Holes	19 Par 72 6142m.
Visitors	Book ahead
Fees	Ptas 5000
Facilities	Bar and restaurant; practice ground; swimming pool; tennis and squash
Pro	Jose Maria Canizares

Club de Golf Escorpion (1975)   25

Phone: 96 1601211

Apto 1, 46180 Betera

North east of Valencia at Betera

Holes	18 Par 73 6239m.
Visitors	Welcome
Fees	Ptas5000
Facilities	Bar and restaurant; practice ground
Pro	Jose Rodriguez Lazaro

Real Automovil Club de España (1967)   26

Phone: 91 6522600

Jose Abascal 10, 28003 Madrid

North of Madrid, off the N1 near the racetrack

Holes	18 Par 72 6502m.
Visitors	Welcome
Fees	Ptas7000
Facilities	Bar and restaurant; practice ground

Club de Golf Girona (1991)   27

Phone: 972 222262

Travesia del Carril 2, 17001 Girona

Just outside Girona, on the west side

Holes	18 Par 72 6230m.
Visitors	Welcome
Fees	Ptas 5000
Facilities	Bar and restaurant; practice ground
Pro	Agustin Gallardo

Granada Club de Golf (1990)   28

Phone: 958 580727

Reyes Catolicos 1, 18001 Granada

On the south west of Granada, off the N323. At the airport take the C340 for Las Gabias

Holes	18 Par 72 6000m.
Visitors	Welcome
Fees	Ptas5000
Facilities	Bar and restaurant; practice ground; swimming pool; tennis
Pro	A P Moreno

Guadalhorce Golf Club (1988)   29

Phone: 952 241677

Apto 48, Campanillas, Malaga

Just west of Malaga at Campanillas

Holes	18 Par 72 6178m.
Visitors	Welcome on weekdays; must book at weekends
Fees	Ptas5000
Facilities	Bar and restaurant; practice ground; short course; swimming pool; tennis
Pro	S B Zaragoza

A restored Andalusian manor house lies at the heart of this club, which has been envisaged as a country club with ample sporting facilities. There is even a family chapel on the site. The golf course has two distinct characters; the first half is open and undulating, with very large greens, while the second nine holes are American in style with water hazards and plateau greens.

Golf Guadalmina (1959)   30

Phone: 952 883375

2960 San Pedro de Alcantara

West of Marbella, off the N340 at San Pedro

Holes	18 Par 72 5825m.
	18 Par 71 6065m.
Visitors	Welcome
Fees	Ptas4000
Facilities	Bar and restaurant; practice ground; swimming pool; tennis
Pro	Francisco Hernandez

Herreria Club de Golf (1968)   31

Phone: 91 8905111

28200 San Lorenzo de El Escorial

North west of Madrid. Follow the A6 and then the M505 to El Escorial

Holes	18 Par 72 6050m.
Visitors	Welcome
Fees	Ptas5000
Facilities	Bar and restaurant; practice ground; swimming pool; tennis
Pro	Luis Benito Fontal

Club de Golf Javea (1980)   32

Phone: 96 5792584

Crta de Javea a Benitachell, 03730 Javea

South of Javea, off the E15

Holes	9 Par 36 3030m.
Visitors	Welcome, but must book
Fees	Ptas4000
Facilities	Bar and restaurant; practice ground; swimming pool; tennis
Pro	J M Carriles

Club de Campo Laukariz (1976)   33

Phone: 94 6740858

14810 Laukariz-Munguia

North east of Bilbao, off the C6313 at Munguia

Holes	18 Par 74 6481m.
Visitors	Welcome
Fees	Ptas3000–5000
Facilities	Bar and restaurant; practice ground; swimming pool; tennis
Pro	Fernando Garcia Perez

Lauro Golf 'Los Caracolillos' (1992)   34

Phone: 952 412767

29130 Alhaurin de la Torre

West of Malaga, off the N340 at Alhaurin

Holes	18 Par 73 6008m.
Visitors	Welcome
Fees	Ptas3000
Facilities	Bar and restaurant; practice ground; horse riding
Pro	Vidal Carralero

The course, designed by Folco Nardi, sits between the mountains and the sea in an area of considerable charm. The design takes full advantage of the rolling terrain, and its lovely trees; pine and cork, olive, orange, lemon and fig. Several lakes add to the difficulty or to the fun, depending on how you play. The clubhouse was made from a splendid 18th century farmhouse.

Golf Llavaneras (1945)   35

Phone: 93 7926050

08392 Sant Andreu de Llavaneras

Just north east of Mataro on the coast road

Holes	18 Par 66 4644m.
Visitors	Welcome
Fees	Ptas5000–7000
Facilities	Bar and restaurant; practice ground; swimming pool
Pro	Francisco Gonzalez

Real Club de Golf Lomas-Bosque (1972)   36

Phone: 91 616750

Urb El Bosque Villaviciosa de Odon

South west of Madrid, off the N5 at Villaviciosa

Holes	18 Par 72 6141m.
Visitors	Welcome
Fees	Ptas7000
Facilities	Bar and restaurant; practice ground
Pro	M Alvarez

Club de Campo del Malaga (1929)   37

Phone: 952 381255

Apto 324, Malaga

West of Malaga, off the N340 and beyond the airport

Holes	18 Par 72 6173m.
Visitors	Welcome
Fees	Ptas5000
Facilities	Bar and restaurant; practice ground; swimming pool; tennis
Pro	Juan Rios

Designed by Tim Simpson this is the senior club on the Costa del Sol and is now owned by the Spanish ghovernment with one of their hotels (Parador) on the course. It is a lovely traditional design, with some of the holes running in links fashion along the sea while the others run through lines of eucalyptus and pine trees.

La Manga Campo del Golf (1971)   38

Phone: 968 564511

30385 Los Belones, Cartagena, La Manga

Off the N332 south of Alicante

Holes	2 x 18 Par 71/72 5780m/6259m.
Visitors	Welcome
Fees	Ptas7000
Facilities	Bars and restaurants; swimming pools; tennis; bowls
Pro	V Ballesteros

The courses were laid out in a shallow valley and thousands of palm trees were planted and several lakes sunk to provide some essential features for the design. The North course is full of interest with its dog-leg holes, ravines and water, while the South course, the venue, for several years, of the European Tour qualifying tournament, is a terrific challenge. The greens on both courses are outstanding, very quick and true. La Manga is an enormous complex of villas and apartments, but there is no sense of being hemmed in by over-development. The other sporting facilities are superb and even include a bowling green.

Campo de Golf de Manises (1964)   39
Phone: 96 3790850
Apto, 22029 Valencia
West of Valencia at Manises
Holes	9 Par 36 3075m.
Visitors	Welcome
Fees	Ptas4000
Facilities	Bar and restaurant; practice ground
Pro	Francisco Pinto

Golf de Mas Nou (1989)   40
Phone: 972 826118
Urb Mas Nou, 17250 Playa d'Aro
South east of Gerona, at Romanya de la Selva
Holes	18 Par 72 6218m.
Visitors	Welcome
Fees	Ptas4000–6000
Facilities	Bar and restaurant; practice ground; swimming pool; tennis
Pro	I Torrado

Up in the Las Gavarros mountains, the views from Mas Nou are breathtaking. With pine and cork trees in abundance, two man-made lakes, several dog-leg holes, large bunkers and the occasional massive boulder to negotiate, it is an entertaining and stimulating challenge.

Golf Club Masia Bach (1989)   41
Phone: 93 7726310
Diagonal 474 5e, 3n 008006 Barcelona
North west of Barcelona. After Martorell, head for Sant Esteve Sesrovires
Holes	27 Par 72 6271m.
Visitors	Welcome
Fees	Ptas7000–9000
Facilities	Bar and restaurant; practice ground; swimming pool; tennis
Pro	Francisco Cabrera

This was Jose Maria Olazabal's first tilt at golf course design and to call it challenging would be an understatement. There are some extraordinary holes here; to play them you need some of the skill and panache of the architect himself. It is immense fun – if you have a well-developed sense of humour.

Golf Club del Mediterraneo (1978)   42
Phone: 964 321227
La Coma, 12190 Borriol
Just north of Castellon. Take exit 46 off the A7 towards La Coma
Holes	18 Par 72 6038m.
Visitors	Welcome
Fees	Ptas 5000
Facilities	Bar and restaurant; practice ground; swimming pool; tennis
Pro	Victor Garcia

Club de Golf de Mijas (1976)   43
Phone: 952 476843
Apto 138, 29080 Fuengirola
Just north of Fuengirola, on the road to Coin; follow signs to the Hotel Byblos
Holes	18 Par 73 6348m (Los Lagos)
	18 Par 71 5896m (Los Olivos)
Visitors	Welcome
Fees	Ptas 6000
Facilities	Bar and restaurant; practice ground
Pro	Juan Rosa Rueda

Miraflores Golf Club (Riviera) (1990)   44
Phone: 952 837353
Urb Miraflores, 29657 Mijas Costa
Between Fuengirola and Marbella, off the N340. Turn off for 'Riviera'
Holes	18 Par 72 5775m.
Visitors	Welcome
Fees	Ptas4000
Facilities	Bar and restaurant; practice ground; swimming pool; tennis

The club is part of an apartment and villa complex but is situated in comparative peace in the foothills of the Sierra Mijas. It is an attractive holiday course with delightful views of the surrounding countryside. Miraflores is a good test of golf, especially over the second half, where there are some tough holes menaced by water. The green fees are reasonable and the clubhouse is superb.

Monte Mayor Golf (1991)   45
Phone: 952 810805
Las Brisas del Golf, 29660 Nueva Andalucia
Off the N340 between Estepona and Marbella. Near Benahavio
Holes	18 Par 71 5685m.
Visitors	Welcome
Fees	Ptas 7000
Facilities	Bar and restaurant; practice ground

This course is privately owned by Francois Perdrix, who encouraged the designer, Pepe Gancedo (of Torrequebrada fame) to indulge his imagination. He hardly needs such encouragement and has created an extraordinary and immensely difficult course. There are long carries to be made, sometimes to island fairways, and if you fail the penalties are severe. It is a wonderful and beautiful course, which any golfer will be eager to play.

Golf La Moraleja (1976)   46

Phone: 91 6500700

Alcobendas

North of Madrid off the A1 near Alcobendas.
Head for Camino de Burgos and then Camino
Viejo

Holes	18 Par 72 6016m.
Visitors	Welcome on weekdays
Fees	Ptas7000
Facilities	Bar and restaurant; practice ground
Pro	Valentin Barrios

The venue for the 1992 World Cup, won by the
USA in the shape of Fred Couples and Davis
Love, the course was designed by the Jack
Nicklaus Company and is a very tough test with
many water hazards.

Golf Los Moriscos (1974)   47

Phone: 958 600412

C Recogidas 11, 18002 Motril

South west of Motril towards Salobrena

Holes	9 Par 36 2885m.
Visitors	Welcome
Fees	Ptas3000
Facilities	Bar and restaurant; practice ground; swimming pool; tennis
Pro	Javier Garralon

Los Naranjos (1977)   48

Phone: 952 815206

Apto 64, Nueva Andalucia

Just west of Marbella, at Nueva Andalucia

Holes	18 Par 72 6457m.
Visitors	Book one day in advance
Fees	Ptas6000
Facilities	Bar and restaurant; practice ground; swimming pool
Pro	M E Merlo

This is yet another Trent Jones creation and
various lakes and streams affect the play on
many of the holes; the first nine are more open
but perhaps make up the more challenging part
of the course. The second half runs through
groves of orange trees which gave the course its
name. Handy if the previous evening's intake of
Rioja has given you a thirst.

Real Sociedad de Golf de Neguri (1911)   49

Phone: 94 4690200

Apto 9, 48980 Algorta

North west of Bilbao near Algorta

Holes	18 Par 72 6319m.
Visitors	Welcome
Fees	Ptas5000
Facilities	Bar and restaurant; practice ground; swimming pool
Pro	Carlos Celles

Golf Novo Sancti Petri (1990)   50

Phone: 956 494450

Chiclana de la Frontera, Cadiz

South east of Cadiz; on the coast at Sancti Petri

Holes	3 x 9 Par 36 (all) 3216/3260/3216m.
Visitors	Welcome
Fees	Ptas6000
Facilities	Bar and restaurant; practice ground; tennis and squash
Pro	Domingo Ruiz

Nuevo Club de Golf de Madrid (1972)   51

Phone: 91 6300820

Ctra de la Coruna, 28290 Las Matas

North west of Madrid, off the A6 at Las Matas

Holes	18 Par 70 5647m.
Visitors	Welcome
Fees	Ptas5000
Facilities	Bar and restaurant; practice ground; swimming pool; tennis
Pro	Marolo Linan

Golf Osona Montanya (1990)   52

Phone: 93 8840170

Masia l'Estanyol, 08553 El Brull

North of Barcelona, off the N152 near Seva

Holes	18 Par 72 6500m.
Visitors	Welcome
Fees	Ptas4000–8000
Facilities	Bar and restaurant; practice ground; tennis; horse riding
Pro	Jaime Roqueñi

Golf de Pals (1966)   53

Phone: 972 636006

Playa de Pals, 17256 Pals

North east of Pals on the coast

Holes	18 Par 73 6222m.
Visitors	Welcome
Fees	Ptas4500–8500
Facilities	Bar and restaurant; practice ground
Pro	Juan Anglada

A well-respected course which has hosted both
the Spanish and the Girona Opens, the holes
meander through avenues of umbrella pines,
unforgiving trees if your ball ends up among
them. The 8th is a severe long hole and is
followed by a short hole where you must carry
your ball over a lake to a two-tiered green.

Golf El Paraiso (1974)   54
Phone: 952 883835
Ctra Cadiz, km 167, 29080 Estepona
Between Estepona and Marbella, off the N340
Holes	18 Par 71 6116m.
Visitors	Welcome, but must book
Fees	Ptas5500
Facilities	Bar and restaurant; practice ground
Pro	Juan Franco

This well-established course was designed by Gary Player and rolls through splendid countryside. Its fairways are lined with palm trees, there are many water hazards and the greens are quick. It is a very enjoyable course.

Real Golf de Pedreña (1928)   55
Phone: 942 500001
Apto 233, 39080 Santander
On a peninsula above Santander
Holes	18 Par 70 5721m.
Visitors	Welcome
Fees	Ptas9000
Facilities	Bar and restaurant; practice ground; swimming pool; tennis
Pro	Ramon Sota

This course is famous as the one near the boyhood home of Seve Ballesteros, who used to sneak on to it for a few clandestine shots. Near the sea, it is a distinguished course which runs through the pine trees and is the more challenging when the wind blows.

Club de Golf La Penaza (1973)   56
Phone: 976 342800
Apto 3039, 50080 Zaragoza
South west of Zaragoza, off the N11
Holes	18 Par 72 6161m.
Visitors	Welcome
Fees	Ptas5000–6000
Facilities	Bar and restaurant; practice ground; swimming pool; tennis
Pro	Pablo Garcia Sanmiguel

Club Pineda de Sevilla (1939)   57
Phone: 954 611400
Apto 796, 41080 Sevilla
Just south of Sevilla, near the hippodrome
Holes	9 Par 35 2867m.
Visitors	Welcome
Fees	Ptas3000
Facilities	Bar and restaurant; practice ground; swimming pool; tennis
Pro	Patricio Delgado

Golf Playa Serena (1979)   58
Phone: 951 333055
Playa Serena, Roquetas de Mar
South west of Almeria at Playa Serena
Holes	18 Par 72 6301m.
Visitors	Welcome
Fees	Ptas7000
Facilities	Bar and restaurant; practice range
Pro	Francisco Parron

Club de Golf Pozoblanco (1984)   59
Phone: 957 100006
S Gregorio 2, 14400 Pozoblanco
At Pozoblanco (north of Cordoba)
Holes	9 Par 36 3020m.
Visitors	Welcome
Fees	Ptas4000
Facilities	Bar and restaurant; practice ground

Real Club de Golf El Prat (1954)   60
Phone: 93 3790278
Aptdo 10, 08080 El Prat
South of Barcelona and a few km from the airport
Holes	18 Par 72 6046m.
Visitors	Welcome
Fees	Ptas7000–9000
Facilities	Bar and restaurant; practice ground; 9 hole course; swimming pool; tennis
Pro	Pedro Marin

The leading Spanish golf architect, Javier Arana, designed the course, which hosted the 1956 Spanish Open won by Peter Alliss. The course has the benefit of having several wells and water affects many of the holes; the pines and palms which line the fairways are intimidating and demand great accuracy of shot. The 9th and 14th holes are especially severe.

Real Club de la Puerta de Hierro (1904)   61
Phone: 91 3161745
Avda de Miraflores, 38035 Madrid
On the north west side of Madrid, near the University
Holes	18 Par 72 6347m.
	18 Par 68 5273m.
Visitors	By introduction only
Fees	Ptas9000
Facilities	Bar and restaurant; practice ground
Pro	Jose Gallardo

This is the oldest club on the mainland of Spain and the home of the first Spanish Open. The championship course is a real challenge, with its rolling fairways lined with trees and thick vegetation. The views of Madrid from the course are well worth the price of the green fee.

Club de Golf Quesada (1989) 62
Phone: 96 6714285
Avda de las Naciones 168, 03170 Rojales
South of Alicante, near the coast at Rojales

Holes	18 Par 72 6185m.
Visitors	Welcome
Fees	Ptas4500
Facilities	Bar and restaurant; practice ground; swimming pool
Pro	Pascal Jimenez

La Quinta Golf & Country Club (1989) 63
Phone: 952 783462
Ctra de Ronda, km 3.5, San Pedro de Alcantara
West of Marbella, off the N340 at San Pedro

Holes	18 Par 70 5413m.
Visitors	Welcome
Fees	Ptas6000
Facilities	Bar and restaurant; practice ground; swimming pool; tennis
Pro	Manuel Pinero

Golf Club Reus Aiguesverds (1989) 64
Phone: 977 752725
Crta de Cambrils, 43206 Reus
Just south west of Tarragona between Salou and Cambrils

Holes	18 Par 72 6314m.
Visitors	Welcome
Fees	Ptas5000–6000
Facilities	Bar and restaurant; practice ground
Pro	Pablo Navarro

This long course winds in charming fashion through olive and cypress trees, with water hazards adding their own diversions on many of the holes. The third hole, with its green encircled by water, is justly celebrated – though not by those players whose shots find the water.

Golf Rio Real (1965) 65
Phone: 952 773776
Apto 82, 29080 Marbella
East of Marbella off the N340

Holes	18 Par 72 6071m.
Visitors	Book in advance
Fees	Ptas6000–8000
Facilities	Bar and restaurant; practice ground; swimming pool
Pro	Angel Miguel

A well-known venue for British golfers, the course is attached to the Los Monteros Hotel, whose guests have priority tee times. Though fairly flat, the course is a good test and it is always pleasant to stroll along the tree lined fairways.

Campo de Golf de Salamanca (1990) 66
Phone: 923 329102
Monte de Zarapicos, 37170 Salamanca
North west of Salamanca off the N620

Holes	18 Par 72 6480m.
Visitors	Welcome
Fees	Ptas3000–6000
Facilities	Bar and restaurant; practice ground; swimming pool; tennis and squash
Pro	Rafael del Castillo

Campo de Golf El Saler (1968) 67
Phone: 96 1611186
Parador Luis Vives, El Saler
South of Valencia on the coast

Holes	18 Par 72 6485m.
Visitors	Welcome
Fees	Ptas5000
Facilities	Bar and restaurant; practice ground; swimming pool; tennis
Pro	Jose Cabo

'Golf World' magazine has consistently rated El Saler as one of the best courses in Europe (it was first in 1989 and second in 1991) and it is indeed a wonderfully challenging course. Parts of it run alongside the Mediterranean through dunes and scrub in true links style and the other holes are protected by clumps of sombrero pines. The greens are superb and often encircled by bunkers, and the finish via the short 17th (at over 200 yards into the wind it seems long enough to most amateurs) and the undulating final hole is very tough indeed. It is hard to imagine how Bernhard Langer fashioned a final round of 62 in the 1984 Spanish Open on such a course.

Golf San Andrés (Chiclana) (1985) 68
Phone: 956 855607
Ctra Cadiz-Malaga, km 14, 11130 Chiclana
South east of Cadiz at Chiclana

Holes	9 Par 36 3150m.
Visitors	Welcome
Fees	Ptas5000
Facilities	Bar and restaurant; practice ground

Golf Club de San Cugat (1914) 69
Phone: 93 674 3908
08190 San Cugat de Valles
Just north west of Barcelona off the A7 at San Cugat

Holes	18 Par 70 5209m.
Visitors	Welcome. Course closed Monday
Fees	Ptas8500–13000
Facilities	Bar and restaurant; practice ground; swimming pool
Pro	Antonio Demelo (and 11 other pros)

San Roque Golf Club (1990)   70
Phone: 956 610649
Postbox 127, San Roque 11360
Off the N340 at San Roque

Holes	18 Par 72 6440m.
Visitors	Welcome
Fees	Ptas7000–9000
Facilities	Bar and restaurant; practice ground; swimming pool

In a lovely setting among wooded foothills, the San Roque course was designed by Dave Thomas, with Tony Jacklin as its golf director. Excellent credentials; and the aim was to produce an exclusive country club along American lines. The Japanese have spared nothing to build a challenging and interesting course and it is likely to be a venue for the European professional tour in the near future. The clubhouse, once owned by the Domecq family, is gorgeous.

Real Golf Club de San Sebastian (1968)   71
Phone: 943 616845
Apto 6, 20080 Fuentarrabia
East of San Sebastian, off the A1 at Fuentarrabia

Holes	18 Par 71 5955m.
Visitors	Weekday mornings only
Fees	Ptas6000–7000
Facilities	Bar and restaurant; practice ground swimming pool; tennis and squash
Pro	Jesus Arniti

Real Aero Club de Santiago (1976)   72
Phone: 981 592400
General Pardinas 34, 15701 Santiago de Compostella
East of Santiago de Compostella near the airport

Holes	9 Par 36 3047m.
Visitors	Welcome
Fees	Ptas5000
Facilities	Bar and restaurant; practice ground; swimming pool; tennis
Pro	Javier Ibarra

La Sella Golf (1991)   73
Phone: 96 5761549
Urb La Sella, 03750 Pedreguer
Jus inland from Denia at Cabo San Antonio

Holes	18 Par 72 6129m.
Visitors	Welcome
Fees	Ptas6000
Facilities	Bar and restaurant; practice ground
Pro	J A Borja

Club Sevilla Golf (1990)   74
Phone: 95 575 0414
Crtras Isla Mayor, km 0.800, 41849 Aznalcazar
South west of Sevilla, off the A49 at Aznalcazar

Holes	9 Par 36 2955m.
Visitors	Welcome
Fees	Ptas3000–5000
Facilities	Bar and restaurant; practice ground; tennis
Pro	Daniel Lozano

Real Club de Golf de Sevilla (1992)   75
Phone: 95 421 4781
Rafael Gonzalez Abreu 3, Sevilla
On the south east side of Sevilla, off the Utrera road

Holes	18 Par 72 6321m.
Visitors	Welcome on weekdays only
Fees	Ptas5000
Facilities	Bar and restaurant; practice ground; swimming pool; tennis and squash
Pro	Salvador Luna

Campo de Golf de Somosaguas (1971)   76
Phone: 91 3521647
Somosaguas, 28011 Madrid
On the west side of Madrid. Head for Pozuelo and then Somosaguas

Holes	9 Par 34 3027m.
Visitors	Welcome
Fees	Ptas5000
Facilities	Bar and restaurant; practice ground
Pro	Manuel Cabrera

Club de Golf Sotogrande (1965)   77

Phone: 956 795050

Paseo del Parque, 11310 Sotogrande

Off the N340 at Sotogrande

Holes	18 Par 74 6224m.
Visitors	Book a day in advance
Fees	Ptas8000
Facilities	Bar and restaurant; practice ground; swimming pool
Pro	Teodoro Gonzalez

This was Robert Trent Jones's first venture into Europe and, to many golf enthusiasts, it was his best. He once stated his credo in these words: 'the players attack the course and it is the architect's job to defend it.' At Sotogrande his defences include great length (the long tees give plenty of flexibility), well-positioned bunkers, dog-leg holes, water which comes into play particularly during the second half, huge contoured greens, and a profusion of cork trees as a backdrop to the holes. It is a magnificent golf course, and away in the distance is the great Rock of Gibraltar.

Club de Golf Terramar (1922)   78

Phone: 93 8940580

Aptdo 6, 08870 Sitges

South west of Sitges on the coast

Holes	18 Par 72 6040m.
Visitors	Welcome
Fees	Ptas4200–7000
Facilities	Bar and restaurant; practice ground; swimming pool; tennis
Pro	Juan Hernandez

Golf La Toja (1970)   79

Phone: 968 730726

36991 Isla de la Toja

West of Pontevedra, on the island of La Toja

Holes	9 Par 36 2996m.
Visitors	Welcome
Fees	Ptas5000–8000
Facilities	Bar and restaurant closed Monday in winter; practice ground; swimming pool; tennis
Pro	Primitivo Medrano

This is rated by some enthusiasts as one of the finest nine hole courses in Europe, a little jewel whose holes run along the coastline of the island and swing through groves of fine trees. The course calls for accuracy, especially off the tee; most notably at the 4th and the 6th holes where you must drive over the encroaching sea.

Golf Torrequebrada (1976)   80

Phone: 952 442742

Apto 67, 29630 Benalmadena Costa

Close to Benalmadena, off the N340

Holes	18 Par 72 5860m.
Visitors	Welcome
Fees	Ptas7000
Facilities	Bar and restaurant; practice ground; swimming pool; tennis and squash
Pro	Juan Jimenez

Pepe Gancedo, a former Spanish amateur champion, designed this very difficult course, which twists and turns and swoops and falls through valleys and hills. It was Gancedo's first project and he used immense wit and imagination in creating a course which both enchants and infuriates. It is certainly not to be missed if you are anywhere nearby.

Club de Golf de Ulzama (1965)   81

Phone: 948 305162

31799 Guerendiain

North of Pamplona off the N121

Holes	9 Par 36 3175m.
Visitors	Welcome
Fees	Ptas5000
Facilities	Bar and restaurant; practice ground; swimming pool; tennis
Pro	Rogelio Echevarria

Club Valdelaguila (1975)   82

Phone: 91 8859659

Apto 9, 28080 Alcala de Henares

East of Madrid off the A2 near Alcala

Holes	9 Par 36 2657m.
Visitors	Welcome
Fees	Ptas5000
Facilities	Bar and restaurant; practice ground

Club de Golf Valderrama (1975)   83

Phone: 956 792775

Apto 1, 11310 Sotogrande

Off the N340 at Sotogrande

Holes	18 Par 72 6326m.
Visitors	By introduction only
Fees	Ptas 9000
Facilities	Bar and restaurant; practice ground; par 3 course
Pro	Juan Guerrero

This was once the New Course of Sotogrande and was designed by Robert Trent Jones. Jaime Ortiz Patino, who made several fortunes in tin mining, bought it in the 1980s and has lavished uncounted amounts of pesetas on the club to make it the best and most exclusive in Europe. It is a reasonable supposition that the Ryder Cup will be played there in 1997, and it is currently the home of the Volvo Masters tournament. It is a magnificent golf course, one of the ultimate challenges even for professionals. David Feherty called it 'the last course Walt Disney designed before they froze him'; but Seve Ballesteros considers it one of the best in the world.

Club de Golf Vallromanas (1969) 84
Phone: 93 5729064

08170 Vallromanas

North of Barcelona, near Granollers

Holes	18 Par 72 6038m.
Visitors	Welcome, but must book. Course closed Tuesday
Fees	Ptas5800–11,500
Facilities	Bar and restaurant; practice ground; swimming pool; tennis
Pro	Jaime Gallardo

Aero Club de Vigo (1951) 85
Phone: 986 242493

Reconquista 7, 36201 Vigo

East of Vigo near the airport

Holes	9 Par 35 2687m.
Fees	Pts3000
Facilities	Bar and restaurant; practice ground; tennis
Pro	Diego San Roman

Club de Campo Villa de Madrid (1932) 86
Phone: 91 3572132

Crta Castilla, 28040 Madrid

Just to the north west of Madrid

Holes	18 Par 72 6118m.
	9 Par 36 2900m.
Visitors	Must book
Fees	Ptas5000–10,000
Facilities	Bar and restaurant; practice ground; swimming pool; tennis; horse riding
Pro	German Garrido

Situated on hilly ground outside Madrid, the course, designed by Javier Arana, has been the venue for many major tournaments including the Canada Cup. The course is laid out over rolling ground with many plateau greens to test the golfer's judgement. As well as the golf course a number of other sports are housed in this large complex.

Campo de Golf Villamartin (1972) 87
Phone: 96 6765160

Apto 35, 3080 Torrevieja

South of Torrevieja, off the N332

Holes	18 Par 72 6037m.
	18 Par 72 5824m.
Visitors	Welcome
Fees	Ptas4000
Facilities	Bar and restaurant; practice ground; swimming pool; tennis
Pro	Emilio Rodriguez

Club de Golf Los Villares (1976) 88
Phone: 957 350208

Ronda de los Tejares, 1–2 Apto 436, Cordoba

Just north of Cordoba

Holes	18 Par 72 5964m.
Visitors	Welcome
Fees	Ptas3000–5000
Facilities	Bar and restaurant; practice ground; swimming pool; tennis
Pro	Juan Jose Nieto

Vista Hermosa Club de Golf (1975) 89
Phone: 956 875604

Apto 77, 11500 El Puerto de S Maria

North of Cadiz, at Puerto de S Maria

Holes	9 Par 36 2837m.
Visitors	Welcome
Fees	Ptas 7000
Facilities	Bar and restaurant; practice ground; swimming pool; tennis
Pro	Manuel Velasco

Real Aero Club de Zaragoza (1966) 90
Phone: 976 214378

Seccion de Golf Coso 34, 50004 Zaragoza

West of Zaragoza, off the N11 near the airport

Holes	9 Par 35 2520m.
Visitors	Welcome
Fees	Ptas5000
Facilities	Bar and restaurant; practice ground

Real Golf de Zarauz (1916)   91
Phone: 943 830145
Apto 82, 20080 Zarauz
West of San Sebastian at Zarauz
Holes   9 Par 34 2546m.
Visitors   Welcome
Fees   Ptas 5000
Facilities Bar and restaurant; practice ground
Pro   Norberto Belartieta

Ibiza

Golf de Ibiza (1989)   92
Phone: 971 315003
Can Micolau, Santa Eulalia del Rio
On the east coast at Roca Llisa
Holes   18 Par 72 6085m.
             9 Par 36 2810m.
Visitors   Welcome
Fees   Ptas8000
Facilities Bar and restaurant; practice ground;
             swimming pool; tennis
Pro   G Casticco

Club de Golf Roca Llisa (1971)   93
Phone: 971 313718
Apto 200, 07080 Ibiza
North east of Ibiza at Roca Llisa
Holes   9 Par 36 2934m.
Visitors   Welcome
Fees   Ptas5000
Facilities Bar and restaurant; practice ground;
             tennis
Pro   German Castillo

Majorca

Real Golf de Bendinat (1986)   94
Phone: 341 405200
c/Formentera, 07015 Calvia
South west of Palma, on the Andraitx road
Holes   9 Par 34 2494m.
Visitors   Welcome
Fees   Ptas5200
Facilities Bar and restaurant; practice ground
Pro   Ricardo Galliano

Canyamel Golf Club (1980)   95
Phone: 971 564457
Urb Canyamel, Crta de las Cuevas de Arta,
Capdepera
Just south of Capdepera
Holes   18 Par 73 5982m.
Visitors   Welcome
Fees   Ptas5000
Facilities Bar and restaurant; practice ground

Club de Golf Pollensa (1986)   96
Phone: 971 533265
Ctra Palma, 07460 Pollensa
On the northern coast at Puerto de Pollensa
Holes   9 Par 36 2652m.
Visitors   Welcome, but must book
Fees   Ptas5000
Facilities Bar and restaurant; practice ground;
             swimming pool
Pro   Carlos Insua

On the more sedate northern coast, this is one of
Pepe Gancedo's designs, a course which runs
through a lush and charming landscape of olive
trees. Lovely old stone walls have been left in
place and the two large lakes are used to good
effect. The rough is often composed of rocks and
the greens are large and contoured. It is a lot of
fun.

Club de Golf de Poniente (1978)   97
Phone: 971 680148
Crta Cala Figuera, Calvia
South west of Palma, on the coast at Cala
Figuera
Holes   18 Par 72 6430m.
Visitors   Welcome
Fees   Ptas5000
Facilities Bar and restaurant; practice ground
Pro   Francisco Ruiz

Club de Golf Roca Viva (1991)   98
Phone: 34 71565875
Apto 6, Capdepera, 07580 Camp Mitja
On the north east side of the island, near Playa
Ratjada
Holes   18 Par 72 6284m.
Visitors   Welcome
Fees   Ptas5500
Facilities Bar and restaurant; practice ground

The course was built on very rocky terrain and
the architect has utilised very large tees, with
four different tee positions suitable for golfers of
differing abilities. There are plenty of bunkers,
several lakes and lovely finishing holes along
the side of a hill.

Golf Santa Ponsa (1976)   99

Phone: 971 690211

Urb Sta Ponça, 07184 Calvia
South west of Palma at Santa Ponsa

Holes	18 Par 72 6170m.
Visitors	Welcome
Fees	Ptas6200
Facilities	Bar and restaurant; practice ground
Pro	Diego Lopez

The Balearic Open was won here by Seve
Ballesteros in 1992 and Jose Maria Olazabal
holds the course record with a 64. There are not
many trees at Santa Ponso but the rough is
rough and there is some water around, most
notably on the 10th hole, a monster of nearly 600
yards.

Club de Golf Son Servera (1966)   100

Phone: 971 567802

Urb Costa de los Pinos, 07550 Son Servera
North east of Son Servera, off the C715

Holes	9 Par 36 2978m.
Visitors	Welcome, but must book
Fees	Ptas5000
Facilities	Bar and restaurant; practice ground
Pro	Santiago Sota

Club de Golf Son Vida (1964)   101

Phone: 971 791210

Urb Son Vida, 07013 Palma
A few kilometres north west of Palma

Holes	18 Par 72 5705m.
Visitors	Welcome
Fees	Ptas7000–9000
Facilities	Bar and restaurant; practice ground
Pro	Sebastian Ruiz

The course was designed by Fred Hawtree and is
the oldest and most popular on the island. It is
by now means long, but the fairways are narrow
and the rough is unforgiving.

Club de Golf Vall d'Or (1985)   102

Phone: 971 837001

Crta Porto Colom, 07660 Cala d'Or
At Cala d'Or

Holes	9 Par 35 2731m.
Visitors	Welcome
Fees	Ptas5500
Facilities	Bar and restaurant; practice ground; swimming pool; tennis
Pro	Antonio Gonzalez

Menorca

Real Club de Golf de Menorca (1976)   103

Phone: 971 373700

Apto 97, 07780 Mahon
North of Mahon in Urb 'Shangri-La' at El Grao

Holes	9 Par 35 2662m.
Visitors	Welcome
Fees	Ptas5000
Facilities	Bar and restaurant; practice ground

Club de Golf Son Parc (1977)   104

Phone: 971 379814

Apto 634, 07703 Mahon
Nedar Mercadal, off the Fornells road

Holes	9 Par 35 2791m.
Visitors	Welcome
Fees	Ptas5200
Facilities	Bar and restaurant; practice ground; tennis
Pro	Peter Garratt

Gran Canaria

Club de Golf Las Palmas (Bandama) (1891)
                                             105

Phone: 928 351050

Apto 183, 35080 Las Palmas
South west of Las Palmas in Bandama

Holes	18 Par 69 5683m.
Visitors	Welcome
Fees	Ptas5000–7000
Facilities	Bar and restaurant; practice ground
Pro	Felipe Santana

Spain's oldest golf club removed itself from the
city in 1956 and the course now perches at the
top of the volcanic area of Bandama. It is a
short and narrow course with excellent greens.

Campo de Golf Maspalomas (1968)   106

Phone: 928 762581

Ave de Africa, 35100 Playa del Inglés, Las
Palmas
South of Las Palmas at Maspalomas

Holes	18 Par 72 6216m.
Visitors	Welcome
Fees	Ptas7000
Facilities	Bar and restaurant; practice ground; tennis and squash
Pro	Angel Gutierrez

Lanzarote

Club de Golf Costa Teguise (1980)   107
Phone: 928 590512
Apto 170, 35080 Arrecife
North west of Arrecife in Urb Costa Teguise

Holes	18 Par 72 5853m.
Visitors	Welcome
Fees	Ptas5500
Facilities	Bar and restaurant; practice ground; swimming pool; tennis and squash
Pro	Nicolas Garcia

Tenerife

Amarilla Golf & Country Club (1990)   108
Phone: 922 785777
San Miguel de Abona
Next to Golf del Sur, near the airport

Holes	18 Par 72 5844m.
Visitors	Welcome
Fees	Ptas5000
Facilities	Bar and retaurant; practice ground; swimming pool; tennis
Pro	E O'Connor

This is a well-designed course with excellent greens, and the Tenerife Open, a European Tour event, was played here in 1990. It is a punishing course if your shots are wayward, since only rock and scrub awaits your ball off the fairway. There are a couple of very pretty holes laid out by the sea.

The club house is spacious and comfortable and after your round you can relax on the terrace, which surrounds the swimming pool. The practice area is only a few yards away. Villas and apartments alongside the course can be hired.

Golf del Sur (1988)   109
Phone: 922 704555
San Miguel de Abona
Close to Tenerife Sur airport

Holes	3 x 9 Par 35/36/36 2602/2762/2781m.
Visitors	Welcome
Fees	Ptas7250
Facilities	Bar and restaurant; practice ground; tennis and squash
Pro	J Golding

The holiday golfer will enjoy this well-kept course, with its springy turf and superb, very fast greens. The twenty-seven holes are undulating and inventive, but there are rather too many blind second shots for some people's tastes.

A round of golf is expensive, but there is a good discount if you are staying on the complex. .

Club de Golf de Tenerife (1932)   110
Phone: 922 636607
Apto 125, 38080 La Laguna
South west of Santa Cruz, towards the airport

Holes	18 Par 71 5922m.
Visitors	Welcome
Fees	Ptas7000
Facilities	Bar and restaurant; practice ground
Pro	Gabriel Gonzalez

SWEDEN

MUCH has been made of the rapid expansion of golf facilities in Sweden. It has indeed been brisk over the last five years with around 50 new courses and many more in the pipeline. But it is interesting to look back and see that during the 1960s the number of courses open for play in Sweden doubled to around 120.

The main population centres are concentrated in the southern part of Sweden and so are most of their 200 or more courses. The weather is milder there but even so most of the clubs close up for the winter.

Despite the limited season, enthusiasm for golf in Sweden has continued to gather momentum. The Swedish Golf Union has done much to foster the enthusiasm, especially by its development of junior golf. The fruits of their enlightened policies are being seen with the arrival on the professional tournament scene of accomplished players such as Anders Forsbrand, Per-Ulric Johannson and Robert Karlsson.

There are some splendid golf courses in Sweden including Falsterbo, a great links course on the south west tip of Sweden, and its neighbours, Flommens and Ljunghusens. They are easily accessible, by ferry from Denmark for example. Halmstad and Bastad, two other splendid courses, are within reach, too, and there are many more which would repay a visit.

The major problem in visiting Sweden is the cost of living. Those commodities which most concern touring golfers – food, drink and accommodation – are much more expensive than in most other parts of Europe.

Unit of currency: Swedish Krona
Rate of exchange (approx. at 1.1.93): SKr10–£1
International dialling code: (010 46)

A6 Golfklubb (1990)	I
Phone: 036 129010	
Central Vägen, 55305 Jönköping	
On the east side of Jönköping. From the E4 turn off at 'Nya A6' and follow sign to 'Golfbana'	
Holes	27 Par 37/36/35
Visitors	Welcome. Course closed November to March
Fees	SKr160
Facilities	Bar and restaurant; practice ground

Ågesta Golfklubb (1958)	2
Phone: 08 6045641	
Agesta, 12352 Farsta	
South of Stockholm. Head for Farsta and then Agesto	
Holes	18 Par 72 5676m.
Visitors	Welcome. Course closed December to April
Fees	SKr150–250
Facilities	Bar and restaurant; practice ground; short course
Pro	R Tomlinson

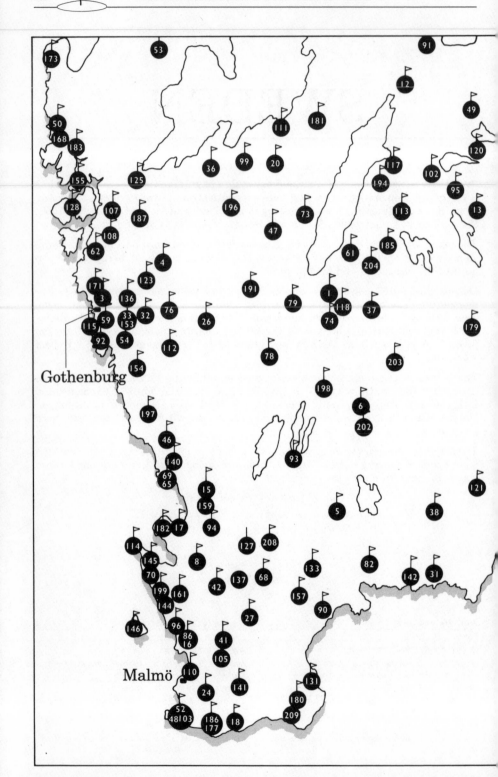

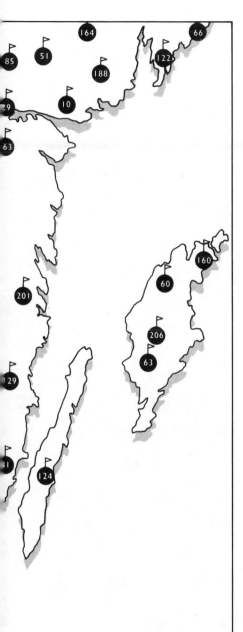

Albatross Golfklubb (1973) **3**

Phone: 031 551901

Lillhagsvagen,42250 Hisings Backa

North of Goteborg off the E6 on the road to Säve

Holes	18 Par 72 6020m.
Visitors	Welcome
Fees	SKr200.
Facilities	Bar and restaurant; practice ground
Pro	P Johansson

Alingsås Golfklubb (1987) **4**

Phone: 0322 52421

Hjalmared 4050, 44195 Alingsås

South east of Alingsås off the R180 towards Borås

Holes	18 Par 72 5600m.
Visitors	Welcome, but must book. Course closed November to March
Fees	SKR150–200
Facilities	Bar and restaurant; practice ground
Pro	A Liljedahl

Älmhults Golfklubb (1975) **5**

Phone: 0476 14135

Box 152, 34322 Älmhult

Just east of Älmhult on route 120

Holes	18 Par 71 5350m.
Visitors	Welcome. Course closed November to March
Fees	SKr120
Facilities	Bar and restaurant; practice ground
Pro	B Märtensson

Alvesta Golfklubb (1992) **6**

Phone: 0472 40140

Kronobergshed, 34036 Moheda

On Route 126, about 7km north of Alvesta towards Moheda

Holes	18 Par 72 5865m.
Visitors	Welcome. Course closed December to April
Fees	SKr150
Facilities	Bar; practice ground

SOUTHERN
SWEDEN

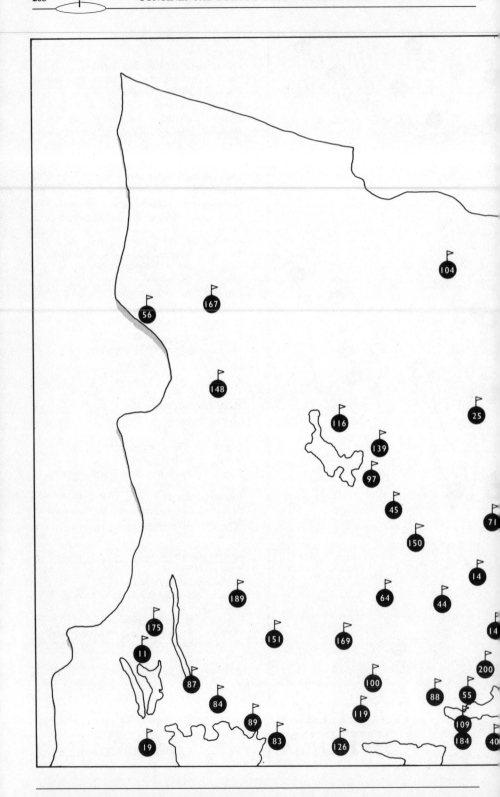

CENTRAL SWEDEN

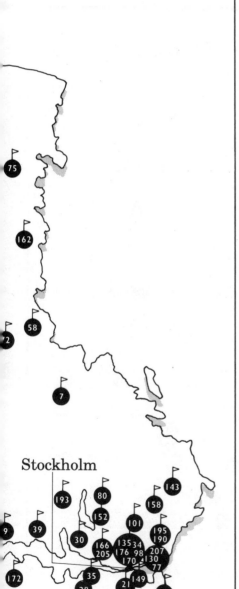

Stockholm

Älvkarleby Golfklubb (1987)   7
Phone: 026 72757
Box 41, 81071 Älvkarleby
Off route 76 between Älvkarleby and Skutskär
Holes   9 Par 35
Visitors   Welcome. Course closed November
             to April
Fees   SKr80–100
Facilities Bar and restaurant; practice ground

Ängelholms Golfklubb (1973)   8
Phone: 0431 30260
Box 1117, 26222 Angelholm
East of Angelholm on the R13/114
Holes   18 Par 72 5760m.
Visitors   Welcome. Course closed December to
             March
Fees   SKr120–150
Facilities Bar and restaurant; practice ground
Pro   Y Mahmoud

Ängsö Golfklubb (1985)   9
Phone: 0171 41012
Skultuna Vägen 7, 72217 Västerås
South east of Västerås off the E18, on an island
Holes   18 Par 72 5825m.
Visitors   Welcome. Course closed November
             to April
Fees   SKr180
Facilities Bar and restaurant; practice ground
Pro   Anders Werthen
Heavy clumps and avenues of trees and water
hazards, which encroach on virtually every hole,
present the major challenges at this course. It is
laid down in the middle of a nature reserve and
is a pleasure to play.

Ärila Golfklubb (1951)   10
Phone: 0155 14967
Nicolai, 61192 Nykoping
South west of Nykoping off the R53
Holes   18 Par 72 5735m.
Visitors   Welcome. Course closed November
             to April
Fees   SKr180
Facilities Bar and restaurant; practice ground
Pro   A Harris

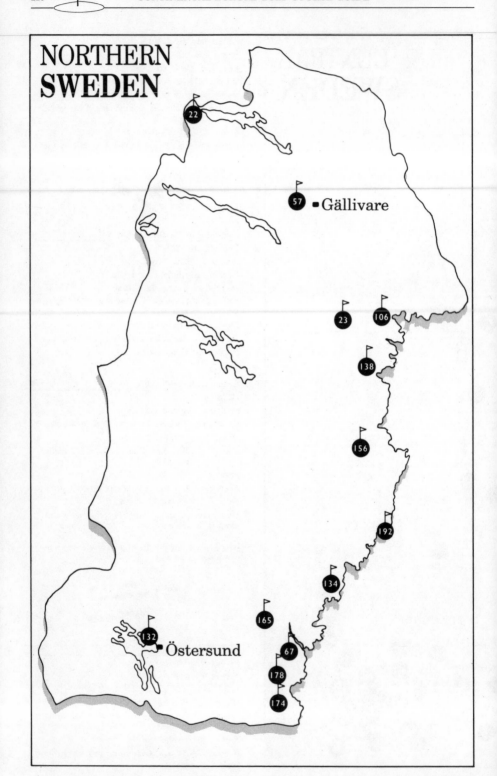

NORTHERN
SWEDEN

Gällivare

Östersund

Arvika Golfklubb (1972) 11
Phone: 0570 54133
Box 197, 67125 Arvika
East of Arvika off the R61

Holes	18 Par 72 5745m.
Visitors	Welcome. Course closed November to April
Fees	SKr120
Facilities	Bar and restaurant; practice ground
Pro	Peter Carsbo

Askersund Golfklubb (1980) 12
Phone: 0583 34440
Box 3002, 69603 Ämmeberg
South east of Askersund off the A50. Head for Ämmeberg and Zinkgruvan

Holes	18 Par 72 5650m.
Visitors	Welcome. Course closed November to April
Fees	SKr150
Facilities	Bar and restuarant; practice ground
Pro	L Johansson

Ätvidaberg Golfklubb (1957) 13
Phone: 0120 11425
Vastantorp, Box 180, 59724 Ätvidaberg
Just south west of Ätvidaberg off the R35. Follow the signs to Bjärka Säby for about 2km

Holes	18 Par 72 5900m.
Visitors	Welcome. Course closed November to April
Fees	SKr140–160
Facilities	Bar and restaurant; practice ground
Pro	Bernt Nygren

Wonderful scenery awaits the golfer at this course whose fairways stretch out alongside a lake and through groves of stately oak and beech trees. The holes offer a real challenge but, however he plays, the golfer cannot fail to be enchanted by his surroundings.

Avesta Golfklubb (1963) 14
Phone: 0226 10363
Box 168, Asbo, 77424 Avesta
Just east of Avesta off the R68. The course is signposted

Holes	18 Par 71 5500m.
Visitors	Welcome. Course closed November to April
Fees	SKr140
Facilities	Bar and restaurant; practice ground
Pro	Gordon Long

Backavattnets Golfklubb (1980) 15
Phone: 035 44271
Box 288, 30107 Halmstad
East of Halmstad off the R25; follow the signs to 'Golfbana'

Holes	18 Par 72 5740m.
Visitors	Welcome
Fees	SKr180
Facilities	Bar and restaurant; practice ground
Pro	Stanley Grant

Barsebäck Golf & Country Club (1969) 16
Phone: 046 776230
Box 274, 24022 Loddekopinge
South of Landskrona off the E6 towards Järavallen

Holes	18 Par 72 5910m.
	18 Par 72 5855m.
Visitors	Welcome, but must book
Fees	SKr240
Facilities	Bar and restaurant; practice ground; swimming pool; tennis
Pro	I Christersson

The original course is an entertaining mixture of parkland, woods and seaside. The Scandinavian Masters tournament has been played here and a mixture of holes from both courses were used.

Båstad Golfklubb (1929) 17
Phone: 0431 73136
Box 1037, 26921 Bastad
West of Bastad off the R116

Holes	18 Par 71 5616m (Old course)
	18 Par 73 5845m (New course)
Visitors	Welcome. Closed November to April
Fees	SKr250
Facilities	Bar and restaurant; practice ground
Pro	Per Hanson

Many Swedish championships have been played on the Old Course, founded by a relation of Alfred Nobel, instigator of the eponymous prize, and laid out by the legendary English golfer, J H Taylor. The fairways are generous and have notably lush turf but the greens have some difficult slopes and tiers and are well-defended by bunkers. A feature of the course is the old windmill beside the first tee, and the views of the sea are superb. The New Course has been criticised for its lack of variety and is never as busy as the Old.

Bedinge Golfklubb (1931)   18

Phone: 0410 25514

Box 20, 23021 Beddingestrand

East of Trelleborg off the R10 at Beddingestrand

Holes	18 Par 70 4500m.
Visitors	Welcome
Fees	SKr100–150
Facilities	Bar and restaurant; practice ground
Pro	I Persson

Billerud Golfklubb (1961)   19

Phone: 0555 91313

Box 192, 66100 Saffle

North east of Saffle off route 45 towards Karlsbad

Holes	18 Par 72 5874m.
Visitors	Welcome. Course closed November to April
Fees	SKr140
Facilities	Bar and restaurant; practice ground
Pro	R Bailey

Billingens Golfklubb (1959)   20

Phone: 0511 80291

St Kulhult, 54017 Lerdala

20km from Skara. Follow the B49 to Axvall, and then head for Lerdala

Holes	18 Par 71 5670m.
Visitors	Welcome. Course closed November to March
Fees	SKr140–170
Facilities	Bar and restaurant; practice ground; short course
Pro	B Falk

Björkhagens Golfklubb (1973)   21

Phone: 08 7730431

Box 4030, 12104 Johanneshov

South of Stockholm in the Bagamossen suburb

Holes	9 Par 33 2250m.
Visitors	Welcome. Course closed November to April
Fees	SKr120–150
Facilities	Refreshments; practice ground
Pro	K Johnson

Bjorkliden Arctic Golfklubb (1989)   22

Phone: 0980 40040

98025 Bjorkliden

In Bjorkliden off route 98

Holes	9 Par 35 2480m.
Visitors	Welcome. Course closed October to May
Fees	SKr100
Facilities	Bar and restaurant

This recently became the most northerly golf course in the world, about 150 miles north of the Arctic circle. The views of the lakes and the mountains are beguiling and for most of Bjorkliden's short season you can play through-out the night as well as the day. The fairways are narrow, the greens tiny and the tundra tough; and there are some local rules: for example 'if a reindeer eats your ball, drop a new one where the incident occurred'.

Bodens Golfklubb (1946)   23

Phone: 0921 61071

Box 107, 96121 Boden

West of Boden by route 97 and route 356 to Hedon; then head for S Bredåber and Degerbåcken

Holes	9 Par 36 2898m.
Visitors	Welcome. Course closed October to May
Fees	SKr100
Facilities	Bar and restaurant; practice ground
Pro	J Gidland

Bokskogen Golfklubb (1963)   24

Phone: 040 481121

Totups Nygärd, 23040 Bara

East of Malmo, off the E14 towards Oxie, then Torup

Holes	18 Par 72 5992m.
	18 Par 70 5419m.
Visitors	Welcome
Fees	SKr180–220
Facilities	Bar and restaurant; practice ground
Pro	J Larsson

This is a rather exclusive club, situated alongside the Ydinggesjö river, and has staged one or two European Tour events. The tees are reasonably open but the fairways tend to close in inexorably as they approach the greens, which can be very quick.

Bollnäs Golfklubb (1966)   **25**
Phone: 0278 50540
Box 1072, 82112 Bollnäs
South west of Bollnäs off route 272
Holes   18 Par 72 5870m.
Visitors   Welcome. Course closed November
            to April
Fees   SKr150
Facilities Bar and restaurant; practice ground
Pro   N Forsberg

Boras Golf Club (1954/1991)   **26**
Phone: 0332 50142
Ostra Vik, 50595 Boras
South of Boras off the B41. Follow signs to
'Golfbana'
Holes   18 Par 72 5920m.
            18 Par 70 5030m.
Visitors   Welcome. Course closed November
            to March
Fees   SKr200–240
Facilities Bar and restaurant; practice ground;
            short course
Pro   Per Johansson

Bosjoklöster Golfklubb (1974)   **27**
Phone: 0413 25858
24395 Hoor
South of Hoor off the R23
Holes   18 Par 72 5890m.
Visitors   Welcome
Fees   SKr150
Facilities Bar and restaurant; practice ground
Pro   Olle Asplund

Botkyrka Golfklubb (1988)   **28**
Phone: 0753 29650
Malmbrogård, 14791 Grödinge
South west of Stockholm off route 225 towards
Nynashamn
Holes   18
Visitors   Welcome, but must book. Course
            closed mid-October to mid-May
Fees   SKr200–250
Facilities Refreshments; practice ground

Bråvikens Golfklubb (1992)   **29**
Phone: 011 40072
Box 6015, 60006 Norrköping
From Norrköping take route 209 east towards
Arkösund. After about 8km turn left towards
Djurön; the golf course is 5km on the left
Holes   3 x 9 Par 36 (all)
Visitors   Welcome
Fees   SKr150
Facilities Bar and restaurant; practice ground
Pro   Jan Monier

Bro-Balsta Golfklubb (1978)   **30**
Phone: 0758 41300
• Box 96 Nygardsvagen, 19722 Bro
Turn off the E18 from Stockholm at Bro, and
follow the golf course signs from the centre of
Bro
Holes   18 Par 73 5895m.
Visitors   Welcome. Course closed November
            to April
Fees   SKr230–280
Facilities Bar and restaurant; practice ground;
            short course
Pro   Anders Sjöhagen

Carlskrona Golfklubb (1949)   **31**
Phone: 0457 35123
Almö, 37024 Nattraby
West of Karlskrona off the E66. After Nattraby
head for Garpen
Holes   18 Par 70 5525m.
Visitors   Welcome. Course closed December to
            March
Fees   SKr160
Facilities Bar and restaurant; practice ground
Pro   Anders Johansson

Chalmers Golfklubb (1991)   **32**
Phone: 031 918430
Post Box 1115, 43800 Landvetter
Off the R40 near Landvetter
Holes   18 Par 71 5560m.
Visitors   Welcome
Fees   SKr150–200
Facilities Bar and restaurant; practice ground
Pro   Patrick Hoibrandt

Delsjo Golfklubb (1962)   33

Phone: 031 406959
Kallebäck, 41276 Goteborg
South east of Goteborg. Take the R40 and turn off at the Delsö area. There are signs to the golf course

Holes	18 Par 71 5703m.
Visitors	Welcome weekdays before 3pm, weekends after 1pm
Fees	SKr200
Facilities	Bar and restaurant; practice ground
Pro	P-O Dahlman

The course is by no means long but makes up for this with its very narrow fairways running through thick woodland. The onus is on straight driving and the golfer must also contend with fairly heavy rough and some tricky dog-leg holes, especially during the first half.

Djursholms Golfklubb (1931)   34

Phone: 08 7551477
Hagbardsv. 1, 18263 Djursholm
North of Stockholm through Rosjagstull, Dauderyds and Djursholm towards Näsby park

Holes	18 Par 71 5590m.
	9 Par 34
Visitors	Welcome, but must book. Course closed November to April
Fees	SKr250
Facilities	Bar and restaurant; practice ground
Pro	G Deverell

Drottningholm Golfklubb (1956)   35

Phone: 08 7590085
Box 183, 17011 Drottnignholm
West of Stockholm, on the Drottningholm road towards Ekerö

Holes	18 Par 72 5825m.
Visitors	Welcome, but must book. Course closed November to April
Fees	SKr250
Facilities	Bar and restaurant

The club is located on an island on Lake Malaren and is close to a summer palace belonging to the Swedish royal family. The course runs through charming and well-wooded parkland for most of its length, although some of the later holes cover more open terrain.

Ekarnas Golfklubb (1970)   36

Phone: 0514 11450
Balders Vag 12, 46700 Grastorp
Just west of Grastorp off the B47 towards Vänerborg

Holes	18 Par 71 5480m.
Visitors	Welcome. Course closed November to April
Fees	SKr170
Facilities	Refreshments; practice ground

Eksjö Golfklubb (1938)   37

Phone: 0381 13525
Skedhult, 57591 Eksjo
On route 33, 5km from Eksjö towards Nässjö

Holes	18 Par 72 5930m.
Visitors	Welcome. Course closed November to March
Fees	SKr150
Facilities	Bar and restaurant; practice ground
Pro	M Wissinger

This delightful course runs through undulating parkland and the fairways are lined with fine and stately trees. There is not too much trouble here; the course is open and inviting.

Emmaboda Golfklubb (1976)   38

Phone: 0471 20505
Kirkogatan, 36060 Vissefjarda
South of Emmaboda off the R28 at Vissefjärda

Holes	18 Par 72
Visitors	Welcome. Course closed December to March
Fees	SKr120
Facilities	Refreshments; practice ground

Enköping Golfklubb (1970)   39

Phone: 0171 20830
Box 2006, 74545 Enköping
Just east of Enköping past the Fanna district

Holes	18 Par 71 5660m.
Visitors	Welcome, Course closed November to Aprl
Fees	SKr120–200
Facilities	Bar and restaurant; practice ground
Pro	D Bäck

Eskilstuna Golfklubb (1951) 40

Phone: 016 142629

Strängnäsvägen, 63349 Eskilstuna

Just south east of Eskilstuna off the E3. From Stockholm take the 'Eskilstuna Östra (East)' exit

Holes	18 Par 70 5590m.
Visitors	Welcome. Course closed November to April
Fees	SKr150
Facilities	Bar and restaurant; practice ground
Pro	A Robinson

Eslövs Golfklubb (1968) 41

Phone: 0413 18610

Box 150, 24122 Eslov

Take the R113 south from Eslöv towards Lund. Follow signposts to Ellinge and Golfbana

Holes	18 Par 70 5630m.
Visitors	Welcome. Course closed December to March
Fees	SKr150–180
Facilities	Bar and restaurant; practice ground
Pro	Mark Dewdney

This is an extremely tight course, with out of bounds areas lurking on many of the holes, especially at the start. If you are wild from the tee this is a course to avoid. Dog-leg holes and plenty of water hazards add to the fun; accuracy is all at Eslövs.

F 5 Golfklubb (1959) 42

Phone: 0435 41467

Flygflottilj, 26070 Ljungbyhed

Just west of Ljungbyhed near the Aviation School

Holes	9 Par 36 2838m.
Visitors	Welcome
Fees	SKr80–100
Facilities	Practice ground

Fågelbro Klubb (1991) 43

Phone: 0766 40130

13900 Värmdö

35km from Stockholm. Take route 222 towards Gustavsberg–Strömma–Stavnäs. Just after the Strömma crossroads there is a sign to Fågelbro Säteri

Holes	18 Par 72 5682m.
Visitors	Welcome. Course closed November to April
Fees	SKr250–350
Facilities	Bar and restaurant; practice ground; swimming pool; tennis and squash
Pro	Mike Sheard

Built in the grounds of an ancient estate this course has first class credentials. The first nine holes meander through hilly terrain with the many streams posing the main problems, along with the dog-leg design of several fairways. You might need a coracle for the second half since there is water everywhere and many deep bunkers.

Fagersta Golfklubb (1973) 44

Phone: 0223 54060

Box 2051, 73702 Fagersta

South west of Fagersta. Take route 65 to Ludvika and then head for Hedkärra

Holes	9 Par 36 2890m.
Visitors	Welcome. Course closed October to April
Fees	SKr75
Facilities	Bar and restaurant; practice ground

Falun-Borlange Golfklubb (1956) 45

Phone: 023 31015

Storgården 10, 79193 Falun

10km from Falun. Turn off route 60 between Falun and Borlange at Ornäs towards Aspeboda

Holes	18 Par 72 6085m.
Visitors	Welcome. Course closed November to April
Fees	SKr130–150
Facilities	Bar and restaurant; practice ground
Pro	A Ryberg

Falkenberg Golf Club (1949) 46

Phone: 0346 50287

Golfvagen, 31175 Falkenberg

East of Falkenberg off the E6

Holes	3 x 9 Par 35/36 2856/2919/2978m.
Visitors	Welcome. Course closed December to February
Fees	SKr120–220
Facilities	Bar and restaurant; practice ground
Pro	S-A Bolten

The design has the variation offered by three loops of nine holes and the courses are rated among the best in Sweden. Variety is the key here since the fairways thread their way through forest and more open parkland with a number of water hazards and well-situated bunkers. The par 4s are notably difficult.

Falkoping Golf Club (1965)   47
Phone: 0515 31270
Box 99, 52102 Falkoping
North east of Falkoping off the B46 towards Skövde

Holes	18 Par 72 5835m.
Visitors	Welcome, but must book. Course closed November to April
Fees	SKr120–150
Facilities	Bar and restaurant; practice ground

Falsterbo Golfklubb (1909)   48
Phone: 040 470078
Fytvägen, Box 71, 23011 Falsterbo
South west of Falsterbo on the tip of the peninsula

Holes	18 Par 71 5895m.
Visitors	Welcome at weekends after 1pm; and by reservation June/August
Fees	SKr200–300
Facilities	Bar and restaurant; practice ground
Pro	David Leet

This classic links course sits on the tip of Sweden's south west peninsula where the Sound and the Baltic Sea meet. The club was founded in the early years of this century and the course was re-designed in 1930 and has remained largely unchanged since then. The scene of many important tournaments, Falsterbo has all the attributes of a great seaside course: superb springy turf, nearly a hundred bunkers, strong and shifting wind and an extra factor: water, which menaces the player especially on the 4th, 5th and 11th holes, and makes its presence felt elsewhere too. It is a severe and unrelenting challenge to any golfer and has enormous charm.

Finspång Golfklubb (1965)   49
Phone: 0122 13940
Viberga Gård, 61292 Finspang
Just south east of Finspang off the R51 towards Norrköping

Holes	18 Par 72 5800m.
Visitors	Welcome. Course closed October to April
Fees	SKr120–150
Facilities	Refreshments; practice ground
Pro	J Kjellvall

Fjallbacka Golfklubb (1967)   50
Phone; 0525 31150
45071 Fjallbacka
Just north of Fjallbacka on the R163

Holes	18 Par 73 5850m.
Visitors	Welcome
Fees	SKr110–160
Facilities	Bar and restaurant; practice ground
Pro	Ture Eriksson

Flens Golfklubb (1988)   51
Phone: 0157 10814
Norrtorps Golfbana, 64200 Flen
Just south of Flen by R55 towards Katrineholm

Holes	18 Par 72
Visitors	Welcome, but must book. Course closed December to march
Fees	SKr160
Facilities	Bar and restauarnt; practice ground

Flommens Golfklubb (1935)   52
Phone: 040 470568
Box 49, 23011 Falsterbo
In Falsterbo-West, off the E6 and the R100

Holes	18 Par 72 5610m.
Visitors	Welcome
Fees	DKr130–175
Facilities	Bar and restaurant; practice ground
Pro	B Kristoffersson

The course is next door to Falsterbo and is another challenging and highly rated golf course. It has some of the links character of its illustrious neighbour, is affected by the winds off the sea and has water hazards on virtually every hole.

Forsbacka Golfklubb (1969)   53
Phone: 0532 43055
Box 136, 66200 Åmål
North west of Åmål by route 164 towards Bengtsfors; turn at the 'Golfbana' sign

Holes	18 Par 72 5860m.
Visitors	Welcome. Course closed November to April
Fees	SKr150
Facilities	Bar and restaurant; practice ground

Forsgardens Golf Klubb (1990)   **54**

Phone: 0300 13649

Gammla Forsvagen 1, 43447 Kungsbacka

East of Kungsbacka toward Fjärås then Hallingsjö

Holes	18 Par 72
Visitors	Welcome on weekdays before 4pm and weekends after 1pm
Fees	SKr200
Facilities	Refreshments; practice ground
Pro	J Moreau

Frösåker Golfklubb (1989)   **55**

Phone: 021 25024

Frösåker Gard, 72597 Västeräs

East of Västeräs; turn off at Irsta towards Frösåker

Holes	18 Par 72
Visitors	Welcome
Fees	SKr130–175
Facilities	Bar and restaurant; practice ground

Funäsdalsfjällen Golfklubb (1972)   **56**

Phone: 0684 21100

PO Box 66, 84095 Funäsdalen

4km from Funäsdalen on the Ljusnedal lake near the Norwegian border

Holes	18 Par 72 5580m.
Visitors	Welcome. Course closed October to May
Fees	SKr150
Facilities	Bar and restaurant; practice ground
Pro	Kalle Arnell

Gällivare-Malmberget Golfklubb (1973)   **57**

Phone: 0970 10660

Box 52, 97221 Gällivare

4km west of Gällivare towards Malmberget; follow the sign to Siktrask

Holes	18 Par 71 5620m.
Visitors	Welcome. Course closed November to May
Fees	SKr100
Facilities	Refreshments; practice ground
Pro	P Mattsson

Gävle Golfklubb (1949)   **58**

Phone: 026 113163

Bönavägen 23, 80595 Gävle

Just north of Gävle off the old E4; turn for Fredrikskaus at Avan airport

Holes	18 Par 72 5658m. 9 Par 36 2910m.
Visitors	Welcome. Course closed October to April
Fees	SKr160
Facilities	Bar and restaurant; practice ground
Pro	B Youngman

Goteborgs Golfklubb (1902)   **59**

Phone: 031 282444

Box 2056, 46020 Hoväs

South of Goteborg on the R158 at Hoväs

Holes	18 Par 70 5460m.
Visitors	Welcome, but must book. Course closed December to March
Fees	SKr200–250
Facilities	Bar and restaurant; practice ground
Pro	E Öster

This is Sweden's senior golf club and, from modest beginnings, it became the venue for all Swedish championships, along with Falsterbo. The last one was held there in 1938 and it is too short a course for modern tournaments. Nevertheless, it is an excellent test over hilly ground and is one of the best-supported clubs in the country.

Gotska Golfklubb (1989)   **60**

Phone: 0498 15545

Box 1119, 62122 Visby

North east of Visby by route 148 towards Fårosund

Holes	9 Par 34 2425m.
Visitors	Welcome
Fees	SKr60
Facilities	Practice ground

Gränna Golfklubb (1990)   **61**

Phone: 0390 10030

Västanå Slott, 56392 Granna

South of Granna. Look for the Hotel Gyllene Utteru and follow signs for Västanå

Holes	18 Par 72 5640m.
Visitors	Welcome. Course closed December to April
Fees	SKr170
Facilities	Bar and restaurant; practice ground; tennis
Pro	Mats Candinger

Gullbringa Golf & Country Club (1967)　**62**

Phone: 0303 27161

44290 Kungälv

14km from Kungälv on the R168 towards
Marstrand

Holes　3 x 9　Par 34/35/36　2520/2790/2810m.

Visitors　Welcome

Fees　SKr200

Facilities　Bar and restaurant; practice ground;
swimming pool; tennis

Pro　Stefan Arnesson

Gumbalde Golfklubb (1988)　**63**

Phone: 0497 82880

PO Box 35, 62013 Stänga

Stånga is on route 144 about 50km south of
Visby on the island of Gotland

Holes　18　Par 72　5870m.

Visitors　Welcome

Fees　SKr180

Facilities　Bar and restaurant; practice ground;
tennis

Hagge Golfklubb (1963)　**64**

Phone: 0240 28087

Box 160, 77124 Ludvika

12km south of Ludvika. Turn off route 65
towards Hagge

Holes　18　Par 71　5519m.

Visitors　Welcome. Course closed November
to April

Fees　SKr140

Facilities　Bar and restaurant; practice ground

Pro　G Wallner

Halmstad Golfklubb (1930)　**65**

Phone; 035 30077

Tylösand, 30273 Halmstad

West of Halmstad towards Tylösand

Holes　18　Par 72　5980m.
　　　　18　Par 72　5720m.

Visitors　Welcome. Course closed December to
March

Fees　SKr250–300

Facilities　Bar and restaurant; practice ground

Pro　M Sorling

Next to Falsterbo Halmstad's championship
course is generally considered to be the finest
test in Sweden, yet, despite its sandy terrain and

close proximity to the sea it is as different from
Falsterbo as Sunningdale is from St. Georges.
Majestic tall pines line the fairways at Halmstad
and a ubiquitous stream provides many of the
challenges. The club boasts two picturesque 18
hole courses, the championship North and the
South. A friendly club which shares the same
latitude as Gleneagles, Halmstad is midway
between Gothenberg and Malmö in the tiny
resort of Tylösand.

Haninge Golfklubb (1983)　**66**

Phone: 0750 32240

Årsta Slott, 13691 Haninge

South east of Stockholm, through Handen
towards Dalarö

Holes　18　Par 73　5930m.

Visitors　Welcome, but must book. Course
closed November to April

Fees　SKr250

Facilities　Bar and restaurant; practice ground;
short course

Pro　B Deilert

Härnösand Golfklubb (1962)　**67**

Phone: 0611 66169

Box 52, 87122 Härnösand

Take the E4 north of Härnösand towards
Alandsbro. Follow the signs for Hemsön and
'Golfbana'

Holes　18　Par 70　5410m.

Visitors　Welcome. Course closed November
to April

Fees　SKr140

Facilities　Bar and restaurant; practice ground

Pro　Fatah Guedra

The course lies between the Bothnia Sea and a
river with a distant backdrop of mountains. It is
a lovely sight and the course is also charming,
as it rolls through wooded parkland. A
Midsummer Marathon is played over 72 holes
and a golf week is held in the second week of
July.

Hassleholm Golfklubb (1977)　**68**

Phone: 0451 53266

Box 114, 28200 Tyringe

Off the R21 between Hassleholm and
Helsingborg. Take the turning marked Skyrup in
Tyringe

Holes　18　Par 72　5830m.

Visitors　Welcome

Fees　SKr130–175

Facilities　Bar and restaurant; practice ground

Haverdals Golfklubb (1989)   69
Phone: 035 59530
Slingervägen 35, 31042 Haverdal
11km north of Halmstad by the R610

Holes	18 Par 72 5840m.
Visitors	Welcome
Fees	SKr130–180
Facilities	Bar and restaurant; practice ground
Pro	Anders Israelson

Helsingborgs Golfklubb (1924)   70
Phone: 042 236147
Golfbanegrand 2, 26040 Viken
By the sea, north of Helsingborg off the R115
towards Höganäs

Holes	9 Par 34 2789m.
Visitors	Welcome on weekdays
Fees	SKr100–120
Facilities	Bar; practice ground

Hofors Golfklubb (1965)   71
Phone: 0290 85125
Box 117, 81322 Hofors
South east of Hofors. Head for Torsåkel and
turn off in Långnäs

Holes	18 Par 70 5400m.
Visitors	Welcome. Course closed November to April
Fees	SKr100–140
Facilities	Bar and restaurant; practice ground
Pro	T Abbreman

Högbo Golfklubb (1972)   72
Phone: 026 45015
Daniel Tilas vag 4, 81192 Sandviken
North of Sandviken on route 272 to Högbo Bruk

Holes	18 Par 72 5670m.
	9 Par 35 2600m.
Visitors	Welcome. Course closed November to April
Fees	SKr150
Facilities	Bar and restaurant; practice ground
Pro	G Sandegard

Hökensås Golf Club (1962)   73
Phone: 0503 16059
Box 116, 54422 Hjo
South of Hjo off the B195

Holes	18 Par 71 5540m.
Visitors	Welcome. Course closed November to March
Fees	SKr120–150
Facilities	Bar and restaurant; practice ground
Pro	Jo Lindström

Hooks Golf Club (1941)   74
Phone: 0393 21420
56013 Hok
At Hok, 39km south of Jonkoping on route 30
towards Växjö

Holes	18 Par 72 5748m.
Visitors	Welcome. Course closed December to May
Fees	SKr170
Facilities	Bar and restaurant; practice ground; 9-hole pitch & putt; swimming pool; tennis
Pro	Bengt Malmqvist

Water is the main enemy of the golfer on this
course, since it is in evidence on eleven of the
holes. The first green, with insidious stretches of
liquid in front and on three sides, gives the
golfer a taste of what is to come, and the
problem is even worse on the third and fourth
greens. Strong nerves and a good technique are
needed here.

Hudiksvall Golfklubb (1964)   75
Phone: 0650 15930
Box 531, 82400 Hudiksvall
South east of Hudiksvall beside the Hudiksvall
fjord

Holes	18 Par 72 5665m.
Visitors	Welcome. Course closed November to April
Fees	SKr120–140
Facilities	Bar and restaurant
Pro	M Larsson

Hulta Golf Club (1983)   76
Phone: 0332 88180
PO Box 54, 51701 Bollebygd
North of Bollebygd off the A40

Holes	18 Par 73 5935m.
Visitors	Welcome. Course closed November to mid-April
Fees	SKr200
Facilities	Bar and restaurant; practice ground
Pro	Bill Byard

Ingarö Golfklubb (1962/1991)　　　**77**
Phone: 0766 28655
Fogelvik, 13035 Ingarö
South of Gustavsberg. Head for Ingarö annd
Brunn and then towards Bjorkvik

Holes	18 Par 71 5603m.
	18 Par 72 5500m.
Visitors	Welcome, except weekends before 2pm. Course closed November to April
Fees	SKr250–300
Facilities	Bar and restaurant; practice ground
Pro	Raymond Morin

Isaberg Golf Club (1970)　　　**78**
Phone: 0370 36330
Box 40, 33221 Gislaved
At Nissafors between Halmsbad and Jönköping

Holes	18 Par 72 5709m.
	9 Par 36 2865m.
Visitors	Welcome. Course closed November to April
Fees	SKr180
Facilities	Bar and restaurant; practice ground
Pro	Stephen Carpenter

The course has a splendid setting amid great banks of trees and long stretches of water from the River Nissan, which in effect divides the main course in two. These two elements have been used to create a fine test of golf.

Jönköping Golfklubb (1936)　　　**79**
Phone: 036 76567
Kettilstorp, 55267 Jönköping
Just south west of Jönköping off the R40

Holes	18 Par 70 5610m.
Visitors	Welcome. Course closed December to March
Fees	SKr180
Facilities	Bar and restaurant; practice ground
Pro	A Turnbull

The course lies in very appealing countryside at the southern end of Sweden's second largest lake, Vattern, and right in the middle of the southern highlands. It is a hilly and challenging course and the surrounding scenery is wonderful.

Kåbo Golfklubb (1988)　　　**80**
Phone: 018 551095
Box 8019, 75008 Uppsala
On the south side of Uppsala

Holes	9 Par 33
Visitors	Welcome. Course closed November to March
Fees	SKr100–160
Facilities	Bar and restaurant; practice ground

Kalmar Golfklubb (1947)　　　**81**
Phone: 0480 72111
Box 278, 39123 Kalmar
North of Kalmar off the E66 at the Linsdal turn

Holes	18 Par 72 5855m.
Visitors	Welcome
Fees	SKr150–180
Facilities	Bar and restaurant; practice ground
Pro	Hans Weinhöfer

Some splendid and testing holes run through great blocks of woodland and the dog-leg designs of many of them put the emphasis on accuracy. The course starts with a mischievous short hole across water, which comes into play here and there in the form of a stream. It is an excellent parkland course.

Karlshamn Golfklubb (1962)　　　**82**
Phone: 0454 50085
Box 188, 37423 Karlshamn
North west of Karlshamn at Mörrums

Holes	18 Par 72 5861m.
Visitors	Welcome. Course closed December to March
Fees	SKr130–160
Facilities	Bar and restaurant; practice ground

A splendid golf course which swoops and rolls through forest and parkland near the river Mörrumsän. There is much to entertain the golfer since the course is nicely varied; easier holes are subtly mixed with more difficult ones.

Karlskoga Golfklubb (1975)　　　**83**
Phone: 0586 28190
Valåson Bricketorp 647, 69194 Karlskoga
South of Karlskoga off the E18

Holes	18 Par 72 5705m.
Visitors	Welcome. Course closed November to April
Fees	SKr150
Facilities	Bar and restaurant; practice ground
Pro	P Glimaker

Karlstad Golfklubb (1957)　　**84**
Phone: 0548 36353
Box 294, 65107 Karlstad
From Karlsbad, take the E18 east and then the R63 north towards Ludvika
Holes　　18 Par 72 5970m.
　　　　　9 Par 36 2875m.
Visitors　Welcome. Course closed November to April
Fees　　SKr160
Facilities　Bar and restaurant; 9-hole pitch & putt
Pro　　Henri Reis
The key to good scoring on this course is to avoid the water which affects the play of almost every hole. The fairways run through wooded country and it all adds up to a very tough course, especially the first hole on the Red nine, which is almost 600 yards in length.

Katrineholm Golfklubb (1959)　　**85**
Phone: 0150 39270
Box 74, 64121 Katrineholm
East of Katrineholm by route 52 towards Nyköping
Holes　　18 Par 72 5860m.
Visitors　Welcome
Fees　　SKr160–180
Facilities　Bar and restaurant; practice ground
Pro　　S Eriksson

Kävlinge Golfklubb (1990)　　**86**
Phone: 046 73 6270
Äboda, Box 138, 24422 Kävlinge
Just north west of Kävlinge off the R104. The course is signposted
Holes　　18 Par 71 5700m.
Visitors　Welcome. Course closed November to February
Fees　　SKr110–150
Facilities　Bar and restaurant; practice ground

Kils Golfklubb (1988)　　**87**
Phone: 0554 40705
Box 173, 66500 Kil
5km north of Kil off route 61 at Frykenbaden
Holes　　18 Par 72
Visitors　Welcome. Course closed November to April
Fees　　SKr120
Facilities　Bar and restaurant; practice ground

Korslöt Golfklubb (1963)　　**88**
Phone: 0221 81090
Box 278, 73126 Köping
North west of Köping off route 250
Holes　　19 Par 71 5636m.
Visitors　Welcome. Course closed October to April
Fees　　SKr120–180
Facilities　Bar and restaurant; practice ground
Pro　　B Malmquist

Kristinehamns Golfklubb (1974)　　**89**
Phone: 0550 82310
Box 337, 68126 Kristinehamn
North of Kristinehamn by route 64 towards Filipstad
Holes　　18 Par 72 5730m.
Visitors　Welcome. Course closed November to April
Fees　　SKr120
Facilities　Bar and retaurant; practice ground
Pro　　A Reumert

Kristianstad Golfklubb (1924)　　**90**
Phone: 044 247656
Box 41, 29600 Ahus
South of Kristianstad off the R118 at Ahus
Holes　　18 Par 72 5810m.
　　　　　9 Par 36 2945m.
Visitors　Welcome. Course closed January/ February
Fees　　SKr150–180
Facilities　Bar and reataurant practice ground
Pro　　D Green

Kumla Golfklubb (1986)　　**91**
Phone: 019 77370
Box 2012, 69202 Kumla
East of Kumla towards Kattineholm
Holes　　18 Par 72 5985m.
Visitors　Welcome. Course closed November to March
Fees　　SKr180
Facilities　Bar and restaurant; practice ground
Pro　　J Skogfeldt

Kungsbacka Golfklubb (1971) 92
Phone: 031 936277
Hamra Gård 515, 43040 Särö
6km north of Kungsbacka off the R158 before Särö

Holes	18 Par 72 5855m.
Visitors	Welcome, but must book. Cours closed December to March
Fees	SKr200
Facilities	Bar and restaurant; practice ground
Pro	P Nellbeck

Lagans Golfklubb (1966) 93
Phone: 0372 30450
Box 63, 34014 Lagan
North of Lungby on the E4 at Lagan

Holes	18 Par 71 5580m.
Visitors	Welcome. Course closed November to March
Fees	SKr120
Facilities	Restaurant; practice ground
Pro	Charlotte Ögren

Laholm Golfklubb (1964) 94
Phone: 0430 30601
Box 101, 31222 Laholm
South east of Laholm off the R24 towards Våxtorp

Holes	18 Par 70 5430m.
Visitors	Welcome
Fees	SKr120–180
Facilities	Bar and restaurant; practice ground
Pro	T Lindwall

Landeryds Golfklubb (1989) 95
Phone: 013 162520
Bogestad Gard, 58593 Linköping
South of Linköping. Take the Brokindsleden sign towards Sturefors

Holes	18 Par 70 5675m.
Visitors	Welcome. Course closed November to March
Fees	SKr150
Facilities	Bar and restaurant; practice ground
Pro	K Kinell

Landskrona Golfklubb (1960) 96
Phone: 0418 19528
Erikstorp, 26162 Landskrona
Just north of Landskrona off the E6

Holes	18 Par 71 5700m.
	18 Par 61 4000m.
Visitors	Welcome, but must book. Course closed December to February
Fees	SKr140–170
Facilities	Bar and restaurant; practice ground
Pro	A Olsson

Leksand Golfklubb (1982) 97
Phone: 0247 14640
Vargnäs, Box 25, 79321 Leksand
Off route 70 north of Leksand towards Rättvik

Holes	18 Par 71 5551m.
Visitors	Welcome. Course closed November to April
Fees	SKr150
Facilities	Bar and restaurant; practice ground
Pro	Per Jönsson

Lidingo Golfklubb (1927) 98
Phone: 0873 17900
Box 1035, 18121 Lidingo
2km from Lidingo

Holes	18 Par 71 5632m.
Visitors	Welcome before 3pm weekdays, after 1pm weekends. Course closed November to April
Fees	SKr250
Facilities	Bar and restaurant; practice ground; short course
Pro	Per Hansson

One of the senior Swedish clubs, Lidingo is quite close to the centre of Stockholm. It offers a fair challenge to the golfer by dint of its tree-lined fairways and excellent bunkering, especially on the angles of the fairways, many of which are dog-legs. Water hazards are also used to good effect.

Lidköping Golfklubb (1977) 99
Phone: 0510 46144
Box 2029, 53102 Lidkoping
East of Lidkoping towards Götene off route 44

Holes	18 Par 70 5540m.
Visitors	Welcome
Fees	SKr110–130
Facilities	Bar and restaurant; practice ground; 5-hole pitch & putt
Pro	Toni Lundahl

Linde Golfklubb (1984)   100

Phone: 0581 13960

Dalkarlshyttan, 71131 Lindesberg

Just south of Lindesberg

Holes	18 Par 71 5700m.
Visitors	Welcome. Course closed November to April
Fees	SKr180
Facilities	Bar and restaurant; practice ground
Pro	J Skogfeldt

Lindö Golfklubb (1978)   101

Phone: 0762 72260

19692 Vallentuna

Take the E3 north from Stockholm; exit at Täby through Vallentuna towards 'Bjorn Borg Sports Club'

Holes	18 Par 72 5980m. 9 Par 36 3030m.
Visitors	Welcome. Course closed October to April
Fees	SKr200–250
Facilities	Bar and restaurant; practice ground

Linköping Golfklubb (1945)   102

Phone: 013 120646

Box 10054, 58249 Linköping

West of Linköping off the E4. Turn at the Hogskolan sign

Holes	18 Par 71 5675m.
Visitors	Welcome
Fees	SKr150
Facilities	Bar and restaurant; practice ground
Pro	Bertil Lemke

Many notable tournaments have been staged at this course, whose fairways run tightly through the encroaching trees. The five short holes, defended by huge bunkers, are the key to scoring well here; and the 16th hole, the 'Bauer', is the most famous, its green dominated by a huge rock.

Ljunghusens Golfklubb (1932)   103

Phone: 040 450384

Kinellsvag, 23642 Hollviken

East of Falsterbo off the R100 near Ljunghusen. The club is signposted

Holes	18 Par 72 5895m. 9 Par 35 2615m.
Visitors	Welcome, but must book
Fees	SKr220
Facilities	Bar and restaurant; practice ground
Pro	Göran Sandegård

Ljunghusens makes up the fine triumvirate of seaside courses in this area and lies on the narrowest part of the Falsterbo isthmus. As with the other courses, the wind constantly tests the golfer's judgement and the sand dunes, heather and a dozen water hazards add to the severe nature of the holes; the last three are especially difficult owing to the prevalence of water.

Ljusdals Golfklubb (1973)   104

Phone: 0651 14366

Box 151, 82700 Ljusdal

Just south east of Ljusdal in the direction of Hybo

Holes	18 Par 72 5725m.
Visitors	Welcome. Course closed November to April
Fees	SKr120
Facilities	Restaurant; practice ground
Pro	Ulf Norrby

Lunds Akademiska Golfklubb (1936)   105

Phone: 046 99005

Kungsmarken, 22592 Lund

Just east of Lund and near Sodra Sandby

Holes	18 Par 72 6140m.
Visitors	Welcome. Course closed November to March
Fees	SKr160–220
Facilities	Bar and restaurant; practice ground
Pro	Van MacDougall

The club has its name because the land belongs to the university of this ancient city, founded well over a millenium ago. Lunds adds up to an excellent course of championship quality and has hosted several important tournaments. It is laid out in two loops, separated by the Gloms brook, and has some tough bunkers and heavy rough.

Luleä Golfklubb (1958)   106

Phone: 0920 56300

Box 314, 95125 Luleä

North of Luleä off the E4 near the village of Rutvik

Holes	18 Par 72 5675m.
Visitors	Welcome. Course closed November to April
Fees	SKr150
Facilities	Bar and restaurant; practice ground
Pro	Leslie Stewart

This is a charming course with reasonably generous fairways which run through archetypal parkland terrain with plenty of trees. Water adds to the fun on a few holes, most notably the 5th, 7th, 10th and 17th. It was once the most northerly course in Sweden, but that distinction now belongs to Bjorkliden. In summer, the real fanatics can play golf throughout the night, as well as the day.

Lyckorna Golfklubb (1967) 107

Phone: 0522 20176

Box 66, 45922 Ljungskile

Just south of Ljungskile off the E6, follow signs to 'Golfbana'

Holes	18 Par 72 5820m.
Visitors	Welcome. Course closed November to March
Fees	SKr160
Facilities	Bar and restaurant; practice ground
Pro	U Ligner

The surroundings of this fine course are captivating; many holes run alongside the fjord with its small wooded islands and most run through avenues of pine, beech and oak. The long holes are quite severe, especially the 16th at nearly 600 yards and a ravine cuts playfully through the course at one point.

Lysegardens Golfklubb (1966) 108

Phone: 0303 223426

Box 82, 44221 Kungälv

North of Kungalv near Lyzegärden

Holes	18 Par 71 5670m.
Visitors	Welcome. Course closed November to March
Fees	SKr130–160
Facilities	Bar and restaurant; practice ground
Pro	G Crisp

This course can delight and infuriate in equal measure, since its difficulties are compounded by the plethora of water hazards. The most spectacular hole is the 13th with a waterfall alongside the green and a ravine to its right. Water threatens most of the holes, especially during the second half where a vast lake impinges on nearly every hole.

Malarbaden Golfklubb (1991/2) 109

Phone: 016 343737

Wernerska Villan, 64436 Torshälla

At Malarbaden by the lake

Holes	9 Par 36 2710m.
Visitors	Welcome. Course closed October to March
Fees	SKr150
Facilities	Driving range

Malmö Golfklubb (1981) 110

Phone: 040 292535

Segesvängen, 21227 Malmö

North east of Malmö, near Segesväng

Holes	18 Par 71 5720m.
Visitors	Welcome, but must book
Fees	SKr140–170
Facilities	Bar and restaurant; practice ground
Pro	H Bergdahl

Mariestad Golfklubb (1975) 111

Phone: 0501 17383

Box 299, 54223 Mariestad

West of Mariestad

Holes	18 Par 72 5885m.
Visitors	Welcome. Course closed December to February
Fees	SKr130
Facilities	Bar and restaurant; practice ground

Marks Golfklubb (1962) 112

Phone: 0320 14220

Brättingstorpvagen, 51158 Kinna

On the east side of Kinna off the B41

Holes	18 Par 69 5410m.
Visitors	Welcome, but must book at weekends. Course closed November to March
Fees	SKr140–180
Facilities	Bar and restaurant; practice ground
Pro	G Nyberg

Mjolby Golfklubb (1985) 113

Phone: 0142 12570

Box 171, 59522 Mjolby

Take route 32 south of Mjolby towards Boxholm. After 3km follow signs to 'Golfbana'

Holes	18 Par 71 5485m.
Visitors	Welcome. Course closed November to April
Fees	SKr130
Facilities	Bar and restaurant; practice ground
Pro	Bo Ackelman

Molle Golfklubb (1943)   114
Phone: 042 347520
Kullagarden, 26042 Molle
Just north west of Molle off the R111 towards
the Kullen lighthouse
Holes   18 Par 70 5640m.
Visitors   Welcome
Fees   SKr170
Facilities   Bar and restaurant; practice ground
Pro   J Pyk-Jargärd
Mölle has a wonderful location in a nature
reserve near the Kulleberg Cliffs and near the
famous Krapperup Castle. The holes run through
some superb woodland and the undulating
nature of the terrain makes up for the compara-
tive shortness of the course.

Mölndals Golfklubb (1987)   115
Phone: 031 993030
Box 77, 43721 Lindome
South of Goteborg off the E6; and 3km from
Lindome towards Hällingsjö
Holes   18 Par 72 5625m.
Visitors   Welcome. Course closed November
    to March
Fees   SKr150–200
Facilities   Bar and restaurant; practice ground
Pro   D Robinson

Mora Golfklubb (1983)   116
Phone: 0250 10182
Box 264, 79224 Mora
Just north of Mora off the R70
Holes   18 Par 72 5630m.
Visitors   Welcome. Course closed October to
    April
Fees   SKr150
Facilities   Bar and restaurant; practice ground
Pro   Thomas Lindh

Motala Golfklubb (1956)   117
Phone: 0141 50840
Box 264, 59123 Motala
South of Motala towards Skänninge/Mjölby and
Långetorp
Holes   18 Par 72 5905m.
Visitors   Welcome. Course closed November
    to March
Fees   SKr140
Facilities   Bar and restaurant; practice ground
Pro   S Johansson

Nässjö Golfklubb (1989)   118
Phone: 0380 10022
Box 5, 57100 Nässjö
Just west of Nässjö off the R33. Follow the sign
to Nässjö Golfklubb
Holes   18 Par 72 5783m.
Visitors   Welcome. Course closed November
    to April
Fees   SKr150
Facilities   Bar and restaurant; practice ground;
    9-hole pitch & putt
Pro   David Nicholson

Nora Golfklubb (1988)   119
Phone: 0587 11660
Box 108, 71323 Nora
South east of Nora off route 244. The club is
signposted
Holes   18 Par 72 5865m.
Visitors   Welcome
Fees   SKr120–150
Facilities   Bar and restaurant; practice ground
Pro   David Kirkham

Norrköping Golfklubb (1928)   120
Phone: 011 35235
Box 2150, 60002 Norrköping
South west of Norrköping off the E4 towards
Klinga Gård
Holes   18 Par 73 5860m.
Visitors   Welcome. Course closed November
    to March
Fees   SKr120–200
Facilities   Refreshments; practice ground
Pro   P Karström

Nybro Golfklubb (1925)   121
Phone: 0480 55044
Box 235, 38223 Nybro
South east of Nybro off the R25
Holes   18 Par 72 5452m.
Visitors   Welcome. Course closed December to
    March
Fees   SKr120
Facilities   Bar and restaurant; practice ground
Pro   J Evergren

Nynäshamns Golfklubb (1977)   122

Phone: 0753 27190
Box 4, 14821 Ösmo
50km south of Stockholm via route 73 at Ösmo

Holes	18 Par 72 5750m.
Visitors	Welcome. Course closed November to April
Fees	SKr200–250
Facilities	Bar and restaurant; practice ground
Pro	S Ohlsson

Oijared Golf Club (1958/1972)   123

Phone: 0302 30604
Box 1082, 44892 Floda
Just north of Floda; signs to Golfbana

Holes	18 Par 71 5655m (Old)
	18 Par 72 5870m (New)
Visitors	Welcome except weekends before 3pm
Fees	SKr160–200
Facilities	Bar and restaurant; practice ground; 9 hole pitch & putt
Pro	Eric Dawson

Oijared is said to be Sweden's biggest golf centre with two full-size courses and a short course. The Old course runs through woodland and has several water hazards, whereas the New course is laid out on more open ground; it also has a lake which comes into play on the short 9th hole.

Ölands Golfklubb (1989)   124

Phone: 0485 11200
Box 79, 38722 Borgholm
Ekerum – south of Borgholm off the R136.
Källatorp – 40km north of Borgholm, near Källa

Holes	27 Par 72/36 (Ekerum)
	9 (Kallatorp)
Visitors	Welcome. Courses closed December to March
Fees	SKr50–100
Facilities	Refreshments; practice ground

Onsjö Golfklubb (1977)   125

Phone: 0521 65830
Box 100, 46221 Vanersborg
Just south of Vanersborg off the B45 towards Gothenburg

Holes	18 Par 72 5735m.
Visitors	Welcome. Course closed November to March
Fees	SKr140–170
Facilities	Bar and restaurant; practice ground
Pro	Neil Goodison

Örebro Golfklubb (1939)   126

Phone: 019 91065
Lanna, 71015 Vintrosa
18km west of Orebro on the E18

Holes	18 Par 71 5870m.
Visitors	Welcome. Course closed November to April
Fees	SKr220
Facilities	Bar and restaurant; practice ground; 6-hole pitch & putt; swimming pool
Pro	Joahim Bloom

This is considered to be one of the best inland courses in the country and has been the venue for several championships. It sits in the lee of a small mountain ridge in charming countryside. The course is varied and the undulating ground with its many trees demands both sound tactics and accuracy.

Örkelljunga Golfklubb (1991)   127

Phone: 0435 54654
Box 149, 28622 Örkelljunga
Situated about 50km from Helsingborg along the E4, in the village of Eket, Örkelljunga

Holes	18 Par 72 5755m.
Visitors	Welcome. Course closed November to March
Fees	SKr120–180
Facilities	Cafeteria (clubhouse planned for 1994); practice ground
Pro	Marie Wennerston-From

Orust Golfklubb (1981)   128

Phone: 0304 53170
Box 108, 44090 Henan
West of Henån on the island of Orust, near the Morlanda church

Holes	18 Par 72 5770m.
Visitors	Welcome
Fees	SKr160
Facilities	Bar and restaurant; practice ground
Pro	S Eriksson

Oskarshamn Golfklubb (1972) 129
Phone: 0491 94033
Box 148, 57201 Oskarshamn
10km south of Oskarshamn on the coastal road.
Head for Fliseryd and there is a sign to
'Golfbana'
Holes | 18 Par 71 5571m.
Visitors | Welcome. Course closed November to April
Fees | SKr150
Facilities | Bar and restaurant; practice ground
Pro | Jan Hult

Österåkers Golfklubb (1989) 130
Phone: 0764 85190
Hagby 1:1, 18492 Åkersberga
30km from Stockholm; take the E3 towards
Norrtälje. After 25km turn right on route 276
towards Åkersberga for 4km
Holes | 18 Par 72 5792m.
Visitors | Welcome, but must book. Course closed November to March
Fees | SKr225
Facilities | Bar and restaurant
Pro | Lars Bröms

Österlens Golfklubb (1945) 131
Phone: 0414 24230
Lilla Vik, 27295 Simrishamn
North of Simrishamn off the R10 at Vik
Holes | 18 Par 72 5855m.
Visitors | Welcome
Fees | SKr120–200
Facilities | Bar and restaurant; practice ground
Pro | G Mueller

Östersund-Frösö Golfklubb (1947) 132
Phone: 063 43001
Box 40, 83201 Frösö
8km west of Ostersund on Frösö island
Holes | 18 Par 73 6000m.
Visitors | Welcome. Course closed October to April
Fees | SKr150
Facilities | Bar and restaurant; practice ground
Pro | G Knutsson

Golf fanatics will adore this remarkable course
which is quite close to the Arctic circle; they
could play for the full 24 hours at midsummer
and there is a Midnight Sun tournament. It is a
staggeringly beautiful course which overlooks
Lake Storsjön and runs through pine forests
with a backdrop of snow-covered mountains.

Östra Göinge Golfklubb (1981) 133
Phone: 044 60060
Box 114, 28900 Knislinge
Just north of Knislinge on the R20 to Broby
Holes | 18 Par 72 5898m.
Visitors | Welcome. Course closed December to March
Fees | SKr150
Facilities | Bar; practice ground
Pro | J Kjellgren

Öviks Golfklubb Puttom (1966) 134
Phone: 0660 82488
Idrottens Hus, 89132 Ornskoldsvik
North west of Örnskoldvik off the E4
Holes | 18 Par 72 5800m.
Visitors | Welcome. Course closed November to April
Fees | SKr140
Facilities | Bar and restaurant; practice ground
Pro | T Mogren

Parkens Golfklubb (1970) 135
Phone: 0762 70055
CBM Business Club AB, 18692 Vallentuna
At Stockholm Lindö Park. Take the E4 from
Stockholm towards Uppsala. After 20km take the
Upplands Väsby-Vallentuna exit; after 9km turn
off at the Lindö Park sign
Holes | 18 Par 72 5800m.
Visitors | Welcome, but must book. Course closed October to April
Fees | SKr225–250
Facilities | Bar and restaurant; practice ground; swimming pool; tennis
Pro | Neil Fossett

Partille Golfklubb (1971) 136
Phone: 031 987004
Box 234, 43324 Partille
East of Goteborg off the E3 near Partille; head
for Öjersjö
Holes | 18 Par 70 5530m.
Visitors | Welcome. Course closed November to April
Fees | SKr150–200
Facilities | Refreshments; practice ground
Pro | R Hutton

Perstorp Golfklubb (1964)   **137**

Phone: 0435 35411

Box 87, 28400 Perstorp

Just south east of Perstorp on the road to Färingtofta

Holes	18 Par 71 5675m.
Visitors	Welcome. Course closed December to March
Fees	SKr120–160
Facilities	Bar and restaurant; practice ground; short course
Pro	Jim Kennedy

Pitea Golfklubb (1960)   **138**

Phone: 0911 14990

Box 12, 94121 Pitea

Just north east of Pitea, along Sundsgtan and Svattuddsvågen

Holes	18 Par 68 5905m.
Visitors	Welcome. Course closed November to April; midnight sun golf played in June/July
Fees	SKr150
Facilities	Bar and restaurant; practice ground
Pro	A Gillard

Rättvik Golfklubb (1954)   **139**

Phone: 0248 11030

Box 29, 79531 Rättvik

Just north of Rättvik off the R70

Holes	18 Par 70 5515m.
Visitors	Welcome. Course closed November to April
Fees	SKr130–150
Facilities	Bar and restaurant; practice ground
Pro	M Ahlgren

Ringenäs Golfklubb (1989)   **140**

Phone: 035 59050

Strandlida, 30590 Halmstad

North west of Halmstad past the airport at Tingenäs

Holes	3 x 9 Par 35/36 5395/5615m.
Visitors	Welcome, but must book. Course closed January to March
Fees	SKr150–200
Facilities	Bar and restaurant; practice ground
Pro	K Wallace

Romeleasens Golfklubb (1969)   **141**

Phone: 046 82012

Kvarnbrodda, 24014 Veberod

South of Veberod off the R802 at Dörröd

Holes	18 Par 72 5783m.
Visitors	Welcome, but must book. Course closed December to March
Fees	SKr100–200
Facilities	Bar and restaurant; practice ground
Pro	J Byard

Ronneby Golfklubb (1964)   **142**

Phone: 0457 10315

Box 26, 37221 Ronneby

Just south of Ronneby

Holes	18 Par 70 5323m.
Visitors	Welcome. Course closed November to March
Fees	SKr160–180
Facilities	Bar and restaurant; practice ground
Pro	F Johnsson

Roslagens Golf Club (1964)   **143**

Phone: 0176 37194

Box 110, Norrtalje

From Norrtalje take the road north east towards Vätö for 6km

Holes	18 Par 72 5512m.
	9 Par 36 2880m.
Visitors	Welcome, but must book. Course closed mid-October to mid-April
Fees	SKr150–200
Facilities	Bar and restaurant; practice ground
Pro	Leif Modin

There are now 27 holes to play at Roslagens and the main course calls for accurate striking, especially from the tee, since the fairways are narrow and fringed by trees. As is usual in Sweden, there are water hazards to add to the fun.

Rya Golfklubb (1934)   **144**

Phone: 042 221082

Rya 5500, 25592 Helsingborg

South of Helsingborg off the R106

Holes	18 Par 71 5691m.
Visitors	Welcome
Fees	SKr180–200
Facilities	Bar and restaurant; practice ground
Pro	J Grant

As befits one of Sweden's senior clubs, there is a very traditional look to the course, a wonderfully varied design which has both parkland and seaside elements.

St Arild Golfklubb (1989)   145
Phone: 042 346860
Box 1726, 26041 St Arild
South east of St Arild on the coast road
Holes   18 Par 72 5730m.
Visitors   Welcome
Fees   SKr190
Facilities Bar and restaurant; practice ground;
           9-hole pitch & putt
Pro   Peter Hansson

St Ibb Golfklubb (1974)   146
Phone: 0418 26363
c/o Box 214, 24022 Löddeköpinge
On Hven island. Take the ferryboat from
Landskrona
Holes   9 Par 64 2550m.
Visitors   Welcome. Course closed January/
           February
Fees   SKr150
Facilities Bar and restaurant; practice ground;
           tennis
Pro   Mikael Rådberg

Sala Golfklubb (1970)   147
Phone: 0224 53077
Fallet, Isätra, 73392 Sala
East of Sala off route 72 towards Uppsala
Holes   18 Par 71 5570m.
Visitors   Welcome
Fees   SKr80–125
Facilities Bar and restaurant; practice ground
Pro   T Borgling

Sälen Golfklubb (1985)   148
Phone: 0280 20670
Box 20, 78067 Salen
2km east of Salen off route 297
Holes   18 Par 72 5730m.
Visitors   Welcome. Course closed October to
           April
Fees   SKr150
Facilities Bar and restaurant; practice ground
Pro   Peter Hamblett

Saltsjöbaden Golfklubb (1929)   149
Phone: 08 7170125
Box 51, 13321 Saltsjöbaden
15km south of Stockholm towards Saltsjöbaden;
head for Ljuskärrberget
Holes   18 Par 72 5685m.
Visitors   Welcome, but must book. Course
           closed November to April
Fees   SKr200–250
Facilities Bar and restaurant; practice ground;
           short course
Pro   B Youngman

Säters Golfklubb (1989)   150
Phone: 0225 50030
Box 89, 78322 Säter
South of Säter towards Smedjebacken, by the
lakeside
Holes   18 Par 72 5781m.
Visitors   Welcome. Course closed November
           to April
Fees   SKr150
Facilities Bar and restaurant; practice ground
Pro   Ulf Sandberg

Saxå Golfklubb (1967)   151
Phone: 0590 24071
Saxån, 68200 Filipstad
15km northeast of Filipstad on route 63
Holes   18 Par 72 5580m.
Visitors   Welcome. Course closed November
           to April
Fees   SKr150
Facilities Bar and restaurant closed Monday;
           practice ground

Sigtunabygdens Golfklubb (1961)   152
Phone: 0760 54012
Box 89, 19322 Sigtuna
Follow road from Sigtuna north towards
Uppsala for 2km
Holes   18 Par 72 5740m.
Visitors   Welcome. Course closed November
           to April
Fees   SKr170–240
Facilities Bar and restaurant; practice ground
Pro   P Michols

Sisjö Golfklubb (1990)	**153**

Phone: 031 286004
Längebergsgarten 26, Gothenburg
On the south side of Gothenburg near
Längebergsgarten and Söderleden

Holes   9 Par 34 2623m.
Visitors   Welcome, but must book
Fees   SKr160–200
Facilities Bar and restaurant; practice ground
Pro   Martin Sternberg

Sjögärde Golfklubb (1991)	**154**

Phone: 0340 52325
43330 Frillesäs
45km south of Gothenburg on the E6; head
inland to Breared, then north towards Gällinge

Holes   18 Par 72 5639m.
Visitors   Welcome
Fees   SKr150–220
Facilities Bar and restaurant; practice ground
Pro   Per Svensson

Skafto Golfklubb (1963)	**155**

Phone: 0523 23211
Box 4476, 45034 Fiskebackskil
Just west of Fiskebackskil towards Grundsund

Holes   9 Par 35 2655m. (18 holes planned
             1993)
Visitors   Welcome. Course closed December to
             March
Fees   SKr100–150
Facilities Bar and restaurant; practice ground
Pro   M Kinhult

Skellefteå Golfklubb (1967)	**156**

Phone: 0910 79333
Box 152, 93122 Skellefteå
Just south of Skellefteå off the E4

Holes   18 Par 72 5767m.
Visitors   Welcome. Course closed October to
             mid-May
Fees   SKr150
Facilities Refreshments; practice ground
Pro   N Fosker

This is often chosen as the best course in the
north of Sweden and the traditional barns which
have been left on the course add to its character.
It is an excellent test of golf on fairways which
run through the forest.

Skepparslovs Golfklubb (1985)	**157**

Phone 044 229508
Uddarps Sateri, 29192 Kristianstad
West of Kristianstad, off the R21, signposted
from Skepparslov's church

Holes   18 Par 72 5844m.
Visitors   Welcome
Fees   SKr100–150
Facilities Bar and restaurant; practice ground;
             short course
Pro   Tony Marshall

The course is situated on the Säteröd heights
and there are splendid views over the
Kristiansand plain. The holes run partly through
forest and partly over more open parkland and
offer plenty of variety. The clubhouse, built in
the old stables, is charming.

Skepptuna Golfklubb (1988)	**158**

Phone: 08 51293069
19593 Märsta
At Lunda (about 45km north of Stockholm) look
for the signposts to Skepptuna Golfklubb

Holes   18 Par 72 5850m.
Visitors   Welcome. Course closed November
             to April
Fees   SKr150–200
Facilities Bar and restaurant; practice ground
Pro   Anders Ageborg

Skogaby Golfklubb (1988)	**159**

Phone: 0430 60190
31293 Laholm
From Laholm take the road east to Skogaby, and
then the R117 towards Knäred

Holes   18 Par 71 5555m.
Visitors   Welcome. Course closed December to
             March
Fees   SKr160–180
Facilities Bar and restaurant; practice ground
Pro   Mikael Eriksson

Slite Golfklubb (1988)	**160**

Phone: 0498 26170
PO Box 24, Slite
3km east of Slite on the island of Gotland

Holes   9 Par 35
Visitors   Welcome
Fees   SKr100
Facilities Cafeteria; practice ground

Söderäsens Golfklubb (1966) 161

Phone: 042 73337

Box 41, 26050 Billesholm

East of Helsingborg, beside the R110 near Bjuv

Holes: 18 Par 73 6590m.
Visitors: Welcome. Course closed December to March
Fees: SKr150–250
Facilities: Bar and restaurant; practice ground
Pro: T Lidholm

Söderhamns Golfklubb (1961) 162

Phone: 0270 51300

Oxtorget 1c, 82632 Soderhamn

East of Söderhamn. From the Town Hall, follow the Kungsgatan, turn right after a wooden bridge and the club is signposted

Holes: 18 Par 72 5825m.
Visitors: Welcome. Course closed November to April
Fees: SKr130–150
Facilities: Bar and restaurant; practice ground
Pro: M Andersson

Situated on the north shore of the Söderhamns Sound, this is one of the most charming courses in Sweden, situated on parkland with fine old trees and a profusion of wild flowers. You will see the occasional deer as you walk the fairways, which have a good number of bunkers.

Söderkopings Golfklubb (1985) 163

Phone: 011 70579

Hylinge, 60590 Norrköping

9km west of Söderkoping on route 210 towards Linköping; there are signs near Vastra Husby to 'Golfbana'

Holes: 18 Par 72 5730m.
Visitors: Welcome. Course closed November to April
Fees: SKr150
Facilities: Bar and restaurant; practice ground
Pro: Lars Cernold

Södertälje Golfklubb (1952) 164

Phone: 0755 38240

Masnaryd, Box 91, 15121 Södertälje

West of Södertälje off the E3 via Ängsgarden and Strängnäsvägen

Holes: 18 Par 72 5875m.
Visitors: Welcome. Course closed November to April
Fees: SKr160–210
Facilities: Bar and restaurant; practice ground
Pro: B Tomlinson

Sollefteä-Langsele Golfklubb (1970) 165

Phone: 0620 21477

Box 213, 88101 Sollefteä

15km west of Sollefteä off route 87 towards Langsele

Holes: 18 Par 72 5769m.
Visitors: Welcome. Course closed November to April
Fees: SKr175
Facilities: Bar and restaurant; practice ground
Pro: Tony Green

Sollentuna Golfklubb (1969) 166

Phone: 08 7543625

Skillingegården, 19177 Sollentuna

Take the E4 north from Stockholm and turn off towards Rotebro. The course is nearby off the Staket road

Holes: 18 Par 72 5868m.
Visitors: Welcome. Course closed November to March
Fees: SKr250
Facilities: Bar and restaurant; practice ground
Pro: Eva Flodberg

Sonfjällets Golfklubb (1992) 167

Phone: 0684 11020

PL 3125, 84093 Hede

The course is in the centre of Hede, which is on route 84 about 150km south west of Östersund

Holes: 9 Par 35 2723m.
Visitors: Welcome. Course closed October to May
Fees: SKr110
Facilities: Bar and restaurant; driving range; swimming pool; tennis
Pro: Peter Widmark

This short nine-hole course (though a further nine should soon be ready for play) is in a national park with a number of other sporting facilities including a swimming pool, canoeing, tennis courts, horseriding, fishing and go-karting.

Sotenäs Golfklubb (1990) 168

Phone: 0523 52390
Önna 45046 Hunnebostrand
8km beyond Hunnebostrand at Tossene (near Tossene church)

Holes	18 Par 71 5630m.
Visitors	Welcome
Fees	SKr175
Facilities	Bar and restaurant; practice ground
Pro	Lennart Härdner

Stjernfors Golf Club (1973) 169

Phone: 0580 41048
Box 11, 71400 Kopparberg
South of Kopparberg towards Hällefors

Holes	10 Par 71 5548m.
Visitors	Welcome. Course closed November to April
Fees	SKr100
Facilities	Bar and restaurant; practice ground

Stockholm Golfklubb (1904) 170

Phone: 08 7550753
Kevingestrand 20, 18231 Danderyd
On the north west side of Stockholm. Take the Norrtälje road to Danderyd's hospital

Holes	18 Par 69 5525m.
Visitors	Welcome. Course closed November to April
Fees	SKr250–300
Facilities	Bar and restaurant; practice ground
Pro	K Gow

Stora Lundby Golfklubb (1983) 171

Phone: 0302 44200
Box 4034, 44006 Grabo
North east of Goteborg, off the R190 to Gräbo

Holes	18 Par 72 6040m.
Visitors	Welcome. Course closed December to March
Fees	SKr150–200
Facilities	Bar and restaurant; practice ground; short course
Pro	L Svensson

Strängnäs Golfklubb (1968) 172

Phone: 0152 14731
Box 21, 64521 Strängnäs
Just south of Strängnäs. At junction of the E3/Route 55 head for Norrköoping

Holes	18 Par 72 5780m.
Visitors	Welcome. Course closed mid-October to mid-April
Fees	SKr150–200
Facilities	Refreshments; practice ground
Pro	K Jansson

Strömstad Golfklubb (1967) 173

Phone: 0526 11788
Box 129, 45223 Strömstad
Just north of Strömstad towards Selater

Holes	18 Par 71 5490m.
Visitors	Welcome. Course closed December to April
Fees	SKr140–160
Facilities	Bar and restaurant; practice ground
Pro	T Hunter

Sundsvalls Golfklubb (1952) 174

Phone: 060 561056
Golfvägen 5, 86200 Kvissleby
South of Sundsvall off the E4. Head for Kvissleby, Skottsund, and then Mjösund

Holes	18 Par 72 5845m.
Visitors	Welcome. Course closed October to April
Fees	SKr160–180
Facilities	Bar and restaurant; practice ground
Pro	T Bjornsson

Sunne Golfklubb (1970) 175

Phone: 0565 14100
Box 108, 68600 Sunne
Just south of Sunne on route 234

Holes	18 Par 72
Visitors	Welcome. Course closed November to April
Fees	SKr150
Facilities	Bar and restaurant; practice ground
Pro	A Olsson

Täby Golfklubb (1968) **176**
Phone: 0762 23261
Skålhamra Gard, 18343 Täby
North of Stockholm, on the western side of Lake
Vallentunasjän. Head for Vallentuna and follow
signs to Hagby and 'Skalhamra/Golfbana'
Holes 18 Par 73 5776m.
Visitors Welcome on weekdays only. Course
closed November to April
Fees SKr275
Facilities Bar and restaurant; practice ground
Pro Thure Holmsfröm

Tegelberga Golf & Country Club (1991) **177**
Phone: 040 485690
Lilla Alstad, Box 140, 23196 Trelleborg
Off the R101 near Alsbad; follow the sign to
Tegelberga
Holes 18 Par 71 5679m.
Visitors Welcome
Fees SKr100–200
Facilities Bar and restaurant; practice ground
Pro Peter Dahlberg

Timra Golfklubb (1988) **178**
Phone: 060 570153
Box 17, 86030 Sörberge
North of Timrå towards the airport and
Fagersvik
Holes 18 Par 72 5715m.
Visitors Welcome. Course closed October to
April
Fees SKr160–180
Facilities Bar and restaurant; practice ground
Pro G Campbell

Tobo Golfklubb (1971) **179**
Phone: 0492 30346
Box 101, 59800 Vimmerby
South of Vimmerby off the R34
Holes 18 Par 72 5950m.
Visitors Welcome. Course closed November
to April
Fees SKr140
Facilities Bar and restaurant; practice ground
Pro L Wiberg

Tomelilla Golfklubb (1990) **180**
Phone: 0417 13420
Box 129, 27323 Tomelilla
Just south east of Tomelilla, towards Bollerup
Holes 18 Par 73 6400m.
Visitors Welcome on weekdays
Fees SKr120–150
Facilities Bar and restaurant; practice ground
Pro M Neal

Toreboda Golfklubb (1965) **181**
Phone: 0506 12305
Box 18, 54521 Toreboda
East of Toreboda by the Mansarud lake
Holes 18 Par 70 5370m.
Visitors Welcome. Course closed November
to April
Fees SKr130
Facilities Bar and restaurant; practice ground
Pro D McLean

Torekovs Golfklubb (1938) **182**
Phone: 0431 63355
Box 81, 26093 Torekov
Just north of Torekov on the R115
Holes 18 Par 72 5701m.
Visitors Welcome, but must book
Fees SKr200
Facilities Bar and restaurant; practice ground;
tennis
Pro Gösta Hall

Torreby Golfklubb (1961) **183**
Phone: 0524 21109
Postlada, 45593 Munkedal
South west of Munkedal towards Torreby
Holes 18 Par 72 5885m.
Visitors Welcome. Course closed November
to March
Fees SKr120–160
Facilities Bar and restaurant; practice ground
Pro J Grahn

Torshälla Golfklubb (Nyby Bruks) (1960) 184

Phone: 016 358722

Box 587, 63108 Eskilstuna

West of Eskilstuna between the E3 and
Torshälla

Holes 9 Par 36 2935m.

Visitors Welcome, but must book. Course
closed November to April

Fees SKr100–150

Facilities Refreshments; practice ground

Tranås Golfklubb (1952) 185

Phone: 0140 11661

Norrabyvägen 8, 57343 Tranås

Just north east of Tranas off the R32. Follow
signs for DHR Tranåsbaden

Holes 18 Par 72 5830m.

Visitors Welcome, but must book. Course
closed November to March

Fees SKr120–150

Facilities Bar and restaurant; practice ground

Pro S Reese

Trelleborgs Golfklubb (1963) 186

Phone: 0410 30460

Maglarp, Post Box 401, 23193 Trelleborg

On the sea 6km west of Trelleborg

Holes 18 Par 69 5160m.

Visitors Welcome

Fees SKr150–180

Facilities Bar and restaurant; practice ground

Pro Göran Malmquist

Trollhättans Golfklubb (1963) 187

Phone: 0520 41000

Box 254, 46126 Trollhättan

South of Trollhättan off route 42 towards Böras.
Turn off at the 'Golfbana' sign

Holes 18 Par 72 6200m.

Visitors Welcome. Course closed November
to March

Fees SKr150

Facilities Bar and restaurant; driving range

Pro G Clark

The course is situated by a beautiful lake, which
affects the play on several holes, many of which
are fringed by ancient trees. There are many
testing shots and the famous Koberg castle is
nearby.

Trosa-Vagnhärad Golfklubb (1972) 188

Phone: 0156 22015

Uddby 15600, Vagnhärad

South of Trosa towards Västerljung and then
Uttervik

Holes 18 Par 72 5840m.

Visitors Welcome. Course closed November
to April

Fees SKr180

Facilities Refreshments; practice ground

Pro C Rose

Uddeholms Golfklubb (1965) 189

Phone: 0563 60564

Risäters Herrgård 610, 68303 Råda

South west of Hagfors by route 62 to Råda

Holes 18 Par 72 5850m.

Visitors Welcome

Fees SKr120

Facilities Refreshments; practice ground

Pro J Linden

Ullna Golfklubb (1981) 190

Phone: 08510 26075

Rosenkälle, 18492 Akersberga

From Stockholm, take the E3 towards Norrtälje.
Exit at Åkersberga then turn left towards
Gribbyland for 1km

Holes 18 Par 72 5805m.

Visitors Welcome on weekdays; at weekends
with a member. Course closed
October to April

Fees SKr300

Facilities Bar and restaurant; practice ground

Pro John Cockin

This is a very fine golf course which is less than
an hour's drive from Stockholm. It has several
times been the venue for the Scandinavian
Enterprise Open, won there both by Ian Baker-
Finch and Seve Ballesteros. Ullna has a design
which is full of tantalising challenges but it will
also delight the eye of most golfers; there are
lovely trees and shimmering stretches of water.
The short 3rd hole, where you play to an island
green, is only one of many memorable holes.

Ulricehamn Golfklubb (1947) 191

Phone: 0321 10021

Box 179, 52324 Ulricehamn

Close to Ulricehamn centre; head towards
Lassalyckans

Holes 18 Par 71 5370m.

Visitors Welcome. Course closed November
to April

Fees SKr140

Facilities Refreshments; practice ground

Pro A Halim

Umeå Golfklubb (1954) 192
Phone: 090 41071
Lövön, 91300 Holmsund
South of Umeå in Holmsund

Holes	18 Par 72 5752m.
Visitors	Welcome. Course closed October to mid-May
Fees	SKr80–125
Facilities	Bar and restaurant; practice ground
Pro	J Anderson

Upsala Golfklubb (1964) 193
Phone: 018 460120
Hamo Gard, Läby, 75592 Uppsala
South west of Uppsala on route 55 to Enkoping

Holes	18 Par 71 5902m.
Visitors	Welcome. Course closed November to March
Fees	SKr225–250
Facilities	Bar and restaurant; practice ground; short course
Pro	Martin Söderberg

This is one of the most challenging courses in the country and is always in excellent condition. Part of it is cut through dense forest and many of the tees are built on high ground from where the golfer has lovely views to Uppsala. A lake and a stream come into play during the first half and the course above all demands accuracy.

Vadstena Golfklubb (1956) 194
Phone: 0143 12440
Hagalund, 59200 Vadstena
Just south of Vadstena towards Väderstad

Holes	18 Par 71
Visitors	Welcome. Course closed November to April
Fees	SKr100
Facilities	Bar and restaurant; practice ground
Pro	C Bolgakoff

Vallentuna Golfklubb (1991) 195
Phone: 0762 77000
Box 266, 18622 Vallentuna
3km from the centre of Vallentuna. Cross the railway line and head for Lindholmen

Holes	18 Par 72 5734m.
Visitors	Welcome. Course closed October to April
Fees	SKr190–250
Facilities	Bar and restaurant; practice ground
Pro	Stefan Kvillstrom

Vara-Bjertorp Golfklubb (1990) 196
Phone: 0512 20260
Bjertorp, 53500 Kvänum
North of Vara at Bjertorp

Holes	18 Par 72 6005m.
Visitors	Welcome, but must book at weekends. Course closed December to March
Fees	SKr120–160
Facilities	Bar and restaurant; practice ground
Pro	Inge Klarqvist

Varbergs Golfklubb (1950) 197
Phone: 0340 37470
Box 39, 43202 Varberg
East of Varberg off the R153 towards Rolfstorp and then Grimeton

Holes	18 Par 72 5700m.
Holes	18 Par 72 6000m.
Visitors	Welcome
Fees	SKr150–200
Facilities	Bar and restaurant; practice ground
Pro	F Englund

Värnamo Golfklubb (1972) 198
Phone: 0370 23123
Box 146, 33101 Värnamo
North east of Värnamo off the E4 and R127 to Näsbyholm

Holes	18 Par 72 5588m.
Visitors	Welcome. Course closed November to April
Fees	SKr170
Facilities	Bar and restaurant; practice ground
Pro	B Ekenberg

Vasatorps Golfklubb (1973)   199

Phone: 042 235058

Box 13035, 25013 Helsingborg

East of Helsingborg, off the E4 near Rää

Holes	18 Par 72 5875m.
	9 Par 36 2940m.
Visitors	Welcome. Course closed December to March
Fees	SKr160–200
Facilities	Bar and restaurant; practice ground
Pro	K Davies

Situated in attractive parkland, the course has been the venue for the Scandinavian Enterprise Open on three occasions. Seve Ballesteros, Sandy Lyle and Greg Norman have been the illustrious winners. Vasatorps has a splendid pedigree and its difficulties lie in the cleverly designed dog-leg holes and the well-bunkered greens.

Västerås Golfklubb (1931)   200

Phone: 021 35743

Bjärby, 72481 Västerås

North of Västerås off the E18

Holes	18 Par 69 5345m.
Visitors	Welcome. Course closed November to April
Fees	SKr140–180
Facilities	Bar and restaurant; practice ground
Pro	T Ljungqvist

Västervik Golfklubb (1989)   201

Phone: 0490 32420

Ekhagen, 59300 Västervik

Just north of Västervik centre, over the bridge to Slottsholmen. Follow sign to 'Ekhagen/Golfbana'

Holes	18 Par 72 5785m.
Visitors	Welcome
Fees	SKr150
Facilities	Bar and restaurant; practice ground
Pro	Pär Johansson

Växjö Golfklubb (1959)   202

Phone: 0470 21539

Box 227, 35105 Växjö

2km by route 23 from Växjö towards Araby

Holes	18 Par 72 5860m.
Visitors	Welcome, but must book. Course closed November to April
Fees	SKr140–170
Facilities	Bar and restaurant; driving range
Pro	L Prick

Vetlanda Golfklubb (1983)   203

Phone: 0383 18310

Box 249, 57423 Vetlanda

West of Vetlanda off the R127 towards Sävsjö and Östanå Värdhus

Holes	18 Par 72 5698m.
Visitors	Welcome. Course closed November to March
Fees	SKr120
Facilities	Bar and restaurant; practice ground
Pro	S Petersson

Viredaholm Golf & Country Club (1992)   204

Phone: 0390 31114

Viredaholm Sateri, 57800 Aneby

Off Route 986 north west of Aneby; in Vireda near the church

Holes	18 Par 71 5600m.
Visitors	Welcome. Course closed November to March
Fees	SKr100
Facilities	Bar and restaurant; practice ground; swimming pool
Pro	Philip Cooper

Viksjö Golfklubb (1967)   205

Phone: 0758 16600

Fjällens Gard, 17545 Järfälla

Take the E18 from Stockholm towards Jakobsberg for 18km; turn off at the Viksjö exit and follow 'Viksjoleden' to the course

Holes	18 Par 73 5930m.
Visitors	Welcome. Course closed mid-October to mid-May
Fees	SKr275
Facilities	Bar and restaurant; practice ground
Pro	Sajed Cherif

Visby Golfklubb (1958)   206

Phone: 0498 45058

PO Box 1038, 62121 Visby

South of Visby off the R140 near the lighthouse

Holes	18 Par 72 5765m.
Visitors	Welcome
Fees	SKr200
Facilities	Bar and restaurant; practice ground

This is a very challenging course by the Baltic, partly because the winds can blow and make every shot difficult. But the golfer must also contend with narrow fairways driven through thick pine forests and with heather that is reminiscent of some of the great Scottish courses. The final element is water, and plenty of it.

Wermdo Golf & Country Club (1966)   207

Phone: 0766 20849

Torpa, 13900 Varmdo

On the archipelago 28km east of Stockholm. The course is near Grisslinge

Holes	18 Par 72 5625m.
Visitors	Welcome except weekends before 2pm. Course closed November to April
Fees	SKr300–350
Facilities	Bar and restaurant; practice ground; sailing; tennis; swimming pool
Pro	Matts Jansson

This is certainly most people's idea of a country club with swimming, tennis, sailing and boule in addition to golf. The restaurant overlooks the marina. The course is an archetypal parkland design which rolls through the woods, and the club is located on one of the larger islands of the Stockholm archipelago.

Wittsjo Golfklubb (1962)   208

Phone: 0451 22635

Ubbaltsgarden, 28022 Vittsjo

On the south side of Vittsjö

Holes	18 Par 71 5461m.
Visitors	Welcome, but must book. Course closed November to March
Fees	SKr120–160
Facilities	Bar and restaurant; practice ground
Pro	G Dahl

Ystad Golfklubb (1930)   209

Phone: 0411 50350

Box 162, 27124 Ystad

East of Ystad off the R10 by the sea

Holes	18 Par 72 5800m.
Visitors	Welcome
Fees	SKr80–125
Facilities	Bar and restaurant; practice ground
Pro	J Grant

SWITZERLAND

S WITZERLAND is unusual among European countries in that very few new courses have been built in the last few years. Only half a dozen new clubs opened their doors and their fairways during the 1980s; indeed, nearly half of the thirty or so clubs in existence were established before 1940. The oldest club is Engadine, founded before the turn of the century, and the other senior clubs include Crans-sur-Sierre, Geneva, Lausanne, Lucerne and Zurich.

There are various clear reasons for this lack of expansion. Switzerland's main sport is skiing and the climate ensures that the golf season is rather limited; typically it runs from May to October. The mountainous terrain makes the building of golf courses difficult and expensive, and land is far from cheap.

Nevertheless, Switzerland is a wonderful place to play golf during the summer months. To play high up in the mountains amid magnificent scenery is a most exhilarating experience.

Unit of currency: Swiss Franc
Rate of exchange (approx. at 1.1.93): SFr2.20–£1
International dialling code: (010 41)

Arosa Golfclub (1946) **1**

Phone: 081 312215

7050 Arosa

Just north of Arosa

Holes	9 Par 33 2227m.
Visitors	Welcome. Course closed October to May
Fees	SFr40
Facilities	Bar and restaurant; practice ground
Pro	Livio Fogliada

Golf Club Patriziale Ascona (1928) **2**

Phone: 093 352132

Via al Lido 81, 6623 Ascona

Just east of Ascona

Holes	18 Par 71 5893m.
Visitors	Welcome
Fees	SFr60–80
Facilities	Bar and restaurant; practice ground
Pro	Michael Buchter

The course, quite long and reasonably flat, runs in charming style along the shore of Lake Maggiore. The climate is mild in this part of the country and the palm trees and magnolias add to the attractions. With its many trees and well-placed bunkers it is an excellent course.

Bad Ragaz Golfclub (1956)   3

Phone: 085 91556

Hans-Albrechtstrasse, 7310 Bad Ragaz

South east of Bad Ragaz, off the E43

Holes	18 Par 70 5750m.
Visitors	Welcome. Course closed November to March
Fees	SFr75
Facilities	Bar and restaurant; practice ground
Pro	Mario Caligari

Only a few miles from Liechtenstein, Bad Ragaz sits in sumptuous scenery of mountains and forests. It is an agreeable holiday course which tests the golfer by dint of its tight tree-lined fairways and the streams which criss-cross the course.

Golf de Basel (1967)   4

Phone: 010 33 89 685091

Geissberg bei 68220 Hagenthal France

South west of Basel, off the D12 at Hagenthal

Holes	18 Par 72 6255m.
Visitors	Welcome
Fees	SFr75–90
Facilities	Bar and restaurant; practice ground
Pro	A Perrone

The club is actually on French territory but it is a Swiss club. It is an extremely tough course, its difficulty emphasized over the opening holes where a number of out of bounds areas threaten the wayward shot. Basel runs through woods and the greens are well-bunkered; it is a real challenge.

SWITZERLAND

Blumisberg Golfclub (1959)   **5**

Phone: 037 363438

Blumisberg 5, 3184 Wünnewil

Between Bern and Fribourg, off the B12. Take the Flanatt exit

Holes	18 Par 73 6048m.
Visitors	Welcome on weekdays. Course closed November to March
Fees	SFr60
Facilities	Bar and restaurant; practice ground; swimming pool
Pro	Fausto Schiroli

The course is located in the Swiss plain between the Alps and the Jura mountains. It was designed by Bernhard von Limburger and therefore demands intelligent play. Some holes are long, the 3rd and 15th for example, while others require shrewd tactics, especially the dog-legged 7th and 18th. The terrain is undulating and there are plenty of trees to add to the interest.

Club de Bonmont (1983)   **6**

Phone: 022 3692345

Château de Bonmont, 1261 Chéserex

North of Geneva, off the N1. Take the Nyon exit and head for Chéserex

Holes	18 Par 71 6120m.
Visitors	Welcome. Course closed mid-December to February
Fees	SFr80
Facilities	Bar and restaurant; parctice ground; swimming pool; tennis
Pro	F Boillet

Donald Harradine designed this course and at its hub sits a wonderful clubhouse formed from an 18th century château. The course is also splendid, a real challenge laid out over undulating ground, with some steep climbs.

Golfclub Breitenloo (1964)   **7**

Phone: 01 8364080

61 Bassersdorf, 8309 Oberwil

North east of Zürich near the airport

Holes	18 Par 72 6125m.
Visitors	Welcome. Course closed November to March
Fees	SFr50
Facilities	Bar and restaurant
Pro	T Villiger

Bürgenstock Golfclub (1928)   **8**

Phone: 041 612434

6366 Bürgenstock

South east of Luzern, off the N2 at Burgenstock

Holes	9 Par 32 2400m.
Visitors	Welcome. Course closed October to May
Fees	SFr100
Facilities	Bar and restaurant
Pro	Grahame Denny

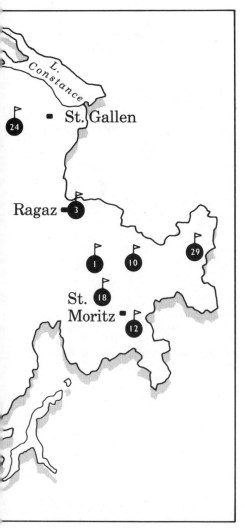

Golf Club Crans-sur-Sierre (1927)   9

Phone: 027 41268

3963 Crans-sur-Sierre

Just west of Crans-sur-Sierre off the N9

Holes	18 Par 72 6165m. 9 Par 35 2667m.
Visitors	Welcome. Course closed November to April
Fees	SFr80
Facilities	Bar and restaurant; practice ground; tennis and squash
Pro	Roger Barras

Sir Arnold Lunn, one of the pioneers of holiday skiing, laid out the first course over nine holes, and the current course came into being in 1951. At 5000 feet above sea level, the views over the Rhone Valley to the Matterhorn are exhilarating and so is the air. It is not a difficult course but it is sheer delight to play in such a setting; and the ball goes much further in the thin air. Crans is the home of the Swiss Open and, on a less exalted level, amateur competitions are held virtually every day during July and August: take your handicap certificate and join in.

Golf Club Davos (1929)   10

Phone: 081 465634

Mattastrasse 25, 7260 Davos-Platz

Just south of Davos

Holes	18 Par 69 5325m.
Visitors	Welcome. Course closed November to May
Fees	SFr60–70
Facilities	Bar and restaurant; driving range
Pro	H Horenz

Golf Club Domaine Impérial (1987)   11

Phone: 022 644545

Case Postale, 1196 Gland

North east of Geneva, at Gland on Lac Leman

Holes	18 Par 72 6297m.
Visitors	Welcome. Course closed December to March
Fees	SFr100
Facilities	Bar and restaurant; practice ground
Pro	Robert Guignet

This is the first design in Europe by the notable American architect, Pete Dye, who built Kiawah Island, Crooked Stick and Sawgrass. When Jerry Pate won a tournament at the latter course he threw Dye into one of the lakes and dived in afterwards – such was the difficulty of the course. Dye moved mountains of earth to build this undulating course by Lake Geneva. It is a fine challenge and has a superb finishing hole.

Engadine Golfclub (Samedan) (1898)   12

Phone: 082 65226

7505 Samedan/St Moritz

North of St Moritz near Samedan

Holes	18 Par 72 6350m.
Visitors	Must book. Course closed November to May
Fees	SFr80
Facilities	Bar and restaurant; practice ground
Pro	A Chiogna

The oldest club in Switzerland is also its highest, perched up in the air at nearly 6000 feet. Surprisingly the course is reasonably flat but the pine trees and streams make it a challenging course, as does the wind which blows down from the Maloja pass.

Golf de Genève (1923)   13

Phone: 022 735 7540

70 Rue de la Capite, 1223 Cologny

Just north east of Geneva on the edge of the lake

Holes	18 Par 72 6250m.
Visitors	Welcome. Course closed January and February
Fees	SFr75–100
Facilities	Bar and restaurant; practice ground
Pro	J M Larretche

Gstaad Golfclub (1962)   14

Phone: 030 42636

3777 Gstaad-Saanenmöser

North east of Gstaad near Saanenmöser

Holes	9 Par 35 2760m.
Visitors	Welcome. Course closed November to May
Fees	SFr45–60
Facilities	Bar and restaurant; practice ground
Pro	Bruno Herrman

Golfclub Hittnau-Zürich (1964)   15

Phone: 01 9502442

Dürstelen bei Pfäffikon

East of Zürich off the N1 near Pfäffikon

Holes	18 Par 71 6020m.
Visitors	Welcome. Course closed December to April
Fees	SFr75
Facilities	Bar and restaurant; practice ground
Pro	E Bauer

Interlaken-Unterseen Golf Club (1964) 16
Phone: 036 226022
Postfach 110, 3800 Interlaken
On the north west side of Interlaken

Holes	18 Par 72 5980m.
Visitors	Welcome, but must book. Course closed November to March
Fees	SFr50–70
Facilities	Bar and restaurant; practive ground
Pro	Bernard Chenaux

Lausanne Golfclub (1921) 17
Phone: 021 7841317
Le Chalet-à-Gobet, 1000 Lausanne 25
Just north of Lausanne, off the N9

Holes	18 Par 72 6295m.
Visitors	Welcome. Course closed December to March
Fees	SFr80–100
Facilities	Bar and restaurant; practice ground
Pro	D Ingram

This is one of the most celebrated courses in Switzerland and is ranked in the top 50 in Europe by 'Golf World' magazine. Golfers have fine views of Lac Leman from the fairways and of the Savoy Alps. The course plunges up and down and avenues of trees line many of the holes (the short 3rd and the 12th holes are especially tough) and it is always in superb condition. The Swiss Open has been held here on several occasions.

Lenzerheide-Valbella Golfclub (1951) 18
Phone: 081 341316
7078 Lenzerheide
Just south of Lenzerheide, off the B3

Holes	18 Par 69 5274m.
Visitors	Welcome. Course closed November to mid-June
Fees	SFr70
Facilities	Bar and restaurant; practice ground
Pro	Helmuth Schumacher

This is another course built at a high altitude, at around 5000 feet. It runs over steep terrain with plenty of pine trees to enliven the round, and the views are splendid.

Lucerne Golf Club (1903) 19
Phone: 041 369787
Dietschiberg, 6006 Luzern
On the north east side of Luzern, off the B4

Holes	18 Par 72 6000m.
Visitors	Welcome
Fees	SFr50
Facilities	Bar and restaurant; practice ground
Pro	Bruno Lagger

Lugano Golfclub (1923) 20
Phone: 091 711557
6983 Magliaso
South west of Lugano off the N2/A9

Holes	18 Par 71 5775m.
Visitors	Welcome
Fees	SFr50
Facilities	Bar and restaurant;
Pro	Denis Maina

Golf Club Mittelland (1988) 21
Phone: 064 438984
Muhenstrasse 52, 5036 Oberentfelden
West of Zurich, off the N1 near Oberentfelden

Holes	9 Par 30 2000m.
Visitors	Welcome. Course closed November to March
Fees	SFr50
Facilities	Bar and restaurant; tennis courts
Pro	Tom McKenna

Golfclub de Montreux (1964) 22
Phone: 025 264616
Rte d'Evian, 1860 Aigle
South of Montreux off the N9; take the Aigle exit

Holes	18 Par 72 6143m.
Visitors	Welcome
Fees	SFr60–80
Facilities	Bar and restaurant; practice ground
Pro	Toribio Cordoba

The beautiful city of Montreux has a superb temperate climate and plays host to many international festivals. The course is a long slog, though fairly flat, and the many trees provide most of the problems along the rather narrow fairways.

Neuchâtel Golfclub (1928) 23
Phone: 038 335550
Rte de Lignières, 2072 Voëns-St Blaise
On the north east side of Neuchâtel

Holes	18 Par 70 5840m.
Visitors	Weclome. Course closed December to March
Fees	SFr50
Facilities	Bar and restaurant; practice ground
Pro	Carlos Duran

Ostschweizer Golfclub (1948)   24

Phone: 071 811856

9246 Niederbüren SG

West of St Gallen, off the N1 near Niederbüren

Holes	18 Par 72 5951m.
Visitors	Welcome. Course closed January
Fees	SFr50–75
Facilities	Bar and restaurant; practice ground
Pro	Campbell Craig

Schinznach-Bad Golfclub (1929)   25

Phone: 056 431226

5116 Schinznach-Bad

South of Brugg, off the B5 at Schinzbach

Holes	9 Par 35 2835m.
Visitors	Welcome. Course closed November to March
Fees	SFr50
Facilities	Bar and restaurant; practice ground
Pro	H H Zimmermann

Golf & Countryclub Schönenberg (1967)   26

Phone: 017 881624

7724 Schönenberg

South of Zürich, off the B4 at Schönenberg

Holes	18 Par 72 6119m.
Visitors	Welcome. Course closed November to March
Fees	SFr70
Facilities	Bar and restaurant; practice ground
Pro	J Wallwork

Golf Club Verbier (1970/91)   27

Phone: 026 311566

Les Moulins, 1936 Verbier

Just east of Verbier

Holes	18 Par 70 5110m.
Visitors	Welcome. Course closed December to May
Fees	SFr60
Facilities	Bar and restaurant; practice ground; short course; swimming pool, tennis and squash; horse riding
Pro	Tony Calvo

Villars Golfclub (1922)   28

Phone: 025 354213

Rte Col de la Croix, 1884 Villars

South west of Villars, off the N9

Holes	18 Par 64 4260m.
Visitors	Welcome. Course closed Nov-May
Fees	SFr50
Facilities	Bar and restaurant; practice ground; swimming pool; tennis and squash
Pro	Jean-Louis Chable

The course is several thousand feet up in the mountains and the skiers take over during the winter. The air and the panoramic views are wonderful but this is a true mountain course where golfers must expect some very hard walking.

Vulpera Golfclub (1923)   29

Phone: 084 99688

7552 Vulpera

In Vulpera

Holes	9 Par 31 2021m.
Visitors	Welcome. Course closed November to April
Fees	SFr50
Facilities	Bar and restaurant; practice ground
Pro	Peter Jones

Zürich-Zumikon Golfclub (1931)   30

Phone: 01 9180051

8125 Zumikon ZH

South east of Zürich, off the A8 at Zumikon

Holes	18 Par 72 6360m.
Visitors	Welcome on weekdays. Course closed November to March
Fees	SFr75–100
Facilities	Bar and restaurant; practice ground
Pro	G C Denny

In the lush countryside near Zurich, this is a very agreeable parkland course, beautifully maintained, scattered with fine trees, and with a river meandering here and there. The terrain rises and falls quite substantially but the fairways are generous; it is an excellent holiday course.

APPENDIX 1

A-Z of French courses

The Guinness Continental Europe Golf Course Guide lists French golf courses in four separate sections, and within those sections courses are listed by region. This appendix provides a complete A-Z listing of French courses, with page references.

Aa-St-Omer GC 58
Golf de l'Abbaye des Sept Fontaines 72
Golf d'Abbeville 58
Golf d'Ableiges 63
GC d'Agen Bon-Encontre 81
Golf de l'Ailette 58
Golf des Aisses 55
GC d'Aix-les-Bains 89
GC Aix-Marseille 98
Golf des Ajoncs d'Or 49
Golf d'Albi (Lasbordes) 85
GC d'Albon 89
Golf d'Albret 81
Golf International d'Allauch 97
Golf d'Amiens 58
Golf d'Ammerschwihr 70
Golf d'Angers 52
Anjou G & CC 52
Club d'Arcachon 81
Golf d'Arcangues 81
Golf d'Arc-en-Barrois 72
Golf des Arcs 89
Golf des Ardennes 72
Golf d'Ardrée 55
GC de l'Ariege 85
Golf d'Arras 58
Golf d'Artiguelouve 81
Golf d'Auriac 95
Golf d'Autun 74
GC des Avenelles 77
Golf d'Avrillé de la Perriere 52
Golf d'Azy 74

Golf de Baden 49
GC de Bagnoles 45
GC Barbaroux 98
Golf de la Barouge 86
GC de Barthe 81
Golf de la Bastide du Roy (Biot) 98
Golf de la Baule 52-3
Golf des Baux de Provence 98
GC du Beaujolais 89
Golf de Beaune 74
Golf du Beauvallon 98
Golf de Bélesbat 63
Golf de Belleme St Martin 45
Golf de Besançon 70
Béthemont Chisan CC 67

Golf de Beuzevat 45
Golf de Biarritz 81
Golf de la Bigorre 86
Golf de Biscarosse 81
Golf de Bitche 72
Golf du Bois de Ruminghem 58
Golf du Boisgelin 49
Golf de Bombequiols 95
Golf de Bondoufle 64
Golf de Bondues 58
Golf de Bordeaux Cameyrac 82
Golf Municipal de Bordeaux-Lac 82
Golf Bordelais 82
Golf International Les Bordes 55
Golf de la Bosse 55
Golf de Bossey 89
Golf de la Boulie 67
Golf de Bourges 55
GC du Chateau de Bournel 70
Golf de Bouvent 89
Golf Municipal de Bréhal 45
Golf de la Bresse 91
Golf de Brest-Iroise 49
Golf de la Bretesche 53
Golf de Brigode 59
Golf des Bruyeres 59
Golf de Bussy-St-Georges 64

Golf Public de Cabourg 45
Golf de Cabourg Le Home 45
Golf de Cabries-Calas 98
Golf de Caen 46
Golf de Cannes Mandelieu 98
Cannes Mougins CC 98-9
Golf du Cap d'Agde 96
Golf du Cap Vert 74
Golf de la Carte 55
Golf de Casteljaloux 82
Golf de Castelnaud 82
Golf de Cavaliere 99
Golf du Cély 64
Golf de Center Parcs 46
Golf de Cergy-Pontoise 64
GC du Chateau de Chailly 74
Golf Public de Chalon-sur Soane 74
Golf de Chambon-sur-Lignon 79
Club de Chamonix 91
Golf du Champ de Bataille 46

Golf de Champagne 59
Golf de Champlong-Villeret 91
Golf de Chantaco 82
Golf de Chantilly 59
Golf La Chapelle en Vercors 91
Golf de Charade 79
Golf de Chateau-l'Arc 99
GC de Chateaublanc 99
Golf de Chaumont-en-Vexin 59
Golf de Cherbourg 46
Golf du Chateau de Cheverny 55
Golf Public de Chevry 64
Golf de Chiberta 82
Golf de Cholet 53
Golf de Cicé Blossac 49
Golf de Clairis 74
Golf du Clécy Cantelou 46
Golf Clément Ader 64
Golf du Clou 92
Golf du Cognac 76
Golf du Coiroux 79
Golf de Combles en Barrois 72
Golf de la Commanderie 92
Golf de Compiegne 59
GC du Connetable 76
Golf de la Cordeliere 72
Golf de Corrençon-en-Vercors 92
Golf de la Cote d'Argent 83
Golf de la Cote des Isles 46
Golf du Coudray 64
Golf de Coulondres 96
Golf de Courson-Monteloup 64
Golf de Coutainville 46
Crécy-la-Chapelle (Golf de Montpichet) 66
Golf de la Criniere 50
Golf de la Croix de Montemart 83
Golf du Cros du Loup 79

Golf de Deauville 47
Golf de Dieppe 47
Golf de Digne 99
Golf de Dijon-Bourgogne 74
Golf de Dinard 50
Golf de Divonne 92
Golf du Domaine de St Donat 99
Golf de la Domangere 53
GC de la Dombes 92
Golf de Domont-Montmorency 64
Golf de la Drome Provençale
Golf des Dryades 56
Golf de Dunkerque Fort Vallieres 59

Golf d'Embats 86
GC d'Esery 92
GC d'Espalais 86
Golf de l'Estérel 99
Golf des Etangs de Fiac 86
Golf d'Etiolles 65
Golf Marin d'Etretat 47
Royal GC Evian 92
Golf d'Evreux 47

Golf de Falgos 96
Golf de Faverges-de-la-Tour 93
Golf de Flaine-les-Carroz 93
Golf des Flandres 59
Golf de Fleurance 86
Golf de Font-Romeu 96
Golf de Fontainebleu 65
GC de Fontcaude 96
Golf de Fontenailles 65
Golf de Fontenay-en-Cotentin 47
Golf des Fontenelles 53
Golf de la Foret d'Orient 72
Golf de la Foret Verte 47
Golf du Forez 93
Golf de Forges-les-Bains 65
Golf de la Forteresse 65
Golf de Fourqueux 68
Golf de la Frediere 75
Golf de Frégate 100
Golf de la Freslonniere 50

Green Golf Gaillon 47
Golf Public de Gap Bayard 100
Golf de Garcelles 47
Golf de Gascogne 86
Golf de Giez 93
Golf de Gourdan 93
Golf de Gouverneur 93
Golf du Grand Avignon 100
Golf de la Grande Bastide 100
Golf de la Grande Motte 96
Golf de la Grande Romanie 72-3
Golf de Granville 48
Golf des Graves et du Sauternais 83
GC de Grenoble 'Les Alberges' 93
GC de Grenoble 'Bresson' 93
GC de Grenoble 'St Quentin' 94
Golf de Guinlet 86
Golf de Gujan Mestras 83

Golf du Haras Lupin 68
Golf de Hardelot 61
GC du Haut Poitou 76
Golf des Hauts de Nimes 96
Golf du Havre 48
Golf de l'Hirondelle 76
Golf d'Hossegor 83
Golf d'Humieres 61

Golf d'Ilbarritz 83
GC de l'Ile d'Abeau 94
Golf de l'Ile d'Or 53
Golf des Images d'Epinal 73
Golf Isabella 68

Golf de la Jonchere 79

Golf de Kempferhof 70
Golf de Kerver 50

Golf du Lac d'Annecy 94

Golf du Lac de Germigny 65
Golf du Lac de Lourdes 86
Golf International de Lacanau 83
Golf Municipal de Laloubere 87
Golf de Lannemezan 87
Golf de la Largue 70
GC de Laval 53
Golf de Léry-Poses 48
Golf Municipal de Limoges 80
Golf de Lolivarie 84
Golf de Lou Rocas 100
Loudun GC 76
Golf de Luchon 87
Golf de Luxeuil-Bellevue 70
Golf de Lyon-Chassieu 94
Golf de Lyon-Verger 94
Golf de Lyon-Villete d'Anthon 94
International Club du Lys 61

Golf de Madine 73
Golf du Chateau de Maintenon 56
GC du Mans 54
Golf de Marcilly 56
Golf de Marmande 84
Golf de Marolles-en Brie 65
Golf de la Marsaudiere 65
Golf les Martines 87
GC de Massane 97
Golf des Meaulnes (de Nançay) 56
Golf de Meaux-Boutigny 66
Golf du Médoc 84
Golf de Méribel 94
Golf du Mesnil St Laurent 62
Golf de Metz-Chérisey 73
Golf de Mezeyrac 87
Golf de Mignaloux-Beauvoir 76
Golf du Mont d'Arbois 94
GC de Mont-de-Marsan 84
Golf du Mont St Jean 70
GC de la Montagne Noire 87
Country GC de Montauban 87
Golf de Monte Carlo 100
Golf de Montgenevre 100
Les Golfs de Montgriffon 66
Golf de Montpichet (Crécy-la-Chapelle) 66
Golf de Morfontaine 62
GC de Mormal 62
Golf du Moulin 101

Golf de Nampont St Martin 62
Golf de Nançay (des Meaulnes) 56
Golf de Nancy-Aingeray 73
Golf de Nantes Erdre 54
Golf de Nantes Vigneux 54
Golf National 68
Golf de Nevers 75
GC de Nimes Campagne 97
GC Niortais 76
Golf de la Nivelle 84

Golf de l'Odet 50

Golf d'Oléron 77
Golf d'Olhain 62
Golf de Bayeux Omaha Beach 48
Golf des Ormes 50
Golf d'Ormesson 66
Golf d'Ozoir-la-Ferriere 66

Paris International GC 66
Golf de Pau 84
Golf de Pen Guen 50
Golf du Perche 56
Golf Public de Périgueux 84
Golf de Pessac 85
Golf du Petit Chene 77
Golf de la Petite Blanchardiere 54
GC de la Picardiere 56
Golf de Pierrevert 101
Golf du Pilhon 95
Golf de la Pinede 97
Golf du Plessis 66
Golf de Ploëmeur Océan 51
Golf de la Porcelaine 80
Golf de Pornic 54
Golf de Port-Bourgenay 54
Golf de la Prée Rochelle 77
Golf de la Preze 77
Golf du Prieure 68
Golf de Prunevelle 71

Golf de Quimper et de Cornouaille 51

GC de Rebetz 62
Golf de Reims-Champagne 73
Golf de Rennes 51
Golf du Réveillon 66
Golf du Rhin 71
Golf du Rigolet (Mont-Dore) 80
Riviera GC 101
GC de Rochebois 85
Rochefort Chisan CC 68
Golf des Rochers Sévigné 51
Golf de Roncemay 75
Golf de Roquebrune sur Argens 101
Golf de Rosny-sous-Bois 66
Golf des Roucous (Sauveterre) 87
GC de Rouen 48
Golf de Rougemont-le-Chateau 71
Golf Les Rousses (du Rochat) 71
Golf de Royan (Cote de Beauté) 77

Golf de Sablé 54
Golf des Sables-d'Or-les-Pins 51
Golf du Sabot 97
Golf de Ste Agathe 80
Golf Public de St Aubin 67
Golf de la Ste Baume 101
Golf de St Cloud 68-9
Golf de St Cyprien 97
Golf St Gabriel 87
Golf de St Gatien 48
Golf de St Germain 69

Golf de St Germain-les-Corbeil 67
Golf de St Jean de Monts 54
Golf de St Julien 49
Golf de St Laurent-Ploëmel 51
Golf de St Malo le Tronchet 51
Golf de Ste Maxime 101
Golf de St Nom-la-Breteche 69
Golf Public de St Pierre-du-Perray 67
Golf de St Quentin 69
Golf de St Saëns 49
Golf de St Samson 52
Golf de St Thomas Béziers 97
Golf de St Walfroy 73
Golf de Saintes 77
Golf de Salbris 56
Golf de la Salette 101
Golf de Salies-de-Béarn 85
Golf de Salives 75
Golf du Chateau de la Salle 75
Golf de Salvagny 95
Golf de Sancerrois 56
Golf des Sarrays 57
Golf du Sart 62
Golf de Saumane 102
Golf de Sauzon 52
Golf de Savenay 55
Scottish Golf d'Aubertin 85
Golf de Seignosse 85
Golf sur Seine 69
Golf du Chateau des Sept Tours 57
Golf de Septemes 102
Golf de Seraincourt 67
Golf de Servanes (Mouries) 102
Set Golf International 102
Golf de Sologne 57
GC de la Sorelle 95
Golf de Spano 103
Golf de Spérone 103
GC de Strasbourg 71
Golf de Sully-sur-Loire 57

Golf du Chateau de Tanlay 75
G & CC de Taulane 102
Golf du Technopole de Metz 73
GC des Templiers 67
Golf de Téoula 88
Golf du Chateau de Terrides 88
Golf de Thiers 80
Golf de Thumeries 62

Golf du Tilbury 88
Golf de Tir Na N'Go 52
Golf Toulouse Borde-Haute 88
Golf de Toulouse Palmola 88
Golf de Toulouse-la-Ramée 88
Golf de Toulouse-Seilh 88
GC du Touquet 63
Golf de Touraine 57
Golf du Tremblay sur Mauldre 69
Golf de Trousse Chemise 77
Golf des Tumulus 88

Golf d'Uzes 97

Golf du Val d'Amour 71
Golf du Val-de-Cher 80
Golf du Val de l'Indre 57
Golf du Val de Loire 57
Golf du Val Martin 102
Golf du Val Quéven 52
GC du Val Secret 63
Golf du Val de Sorne 71
Golf de Valbonne (Opio) 102
Golf de Valcros 102
Golf de la Valdaine 95
Golf de Valence le Bourget 95
Golf de Valence-Chanalets 95
Golf de Valence-St Didier 95
Golf de Valenciennes 63
Golf de Valescure 103
Golf du Valois 63
Golf de la Vaucouleurs 69
Golf du Vaudreil 49
GC de Vaugouard 57
Sporting Club de Vichy 80
Golf de Vieille Toulouse 88
Golf de Viévola 103
Golf de Villarceaux 67
Golf de Villennes-sur-Seine 69
Golf de la Vitarderie 73
Golf de Vittel 73
Golf du Vivier 63
GC de Volcans 80

Golf de la Wantzenau 71
Golf de Wimereux 63

Golf des Yvelines 70

APPENDIX 2

A-Z of German courses

The Guinness Continental Europe Golf Course Guide lists German courses in two separate sections, Northern and Southern. This appendix provides a complete A-Z listing of German courses, with page references.

PLAY AROUND
ON THE CONTINENT

Drive off with P&O European Ferries to the Golf Courses of Europe.

Wherever you're aiming for, we've a route to set you on your way in style.

Our Dover-Calais route has superferry sailings every 45 minutes in peak periods. And with a high-speed check-in and a crossing of just 75 minutes, you could be teeing off at Le Touquet or Hardelot before you can say 'Fore'.

If you're planning to conquer some courses in Normandy, the Loire Valley or the West Coast, our services from Portsmouth to Le Havre and Cherbourg will give you a head start. While our route from Felixstowe to Zeebrugge and Dover to Ostend set you on course for Belgium and Germany.

New Cruise-Ferry to Spain

And now you can cruise direct to the great courses of Spain and Portugal with P&O European Ferries. Our new Portsmouth-Bilbao service opens in the Spring with a twice weekly cruise on the magnificent 'Pride of Bilbao', the largest, most luxurious cruise ferry ever to operate from Britain.

Across to the Emerald Isle

And our Cairnryan-Larne route is the shortest way to the lush green greens of Ireland.

For more details ask your Travel Agent for P&O European Ferries Car Ferry Guide. Or phone 0304 203388.

P&O
European Ferries

DON'T JUST GET ACROSS. CRUISE ACROSS.

Your comments about any aspect of the Guide will be very welcome and so
will your opinions on any of the courses we have listed. Please send the
form to The Guide to European Golf Courses, c/o Hamer Books Ltd,
Freepost, London SW13 9BR

Name of Club :

Address   :

Country   :

Comments   :

Your name   :

Address   :

Name of Club :

Address   :

Country   :

Comments   :

Your name   :

Address   :